In this brilliant account of the civilisation of
ancient Egypt Professor Montet gives a pic-

1

HISTORY OF CIVILISATION

Eternal Egypt

Eternal Egypt

PIERRE MONTET

*Member of the French Institute and Honorary Professor at the
Collège de France*

Translated from the French by

DOREEN WEIGHTMAN

57114

WEIDENFELD AND NICOLSON
20 NEW BOND STREET LONDON W 1

SET IN 11-ON-12 POINT BASKERVILLE
PRINTED IN GREAT BRITAIN
BY EBENEZER BAYLIS AND SON, LTD.,
THE TRINITY PRESS, WORCESTER, AND LONDON

CONTENTS

CONTENTS

LIST OF PLATES

(Between pages 170 and 171)

ACKNOWLEDGEMENTS

The author wishes to thank the following for supplying photographs:

Aerofilms, 7; Anderson-Giraudon, 60; British Museum, 49, 85, 86, 87, 88, 89; The Brooklyn Museum, 44, 59; R. B. Fleming, 57; Gulbenkian Museum, 42; Hirmer Fotoarchiv, 41, 52; Lehnert & Landrock, 19, 24, 25, 26, 27, 38, 39, 43, 51, 55, 56, 62, 67, 72, 75, 76, 77, 79, 80, 81, 82, 83, 84, 90, 91, 92, 93, 94, 95, 96, 97, 100, 104; Metropolitan Museum of Art, New York, 40, 45, 46, 103; Musées Nationaux, 22, 36, 50, 58, 64, 66, 69, 71, 74, 107; Museum of Fine Arts, Boston, 23, 29, 30–33, 34, 35, 38, 63; Paul Popper, 3, 9, 14, 17, 53, 54, 98; Josephine Powell, 18; P.A.-Reuter, 8, 15; Roemer–Palizaeus Museum, 28; Roger Wood, 6, 11, 16, 20, 78.

LIST OF FIGURES

LIST OF MAPS

PREFACE

THE history of ancient Egypt began at the point when the unification of the country under a single leader became an accomplished fact. It came to an end when Alexander incorporated Egypt into his empire. Manetho, an Egyptian who wrote a history of Egypt in Greek at the beginning of the third century BC, lists, between Menes, the first Pharaoh, and Alexander the illustrious conqueror, thirty dynasties, not all with the same number of kings. There must have been, in all, about three hundred and thirty monarchs. Modern scholars have tried to discover what their original names were, what monuments they erected, to place them in chronological order and, wherever possible, to describe the events which occurred during their reigns. This task, which is still being pursued today, has not been undertaken in vain. Although much remains obscure, it can be said that a great deal is now known about several dynasties – the one during which the Great Pyramids were built, the one during which the Labyrinth was constructed, and the Eighteenth, Nineteenth and Twenty-sixth Dynasties. A few sharply-defined figures stand out among the endless series of rulers: Queen Hatsheput who succeeded, throughout her lifetime, in preventing her nephew from taking over the throne, and who was responsible for one of the most beautiful buildings in the whole of Egypt; Tuthmosis III, the warrior; Amenophis III who expressed a wish to see the gods, and his son Akhenaton, who persecuted them and who moved his capital to the provinces; and, of course, Tutankhamen, who won fame overnight as the result of an astounding discovery. These are happy exceptions. There is little to record of many Pharaohs, apart from their accession, the wars inflicted on them or the wars they embarked upon, the one or two monuments they erected and the site of their tomb. Some are known only as names. Egypt was a land of tradition where the same things went on recurring indefinitely. The Egyptians very rightly maintained that there had been no change since 'the time of the god'. The historian who undertakes to write an account of the Pharaohs is soon aware that there is very little information available; on the other hand, if his aim is to define the institution created by the Pharaohs and to describe the preoccupations and duties of these kings, he has a vast mass of material at his disposal. Within this context, so little change took place that in order to conjure up a picture of that extraordinary being the Pharaoh – more like a god than a man – he can choose illustrations from widely divergent periods.

What is true of the king is true of the country and its inhabitants. Apart from a few minor changes, the climate, the configuration of the Nile, the flora and fauna, the cultivation of the land and stock-breeding, as well as arts and crafts, were virtually the same at the time of the last independent kings as they had been under the Pharaohs who built the pyramids. Some animal and vegetable species were no longer found, while others made their appearance – the horse under the Hyksos, then later the persea and the cock during the Late Period. Important though such changes were, they must never allow us to forget that it is the Nile which, by overflowing its banks regularly every year at a fixed time, gives life to Egypt, that narrow valley enclosed between two barren cliffs. The river is an imperious if benevolent master, who determines the life of the nation once and for all.

Subject to natural conditions which remained virtually unchanged, Egypt created a completely original civilisation, the most obvious feature of which is its immutability. Hieroglyphic writing which had been invented towards the end of the prehistoric era and was used regularly at the time of Menes, covers the walls and columns of the Ptolemaic and Roman temples. It died out when Christianity replaced the old religions. Until then, the Egyptians remained faithful to their gods and continued to place their mummies in elaborate tombs. Evidence supplied by classical historians from Herodotus to Strabo, Plutarch and Juvenal confirms and completes what we learn from the original documents.

The object of the present work, which we have called *Eternal Egypt*, is to try to define the permanent cultural features of the country. It will, nevertheless, be necessary to point out certain innovations which inevitably occurred in a land where tradition, however respectfully adhered to, was from time to time swept aside by passion. In the first five chapters, the natural and political conditions of Egyptian life will be studied. In the four subsequent chapters some account will be given of Egyptian ideas about the gods and the future life, of their contribution to the general field of literature and science, and finally of their brilliant achievements in the various realms of art. The last chapter assembles evidence about the Egyptians given by the various peoples who had dealings with them, and in particular by the

Hebrews and the Greeks. In conclusion, some account will be given of the birth and progress of Egyptology and of its gradual disclosure of a marvellous civilisation.

As reference will be made throughout the following pages to empires, dynasties, intermediate periods and the late period, we feel we should at this point fix the boundaries of Egyptian history as well as the limits of the various stages through which it passed. When Bonaparte said to his soldiers, 'Remember that forty centuries gaze down upon you from these pyramids', he settled, with Alexander-like authoritativeness – and his estimate was not far out – a problem the difficulties of which still beset us.

The problem is caused by the fact that the Egyptians, instead of counting the years from an actual or imaginary event, which might have been the founding of Memphis, or the union of the two lands, considered every reign as a fresh dating point. At the beginning of a great many documents, we find: 'The Xth year of the reign of King N'; however, even when the years attributed to the same king have been added together, we can rarely be sure of knowing exactly how long he reigned. We do know in the case of Ramses II.[1] We possess ostraca bearing the date, year 66, and Ramses IV, on a stela found at Abydos, expresses a wish to rule as long as his ancestor, who reached the sixty-seventh year of his reign. This is an exceptional instance. Very important kings left only a few dated documents, referring only to the earlier parts of their reigns. If we were to add together the known years of the various individual reigns, the total would in all probability amount to far less than the duration of the Pharaonic era. Also, there is the task of arranging the many and various kings in chronological order. One or two officials have helped us in this task by relating the stages of their careers to the reigns of several consecutive kings. This information is indeed welcome, but it is far from adequate. At most, it enables us to check the famous lists of the ancestral kings, the most important of which are those made by Seti I at Abydos, which contains seventy-six names, and the Saqqara list, made under Ramses II, which has only fifty-eight.[2] However, these lists, which are not easy to reduce to any kind of unity, omit names and take liberties with the chronological order. If the Turin Papyrus had been intact, we should have had no need to turn to other sources. This was a splendid document, drawn up with great care under Ramses II in a government department where an authentic list was required.[3] Each name was followed by the duration of the reign, and at intervals series of reigns were added together. The Royal Papyrus unfortunately exists only in fragments, the exact placing of which is not immediately discernible. Many names and figures were lost. We should consider ourselves fortunate in knowing that, according to the Egyptian archivist's reckonings, 955 years and a few days elapsed between Menes and Ibi, at the end of the Old Kingdom; that he estimated the reigns of the kings of the court of Itht-toui, Manetho's Twelfth Dynasty, at 213 years, 1 month and 19 days: that the Hyksos ruled for 108 years. The Annals of the Old Kingdom, the main fragment of which is to be found in the Palermo Museum,[4] while the others are in the Cairo Museum, originally contained the names of all the kings from the Divine Dynasties to the Fifth Dynasty, together with the important events of each year. We possess only a small part of this priceless document. Manetho's history, too, is lost.[5] In its place, we have a few extracts quoted by the author of a treatise, *Contra Apion*, and a few abridged accounts in which the numbers are either fictitious or inaccurate. Not all the affirmations they contain are untrue. It used to be considered uncertain that King Nefercheres was Psusennes' successor, as Africanus and Eusibius claimed him to be. But the two names are associated on a document found during the excavations at Tanis.

Were it not for the dates determined by the Sothic Cycle which provide a few fixed points of reference, Egyptian chronology would be a very uncertain field. The Egyptian year of 365 days began theoretically on the day of the heliacal rising of Sothis (Sirius, the dog star). This seemed to occur just before the Inundation of the Nile. Every fifth year, the star rose one day later, so the Egyptian calendar lost a whole day every four years. The discrepancy went on increasing until it reached a maximum, then it decreased and, after 1,457 civil years, there was again no discrepancy. For four years the day on which the new year began was in its true place: theory and practice coincided. Such a coincidence is mentioned as having occurred in AD 139, from which we can establish the fact that it had previously taken place about 1320 BC, and about 2780 BC. It so happens that the Egyptians marked the dates of the feast of Sirius on their calendars for the reigns of Ptolemy Evergetes, Menophres (Ramses I), the founder of the Nineteenth Dynasty, Tuthmoses III and Amenophis I of the Eighteenth Dynasty, and Sesostris III of the Twelfth Dynasty. We can therefore fix the beginning of the Twelfth Dynasty at about 2000 BC, the beginning of the Eighteenth at about 1580 BC and the beginning of the Nineteenth at about 1380 BC. The documents referred to above allow us to determine the dates of most of the kings after Amenemhat I. An important lacuna remains; the period which elapsed between Aha (Menes) and Amenemhat I has been estimated at anything between one century and two and a half centuries. This uncertainty naturally affects the total duration of the Pharaonic era and means that we can offer only approximate dates for the whole of the Old Kingdom.

In recent years this method of calculation has been criticized, sometimes by those who had fiercely defended it. We should not, however, try to extract from it more information than it can give. The dates obtained are accurate within a margin of four years, perhaps a little more. Egypt lies within seven degrees of latitude, therefore the heliacal rising of Sirius was observed at Aswan seven days before it was seen on the Mediterranean coast. We do not know the position of the observatory, from which the Egyptian astronomers watched for the appearance of the star; it may have been at Memphis or Heliopolis, although we cannot be sure. It is assumed, and this is highly probable, that the calendar year of 365 days was brought into use at the beginning of a Sothic cycle, that is to say, about 2780 BC. It is convenient to accept this date for the reign of Zoser, the founder of the Third Dynasty, under whom Egyptian civilisation took a spectacular leap forward. This date is as good as any and we suggest it be adopted until such time as, through one of those discoveries which can happen only in Egypt, an authentic copy of Manetho's history, or better still a complete and intact Turin Papyrus, comes into our possession. The application of the Carbon-14 method of dating has as yet added nothing new to Egyptology.

The proof of the pudding is in the eating, and the method proposed can be verified by the fact that events in Egyptian history, and even in the history of neighbouring countries from the New Kingdom onwards, fit into it without any difficulty. It is no longer possible for each individual scholar to deduct a number of years from one reign and add them to another. If the following chronological table were to be changed in any way, it would no longer correspond to what is already known about the lands of the east. Here then, with their dates, are the kings who will be mentioned in this work:

DYNASTY	KINGS	SIGNIFICANT EVENTS	DATES
		Beginning of the 3rd millennium	
	Scorpion		
	Narmer	*Conquest of the Delta*	
I	Menes	*Founding of Memphis*	
II	Khasekhemui	*Relations with Byblos*	
III	Zoser	*His adviser Imhotep*	
		Step Pyramid	2780
	Huni	*Pyramid at Medum*	

DYNASTY	KINGS	SIGNIFICANT EVENTS	DATES
IV	Snofru	*Two pyramids at Dahshur*	
	Cheops	*The Great Pyramid at Giza*	
	Rededef		
	Dedefra	*Pyramid at Abu-Roash*	
	Chephren	*Second pyramid at Giza*	
	Menkaura	*Third pyramid at Giza*	
	(Mycerinus)		
	Shepseskaf	*The El Faraun mastaba*	
V	Userkaf		
	Sahura	*His funerary temple*	
	Unas	*Appearance of Pyramid Texts*	
VI	Teti		
	Pepi I		
	Merenre		
	Pepi II		
	Ibi	*955 years after Menes*	
X	Kheti	*Author of a Treatise of Wisdom*	
	Merikara		
XI	Three Intefs		
	Four Mentuheteps		
XII	Amenemhat I	*Capital removed to Ithy-taui*	2000
	Sesostris I		
	Sesostris II		
	Amenemhat II		
	Sesostris III		
	Amenemhat III	*Abichemu at Byblos*	
		Building of the Labyrinth	
	Amenemhat IV	*Ypshemuabi at Byblos*	
		End of the dynasty	1783
XIV	Neferhotep	*Yinaten at Byblos*	
XVI	Six Hyksos kings	*The Hebrews in Egypt*	
XVII	Sekenenra	*At Thebes*	
	Kames	*Fought Apophis, King of Avaris*	
XVIII	Ahmosis	*Expulsion of Hyksos*	1580
	Amenophis I	*Splendour of Thebes*	
	Tuthmosis I	*Tomb in the Valley of Kings*	
	Tuthmosis II		
	Queen Hatsheput		
	Tuthmosis III		
	Amenophis II		

DYNASTY	KINGS	SIGNIFICANT EVENTS	DATES
	Tuthmosis IV	*Relations with Babylon*	
	Amenophis III		
	Amenophis IV	*Took name of Akhenaton*	
		Capital at Akhetaton	
	Tutankhamen	*Brought court back to Thebes*	
	Ai	*Relations with the Hittites*	
	Horemheb		
XIX	Ramses I	*Era of Menophres*	1320
	Seti I		
	Ramses II	*Founded Per-Ramses*	
		Battle of Kadesh	
	Merneptah	*Exodus of Hebrews*	
XX	Ramses III	*Sea Peoples repulsed*	
	Ramses IX	*Disorder and pillaging throughout*	
		the country	
	Ramses XI	*The War of the Unclean*	
XXI	Smendes at Tanis	*Herihor at Thebes*	
	Psusennes	*Tomb intact at Tanis*	
	Nefercheres		
	Amenemopet		
	Siamon		
XXII	Shashank I	*Seized Jerusalem under Jeroboam*	950
	Osorkon II		
	Shashank II		
	Shashank III		
XXIII	Pedibast		
XXIV	Piankhi	*King of Nepata conquered Egypt*	
	Tirhaka		
XXVI	Psammeticus I	*Re-establishment of Egyptian unity*	
	Neko	*Circumnavigation of Africa*	
	Psammeticus II		
	Apries	*Unsuccessful expedition against*	
		Cyrene	
	Amasis		
XXVII	First Persian		525–404
	domination		
XXX	Nectanebo I		378
	Nectanebo II		
	Second Persian		341
	domination		
	Alexander		333

CHAPTER 1

THE BLACK LAND, THE LAND OF KEM-T

The Nile valley in prehistoric times

AT the end of the eighteenth century, the scholars of the Egyptian Commission saw a very different Egypt from the Egypt of today. The population, although considerable, was far below recent census figures. There were no Europeans, or hardly any. There were no dams, railways, macadamized roads, or sky-scrapers. Industry was confined to arts and crafts.

The Islamic Egypt they saw was also appreciably different from Ancient Egypt. The Pharaonic era lasted for a very long time and we must not forget that, by Alexander's time, the Nile valley no longer looked the same as it had done under the kings who built the pyramids. Even greater changes had occurred since the time when man first appeared on the banks of the great African river. At that

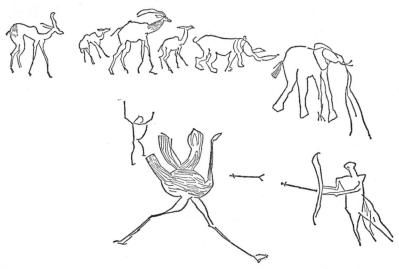

Fig. 1. Procession of animals and ostrich-hunting, from H. A. Winkler, *Rock-drawings of South Egypt*, I, pl. XX. The elephant, the rhinoceros and the giraffe emigrated to the South before the First Dynasty. Ostriches and antelopes remained in the Egyptian deserts.

I

remote period, the Nile flowed into a triangular-shaped gulf dotted with islands and islets. It was very wide, turbulent and fed by tributaries, since north-east Africa enjoyed a warm, humid climate, which produced a rich vegetation. Animal species which are now to be found only along the Upper Nile or in the Congo basin – elephants, rhinoceroses (fig. 1), lions, tigers and serpents such as the python (fig. 2) – made life dangerous for the first human beings who were cautious about approaching the valley and preferred to live on the plateaux. At the beginning of the Neolithic era, the climate changed. It became dry, while still remaining warm. The tributaries of the Nile no longer supplied it with water. The river gradually assumed the configuration it is known to have had during the Pharaonic era. Many animals emigrated to the south. Man moved closer to the Nile and to the big fresh-water lakes. To the south of Gebel Silsileh, there used to be a lake fed by the Nile tributaries. When the lake dried up, those who dwelt on its shores scattered over the black land – kem-t – by which name the country was to be known.

Fig. 2. Elephant and serpent, from *J.E.A.*, V, pl. II. The animosity between these animals was mentioned by the Greek and Roman historians.

The Nile

The Nile makes a noisy entry into Egypt. It has had to carve a passage for itself through a barrier of granite, about eight and a half miles broad, and parts of which survived as rocky islands whose names have become famous: Sehel, Philae, and Elephantine. Above the island of Sehel, where the river has to squeeze its way between a cluster of islands and the eastern bank, its course is today more turbulent than at any other point. Two thousand years ago, there must have been a cataract at this spot. Classical historians maintain that the people living in the neighbourhood were deafened by the roar and that the Persians were unable to stand the sound of the gushing waters for very long.

To the north of the Aswan archipelago, the Nile flows for about fifty miles along a narrow valley until its passage is barred by yet another obstacle – the Gebel Silsileh which, during the Paleolithic Age, held back the waters sweeping down from Abyssinia. The river succeeded in forcing a passage, but not without difficulty, since for more than twelve hundred yards it flows through a narrow gap between two cliffs which might be compared to the side-posts of some monumental door. Here the Nile, Hâpi, was worshipped as a god. Kings and dignitaries of the New Kingdom carved niches for themselves and engraved inscriptions and bas-reliefs to celebrate the blessings of the Nile.

Having passed through Gebel Silsileh, the Nile lazily pursues a meandering course towards the Mediterranean, sometimes encircling groups of islets. At first, it appears to be drawn towards the Red Sea, for at Kene it is no more than one hundred and fifty miles away; however, it is then forced to take a westerly direction and, a little further on, near the village of Hou, to bend northwards. At this point the valley becomes much broader, but the two banks are not alike. The river is attracted towards the eastern desert and for several miles flows so close to it that there is hardly any room for the cultivation of crops, an activity which is carried out extensively on the left bank.

To right and to left, but more especially to the left, the Nile throws out a number of smaller branches which irrigate the land bordering on the desert. One of these streams flows towards Sohag, skirting the mountain of Assiut and leading into a series of swamps. At Deirut it is joined by a very important stream, the Bahr Yusuf, whose winding course is confined almost entirely to desert land. This stream flows through the towns of Oxyrhynchos and Heracleopolis. After reaching El Lahun, it runs due west and threads its way between two high desert plateaux. Its off-shoots water the Fayum depression, which gradually emerged from the Neolithic period onwards to form, in Roman times, the nome called Arsinoe which, according to Strabo, was the best part of Egypt. In the days of the kings who built the Labyrinth and erected a famous temple to Sebek, the crocodile-god, a large area of the Fayum consisted of arable land. The rest was under water and attracted hunters and fishermen. This region was called *Ta-she*, the Lake land, and also *wadj-ur*, to emphasize the fact that it was 'very green', like the real sea. During the New Kingdom a new name appeared, *Pa-ym*, the sea, which remained in Coptic, Arabic and the modern dialects as the Fayum. Even during the Roman period, this sea was much more vast than the stretch of salt water we know today.

The Nile pursuing its course towards the sea reaches Memphis. Near the old capital, between Gebel-Turah and the plateau which is the site of the pyramids, the valley narrows down to half its size, but to the north of Heliopolis the gap between the two cliffs widens again. The gulf, which they overlooked during the Paleolithic period,

3

was already partly silted up, yet Lower Egypt, a rich, thickly populated, and well cultivated area, consisted of enormous swamps as well as of sandy islands. For this reason it was called *ta-meh*, the land under water, and it was to retain this name until the end of the Roman period. What happened in the Fayum happened also along the Mediterranean sea-board. The huge lakes which stretch almost without interruption from Alexandria to Port Said – Mareotis, Burlus and Menzaleh – were formerly fresh-water lakes, covered with water-lilies, where the papyrus plants and reeds grew in profusion. As a result of a subsidence in the coast-line, sea-water rushed in and all vegetable life disappeared. Vast stretches of land around the Isthmus of Suez, which had been thickly populated and cultivated, were impregnated with salt and became unfit for growing crops.

Soon after entering the Delta, the Nile splits up into several channels. One of these, the Ithi canal, which flows eastwards, used to water Heliopolis, skirt the desert and join the Wadi Tumilat which was navigable for part of the year. Finally it disappeared into Lake Timsah, which still retains today the Egyptian name for the crocodile, *meseh*. The name was well-deserved, because an official document shows us another stretch of water situated to the north of Timsah, in the Isthmus of Suez, which was infested with crocodiles (fig. 3). Near Heliopolis another branch of the Nile took a north-westerly direction and entered the Mediterranean near Pelusium. The Egyptians and the Hebrews called it *Shi-Hor*, Lake Horus. It marked the frontier between Egypt and Palestine. Being overgrown with reeds, it was always unsuitable for navigation. To the north-west of Heliopolis, rather more than thirty miles below Memphis, the Nile divides up into its two main arms: the Damietta arm, known in the ancient world as the great river, and the Rosetta branch, the Western Nile, which flowed near the large town of Sae. Not far from Athribis the Tanite arm broke away from the main river; for the Egyptians, this was the water of Avaris down which navigators sailed on their way to Syria, whereas those who came from the Hellenic sea sailed up the Western Nile. The many streams which broke away from the main arms helped to irrigate the inland areas and maintain communications there. One of the most important was the Anpi Canal, which flowed near the two large neighbouring towns of Thmuis and Mendes.

The Greeks considered that the Egyptian sea-board was far from hospitable. At a very early period the Egyptians established observation posts to prevent pirates entering the river mouths. It should be noticed that in Pharaonic times there were no important towns

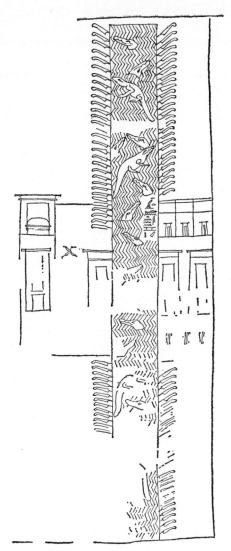

Fig. 3. Crocodile-infested lake in the Isthmus of Suez, a bas-relief from Karnak. The lake marked the boundary between Egypt and the desert inhabited by nomads.

along the coast. Edfu, which was considered to be Egypt's most northerly town, was more than thirty miles inland. Before Alexander founded the capital to which he gave his name, only a small market-town stood on the spot – Rakotis. Ports such as Naucratis, Tanis, formerly Avaris, and Pernefer near Basti (Bubastis) were river ports.[1]

Long before Herodotus described their country as the gift of the Nile, the Egyptians were fully aware of their debt to the river. In their everyday language they referred to it simply as *itr-âa*, the river: the addition of the article *na* gave the Greek word *Neîlos*, and Nile in the modern languages. However, they honoured and gave thanks to their river under the name of Hâpi. They imagined him as a well-nourished man, with huge breasts hanging heavily over his chest and his belly bulging out over his belt. Before his entry into Egypt, he hid in a cave on the island of Senem (fig. 4), holding a libatory vessel in each hand, for the Egyptians imagined the inundation as one vast libation: the libation of Seth spread over Upper Egypt from Elephantine to Per-Hapi, not far from present-day old Cairo, and the libation of Horus spread over Lower Egypt from Per-Hapi to Edfu.

Fig. 4. The source of the Nile, from a bas-relief at Philae. Hidden away in his cave, Hâpi causes the beneficial waters of the Nile to rise over both Upper and Lower Egypt.

These three points interested the geometricians who had worked out the distance between Elephantine and Per-Hapi to be 86 atours (430 miles), and that between Per-Hapi and Edfu[2] to be 20 atours (100 miles). As early as the Twelfth Dynasty, nilometres had been introduced in these three towns, in order to measure the progress, the height and duration of the inundation according to which the state income was calculated. At Elephantine, the level of the water was 21 cubits, 3 fingers (about 11·52 metres), at Per-Hapi, 12 cubits, 3 hands, 3 fingers (about 6·62 metres), and at Edfu 6 cubits, 3 hands, 3 fingers (about 3·17 metres). According to another method, which the people perhaps considered to be a fairer one, the level of water covering the fields was measured when the inundation was supposed to be at its highest point: in Upper Egypt this must have been: 3 cubits, 3 hands and ⅓ of a finger: in Lower Egypt 4 cubits, 3 hands.

Since the Nile was a source of wealth both for the public authorities and private individuals alike, it was right and proper to show gratitude. Ramses III has left an account of all the offerings he made to the Nile at Per-Hapi, in the Lake of the Libation, in the temple of Ra Harakhte, and in the temple of Anubis at Troia, as well as of previous offerings over a period of thirty-one years, together with what was offered up to Hâpi at Memphis during a period of three years.[3] There was a little of everything that the Egyptians valued – bread, beer, cattle, poultry fodder, wine, honey, grapes and other fruit, not to mention statues made of gold, silver, lapis-lazuli, turquoise and many other comparatively rare materials. Things only flourished in Egypt when human piety equalled the liberality of the gods.

The time would come for Hâpi to show himself. Nature would be in a state of exhaustion, and the trees grey with dust; a few vegetable plots, kept alive with great difficulty, provided the only patches of green on the landscape. The White Nile and the Blue Nile, one swollen with the equatorial rains, the other with the melted snow from the Abyssinian highlands, would reach Khartoum at the same time, driving forward debris which for several days coloured the water green. The rising of the waters was observable at Aswan about the 8th June, at Cairo from the 17th to the 20th and two days later in the Delta. The green Nile was succeeded by the red Nile. The river would rise, filling up its former bed, and begin to spread over the countryside. When the flood was at its height during the second half of September, the whole valley became a shallow river flowing between two deserts. The towns and villages built on mounds became tiny islands joined by causeways. Nature would suddenly spring to life again. Man and beast rejoiced together; Sebek, the crocodile god, splashed about in his lake. All work ceased; the only necessary task was to protect causeways and walls. This was the time when the sacred barges left their home-ports and carried the faithful to the places of pilgrimage.

Sometimes, the river would rise again after the first subsidence. Under one of the Saïte kings, there was a second flood because of unseasonable rain on the mountain of Punt, that is, in Abyssinia.

At about the beginning of October the Nile returned to its normal bed and continued to shrink until the following summer. The

inundation lasted for four months. The period between two inundations was divided into two equal seasons of four months: *perit*, the
going out into the fields, or the sprouting of cereals, and *shemu*, the
harvest. These words soon came to signify winter and summer. It
was therefore the inundation which controlled the agricultural life
of the country and which provided the basis of the Egyptian calendar.

From a distance, the desert cliffs bordering the Nile valley look
like two walls of uniform height. A closer view reveals amphitheatres,
gorges isolating massive, fortress-like blocks of stone, which sometimes take the shape of a human head or a recumbent lion, or even
pyramids, as is the case to the west of Karnak. Many of the wadis
are soon lost in the desert sands. Others, beyond a certain point,
turn into desert tracks, which were closely guarded by the Egyptian
soldiers, because they led to wells, gold-mines and quarries. From
Coptos three tracks led eastwards and ran into the Red Sea at points
where, during the Hellenistic period, the ports of Berenice, Kosseir
and Myos Hormos enjoyed a certain prosperity. The middle track
was used mostly by miners and quarrymen on their way to work in
the Rohanu valley, which was three days' walk from the gold-mines
and shale quarries. The Wadi Tura, which ran alongside the
Mokkatam and the Gebel Tura, was the starting point of a track
which finally emerged in the Suez area. A road, called the Philistines'
Road at the time of the New Kingdom, began at Tjaru in the
Isthmus (the present-day El Kantara) and led back to the shore.
Another, which also started at Tjaru, followed a series of water-holes,
and terminated in the land of Canaan. The towns of Erment, Hu,
Saka, Nennesu and Memphis were the starting points of the chief
tracks which maintained communications between the Nile valley
and the string of oases in the Libyan desert. The valley appeared
to be well protected but there were gaps, which were both easy to
pass through and easy to guard. This was a great advantage to the
Egyptians, who needed to carry out prospecting in the desert and
who sent both merchants and soldiers to foreign countries. At the
same time, however, invaders came into their country on several
occasions by these same routes.

Flora

The nature of the soils and the pattern followed by the inundation
meant that the Nile valley was predominantly a land which produced
annual plants – for food, for the making of textiles and dye-stuffs,
for medicinal purposes, and simply for decoration.[4] It is still a
debatable point whether barley and wheat were indigenous to

Egypt or whether these plants had been imported from Mesopotamia in prehistoric times. Whatever the truth of the matter, barley (*iot*) and emmer-wheat (*boti*) were the oldest cereals known to the Egyptians, because their names were written in the most primitive ideographic script: barley was represented by three grains, wheat by an ear. The names of other varieties of cereals introduced later were written in phonetic characters. On the bas-reliefs of the Old Kingdom, the cultivation of flax is often included along with that of cereal plants. On the reliefs just mentioned, lettuces, onions, watermelons and cucumbers can be recognized. In later Egyptian texts, in the Bible and in classical authors, garlic, leeks, beans and lentils are mentioned. Sesame and the castor-oil plant provided oil. The doctors had discovered that castor-oil could be used as a purgative, that it made hair grow, and alleviated certain skin ailments. Classical authors refer to Egyptian cotton, but the local word for it is not known. The plants used by the dyers were alkanet, madder, henna, and indigo.

The vine, which was supposed to be a gift from Osiris, was cultivated during the Old Kingdom in the Delta, chiefly round lakes Mareotis and Menzaleh. The vine obligingly supplied dessert grapes and grapes for wine-making in Middle and Upper Egypt, as well as in the main oases. One district near the cataract was called Irp, the word for wine. It is difficult to believe that the vine grew so far south; the name is perhaps an indication of the fact that wine was taken there to be sold.

Egypt was not a land of forests, yet, as can be seen from certain Theban paintings, the Egyptian landscape was not entirely treeless. The Egyptians loved trees because of their intrinsic beauty, their cooling shade, and their fruit. In every nome, not far from the chief temple, there was a sacred orchard. Ani, a landowner of the Eighteenth Dynasty, had his garden, in which he had assembled twenty-three varieties of trees, painted on his tomb.[5]

The sycamore, *nehet*, was the Egyptian tree *par excellence*. It grew in the villages, at cross-roads, even on the edge of the desert provided its roots could reach down to the water in the subsoil. It was a sturdy tree, nearly as broad as it was high and extremely leafy. The date-palm, with which it was often associated, was on the contrary tall and slender. Copses, even fairly extensive plantations, of palm-trees used to be found – and are still found, like the one which now covers the old site of the town of Memphis. The dôm-palm, the trunk of which divides into branches a few yards from the ground, was only found south of Thebes. Ani must have been very proud indeed to show visitors the exceptionally tall palm, known as the kuku, concerning which a somewhat botanically-minded scribe supplies the following information:

'Oh dôm-palm, sixty cubits high, in which coconuts are to be found. Inside the coconuts are husks. Inside the husks is water. The place where this water is collected is far away.'[6]

There was, in fact, only one coconut palm among the 481 trees in the garden. Fig-trees were abundant, and when the figs were ripe both children and monkeys took part in the harvest in their own way. Willows and tamarisks, jujube, balanos, moringa, carob, pomegranate and chaouaba trees, not to mention several other unidentified varieties, completed the collection. The pomegranate tree appears to have been introduced into Egypt at the beginning of the Eighteenth Dynasty. It can be recognized in the garden created by Tuthmosis III and depicted in the great temple of Amun. Naturalists have identified the chaouaba with the mimusops shimpera, which was known to the Arabs as *lebbakh*, and to the classical authors as persea. Diodorus wrongly imagined that it had been imported by Cambyses. The moringa supplied an oil which was highly prized by perfumers and doctors. No mention is made before the New Kingdom of the olive tree, *djede*, which was not to be found in Ani's garden. It soon became acclimatized in Egypt and Theophrastes noted a forest of olive-trees in the Thebes area. According to Strabo, the olive-trees in the Fayum gave the best fruit. The seyel acacia supplied the carpenters and boat-builders with good quality wood. The terebinth, the resin of which, *sonté*, was used as incense to burn before the gods, and to anoint the dead, grew in the oases and on the desert to the east of Memphis. The orange-tree, lemon-tree, rose-tree and others, which today adorn squares and gardens, were unknown in ancient Egypt.

For the Egyptians, who never saw a rose until the Roman period, the queen of flowers was the white or blue lotus (fig. 5). Huge bunches of it decorated the banquet halls. Women receiving at home or out visiting used to hold lotus blooms in their hands or pin them in their hair. Even the men wore crowns of lotus flowers during

Fig. 5. White lotus and blue lotus from the tomb of Ti. Both these plants are frequently depicted. The pink lotus, which Greek and Roman writers mention as growing in Egypt, has been discovered only in the Graeco-Roman necropolises.

their rustic festivals. The tuberous root of the plant could be grilled or boiled, and a sort of pastry was made from the ground seeds.

The papyrus plant was put to several uses. The lower part of the stem was chewed, just as cane sugar is chewed today. The rest of it was used to make panniers, baskets, cages and light skiffs. The basket in which the baby Moses was placed was made of papyrus. Its principal use, nevertheless, was for the manufacture of paper, which was suitable for both writing and drawing and which lasted indefinitely. There were dense clumps of papyrus plants in the north of Egypt. The spreading umbels of the plants, the stems of which were five or six times the height of a man, provided nesting places for kingfishers and other river birds, which were under constant threat

Fig. 6. Umbels of the papyrus plant, tomb of Ti. Many writers have failed to distinguish between the lotus and the papyrus plant. They were, in fact, quite different, and are shown to be so on Egyptian bas-reliefs.

of attack from civets, rats and wild cats (fig. 6), while fish, otters, hippopotami and crocodiles sported and chased each other among the roots of the plants.

In Upper Egypt, at least according to paintings of the Middle and New Kingdoms, the papyrus plant was less tall and grew less profusely than in the Delta. The plant has now completely disappeared, apart from a few specimens which are to be found in the gardens of Cairo. On the other hand, it grows wild in the Upper Jordan valley and along the shores of Lake Huley, which has kept its old name *hely*, as is confirmed by some documents and especially by the hieroglyphic sign, *hl*.

Fauna

The elephant, the rhinoceros, the giraffe and the python, which were to be found in Egypt during the Neolithic period, emigrated southwards at the beginning of historic times; other beasts were driven back into the desert, and some, such as the dog, the ox, the ass, the goat and the sheep[8] became domesticated. Two different species of oxen can be distinguished on the numerous reliefs depicting rural life in the Old Kingdom. The *nega*, long-legged, lean, wild and with powerful horns, lived and bred in the grass-lands. The cows were trained to the plough, and the bulls were sometimes used for pulling heavy loads. The name of this animal still survives in some African languages. The *ioua* was the *bos africanus*; heavier and fatter than the *nega*, it was used chiefly as butcher-meat. The Egyptians imported whole boat-loads of them from the Sudan, where huge herds of oxen roam freely even today. Except in a few Delta districts there are more buffaloes than oxen in present-day Egypt. The horse was only introduced into Egypt at the time of the Hyksos. It was trained for war and used as a means of transport. The ass, which has always been the companion of the fellah, was used for various purposes.

Other quadrupeds, which had resisted domestication, lived either singly or in herds in the desert wadis. The Egyptians tried to capture them and were still trying to tame them during the Old Kingdom. These were the oryx, with long straight horns, the deer, the ibex, the mouflon, the addax, and the graceful gazelle. During their hunting expeditions, the Egyptians met with various flesh-eating beasts, which were in search of the same game as they were: the lion (fig. 7), which was gradually to disappear with the result that the Pharaohs of the New Kingdom had to go lion-hunting in Mesopotamia, the panther, the wolf, the fox, the jackal, and the hyena. Attempts to train the hyena for hunting met with little success.

Naturalists have been able to identify these and other animals because Egyptian artists had an exceptional gift of observation, which enabled them to recognize the features peculiar to each species, and even to each variety. They applied the same skill to the depicting of fish and aquatic animals.[9] The perch, in Egyptian, *âha* (the fighter) was nearly as big as the men who caught it, and had to be slung on an oar to be carried away. Sea mullet swam up the Nile tributaries, as did dolphins. There was a sort of synodontis which developed the habit of swimming on its back, so that its belly had darkened – hence its name, *batensoda*. The *chromis niloticus*, which is rather like our carp, is still found in Egypt today, and also in Lake Huley in Palestine, perhaps because it feeds on the papyrus plant. A very curious fish is the fahaka, which fills itself with air, turns over on its back and drifts along with the current, showing its silvery under-side. Maspero says that Nature must have created it as a joke.

Fig. 7. A lion carrying off a gazelle from an enclosure, Tomb of Ti. On the tomb of Ptah-hotep, which belongs to the same period, hunters are shown with a lion and a panther they have captured.

Larger creatures also inhabited Egyptian waters. The crocodile, strong enough to pull an unwary traveller beneath the surface, was to be found along the whole length of the Nile, as well as in the lakes and swamps – and usually in conjunction with the hippo-potamus. The two were enemies. The crocodile would keep a watchful eye on the female hippopotamus, waiting for her to give birth; whereupon he would gobble up the new-born calf. The male hippopotamus would arrive too late on the scene and engage the villain in a fatal struggle. The Egyptians mummified crocodiles by the thousand, and harpooned hippopotami, which often overturned their papyrus skiffs. Innumerable migratory birds, attracted by the fruit trees, the fields and the huge swamps, used to spend the winter in Egypt and often settled there. The ibis, which was mummified and interred as a god, disappeared at the same time, no doubt, as the lotus flower and the papyrus plant. Even today, flocks of often

13

destructive little birds give a picturesque note to the countryside; when the grain-harvest is unloaded, clouds of quails swoop down to the threshing-floor, and the peasants make no attempt to chase them away, because is it not true that everything must be allowed to live? During the ancient period, birds of prey nested in hollows among the rocks on both sides of the Nile; they included several species of vulture – the kite, the buzzard, the falcon and the hawk, without which Egypt would perhaps have been uninhabitable. The kite was considered to be a thief but the falcon and the vulture were venerated as divine creatures. Ostriches lived on the edge of the desert and in the mornings would run towards the rising sun. The scorpion, the viper and the cobra stung and killed a great number of people. They even attacked the gods. Certain pious and clever men acquired great reputations during their lifetimes and remained famous after death because they had succeeded in protecting their entourage from this terrible threat.

The two faces of nature

It was most fortunate – the Greeks considered it to be nothing short of a miracle – that the flood should occur just when the whole of nature was parched by the summer sun. The heat was often very intense throughout the entire *shemu* season. It was a relief to breathe in the sweet north wind. The Egyptians never complained about their climate. References to rain, cold, heat, and thunder occur frequently in the surviving documents. It was said for instance of the king:

'He is a parasol during the season of the inundation,
A cooling draught in summer
He is a warm dry shelter during the winter season
He is the mountain protecting us from the wind when there are storms
in the sky.'[10]

Harvesters would ask to be supplied with beer. One of them mentions the fact that the sun is hot. Such comments are very moderate, and it can be said that the Egyptians of Upper as well as of Lower Egypt were quite satisfied with their climate, both in winter and summer. The children ran about naked. Men, rich or poor, wore only a loin-cloth; the peasants wore a belt, the women a shift. The shepherds would settle down for the night, or take shelter from the wind, in a sort of cabin made from reeds. Sometimes they would put on a knitted jersey. During the New Kingdom men wore a flimsy pleated robe over the loin-cloth – more as a concession to

14

fashion than as a means of protection against the cold. They left
woollen garments to Asiatics. It is clear that the people of Egypt
were not unduly inconvenienced by the variations in temperature –
although these were appreciable.

This might seem too favourable an estimate of Egyptian life and
it is corrected to some extent by the Bible story.[11] The plagues that
the prophet inflicted on Egypt in order to frighten the Pharaoh are
a summary of the disasters which could occur without any sort of
supernatural intervention and from time to time made life very
difficult. It will be remembered that frogs, lice and flies constituted
the second, third and fourth plagues. The Egyptians paid little
attention to frogs, but they did everything they could to protect
themselves from lice, mosquitoes and flies, as well as from rats.
Locusts – the eighth plague – were a much-feared scourge, so much
so that the peasants were in the habit of praying to a locust god. The
fifth plague was a disease which attacked live-stock, the tenth an
illness which killed off new-born babies, and the sixth an epidemic
affecting the whole of the population. Hail, the seventh plague, often
damaged the harvest. Lastly, there was the eleventh plague – a west
wind which on certain days in spring raised a cloud of dust so dense
that the whole countryside was plunged in darkness.

Such disasters actually occurred, but they were not peculiar to
Egypt, as the children of Israel well knew since they sought asylum
in Egypt when famine raged in the land of Canaan. The Egyptians
suffered from famine more than once during the course of their long
history. It could be caused by an insufficient flood, and might be
aggravated by anarchy and inefficiency. Epidemics were thought to
be the work of Sekhmet, the lion-headed goddess who also had the
power to bring them to an end, for her priests were also doctors.
All things considered, it can be said that Egypt was most lavishly
endowed by nature. She had a temperate climate, in which snow
and ice were unknown, and the heat was never excessive even at the
height of summer; a land regularly and naturally fertilized by the
inundation and exceptionally suited to the cultivation of necessary
foods; and two deserts which appeared to have been created for the
express purpose of protecting the valley from invasion, and which
concealed an incalculable wealth of ore and minerals. These various
factors created ideal conditions for the founding of a great civilisation. By regulating agricultural activity, and by imposing a discipline
which facilitated the exercise of authority, the Nile, which was
worshipped as a god, established concord among all those who lived
along its banks. Surely no other country could provide a more
delightful picture.

CHAPTER 2

THE EGYPTIANS IN THE NILE VALLEY

Prehistoric man

MAN appeared in Egypt at a very early date. The tools found by the geologists Sandford and Arkell on the terraces overlooking the Nile date from the early Abbevillian period to the Mousterian period.[1] Previously, Bovier-Lapierre had found tools belonging to these same periods in the quarries at Abbassieh, at a spot where the Nile widens; they had been unearthed by the river and deposited in regular layers.[2] Implements belonging to the Acheulean period have also been found in the Khargeh oasis. Relics of the Mousterian period abound in the oases, particularly in an area a little to the west of Nag Hamadi. In the neighbourhood of Kom Ombo, quite a numerous population known as the Sebilians lived for a long time on the shores of a lake, fed by two tributaries of the Nile, and hemmed in by the extension of Gebel Silsileh.[3] Although at the beginning they used typically Mousterian weapons, they finally learnt to arm their arrows and javelins with microliths. When the lake dried up they spread across the valley as far as the Fayum. Chisels and microliths have been found at Aswan, Medamud, in the Fayum, at Khargeh and in the Libyan desert. They have been found too on the other side of the Nile at Helwan and in the Arabian desert. The same type of tool was discovered in Tunisia, while the flint blades and small chisels found in the Fayum have a close affinity with the objects discovered in the Regina grotto in Cyrenaica, and the arrowheads of Helwan with those found in Palestine. It follows that the tribes of the Upper Paleolithic period roamed extensively over north-eastern Africa, crossing the Nile in both directions, and teaching each other their various skills.

At the beginning of the Neolithic period, about 5000 BC, a change of climate forced the descendants of these nomadic tribes to move nearer to the Nile and the lakes, although they kept away from the flooded area. They worked the land, cultivated barley, wheat and flax, built rudimentary houses with mud, tried to domesticate a few animal species, and developed a liking for adornment. Evidence of their existence has been discovered at Tasa in Middle Egypt, in the Fayum,[4] near Helwan and at Merimdeh Beni-Salameh, to the north-west of the pyramids.

The necropolis which Brunton explored at El Badari in Middle Egypt contained proof of progress in the various spheres of activity.[5] By now, copper had made its appearance, and the tombs contained stone vases and statuettes. The Badarians, who had inherited much from the Neolithic civilization, bequeathed their techniques to the Amratians, who settled between Erment and Siut. They in turn were succeeded by the Gerzeans who spread over a wider area; in fact they occupied all the sites which had been inhabited by the Amratians. Evidence of their presence has also been discovered at Nekhen in Upper Egypt and at various points in the valley opposite the Fayum, at Helwan, where the archaeologists of Cairo University are exploring a village in the dwellings of which tools, stone vases, pottery, copper and toilet accessories have been discovered.[6] The skeletons found in the above-mentioned cemeteries and villages were chiefly of Mediterranean and negroid types: a small section belonged to the Cromagnon types, and an even smaller proportion to the brachycephalic types. Judging by the clay and ivory statuettes, the men and women were thin, tall, of rather delicate build and with pointed chins. Dwarfs and steatopygous women also occurred. At this period, then, Egypt was a meeting-point. Strangers who had come from east, west, north and south, some by way of the Mediterranean coast, others by way of the Nile, now mingled with the natives and the desert dwellers who had turned back towards the valley.

The Gerzeans were a sedentary people who knew how to build long, large boats with cabins, each boat being provided with a distinctive ensign fixed at the top of a vertical pole. Later, several of these emblems were used to designate territories, towns, or gods (fig. 8). For instance:

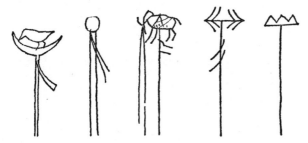

Fig. 8. Prehistoric ensigns, from Loret, *Rev. Egypt.* XI. Other emblems are less easy to identify.

the elephant	the island and town of Elephantine
the solar disc	the god of On, the Greek Heliopolis
the belemnite	the god Min: the Seventeenth Nome of Upper Egypt
two crossed arrows	the goddess Neith: two nomes of Lower Egypt
a falcon in a basket	the god Anzti: the Eighteenth Nome of Upper Egypt
a harpoon	two nomes of Lower Egypt
a mountain chain	the god Ha: a western arm of the Nile.[7]

For these clans life was not easy, as we can see from the slate palettes and the decorated ivory objects which belong to the era immediately prior to the beginning of the historical period.[8] They organized large-scale hunts, and succeeded better than their Neolithic ancestors in taming the various beasts which had already got used to living in proximity to man. There was bitter warfare between the clans; two or more clans would join forces against their neighbours or against aggressors who had come from further afield. The Falcon and the Ibis formed an alliance against bearded warriors, with frizzy hair. Their warriors, allied to those of the Belemnite and the Wolf, attacked these same enemies who had entrenched themselves inside circular enclosures. Another episode in this struggle for survival is depicted on one side of the palette known as the Libyan Tribute. The Falcon, the Lion, the Scorpion, and the Two Falcons

Fig. 9. Boats used by invaders from the East, from Winkler, I, pl. XXII. This type of boat was no longer in use during the historic period.

can be seen vigorously destroying the fortresses in which the Great Duke, a Plumed Bird, the Twins and other clans symbolized by a sort of fence, a plant, and some indefinable object, have taken refuge. If we could be certain that the two sides of the palette referred to the same event, it would be possible to assume that the conquered clans were Libyans, since this other side depicts the tribute sent from the land of the Tehenu, where there are trees which have, justifiably, been taken to be olives. The tribute consisted of cattle, donkeys and sheep, and since Egypt was a land of habit the same tribute sent from the same country is found on a bas-relief of the Fifth Dynasty. Other invaders came from the East in long boats, the prows and poops of which were set almost at right-angles (fig. 9). Boats of this type are depicted on the ivory handle of a knife found at Gebel-el-Arak,[9] as well as on rocks a long way away from the Nile valley. Similar drawings have also been discovered in Mesopotamia (fig. 10). The invaders had as their leader a personage with clawed feet,

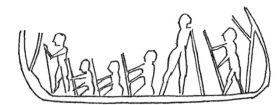

Fig. 10. Mesopotamian boat, from P. Amiet, *La glyptique mésopotamienne*, Pl. 13 bis. Boats of this type probably served as models for those shown in Fig. 9.

a beard and a tiara, who could, with each hand, force a lion up on its hind legs, and who looks very like the Gilgamesh of the Babylonian epics.

At the beginning of historic times, King Scorpion did not yet reign over the whole of Egypt, for he wore the crown of the South. He became the head of a confederation which united two new clans, whose ensigns were later to represent the god Seth and the god Khonsu, to the already mentioned clans of the mountain and the belemnite. Together these various clans conquered two other groups, the Lapwings and the Bows, who continued to play an important part in Egypt.

Narmer, the Scorpion's probable successor, wore the crown of the South and the North, as occasion required. His god, the Falcon, brought to him as captives the inhabitants of Ta-meh, Lower Egypt, who can be assumed to be of Asiatic origin because of their aquiline noses, thick heads of hair and beards (fig. 11). These people are not referred to by name on the slate palette, but they were in fact none other than the Lapwings.[10]

The fact that the Falcon was represented on various documents

Fig. 11. The Falcon brings the Men of the North to the King (Palette of King Narmer). He will club one of them to death.

as being the chief instrument of the unification of Egypt has a philological explanation. The name Heru, the name of the god whom the Egyptians were soon to represent as a falcon (they continued to do so until the end of the pagan period), was the same as the name of the falcon *huru*, recorded in Arab dictionaries. The Falcon came from the Arabian peninsula, whose inhabitants have so often invaded Egypt during the course of history, and entered the Nile valley. It settled at Edfu, where there still exists a magnificent Temple of Horus, in which a series of bas-reliefs depicts the routing of Seth by the god and his allies – a distant echo of what very probably occurred at the time of Scorpion and Narmer.

The races of man

The inscriptions of the historical period often state that the enemy has been completely wiped out. It must be admitted that this is an obvious exaggeration, since the enemy in question soon showed himself to be every bit as aggressive as before. We must suppose, therefore, that the kings who achieved the unity of their country in those distant times, did so not by destroying their enemies but by bringing them into subjection, whether they were native Egyptians or invaders who had come from east or west. At the dawn of her history, Egypt's population in the Nile valley was extremely mixed, and it remained so later.

However diverse their origins may have been, Egyptians of the classical period were conscious of themselves as a nation. In several royal tombs of the New Kingdom – the best-known example is in the tomb of Seti I – there is a picture (fig. 12) showing representatives of four races. First, the *remtu*, the Egyptians themselves, recognizable by their round heads, their short square beards, and their scanty loin-cloths. Beside them are the Asiatics, the Amu, clad in woollen loin-cloths decorated with acorns. With their aquiline profiles, very different from the Egyptian profile, bushy beards and abundant hair, they bear a close resemblance to the people of Ta-meh, who were subjugated by Narmer. Then there are the Nehesiu who lived in the south of Egypt. They had all the charac-

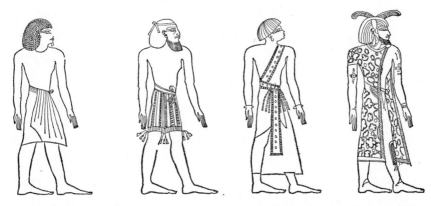

Fig. 12. The human races as shown on the tomb of Seti, Lepsius, *Denkmäler* III. Each race is represented by four persons of rank.

teristics of a black-skinned people, flat faces, and woolly hair. They wore a long loin-cloth and wound bands of cloth round their bodies. Lastly, the Timihu, who lived to the west of Egypt, were fairly close to the Asiatics in respect of profiles and beards, but different from them in that they left a long tress of hair hanging over one shoulder, and fixed ostrich feathers in their hair. Over their loin-cloths, they wore a sort of short, open jacket, with only one sleeve. The Egyptians, then, had no difficulty in distinguishing themselves from the peoples of the east, the west and the south, who figure on bas-reliefs as early as the Fifth Dynasty, and who were represented as being somewhat similar of feature.

Throughout this book, we shall often be obliged to make use of the various word lists in which the Egyptians painstakingly grouped essential terms into categories: heaven, earth, water, persons, offices and professions, human types, the towns of Egypt, buildings and their component parts, agriculture, drink, food.[11] The first section opens with a word already mentioned, *remt*, men, as opposed to gods, and, in the picture representing the human races, men *par excellence*, the Egyptians. Similarly *niut*, the town, in New Kingdom documents meant the queen of towns: Thebes. After *remt*, we learn that there were three categories of human beings: the *Pat*, the *Henemmt*, and the *Rekhet*.

In everyday language, all these words could be synonymous with *remt*, human beings, but more often they referred to sections of the same word, *remt*, in the sense of Egyptian. For instance, they were used on his triumphal stela by Ahmosis, the founder of the Eighteenth Dynasty who freed Egypt from the hateful Hyksos.

'He seized the *Henemmt*. He captures the *Rekhet* and the *Pat* adore him.'

The three groups are not presented as being on the same level. The *Pat* welcomed the victory with unmitigated joy, whereas the *Henemmt* and the *Rekhet* were subject to constraint. It so happened that when the Hyksos occupied Egypt as far as Cusae, they found, both in the occupied zone and in the oases, people who were ready to come to terms with them, and even to become their allies. When the father of Ahmosis undertook to free the country, the *Pat* probably rallied enthusiastically round him, while the two other groups gave very half-hearted support, thus justifying their bad reputation. As early as the Pyramid Texts, the *Pat* were associated with Horus whose earthly representative was the king. On the day of his coronation the king received the *Pat* as if they were his own flesh and blood. When the king died, he was mourned by the *Pat*, while the *Henemmt* and the *Rekhet* appeared to be unmoved by the event. An inscription on a certain stela states that magistrates must distinguish between the *Patu* and *Rekhet*. A certain vizier put the precept into practice and prided himself on having praised the *Patu* to the detriment of the *Rekhet*. The former were, as we would say today, respectable, high-class people, the others were not.

As the word *Patu* was a collective noun, the Egyptians invented the expression *iry-pat*, *iret-pat* in the feminine, which signified those who belonged to the *Pat*. As far as we can tell, the first people to whom this appellation was given were Imhotep, Zoser's adviser and architect, and a high priest of Re. Queens of the Old and New Kingdoms were *iret-pat*, but we cannot be sure that they bore this title automatically.

Under the Old Kingdom, a great many important personages were given the title – the sons of the royal household, governors of provinces and high-ranking magistrates. But high rank did not necessarily carry the title with it. Men who had been honoured with a letter in the king's own hand, who had been granted a tomb by him, who occupied important positions and led missions to foreign countries, were not *iry-pat* although they held several honorary titles and were *hati-a* (princes), Unique Friends of the King. It seems possible that the title of *iry-pat* was reserved for a fairly numerous special class.

A provincial nobleman called Khnumhetep, who, under the Twelfth Dynasty, was governor of the town which was Cheops's birthplace, tells us that his mother, the daughter of a Regent of the Oryx Nome was sent to finish her education in a royal castle and rose to the rank of princess. She married a noble who was also a prince, and her son Khnumhetep inherited from his mother's father the titles of *iry-pat* and prince, and was given the governorship of the town of Menat-Khufu. A certain Zasu, whose two sisters were in turn the wives of Pepi II, declared himself to be a true *pat*. He was, moreover, the son of an *iry-pat* and the adjective 'true' perhaps differentiated him from those whose claim to nobility was of more recent date. The coveted title may have been attached to certain functions, and certainly the king had the power to confer it when he appointed someone who did not yet possess it. How many of the *Pat* of the Late Period could have traced the ancestry back even as far as the Ramses? The *Pat* obviously represented an aristocracy, but an aristocracy which was renewed on numerous occasions. At all periods, it included the faithful servants of the King.

The other two groups are more difficult to define. There is no actual evidence to prove that any individual belonged to either the *Rekhet* or the *Henemmt* or that any particular profession was associated with them. The *Henemmt* were the most mysterious. According to one of the Pyramid texts the sky was their domain. Their name was written as a radiant sun, which was also used in the word *akhu*, the brightness of the sun. Perhaps they were descendants of the old clan of the sun, which had already been depicted on Gerzean vases; perhaps they can be considered as the founders of the town of the sun, On (Heliopolis), which was to remain one of the greatest religious centres in Egypt.

The name of the *Rekhetu* was represented by a lapwing. There are therefore some grounds for believing that the somewhat despised *Rekhetu* of the historical period were the descendants of the Lapwings who were pathetically hung up by the neck below the emblems of King Scorpion's allies (fig. 13). On the pedestal of Zoser's statue they are still treated as enemies, although in a less cruel manner.

Their feathers are intertwined two by two, according to the method that hunters employed with captured birds to prevent them flying away. An old title of Horus still in use under the Twelfth Dynasty was 'The Smiter of Lapwings'. We are tempted to associate King Scorpion's birds with the inhabitants of Ta-meh, who were conquered by King Narmer, which means that we can assume them to have lived in the northern part of the country. As a matter of fact, the Mediterranean coast was called 'The circle of the Lapwings'. A fragment of a sarcophagus belonging to the Thirtieth Dynasty, now in the New York museum, provides two interesting items of information.[12] The Lapwings are depicted as men bearing on their heads

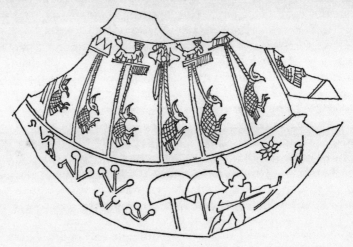

Fig. 13. Lapwings on the mace of King Scorpion. On another fragment of this mace, the Bows are shown hanging from the ensigns.

the tiny crest characteristic of the bird. Their position indicates that they were associated with the Delta. Moreover, during the course of history the inhabitants of the Delta often came into conflict with those of Upper Egypt.

In short, everything seems to indicate that the Egyptians preserved in these names some faint echoes of their most remote past. The *Henemmt*, who worshipped the sun, could be said to represent the first inhabitants of the Nile valley, the original natives whose history had been lost in the mists of time. The Lapwings, who had come from either the east or the west, or perhaps from both, had firmly established themselves along the Delta. The *Patu*, led by the Falcon god, had imposed their authority on their predecessors, and remained as a sort of aristocracy, and the Pharaoh's staunchest supporters in times of crisis. It will be seen in the following chapters that the real aristocracy, consisting of those people who occupied the highest offices and owned the country's wealth, was perpetually being renewed by the king, who made all the important appointments. As for the individuals of the lower and middle classes, they could be distinguished from each other in two ways; firstly, by the nome or the town in which they lived, where their parents had their tomb, where they intended to build their own tomb, and where they worshipped the local god: secondly, by their trade or profession, which was usually handed down from father to son – priest, warrior, scribe, artisan or farmer. We know of no law forbidding people to move from one province to another, or from one profession to another. Some who climbed to positions of authority came of lowly parentage, started in a very humble way and their talent was recognized by the king or by some nobleman. However, such instances seem to have been rare. In times of peace, people did not move from the town, or class, or profession into which they had been born.

Human types

The innumerable statues and statuettes which have been discovered in Egypt provide a magnificent contribution to the world of art. We will come back to this subject later. In this chapter we propose merely to draw attention to those statues which represent the types most common among the population of ancient Egypt, and to distinguish, as far as possible, the original inhabitants from those who were most probably foreign in origin. It must not be forgotten that, as far as the Old Kingdom is concerned, our information comes almost exclusively from the Memphis area. For the later periods it can be drawn from the whole of Egypt. For the New Kingdom, Thebes is the chief source and during the short intermediary period when the Solar disc of the Aton with its human-handed rays was in the ascendancy, the source is Akhetaton, in Middle Egypt.

The men were on the whole rather tall, although never exceptionally so. They had broad, strong shoulders, a firm flat belly, and well-developed limbs. They had clearly defined features, prominent eyes, usually large, almost flat, noses, thickish lips and somewhat low foreheads. Such were without exception the kings of Egypt at the time of the Old Kingdom. Many individuals presented the same features – for instance, Ranefer, who lived during the Fifth Dynasty, and of whom there are two statues in the Cairo Museum. This resolute-looking man represents the perfect aristocratic type, a true *iry-patu*. Rahotep, the fortunate husband of Nefert, and also the seated scribe now in the Louvre, have the same stamp, although they are rather stouter, a fact which in the scribe's case can be explained by the sedentary nature of his profession and in Rahotep's by middle age. The faces differ slightly in some respects, chiefly in expression. It would not be difficult to find similar types in Egypt today.

The famous Sheikh el-Beled is quite different. (He was so named by Mariette's workmen when they unearthed him because of his resemblance to the contemporary headman.) Solid without being muscular, a trifle stout, with a round head set on a powerful neck, he gives an impression of liveliness and vigour. He is the typical landowner, who inspects his vast domains with the stern authority of the master.

These three statues represent three perfect specimens of the Egyptian élite at the time of the pyramids: the man of action, the official and the landed proprietor.

With the scribes, who are shown seated or kneeling, the craftsmen and the manual workers, we have moved one step down the social scale. The scribe in the Louvre, whose penetrating gaze seems to read his master's thoughts before they are expressed, belongs to a higher type than was usual in his profession. His colleagues are different; their respectful attitude is accompanied by a certain coarseness of feature which is characteristic of many statues of this period, although the scribes were justly proud of their superior calling. Their heavy features and prominent eyes do not reveal a very keen intelligence.

The narrow shift worn by Egyptian women concealed a long, slender body and a small waist. The sculptors may be to blame for the rather too broad shoulders, the thick ankles, the rather too masculine hands and feet, although we can hardly hold them responsible for the fact that the women's faces had little charm and were too much like those of their husbands and fathers. Even the most beautiful were not without blemish. Nefert, Rahotep's wife, has been criticized for her receding chin, and for the lifelessness of her expression, and Menkaura's wife for her excessively masculine features.

In Egyptian art, at almost every period, aristocratic types and popular types exist side by side. In this connexion, it would be interesting to compare two female statuettes in inlaid bronze, which are more or less contemporary: Queen Karomama, wife of Takelot II, and the lady Takushit in the Athens Museum. The latter can be praised for her pleasing curves, although her face is totally without expression. Karomama's proud features are in keeping with her truly regal bearing.

We have already pointed out that Egypt was a meeting-point for different races in prehistoric times. It is therefore not surprising to find that several statues – often the most remarkable – display characteristics which denote some foreign origin. The Salt head in the Louvre, because of the shape of the skull, the prominent cheek-bones, and hollow cheeks, is more reminiscent of a Sahara type than of a city-dweller or a Nile valley farmer. Hemiunu, whose statue is in the proud possession of the Hildesheim Museum, was a noble prince, the son of a king, perhaps a nephew of Cheops, and the holder of many religious titles. He is, however, a most curious figure. The huge body in an advanced stage of cellulitis, with its rather too small head set on a bull-like neck, looks as if it belonged to a man who was in the habit of over-eating. But the thin, aquiline nose, the set lips, and the determined chin are characteristics that he must have inherited from some ancestor born in an Eastern land. Long before Joseph made a brilliant career for himself at the court of the king of Avaris, certain Semites had succeeded in winning favour with the Pharaoh. Other foreigners were no less skilful. The bust, now in the Boston Museum, of another famous personage of this period, Ankhaf, bears no resemblance to either the authentic Egyptians or to Hemiunu. Ankhaf is, incidentally, a fine figure of a man, with his broad chest, his lordly bearing, his straight, delicate nose, stern mouth and powerful chin. He could well have been of Greek extraction, a descendant of the sailors we shall discuss in a later chapter, and who were driven by the north wind towards the Egyptian coast.

At the same time, the Nile brought several southern types to Egypt. A head, which is not the original but a replacement, and which was found, like the other works referred to, in a Fourth Dynasty tomb, is undoubtedly negroid in type. The kings and rich Egyptians were fond of dwarfs, whom they brought in from the Upper Nile areas, and from the distant land of Punt, which lay at the far end of the Red Sea. They were gifted dancers and were employed as entertainers, as well as being given the task of looking after the monkeys and greyhounds which were also imported from the south, along with hunchbacks (fig. 14). They often attended to the household linen.[13] At Memphis, there were also native Egyptian dwarfs who were jewellers by trade. Their patron was the god Ptah, whom they worshipped in the form of a pataïkoi (dwarf deity). The Cabires, the sons of Ptah, were themselves dwarfs and jewellers. The statue of the dwarf Khnumhotep in the Cairo Museum was the

Fig. 14. A dwarf and a hunchback, Tomb of Ti. Dwarfs and hunchbacks are also portrayed at Beni-Hasan.

only one of its kind for a long time. However, recent excavations at Giza have provided Khnumhotep with a companion – Senb, who, in spite of his deformity, married a woman of normal size, and became the father of normal-sized children.

Under the Old Kingdom, then, immigrants came to Egypt from all directions. So far, we have mentioned only sculpture found in the region of Memphis. The statuary of more recent periods reveals human types which were common in other provinces. The excavations carried out by Mariette, about a century ago, at San el Hagar in the eastern section of the Delta, yielded a series of sculptured figures which caused a tremendous stir at the time of their discovery, and are still a subject of discussion today; I refer to the four lions with human faces and the group of the two bearers of offerings, now in the Cairo Museum. Mariette was quick to draw attention to their rugged faces, their powerful, aquiline, yet rather flattened noses, their flabby yet sunken cheeks, and their mouths which drooped at the corners. He claimed that he had seen people on the shores of Lake Menzaleh who had exactly the same features. This view has been disputed, although the question has not been made the subject of any serious research. The full flowing beards worn by the two bearers are the only examples of their kind in Egypt, although such beards were common in Mesopotamia; King Hammurabi had a full flowing beard of this variety. The eastern section of the Delta had always been visited at frequent intervals by foreigners who came from far-off lands. Some promptly returned to their own countries, while others merged with the local population. During the early years of the Nineteenth Dynasty, a new type, the Ramesside type, appeared in the statuary, and on the bas-reliefs. It has now been proved that the Ramses family came from the Tanis region, where today their descendants are to be seen at every turn. Baz Ismaïl, who was for a long time the overseer of our excavations, was a remarkable example of the type.

Under the Eighteenth Dynasty, Thebes became the queen of Egyptian cities. The statuary, bas-reliefs and paintings there reveal a type which is in sharp contrast to those represented in the art of the preceding periods. The magnificent head of Amenophis III in the British Museum, the canopic jars found in a tomb said to be that of Queen Tiy, the canopic jars of Smenkhara, and the bas-reliefs on the tombs of Ramose and Khamhat, are very fine examples, as are too the extraordinary contents of Tutankhamen's tomb. Foreign types are not absent from this group. The kings of the New Kingdom often married princesses from far-off lands. The exquisite Nefertiti is of pure Eurasian stock, while Queen Tiy, the daughter of two well-known Thebans, is a perfect example of a Nubian beauty. The numerous prisoners brought back at this period from foreign countries were for the most part compelled to undertake extremely painful and arduous tasks. There are, however, clever people to be found in all situations. Many a slave succeeded in improving his lot, in founding a family which eventually became an integral part of the population. In this way, the influx of foreigners continued to add variety to the native types.

In Ptolemaic times, when the Greeks spread throughout the whole of Egypt, statues began to acquire a different look. This was perhaps because new kinds of faces were to be seen among the male members of the population, or resulted from unions between Greeks and Egyptians, or it may simply be that the Greek look became fashionable.

Population numbers

The Egyptians themselves left no document which allows us to estimate the population figures for the country at any given moment. Periods of conquest and expansion, such as the beginning of the Old Kingdom, the Twelfth Dynasty, the Eighteenth (except towards its end), the reigns of Seti I and Ramses II, and the beginning of the Saïte dynasties, were obviously also times when the population was steadily increasing. In the reign of Amasis, there were, according to Herodotus, twenty thousand highly-populated towns.[14] They must have supplied enough farmers to extract the maximum amount

Fig. 15. Crippled shepherds, from Blakman, *The Rock-Tombs of Meir*, II, Pl. XIX–XX. The tombs at Meir in Middle Egypt contain a whole assembly of the halt and the lame. One or two cripples can be seen on the tombs of Ti and Ptah-hotep.

of food from the land, as well as an adequate number of craftsmen and scribes, soldiers and sailors. The quarries and the sculptors' workshops were veritable hives of activity. The building of the pyramids, the work of hollowing out and decorating the hypogea, called for a virtual mobilization of labour, and yet the more vital occupations had to be carried on as usual.

Periods of expansion were followed by equally long, if not longer, periods during which the Egyptians seemed to lose all initiative, and when the birth-rate must have dropped. However, if the birth-rate had remained constant for several thousand years, the population of Egypt, even before the Ramessides, would have run into astronomical figures.

Herodotus noted that the Egyptians were a sound, healthy people. They were meticulous in matters of personal hygiene and consulted their doctors on the slightest provocation. This did not prevent epidemics taking a heavy toll of the population. The tenth plague, the death of the first-born, must have been an epidemic affecting all young babies. There was an outbreak of the plague almost every year, and it often wrought great havoc. The records contain reference to certain infectious diseases, which called for precautionary measures, such as the isolating of the victims. During troubled times, the lack of security and order completely disrupted commerce and irrigation. Famine became widespread and children were the first to suffer.

Various sculptors have depicted people with physical disabilities going about their daily business – the obese, the under-nourished, the club-footed and the hunchbacked (fig. 15), but they represented only a minority. Such was the vitality of the Egyptian people that great disasters had only to be followed by a prosperous reign for order to be restored, the damage made good, the population once more large enough to cope both with essential tasks and the demands of the luxury trades, and again ready and able to add fresh master-pieces to the treasures of the past.

CHAPTER 3

THE PHARAOH

Definition of the Pharaoh

MODERN languages use the biblical term which described the master of Egypt: Pharaoh. It was Pharaoh who received Abraham. It was Pharaoh who was responsible for Joseph's success and who settled his brothers in the land of Goshen. Then there arose in Egypt a Pharaoh who knew not Joseph. Pharaoh persecuted the sons of Israel. Pharaoh perished in the Red Sea. Finally Pharaoh gave his daughter in marriage to Solomon. Modern scholars are faced with the baffling problem of a single title applied to six different sovereigns. The term is a literal translation of the Egyptian expression *per-aa*, the great house, in other words, the royal palace. We know of the existence of officials of the 'great house' at the time of the Old Kingdom. A courtier was brought up *m per-aa n nesu*, in the king's great house. When certain people referred to themselves as chief singer or chief wig-maker of the *per-aa*, they were thinking not so much of the palace as of its principal occupant. By the time of the Eighteenth Dynasty, *per-aa* was undoubtedly the current expression for the sovereign himself.

The king was certainly far above ordinary mortals. In official stelae he was often called *neter nefer*, the perfect god. A courtier even described him as *neter aa*, the great god. In the section of the ono-masticon dealing with people, he was put before all other humans, immediately after the supernatural beings: *neter*, god; *neterit*, goddess; *akh* and *akhit*, male and female spirits. *Nesu*, the king, is followed by *nesit*, the queen, then by the royal spouse, the royal mother and the royal children, who come before other human beings, the latter being headed by *iry-pat*, the noble.[1]

The royal infant was an exceptional being who was not born in the same way as other children. Certain ingenious theologians worked out a theory of the divine birth of the king which was depicted in wall pictures with inscriptions in the temple of Queen Hatsheput in Deir el Bahari, in the temple of Amenophis III at Luxor, and also in many other buildings which have been either destroyed or damaged.

The real father of Hatsheput was Amen-Re, king of the gods, who took the form of the reigning king, Tuthmosis I.[2] Having resolved to give Egypt a new sovereign, he summoned the Great Ennead, an assembly of twelve gods, and made known his intentions. Thoth led him to the queen who was lying in the splendour of the royal palace. She awoke at the scent of the god and laughed. Filled with desire, the god moved towards the queen. The god's love flowed through her limbs. When His Divine Majesty had accomplished what His will desired, He revealed to her the name of the

Fig. 16. A royal birth, from Naville, *Deir el-Bahari*, Pl. 50–51. The reigning king is kept out of this scene and out of those preceding and following it.

Divine Majesty to whom she would give birth and Who would reign benevolently over the whole earth. Having been apprised of the matter, Khnum, the potter-god, modelled the child together with his Ka (guardian spirit). His mistress, Heket, breathed life into it. When the appropriate time had elapsed, the same divinities led the divinely pregnant queen to the place where she was to give birth (fig. 16). Meskhent acted as midwife and Hathor as wet-nurse, helped by the Nile god and a Milk goddess. A great future was promised for the child. Amun kissed him in the presence of the gods of Upper and Lower Egypt. Everyone was, of course, aware that the father of the royal prince was Tuthmosis, that his mother was a daughter of King Ahmosis, and that he was being entrusted to the great wet-nurse, Sat-Ra, the daughter of Ra, and who was referred to by the name of Ini.[3] It was no doubt believed, that while events were taking their natural course on the earthly plane a similar sequence was being enacted by the gods. The king and queen felt themselves to be taking part in a truly sacred drama, on which the future of the dynasty and the country depended.

The theory of the divine birth was not an invention of the Eighteenth Dynasty: it had already been in existence under the Old Kingdom, but very little remains of the royal funerary temples of this period. A surviving bas-relief from the temple of Sahura shows the king being suckled by the goddess Nekhebet, a young and beautiful woman with a headdress in the form of a vulture, while Khnum, the potter-god, who had modelled the child,[4] looks on. The other episodes of the story were no doubt represented here too, although with variations. The gods of Nemphis and Heliopolis performed several functions which were later attributed to the Theban gods. Hathor was soon to assume the rôle of divine wet-nurse. A famous piece of sculpture shows us Amenemhat III lying underneath Hathor the great cow goddess and being suckled by her. Later Tuthmosis III and Psammeticus I are depicted in the same way.

A story invented perhaps under the Fifth Dynasty and certainly before the end of the Old Kingdom shows how the theories put forward by the theologians were interpreted by the common people.[5] The god Ra, like Zeus, was said to have had intercourse with a mortal, the daughter of one of his priests at Sakhebu, an actual town in the Thigh Nome, to the north-west of Memphis. The reigning king, who was none other than Cheops, did not even know of the existence of this person. However, a magician, who was better informed than the king, was aware that she was carrying three children who would fill the beneficent office (of king) over the whole earth. When she experienced the pangs of childbirth, Ra instructed several goddesses – Isis, Nephthys, Meskhent and Heket – to deliver her. Khnum went with them, to carry their baggage. The goddesses delivered three children – Userkaf, Sahura, and Kakai, who did indeed reign in succession at the beginning of the Fifth Dynasty. According to certain historical evidence, they were not brothers, but this circumstance was not likely to deter the creators of legends. We do not know the end of the story, but it is not difficult to imagine what happened. Cheops, alarmed by what the magician told him, tried to seize the three children. Naturally he did not succeed, because, as some wise man was to write later, the will of the gods must be accomplished, not the whims of men.

Great care and attention was given to the young princes' up-bringing. Certain ancient documents refer to royal establishments for the sons of noblemen, but there is no proof that the heir to the throne ever attended one. He most probably grew up in the palace under the care of a mentor. The author of one of the oldest known books of wisdom, the Vizier Ptah-hotep, was ordered by his sovereign to choose a pupil to whom he would communicate his wisdom. It is possible that the disciple he chose belonged to the royal family. A king of the First Intermediate Period took upon himself the task of enlightening his son, Prince Merikara, about the difficult task with which fate had faced him.[6] He described how the Nomarchs were ready to rebel, how any sign of weakness would be a signal for the Amu to cross the frontier and pillage the country, and how the formidable armies of the southern princes were contending for possession of the southern part of Upper Egypt. After dealing thus with the external situation, he went on to explain that, within his kingdom, the sovereign must rely on the support of a powerful élite who would be all the more eager to apply his laws with impartiality if they themselves felt fully satisfied:

The élite should be chosen on merit and not by birth:

'Great is a great (king) who has great counsellors.
Strong is the king who has a court. Magnificent is the king who is rich in nobles.'

No one should act contrary to Justice:

'Do not distinguish between the son of a noble and the man of humble birth. Take men into your service according to their capacity.'

'Do not oppress the widow; do not strip a man of his father's possessions.'

Punishment should be meted out with discrimination and the death penalty should not be pronounced too often. If the king lived in accordance with these maxims, his soul would progress serenely to the life beyond, and confront the formidable judges 'who see a whole life's span in a single instant'.

The teaching given to the prince and heir was, at least to a certain extent, determined by circumstances. Merikara's father reigned over only a small part of Egypt. We can compare, in this connexion, two texts obviously inspired by the court and composed one at the beginning of the reign of Amenemhat I, the founder of the Twelfth

Dynasty, the other at the end of the same reign.[7] The prophecy attributed to a Seer living at the time of Snofru, boldly looks five hundred years ahead, and, after recalling recent disasters and the panic caused by them, stresses the efforts made by the king to strengthen his precarious position. The teachings composed by the king himself recall that he has strengthened his frontiers, restored the administrative system, brought back prosperity, and yet met with nothing but ingratitude. His life was, in fact, cut short by a plot the aim of which was to prevent the lawful heir inheriting the throne. A century later the dynasty was consolidated, and the new king showed himself to be conscious of the great services his dynasty was rendering to the country. He was justly proud of it and launched into a series of panegyrics and 'instructions'. He was a *Ka* (guardian spirit), a *Hu* (eloquence), an Atum, a Khnum dispensing life and abundance. He was a creator, a generative force giving life to all human beings. He was therefore in a position to provide for all the needs of his faithful subjects; those whom he hated would live in poverty in this world and the next:

'He whom the King loves will be an *imakhu* (i.e. one who has been granted a pension and a tomb): there will be no tomb for those hostile to His Majesty: their bodies will be thrown into the water.'

The king was adamant on one point – the defence of his frontiers. Merikara's father, king of only a limited area of Egypt, was already conscious of the problem. Sesostris III, however, who had extended Egyptian territory expressed himself on the subject with gruff outspokenness:

'A valiant man must attack. To retreat is cowardly. He who goes no further than his own frontier is a real . . . (the text contains an obscene term). Consequently, any son of mine who strengthens the frontier which My Majesty has created, is truly my son, who is born for My Majesty, the image of the son who avenges his father (Horus), who strengthens the frontier of him who engendered him; but he who runs away from the frontier and no longer fights to defend it, is not my son. He was not born for me . . .'[8]

It was truths such as these, illustrated with examples, that had to be instilled into the young prince, by the wise man who had the honour and the responsibility of teaching him.

The Eighteenth Dynasty, even more than the Twelfth, was a period of warrior kings. These no doubt did not fail to instruct their heirs in ancient wisdom, to give them a basic knowledge of history and geography, but they seemed to have laid special emphasis on sports and athletics. Evidence of this can be found on the huge stela of Amenophis II, found at Giza in 1936:[9]

'So His Majesty rose up like a King, a fully-grown young man. At eighteen, he was completely mature. He had learned to master every craft of Montu (a warrior god). On the battlefield he had no equal. He learned to ride and train horses. There was none like him in this great army. There was not a single man who could draw his bow. He could not be overtaken in the races.'

Amenophis goes on to give details of his prowess as an oarsman, an archer, and a horseman. News of his exploits reached his father, the terrible Tuthmosis. His Majesty thereupon said to the members of his entourage:

'Let him be given the very best horses of the stable of My Majesty which is within the Wall (Memphis) and tell him to take charge of them, to make them obedient, to train them, to look after them.'

After this pronouncement, the king's son was invited to take charge of the horses of the Royal Stable, and he did so. Reshpu and Astarte (Asiatic gods of the country from which the horses came) were delighted when they saw him throw himself heartily into the task. He trained horses which had no equal. They never tired when he held the reins; even after a long gallop, they were never lathered with sweat.[10]

Seti I supervised his son's upbringing in the same way, from before birth until the day when he could take part in the royal duties. Seti taught him the art of soldiering, but attended to his sensual pleasures too. Thanks to his father, the young Ramses was surrounded by beautiful women and he was allowed to have both a mistress and a wife.[11]

Education, religion, sport, soldiering, hunting, warfare, sensual pleasures – these were the various fields in which the future Pharaoh was instructed in preparation for his rôle.

The coronation

Let us, in the interests of simplicity, suppose that the reigning king died a natural death and there was no attempt to prevent the lawful heir acceding to the throne. An Egyptian story-teller describes what happens to the dead king:

'The god was lifted up into heaven and there united with the solar disc; the divine body was assimilated into that which had created it. The court was plunged in silence and hearts were sad; the great double door remained closed; the courtiers bowed their heads and the Patu lamented.'[12]

The court remained in mourning until the king was buried. This could not happen until the work of mummification was completed, and even in the case of ordinary individuals it took seventy days. The civil and military leaders saw to the running of day-to-day affairs. The king's son was no doubt invested with some measure of regal authority even before the ceremony which would make him sovereign of Egypt. This was, in fact, an essential step in order to settle the details of the funeral ceremony and to quell seditious elements. Many princes were given some share of power months, or even years, before their father died. Such, for instance, was the customary procedure throughout the whole of the Twelfth Dynasty, and it meant that there was no break in the continuity of government between one reign and the next. During the Thirteenth and Fourteenth Dynasties, kings followed each other in rapid succession, some hardly even occupying the throne for the legal period of mourning. This was not the case during the Nineteenth Dynasty, after the death of Seti I. When his son and successor appeared in public after paying final homage to his father, he had already been granted divine favour. Seti made a point of thanking him from the other world: 'See, every day I am full of joy, because I come back to life.'[13]

Since the birth of the heir to the throne was the work of the gods, they could hardly remain indifferent to the coronation ceremony which would consecrate his authority in the eyes of his subjects and of foreigners alike, whether friendly or hostile. The chief episodes of the ceremony, which had a significance at once human and divine, supplied obligatory themes for the artists who decorated the temple walls. Although we do not possess the complete series, a few episodes have been preserved: Horus and Thoth, or Horus and Seth surround the young sovereign with symbols of life, or sprinkle him with water from their ewers.[14] Gods place crowns on his head, and inscribe his name on the leaves of the sacred tree of Heliopolis, the *ished*. They release birds which fly off in all directions. There is no need to suppose that, before performing these actions, priests donned masks which made them look like gods. What we said earlier about the birth of the king also applies to his coronation. While the earthly ceremony was being enacted in all its splendour, a parallel and no less important ceremony was being performed by the gods. The artists who depicted the episodes of the divine ceremony could only visualize them in terms of the earthly one; the transposition throws light on both.

The coronation celebrations were the signal for great rejoicing among the people.[15] Horemheb, Merneptah, and Ramses IV bear witness to this joy: 'The glorious days are upon us,' said Merneptah, 'a lord has appeared throughout all the land.' And Ramses IV: 'Days of gladness! Heaven and earth are filled with joy, because you are the great lord of Egypt. Those who had fled come back to their towns, those who were in hiding come forth (obviously because a general pardon had been granted); the famished eat their fill and are no longer hungry; those who were thirsty get drunk; those who were naked are clad; those who were dirty put on linen garments (clothing and food were distributed to the poor).' However valuable such documents may be, they do not state where the ceremonies took place. Probably in the capital, but as the kings did not always reside in the same place, several towns must have shared the honour at different times. The Ptolemies who lived in Alexandria were crowned at Memphis; the kings named Nectanebo, and before them the kings who belonged to what we call the Saïte Dynasty, probably preferred the town of Neith, because the goddess Neith was their patroness. Kings of the Eighteenth Dynasty naturally chose Thebes, the town of Amun, and Ramses II, who did not care much for Thebes, followed their example, since he left for Abydos and the Delta immediately after his coronation. Ramses III probably chose to be called Lord of Heliopolis in memory of his coronation. For the same reason, perhaps, the Turin Papyrus refers to the kings of the Twelfth Dynasty as kings of the court of Itht-toui, which was situated between Memphis and the Fayum. We have proof that the kings of the Old Kingdom, who all resided at Memphis or in the area around Memphis, and built their pyramids in the near-by desert, were crowned in Memphis. However, the Annals of the Old Kingdom, which supply the information, do not state whether the ceremony took place in the Temple of Ptah or in some other building.

The Annals of the Old Kingdom also provide, in four brief lines, an extremely succinct account of the coronation rites:

The Rising of the King of the South, the Rising of the King of the North
The Union of the Two Lands
The Procession round the wall
The Placing of the Diadem in the hall.[16]

Before the time of Menes, Egypt was not a united country. There were kings of the South, and kings of the North, some of whose names are preserved on the Palermo Stone. The memory of the division of power haunted the Memphite monarchy – indeed one might almost say, it haunted the whole of Egypt. Since he succeeded two kings, the prince had to be crowned twice. He had to receive the crown of the South, a high conical hat with a bulbous tip, and the crown of the North, which was a sort of cap with a high peak at the back, and a metal projection, terminating in a spiral, standing out from the front. The double crown was a combination of both. In theory the gods were responsible for placing both crowns in position. There is no evidence to prove that the priests performed this action. We can assume that the insignia were handed to the king on a tray, or placed on a piece of furniture, and that he himself put on first the crown of the South and appeared to his subjects, then repeated the operation with the crown of the North, and with the double crown. Once the unity of Egypt had been established – and it was always to be considered as a most precarious and valuable achievement – it was symbolized by a monogram, consisting of the southern plant (a lily perhaps) and the northern plant (the papyrus), wound round a hieroglyphic sign meaning union. The monogram dates back to a very early period. A crude representation of it can be found on vases of the First Dynasty; it is very clearly engraved on the base of statues of Chephren; on the statues discovered by Lisht, Seth, Lord of Upper Egypt, and Horus, Lord of Lower Egypt, represent the binding together of the two parts. During his coronation, the king was perhaps presented with the monogram worked in gold and graduated stones. Either before or after, the other symbols of royal power must have been handed to him; these were the sceptre and flail, which formerly belonged to Anzti, an ancient god of the Delta, the Osirian *atef* (emblem), necklaces, rings, pendants, and the blue helmet, a most becoming piece of headgear, which is only known for certain to have become part of the regalia from the Eighteenth Dynasty onwards. The following is an account by Amenophis II of the handing over of the royal insignia:

'After mounting the great throne, he put on the two magical emblems (the white crown and the red crown). On his head, the two crowns combine in the *pa sekhemty*. The *atef* of Re is on his forehead. His head is adorned with the crown of the South and the crown of the North (fig. 17). He takes possession of the diadem and the blue helmet. The *ibes* with its pair of tall feathers is on his head. The *nemes* (cope) covers his shoulders.'[17]

These and other symbols which formed part of the king's regalia were sacred and anyone who touched them, even inadvertently, ran the risk of heavy punishment, perhaps even death. Once, during a procession, the priest Rauer, who, as his position demanded, was

Fig. 17. Royal crowns in the Temple of Sahura. During the New Kingdom and especially during the Late Periods, many varieties of head-gear were worn by kings and queens.

walking in front of the king, narrowly escaped punishment because of an incident for which he was not to blame. The sceptre slipped out of the king's hand and fell on the priest's foot. The king had the presence of mind to call out to Rauer: 'Do not be alarmed', and to issue orders to the guards who were no doubt about to close in on the priest and seize hold of him: 'My Majesty wishes that he should be left in peace and that no one should lay hands on him.' The king, who thought more highly of Rauer than of anyone else, decreed that the incident should be inscribed on his tomb: instructions to this effect were engraved on one of the stones of the Great House, in the presence of the king himself.[18] Rauer had indeed had a narrow escape.

The names to be assumed by the new king were automatically proclaimed on the day of his coronation. Until then, the heir to the throne had only one name, the one given him at birth by his parents, and which the scribes of the Great House, and later the scribes of the House of Life, carefully recorded. He was the king's son – Pepi, Tuthmosis or Ramessu. From now on he would be given a titulary comprising five titles and as many names. The following is the titulary of Tuthmosis I: The Falcon, Mighty-Bull-beloved-of-Maat; the Vulture-Cobra-who-appears-in-the-Uraeus; the all-powerful; the Golden Falcon, Blessed-in-Years-who-makes-all-hearts-live; the Reed-Bee Akheperre (in a cartouche); Son-of-Ra-Tuthmosis (also in a cartouche).[19]

These titles recall early events in Egyptian history when the Falcon led the inhabitants of the Delta, as captives, to Narmer. The Reed, the Bee, the Vulture and the Cobra were also emblems of clans which rallied in turn to the banner of the Falcon and, following the example of the Falcon who became Horus, were eventually transformed into divinities after whom towns or regions were named. The Vulture Nekhebt represented both a goddess and a town – the present-day El Kab in Upper Egypt. The Cobra was a formidable divinity worshipped in both Upper and Lower Egypt. It was also the name of the Tenth Nome of Upper Egypt, the capital of which was called by the same name, Wazet. The old name of Nen-nesu (the present-day Ahnas), the children of the Reed, indicates that this clan settled there, while the clan of the Bee chose to reside in Saïs where they had a castle in historic times. During the first two dynasties, the king had, officially, two titles: the Falcon, and the four emblems grouped into a single unit, and two names – the Horus name and the personal name, which was generally the one recorded by the annalists. Only after long and laborious efforts have modern historians succeeded in making the two lists correspond.

The titles of Zoser, founder of the Third Dynasty, are engraved in beautiful hieroglyphics along the frame of his stelae in the sub-terranean chambers of the pyramid he built. Neterkhet, divine body (in the sense of corporate body) is the name of the king as Falcon and holder of the four emblems. This was followed by a series of signs, which have not been satisfactorily explained; one is perhaps a golden sun and another a circle set on a stone base, in Egyptian *shenen*, which means simply a representation in miniature of the course of the sun round the world. Very often the falcon and the vulture, the two protectors of the monarchy, hold the *shenen* in their claws above the royal effigy. Finally, it became more elongated in shape, so that one of the king's names could be inscribed in it. However, on Zoser's memorial stela the *shenen* is empty. The reason for thinking that the name relating to the cartouche was that of Zoser the Magnificent is that the name of the architect Imhotep was associated, on contemporary monuments, with Neterkhet and during the Late Period was linked with that of Zoser.

The kings of the Fourth Dynasty generally had four titles and four names: Falcon, Reed-Bee-Vulture-Cobra, Golden Horus and a cartouche containing the name by which the individual king was best known: Snofru, Khufu, Khafra, Dedefra, Menkaura, or Shepseskaf. A fifth title, Son of Ra, made a tentative appearance under the Fifth Dynasty, but for a long time there was some uncertainty when and how to use it. Pepi II placed it inside a second cartouche. It was the not very powerful kings of the First Intermediate Period who gave the titulary its definitive form. The complete list of titles however was only found on official documents and was sometimes omitted from these. Often only the Horus name and two cartouches were given. Foreign monarchs referred to the Pharaoh of their time by his fourth name, for example Usirmare and not Ramessu; this was justified by the fact that Usirmare was a king's name and Ramessu only the name of a prince. Modern historians, for the sake of convenience, have assigned numbers – about which they are not always in agreement – to the various kings with the same name, such as Amenemhat, Tuthmosis, Ramses or Ptolemy. Egyptians distinguish between them by making additions to the names and epithets attached to each title. To Usirmare they added Sotep en Re (chosen by Ra). After the Amarnian crisis it became customary to inscribe Beloved of Amun in the second cartouche which might also contain one or two epithets carefully chosen by the court. Sometimes they commemorated an important event; for instance, Ramses III was Lord of Heliopolis (On) because he was, we think, crowned in that town. Most of the Bubastites kept the title,

adding Son of Bastet to show devotion and gratitude to the goddess
Bastet. Sometimes the adjectives indicated a secret ambition conceal-
ing an actual weakness. This is true in the case of Psammetichus,
who styled himself star who rises from the town (Thebes), gift of
Amun, chief prophet, great in monuments at Karnak, writing
to the lands and conquering the Nine Bows – whereas in actual
fact his authority hardly extended beyond the frontier of Lower
Egypt.

Once the names had been proclaimed before a huge crowd, the
announcement that Egypt had a new master had to be made to the
inhabitants of the provinces, or rather to the governors, the officials
on special missions, and to friendly kings. What we know for certain
to have happened on the occasion of Tuthmosis I's accession, through
an inscription sent to Thuroy, Viceroy of Nubia, must have occurred
at the beginning of every reign. The scribes who prepared these
missives also had to record the new titulary in a special office, where
it was readily accessible, should the Pharaoh decide to change it to
suit the circumstances; for instance, to commemorate the capture of
some town, or the conquest of some region. New seals were engraved
for the use of officials in charge of the royal seal. Such an official
always stood by the king's side, in order to affix the royal seal,
whenever His Majesty dictated letters or issued decrees. We know,
however, of one instance when the king's seal could still be used
after his death. The official guarding the pyramid of Amenemhat III
used this king's seal when the monument was opened for the purpose
of burying King Hor, several decades after the death of Amenemhat.
This departure from custom can be explained by the fact that, for
Egyptians, the pyramid was intimately associated with the king who
was resting there in the final sleep of death. The pyramid was, in
fact, the king himself, not the mortal king, although he too had been
obeyed and worshipped like a god, but a being who had signed a
lease with eternity. The seal of each king remained valid, therefore,
within the precincts of the pyramid, as long as the monument remained in a good state of preservation.

The day of the king's coronation was considered as inaugurating
the year 1 of a new era. The Egyptians could never bring themselves
to count the years from some real or imagined event, such as the
founding of Memphis, or the unification of the South and the North.
They considered every reign as a fresh dating point, which means
that, in spite of the achievements of recent research, the modern
scholar, when attempting to estimate the total duration of the
Pharaonic era, of the various dynasties, and sometimes of individual
reigns, is faced with difficult problems, not all of which have been

solved. The Egyptians were not incapable of inventing and applying another system. A famous document surviving from the reign of Ramses II is dated year 400 from the accession of a king, of whom it is not known for certain whether he was a real or a mythical figure.[20] This year 400 seems to coincide with the beginning of the epoch called the epoch of Menophres which, by the end of the Augustan era, had reached the year 1606. There were, then, administrative departments, either civil or religious, where the number of years was recorded without taking the various reigns into account. Kings and their scribes preferred, however, to keep to their inconvenient method of reckoning, as if each monarch wanted to make himself master of time.[21]

One of the final stages in the coronation ceremony was the royal

Fig. 18. The King running from a plaquette of King Den, Fl. Petrie, *Royal Tombs*, Vol. I, Pl. XI and XV. Such scenes are often depicted on the lintels of monumental doors.

procession round the wall. An old name for Memphis was *ineb-hedj*, the white wall, which can be shortened to *ineb*, the wall. Was the king obliged to run round the wall of his capital, as Achilles and Hector went round the ramparts of Troy? This seems unlikely, and we can suppose that the procession was more in the nature of a symbolic act. A representation of it has been preserved on a stone slab of the First Dynasty. The King Den (fig. 18) is shown coming down from the platform where he had been sitting under a canopy. With the double crown still on his head, he is holding a sceptre in one hand, a flail in the other. He is seen pacing energetically up and down, within the confines of a semi-circular enclosure similar to those which have been found inside one of the inner courtyards of Zoser's monument. This particular ritual was not confined to Egypt.

45

Its aim was no doubt to symbolize ownership of a far larger area than the 'runner' was actually covering.

The royal palaces

After the king had been officially enthroned, he lived in the palace and to begin with, most probably in the palace which had belonged to his father. However, it was the ambition of each sovereign to construct his own palace, provided he had both time and means, and to choose a name for it with as much care as he chose the various elements of his titulary. Some of these names have become very famous, since they were also applied to the city which very soon grew up around the palace; examples are: Zedet (Mendes) at the beginning of the Sixth Dynasty; Mennofre which, from the time of Pepi I onwards, was to take precedence over the other names of the capital and was to be adopted in the form of Memphis by the Greeks and by modern scholars; and later Per-Ramses, during the Nineteenth Dynasty.

Visitors to Egyptian temples may get the impression that the king's time was entirely taken up with presenting every sort of offering to the gods and with building new shrines. In actual fact in every temple there were professional priests whose function it was to perform the rites. The Pharaoh's duty, which he never tried to evade, was to demonstrate his gratitude. The splendid document known as the Great Harris Papyrus contains a long list of the acts of piety undertaken by Ramses III in honour of Amun, Atum and Ptah, and other less important deities. The texts also state that the Pharaoh resided in his palace and spent his time on tasks which would give pleasure to the gods. It was after all in the interest of the gods that the king should perform his duties conscientiously. Every day, and as often as necessary, the king, surrounded by his advisers, would listen to reports, read letters, dictate replies, receive officials, technicians – for instance, engineers from the gold mines who complained about the lack of water – criminals like Sinuhe, or people deserving of praise and rewards. All had to kiss the ground in front of the king, or, as a great favour, his foot. When they were given permission to rise and speak, etiquette demanded that they should first praise their lord before broaching the matter in hand; it was up to the king to cut short these preliminaries, if he chose.

Hunting was certainly one of the king's greatest pleasures. A magnificent bas-relief from the temple of Sahura portrays a royal hunt.[22] The game was lured into a part of the desert where there were natural barriers such as steep rocks; artificial barriers were also provided by means of netting hung on posts. When everything was ready, the king would move towards the entrance, which was probably fairly narrow, followed by his servants carrying weapons and provisions and holding greyhounds on the leash. Arrows were showered with unfailing accuracy on antelopes, gazelles, and deer. It was a dignified sport and involved no danger. Hunting the lion and other wild beasts entailed far greater risks, and there is no evidence to prove that the sovereigns of the Old Kingdom ever ventured on this type of expedition, although the kings of the New Kingdom certainly did. Since big game had become scarce in the deserts flanking the Nile, the kings had to go beyond the Euphrates in order to hunt the lion and the elephant. Tuthmosis III and his escort once came across a horde of elephants at Niy. Amenophis III claimed that he had killed one hundred and ten lions. Ramses III hunted antelopes and wild bulls. Once, during an expedition, he was attacked by lions while he was riding in his chariot, and had to defend himself with his spear.

If there were hunter kings there were also warrior kings who were not afraid to face their enemies. The Theban kings, who freed Egypt from foreign domination, certainly belonged to this category. One of them, Sekenenra, had his skull smashed. Ahmosis, Tuthmosis III, Seti I, Ramses II, and Ramses III could certainly all be classed as fighters. The last two kings and probably many others, too, spent a lot of time and vast wealth on their army. On the eve of battle, Ramses III would inspect his troops, and visit his stables which were full of magnificent horses.

The Egyptians can claim to have drawn up a military code before the Greeks and Romans. Treachery was not admissible. Far from trying to take the enemy by surprise, they would fix a day for the battle, and then postpone it if the enemy were not ready. It was thought that either side should have a fair chance, and that the gods would grant victory to the better army.

If we are to believe the texts and bas-reliefs, there was one pleasure which the kings did not deny themselves, that of massacring, with great pomp and ceremony, the enemy chiefs whom they had captured alive. From the palette of Narmer to the pylon of Edfu, we are shown a whole series of kings who, seizing one or several of their enemies by the hair, brandish their formidable maces, while the captives helplessly shake their bows or boomerangs. This was merely a symbolic representation of Egypt's supremacy over the Barbarians. Sometimes, however, the king's mace did actually crash down on the skulls of his captives. Using his club, Amenophis II massacred the seven kings of the land of Tekshi (in Asia), after they had been placed head downwards in the prow of the royal ship. Six of these unfortunate kings were hanged before the wall of Thebes, and their hands were cut off and were hung up beside them. The seventh was taken as far as Nepata so that the victories of His Majesty might be visible for ever throughout the country.[23] The royal prince of Libya, who fell into the hands of the Egyptians, was condemned to death. His father wrote to Ramses III and offered to die in his place, but the Pharaoh remained unmoved. Meshauer was killed with great pomp and ceremony, and so was Kaper. There was no Homer to celebrate these exploits, or to try to plead the cause of the conquered chieftains. Such emotion was, and would always remain, unknown in Ancient Egypt.

It was the king's duty to get to know his subjects and to show himself to them. The Annals of the Old Kingdom refer on several occasions to visits to the palace at Elephantine. Amenemhat I declares that, after his accession to the throne, he travelled as far as Elephantine and then went in the opposite direction to the Delta marshes. Two inscriptions engraved on the rocks of the island of Hesse, the most southerly island of the Aswan archipelago, commemorate a visit by King Merenra, to whom the chieftains of the region paid homage. We must suppose, then, that the king lost no time in going as far as the cataract. He visited the shrines, received various officials, then went back on board his great barge, which was similar to the one recently discovered near the pyramid of Cheops. Escorted by a whole flotilla, the royal vessel sailed slowly downstream, stopping at several points on the way. The king never failed to call on the local chiefs, and to distribute amid the cheers of the populace, those generous gifts which never fail to win the affection and support of the common people. He renewed offerings made by his ancestors, added fresh gifts of his own, decided on the construction or embellishment of certain buildings and then set off for the next town, where the whole procedure would be repeated.

It is interesting to see how the king, if he were not already married, chose his wife, or how the court chose a wife for the heir to the throne. During the Old Kingdom, most of the kings married their sisters. The parents of Ahmosis had a common mother, Queen Tetashera, and Ahmosis himself married his sister Ahmose-Nefertari. One of the daughters of Ramses II, Bent-Anta, also became his wife. There were, however, deviations from this pattern. The wife of Amenophis III, Tiy, was the daughter of Yuyu and Tuya, two Thebans, who were not, as far as we can ascertain, of royal blood. During this period certain kings – Tuthmosis IV, Amenophis III, and Amenophis IV – married foreign princesses. Although a peace treaty had been signed between Ramses II and the Hittite king, fighting was still going on in Syria. It only came to an end when the Hittite king decided to offer his daughter in marriage to Ramses. It was the winter season, but because Ramses was loved by the gods, especially by Seth, the journey took place in summer weather. The king fell in love with the princess as soon as he saw her. Hittite and Egyptian soldiers fraternized for the first time.[24] During the Twenty-sixth Dynasty, Psammetichus married a Mesopotamian princess, Napalta, who brought him, along with other gifts, lapis-lazuli stones.[25] On occasions in the past, kings had married foreigners. Sahura sent his fleet to fetch a princess from a far-off land. In his funerary temple are the remains of a double bas-relief, representing the departure of his fleet, and its return with a large number of Syrians, who insisted on accompanying their princess and are rejoicing along with the Egyptians.

The general rule seems to have been that the Pharaoh, Son of Ra, cherished and crowned by the gods, could only marry a princess of his own family, or a foreign princess who, as a king's daughter, could claim to be of divine origin. This is what the widow of Tut-ankhamen, the last princess of the Eighteenth Dynasty, seems to be implying when she writes to Shubbiluliuma, the most powerful king of her time, asking him to send one of his sons to her, so that she will not have to marry one of her slaves, in other words, one of her subjects.

So tenaciously did the Egyptians cling to these time-honoured customs, that when a usurper seized the throne and founded a dynasty, he himself either married a princess of the vanquished dynasty, or arranged such a marriage for his son. Horemhab, for instance, married Akhenaton's daughter, who would have preferred the son of the Hittite king. Similarly, Osorkon I, the son of the founder of the Twenty-second Dynasty, married a certain princess Makere, who belonged to the previous ruling family.

The information at our disposal is too fragmentary to enable us to draw up a genealogical table of all the royal wives. Tuthmosis III would seem to have been the son of a concubine. The close resemblance between Menkaura and his wife, as they appear in the group in the Boston Museum, points almost certainly to the fact that they were brother and sister. Similar cases occurred during the Old Kingdom. Mertityotes, wife of Snofru, and his daughter according to Sethe, became the wife of Cheops, Snofru's son. She outlived both her husbands, as well as Dedefra, and spent an honoured old age, as an *imaket*, one might almost say a dowager, under King Chephren.

There was neither law nor custom prohibiting the king from

having two or more wives at the same time, or enjoying himself as he thought fit.

If the Annals of the Old Kingdom had not suffered so much damage, they would have provided us with an account of all those actions performed by the king which were deemed worthy of being remembered. In the fragments which remain, great prominence is given to charitable institutions, building projects, statues, punitive expeditions and travel. Ceremonies of which the Egyptians were very fond are frequently referred to. The anniversary of the coronation, especially when it coincided with the feast day of an important god, as in the time of Ramses III, was made the occasion of sumptuous and elaborate celebrations. The royal festival *par excellence* was the *Sed*, which was held at only infrequent intervals: this explains why it is often referred to as the jubilee. It bears very little resemblance to the jubilee celebrated by the ancient Hebrews, which occurred every fifty years and was marked by a year of grace and pardon.

As far as possible, every Pharaoh was anxious to celebrate the *Sed* at least once. Nebtouire Mentuhetep lost no time at all, since he celebrated his in the second year of his reign. Queen Hatsheput waited fifteen years: Pepi I held his in the year after the '18th occurrence' (of the census of live-stock) which, if we are not mistaken, was the year 36 of his reign. Pepi II, who reigned for a very long time, held at least two *Sed* festivals, but the dates are not known. The first *Sed* festival held by Amenophis III took place in the year 30, the second in the year 36. The thirtieth year of the reign seems to have been generally accepted as a jubilee year, since this was also the year chosen by Ramses II for the first celebration of the *Sed* festival. From year 34 onwards, he held it on seven different occasions. It is not known whether these subsequent celebrations were prompted by the king's state of health, by a spirit of thanksgiving for his escape from danger, or by some happy occurrence.

The god Ptah, lord of Memphis, was more intimately connected than any other Egyptian god with the jubilee celebrations. He is often called the lord of the jubilees. People begged him to grant every sovereign an infinite number of jubilees, no doubt because it was at Memphis that the kings of the Old Kingdom celebrated their *Sed* festival. When Memphis ceased to be the capital, the honour fell to other towns. According to one document, a dignitary from Nekhebet in Upper Egypt travelled to Per-Ramses for the occasion of Ramses III's jubilee.[26] The latter was following the example of his famous ancestor Ramses II, founder of Per-Ramses. We know that within Per-Ramses there existed jubilee castles built by Usirmara.

During the Tanis excavations, blocks of stone, statues and columns which had formed part of them, were discovered, and also a bronze stove. Long after the time of Ramses, Shashank V and several of his successors erected jubilee temples at Tanis. Osorkon II had various episodes of his jubilee engraved in the most minute detail on the monumental gate of Bubastis.[27] This does not prove conclusively that the town of Bubastis was the scene of Osorkon's jubilee. Egyptians attached so much importance to the festival that bas-reliefs and inscriptions relating to it have been found in places very far away from the chosen site: for instance at Soleb in the Sudan, on rocks in the valley of Rohanu, which was a much frequented spot, in the tomb of Kheruf, a courtier, at Thebes, in the king's funerary temples, and in the solar temples around Memphis. Pepi I and Pepi II sent jubilee vases to Byblos to be laid in the temple of the Lady of

Fig. 19. The king is seated in the double pavilion used on the occasion of his jubilee, Rohanu valley, *Ham.* 62. Similar scenes can be found in the Temple of Luxor.

Fig. 20. Erection of the Zed pillar on the Tomb of F

Byblos. The Pharaohs were clearly most anxious to announce to the whole kingdom, and to friendly and conquered territories alike, that they had celebrated the *Sed* festival with the customary splendour.

In spite of a wealth of documentary evidence, only certain episodes of the *Sed* festival are known to us, and it is difficult to determine what its true meaning was. Many monuments exist only in a fragmentary state. The one at Bubastis, which is in the best state of preservation, was in ruins when it was discovered, with a large number of stone blocks missing.[28] The *Sed* festival is discussed at great length in works by Egyptologists; the vast amount of literature on the subject is, in fact, proof of the difficulties it presents.

It is known that the queen and the royal children were present at the festival; there were also a considerable number of delegates,

...lar is a symbol of lastingness and stability.

who, like Setau, had brought with them the statue of their local goddess; there were royal officials, such as the ensign-bearers who preceded or accompanied the king on other occasions as well as foreigners anxious to retain the king's favour. Tambourine players, dancing-girls, figurants, amateur or professional singers were called upon to perform at a signal from the priests directing the ceremony. Certain officials had the task of seeing that the people prostrated themselves on the ground or stood up, at the appropriate times, and of keeping the crowd at a respectful distance from the actual ceremony.

An event which took place on the morning of the festival was the setting up of the Zed pillar, a fetish which vaguely resembled a lopped tree and which gave its name to two important cities of the central Delta, Zedu and Zedet. Osiris became connected with the first, which was afterwards called Per-Osiris, and Banebded, the ram, with the second. The ceremony took place in front of a statue of Osiris, which also represented his fetish, and in the presence of the queen and the royal children. The king himself, helped by workmen, pulled on the rope which set up the Zed (fig. 20). After an interval of singing, instrumental music and dancing, or perhaps even while it was still in progress, the people joined in the ceremony. The figurants divided up into two groups, the inhabitants of Pe and the inhabitants of Dep, two neighbouring towns, which finally merged into a single group. They exchanged blows. Some shouted, 'I have taken Horus Kha-maat' (the king himself), while the others replied, 'Hold him fast.' Asses and oxen walked four times round the wall.[29]

For the subsequent episodes a platform had to be set up, and on it a double pavilion. The king occupied each part of the pavilion in turn, assuming the white crown of the South in one, and the red crown of the North in the other. He also wore a sleeveless cope which was used only in the *Sed* ritual. At Bubastis the scenes relating to the king of the South were depicted on one of the towers of the monumental gate, and those relating to the king of the North were on the opposite gate-post. They are very different indeed. In the South the king, accompanied by his family and surrounded by ensign-bearers, is shown offering incense to, and worshipping, various divinities set in tiny chapels, as well as masts and obelisks, which were copies of those to be seen in the city of the sun. In the North, a long procession, of which only the beginning and the end have survived, is in progress; it consists of priests bringing a bird and a fish as gifts. They are all associated with Lower Egyptian deities: Horus, Seth, Osiris Khenti-irty, Isis, Nephthys, and Thoth. The fact that they were all together on this occasion was no accident. In one chapter of the pyramid texts, the same deities are invoked, reviled and most strongly urged to return to their place of origin and the king is forbidden to welcome them. Yet, with the exception of Seth, they were very popular gods with shrines and followers all over Egypt. It is difficult to understand why they should have been treated so harshly. It has been supposed, perhaps rightly, that the towns which honoured these gods had, in the past, formed a confederation to resist the power of the king or the influence of the great solar god. The better cause had, however, triumphed, so in the end the gods went over to the side of the ruler who would one day be master of the Two Lands. On the occasion of the *Sed* festival, their priests came to offer a profession of allegiance, were pardoned, fell into line and handed over their offerings. After this reminder of more turbulent times, the ceremony pursued its course. The king ran, drew his bow

54

and released birds towards the four cardinal points of the compass. Sacrifices were offered up. Incense was burnt before each deity, who received his share of gifts, and the festival ended with a tremendous banquet. According to a New Kingdom text, the king felt rejuvenated by the proceedings. The people were pleased to have seen the royal family and to have relived the distant past. The unification of Egypt had been no easy achievement. People were conscious of the blessings of peace, yet the faint memory of past struggles remained, and peace was felt to be precarious. The ceremony had served to neutralize the forces threatening peace. The day of the coronation, *sma taui* (the union of the Two Lands), had kindled a cherished hope; the *Sed* festival was proof that this hope had been fulfilled.

Royal funerals

Although the king delighted in consecrating temples, distributing bounty, and restoring institutions which had fallen into disuse, the action which afforded him the greatest happiness was the preparation of his own tomb. It is obvious that the pyramids at Giza and Saqqara were not built in a day, and that the king did not wait until old age was upon him before drawing up his plans. Some Egyptologists have put forward the somewhat naive idea that the lengths of the various reigns could be determined from the size of the particular pyramids. In spite of a plentiful supply of labour, both foreign and Egyptian, the smallest of these prodigious monuments must have demanded several years' work. After the preliminary survey and preparation of the site, all the necessary materials had to be assembled; engineers had to be sent long distances in order to procure the best quality stones – alabaster, granite, and diorite. Limestone could be found close at hand, at Tura, opposite Saqqara, but it had to be brought across the Nile. The wood, metals and precious or semi-precious stones required by cabinet-makers and jewellers came largely from foreign countries. The pictures on the walls of the funerary temples no doubt give a complete or partial account of these vast labours. A bas-relief on the causeway leading to the pyramid of Unas shows two barges transporting two monolithic granite columns exactly like those found in the funerary temple itself.

The king supervised the building operations personally. One of Menkaura's contemporaries informs us that: 'His Majesty King Menkaura, may he live for ever, ordered his tomb to be built when His Majesty was on the road leading to the necropolis in order to inspect the work in progress on the pyramid. Divine is Menkaura.'[30]

We can see from the above quotation that the pyramids, or rather the whole of the funerary monument, including lower temple, causeway, upper temple and pyramid, was referred to by a name. It was a current practice to give a name to all civil, military or religious buildings, and even to their various parts, the doors in particular. The name of the pyramid consisted of a sentence, the subject of which was the king's name, and the predicate an adjective or participle: Snofru is resplendent; Cheops is an inhabitant of *Ahket* (the Eastern horizon); Dedefra is a *Sehed* (the name of a constellation); Chephren is great; Menkaura is divine. When most adjectives had been used up, a complement was added: Unas is beautiful in situation (i.e. beautiful is the setting of Unas); Pepi is stable in perfection. Some of these names have remained as names of towns, such as Djed-Esout (Zedet or Mendes) and Men-neferu (Memphis).

A word of explanation is necessary here. It is very probable that the pyramid gave its name to a town somewhere in the neighbourhood. What actually happened was that the town, and subsequently the pyramid where the king would remain throughout eternity, were called after the royal palace.

As soon as the building of a pyramid had been decided upon, the king appointed officials and workers to be employed on the site. A town would soon spring up in the vicinity. Later, when the pyramid had been completed and its august inhabitant laid to rest in the funerary temple, the town would still be inhabited by the priests who saw to the observance of the royal rites, and by all the officials whose task it was to keep the monument in good order and to look after the property, which supplied revenue for the maintenance of the monument and the continuation of the ceremonies. It is a curious fact that Egyptian government officials were often tempted to conscript the people employed in the service of a dead king and to use them for other purposes. The king might then intervene and issue a decree to enforce respect for the provisions laid down by his ancestor. They would remain valid for a certain length of time. The worship of some Old Kingdom kings went on for several generations, and even for several centuries. Finally, the burden would become too heavy to be borne even by those kings who were most respectful of the past. The monument, after being abandoned by the priests and officials, would fall into ruins, and become an object of curiosity. Certain learned princes might undertake to restore it, rather in the manner of the scholars of the present-day *Service des Antiquités*. A son of Ramses II, Khamuas, won a great reputation for himself as a restorer of monuments.

The institutions of the monarchy

If we consider that the average length of the dynasties between Menes and Cambyses was just under a century, it must be concluded that the Egyptians did not always wait for the absence of a male heir of the royal line to oust the royal family from the throne. The history of the dynasties is marked by attempted assassinations and plots, of which probably only a few are known to us. From the following accounts of these plots it will be seen how precarious an institution the monarchy was.

Fig. 21. An officer of the law, with prisoner and scribes, from Junker, *Giza*, V, 76. This, and similar, scenes were often depicted on Old Kingdom tombs and were of frequent occurrence in real life.

When, in 1961, I was visiting the huge workshop where Cheops' great barge was reassembled, Sheik Ahmed Yussef, who had played an important part in the restoration work, showed me a wooden construction, the dismantled parts of which he had found packed in a chest and buried at the bottom of a well by the side of Chephren's pyramid. About twelve centuries after Chephren, the Egyptians were still in the habit of confining their political prisoners in wooden structures of this very kind (fig. 22). It is interesting to speculate about possible occupants of these cramped quarters in Chephren's time, and about the latter's reasons for putting the structure in a safe place so close to his pyramid.

Reisner, the archaeologist, who has carried out many excavations in the area around the pyramids, put forward the theory that Dedefra, who had been crowned king after the murder of his elder brother, the true heir to the throne, was himself assassinated, after reigning for eight years, and his place taken by Chephren. If we suppose that it was Dedefra who was shut up in the wooden cage, everything fits in perfectly.

It seems likely that the founder of the Twelfth Dynasty met with the same fate. He was vizier before he became king, but he was certainly not the heir to the throne. After becoming king, he ruled for some twenty years before a conspiracy brought his reign to an end. At the end of the reign of Ramses III, a plot was hatched to prevent the lawful heir, the future Ramses IV, acceding to the throne. The plot failed but it was the cause of the king's death.

Herodotus has given an account of the events which cost Apries his throne. The Libyans, to whom he was bound by a treaty of mutual aid, appealed to him to help them rid their country of the Greeks who had invaded Cyrene in large numbers. Convinced that his soldiers would easily get the better of the Greeks, Apries dispatched an army which the Cyrenians routed at Irasa. When the survivors returned to Egypt, they accused Apries of having used the expedition as a means of getting rid of them. In view of the threatened rebellion, Apries asked Amasis, his army chief, to re-establish order. He succeeded, and since he had the troops well under control, he also seized the throne and proclaimed himself king.[31]

The perpetrators of such plots did not have a very sincere belief in the divine nature of the king. At court and in the army, there were plenty of adventurers ready to conspire against their lord and usurp his authority.

If we are to believe Herodotus and the Egyptian story-tellers, the popular belief in the king's divinity was hardly stronger. The information supplied by Herodotus about Rhampsinitus, Cheops, Chephren and Menkaura was not invented, but based on what he had actually heard at Memphis and throughout his travels. Cheops shut the temples and imposed every sort of hardship on the people in order to build his pyramid. As he was running short of money he is supposed to have put his daughter into a brothel and collected the proceeds. Rhampsinitus had also used this highly convenient method, not to get money but to find a criminal; the princess had to induce her visitors to say what was the most ingenious and villainous act they had committed. It is true that Cheops, Chephren and Ramses II – if it is Ramses II the narrator is referring to under the name of Rhampsinitus – are among the greatest builders of Egyptian antiquity, and the erection of monuments has always been a costly business. Yet all the kings of the Old and Middle Kingdoms built pyramids; and the rest tried to ensure their immortality by constructing some edifice or other. Yet Snofru, who built two pyramids, had the reputation of being a good and kindly king.

Certain modern historians have claimed quite seriously that the pious Egyptian people accepted all the hard work involved because they believed their fate to be linked with that of the god reposing in his sarcophagus. Maspero was perhaps nearer the truth when he maintained that if they paid heed to the stories about the king being beaten, deceived, kidnapped or having so limited an intelligence that he could be made to believe anything and was incapable of making any decision himself, the funerary monument must have given them the feeling that they were getting their own back on him. But they had very little choice. The alternative to obedience was rebellion, and rebellion would merely replace one proud and dictatorial master by another. The plots and assassination attempts were not an expression of popular feeling; they originated either among the nobility or in the army.

Midway between the unscrupulous ambition of a few high officials and the naive gossip circulating among the common people, we have the writings of scholarly, serious-minded scribes who undertook to defend the Pharaoh. Sinuhe, whose memoirs are among the best known and most widely appreciated of all Egyptian literary texts, belonged to this category. When he spoke about his lord to the Sheik of Retenu who had welcomed him, Sinuhe referred to the king as a master of wisdom, perfect in the position he held, benevolent in the orders he issued, an invincible hero yet at the same time a master of affection, an extremely gentle man who had won great love. The land of Egypt was the first to benefit from the goodness of Sesostris but any foreign country which remained loyal to him would also feel its effects.[32] In the teachings which were written down during the Twelfth Dynasty and intended to give advice on good behaviour and peaceful living, the Egyptian people were told above all to venerate the king in their innermost hearts, and to associate His Majesty with their thoughts. The king is worthy of such devotion because he is the equal of Sa (knowledge), Ra, Hu (eloquence), Atum and Khnum (the gods of creation), Bast, and Sekhmet, the patron goddess of doctors. He can therefore satisfy every need. The conclusion goes without saying: 'Honour the crown of Lower Egypt, worship the crown of Upper Egypt, exalt him who wears the double crown. Do this; it will be beneficial to your persons and you will derive benefit from it for ever more.'[33]

The poets vied with the story-tellers and moralists. A hymn in honour of Sesostris III likens him to an asylum sheltering the timid from his enemy: 'He is a warm dry corner in the winter season; he is a Sekhmet (the patron goddess of doctors also had the power to start epidemics) to the enemies who attack his frontier. He has come; he has united the two lands; he has joined the reed of Upper Egypt to the bee of Saïs; he has given life to Egypt.' Encouraged by these examples set by people in high places, private individuals vied with each other in praising the king's virtue, on their stelae and funerary inscriptions.

The king expected to be revered in this way. On the whole, the adulation lavished on him was deserved. It was, however, inevitable that he should not remain unaffected by the conditions of extravagant luxury in which he lived, and by the fact that from childhood onwards, at every possible opportunity, he had been proclaimed a god. In the official texts, it is always the king himself who is responsible for all achievements, never the members of his entourage. Ramses II alone was responsible for routing the huge Hittite army, and for forcing the survivors to ask for the cessation of hostilities. Tuthmosis III is said to have killed the largest elephant single-handed during a hunting expedition. One of his officers, however, records on his tomb that he cut off the elephant's trunk (it is referred to as a 'hand'). But the Pharaoh did not go so far as to claim to be able to control the seasons. When his soldiers had to undertake a long and arduous journey in mid-winter in order to bring back a Hittite princess, he requested Setekh to calm the elements; the god heard his prayer and provided a succession of summer days. Nor was it through an act of will on the king's part that the well-diggers struck water in the Ikaïta desert. The gods caused the water to gush forth because they loved Ramses more than his predecessors.

In the opinion of Herodotus, the Egyptians were a deeply religious people. The king could not afford to be an exception, and we have innumerable proofs of his piety. Even if we disregard the official imagery which presents only one human being, the king, as being equal to the gods, it is nevertheless true that Ramses' appeal to Amun when he found himself suddenly surrounded by his enemies, sounds like the cry of a sincere believer. When Ramses III's son and heir was threatened by grave dangers, the king commended him to Amun, Ptah and Atum and even to lesser deities, in tones of moving sincerity. Akhenaton, the reformer, seems to have rejected the innumerable divinities which had been invoked by previous kings and were to be again, by others, after Akhenaton's time. His piety towards the one god he retained, the disc with the human-handed rays, was all the more fervent and found expression in extremely lofty terms. According to Josephus, the historian, a king called Amenophis – perhaps Amenophis III – said to his confidant, who was also called Amenophis, that he would like to see the gods.[34] In this instance, royal piety was verging on madness, but the author of the *Treatise against Apion* is not always a reliable source. If we confine ourselves to authentic documents, we can see that the Pharaoh, in both thought and deed, behaved towards the gods in the manner of an obedient and respectful son.

On numerous occasions, the king showed himself to be a reasonable, sensitive human being. The instance in which he suspended the law, which decreed punishment for anyone who had touched the royal insignia, in favour of a respected priest, has already been quoted. The king liked to visit the site of his pyramid while it was in process of construction. On the way there, he would often promise some faithful servant that he would build him a tomb. During one of these visits, Uash-Ptah, the architect, fainted. The king, Neferir-kera, immediately sent for his doctors to come with their books, but they failed to revive the architect. The king was most grieved and had an ebony coffin made for him.[35] Once when he received an elderly courtier he allowed him to kiss his foot instead of the ground. It is again Sinuhe, in his biography, who reveals most clearly how the kings of Egypt could combine simplicity with grandeur, and sternness with clemency.

While he was serving in the Libyan army, Sinuhe deserted because he overheard a secret which he was not intended to hear. He remained in exile until he was an old man. The king, not wanting him to die on foreign soil, authorized his return. Sinuhe presented himself at the palace, but when he perceived his sovereign seated on the golden throne he fainted: 'Lift him up,' the king said to one of his nobles, 'and let him speak to me.' Sinuhe stammered out a few words and the king turned to his wife and said: 'Just look at Sinuhe who has come back looking like an Asiatic, a real Bedouin.' She uttered a cry and the royal children shouted all together: 'It is not really he, Your Majesty, my Lord.' 'Yes, it is,' replied the king. The princes presented the king with the *menat* (crotals) and sistrums, the ornaments of Hathor, goddess of joy, and then asked that the fugitive Sinuhe should be pardoned.

In his leisure hours, the king liked to listen to each one of his sons in turn telling stories about magicians; he also took pleasure in the society of scholarly people who could discourse on the past and the future. He appreciated the company of pretty girls and liked to watch them dance. Having heard from his officials of the beauty of Sarah, whom Abraham was passing off as his sister, the king summoned her to his palace; however, he dismissed both her and her people when the great plagues sent by Jehovah made him realize that she was Abraham's wife.[36] In Egypt the adulterous wife and her paramour were severely punished. Yet we could perhaps apply to the country as a whole what was said to Cambyses: The law allows the Pharaoh to do as he pleases.

It must be admitted that we have very little information on the general behaviour of the great Pharaohs. Egypt had no historians like Quintus-Curtius or Plutarch. In so far as we can attempt to draw a comparison between the best known of the Pharaohs and the sovereigns of the other nations of antiquity, we can conclude that Egypt fared no worse than the others. Her warriors lacked the prestige of Alexander; her statesmen were without the great ability of men like Augustus or Constantine. The kings who wrote Books of Wisdom can hardly be put on the same level as Marcus Aurelius, but on the other hand the throne of Horus was probably never disgraced by monsters such as Cambyses or Nero. Although we cannot be sure of this, it is a fact that in all countries the bad kings are remembered longest. Many Pharaohs performed their duties conscientiously, defended their frontiers, maintained law and order within their borders, urged judges and scribes to be impartial, and expressed their gratitude towards the gods by generous gifts. They thus pleased the gods who, at the appointed time, brought about the Inundation of the Nile, that inexhaustible source of prosperity and joy.

CHAPTER 4

THE DEVELOPMENT OF EGYPT

The royal lands, sacred and private

As Pharaoh was master of the Two Lands, he considered that every-thing in Upper and Lower Egypt – people and live-stock, buildings and land, tools and furniture – belonged to him, and that he could dispose of everything as he wished. In theory, he was also the only intermediary between the gods and men, but in practice the ritual of worship was carried out by professional priests. We may also ask to whom land in Egypt really belonged.

The king was without doubt the biggest landowner in the country. Snofru, founder of the Fourth Dynasty, had engraved on his funerary temple a list (which has not been preserved in its entirety) of the estates which he personally owned.[1] A fragment from a similar list is to be seen in Sahura's temple.[2] The king owned three, four or five domains in each nome. They were referred to by a name which always included that of the king: for instance, the Nurse of Snofru, the Way of Snofru in the Fourteenth Nome, the Sandal of Snofru in the Thirteenth, the Fishing-ground of Snofru in the Fifteenth, the Opulence of Sahura in the Black Bull.

We know neither the extent nor the origin of these lands. Snofru, as the founder of a dynasty, no doubt confiscated the royal domain which had belonged to his predecessor. It is possible that he enlarged it by adding land reclaimed from the marshes, and waste land made cultivable by draining and irrigation, he alone being in a position to begin such operations and carry them to a successful conclusion.

These royal estates had clearly marked boundaries, were officially registered, and were administered by a man chosen by the king. A certain Meten, a contemporary of Snofru, has left a list of the lands and castles of which he was overseer.[3] It is a very long one and includes lands and castles situated in every nome in Lower Egypt; it is hardly likely that they were all entrusted to Meten's overlordship at one and the same time. Perhaps he had to give up the estates listed first; if so, he gives no explanation of why this happened.

63

Changes certainly occurred in the royal estates. The names which linked the various areas with Snofru must have been changed when Cheops replaced him on the throne of Horus. Mention is made, on an inscription in the Middle Kingdom, of a town called the Nurse of Cheops, situated in the Oryx nome, as was Snofru's domain of the same name. It seems possible that certain royal domains were given their freedom in the same way as some European towns in the Middle Ages were allowed to become city states. Two towns in the Rural, the Second Nome of Upper Egypt, Per-Sahura (Sahura's domain) and Hut (castle) of Snofru, later known as *hesfen*, were probably also former royal domains which had become independent towns.[4] It would seem that the king constantly acquired new estates – sometimes by taking over the property of men who had been condemned to death, or by buying up property from people who had lost their wealth. We can draw evidence from the Bible on this point: during the period of the ill-favoured kine, landowners came to Joseph, who was Pharaoh's trusted adviser, and handed over their estates in exchange for food. After the Hyksos had been driven out of Egypt, there was a fresh distribution of land. Pharaoh kept for himself some of the estates confiscated from those who had collaborated with the invaders, and he shared out the rest among his loyal soldiers.

The temples provide us with an additional source of information. In spite of their fragmentary state the Annals of the Old Kingdom show kings of the Fifth Dynasty allotting extensive areas of land to the chief gods – Hathor and Ptah, the souls of On. The priests of these gods were not content with having obtained estates from the king; they were also anxious to have some guarantee that they would not be subject to taxation either in the present or the future. Kings of the Sixth Dynasty and their successors signed several decrees to this effect.[5] It is curious to find the royal authority working against its own interests, by exempting the personnel of ecclesiastical or funerary property from taxation in the form of services or goods. As the number of exemptions increased throughout the land, the resources of the state dwindled. At Coptos, the capital of the nome called The Two Falcons, officials of the king's household were not allowed either to press the temple personnel into service, or to make use of funds which had been set aside for the worship of Min, the god of Coptos.[5] Near Memphis, the town adjoining the two pyramids built by Snofru was not required to supply men to work in the king's palace or provisions for the messengers who journeyed up and down the country either by river or by land. After listing further equally generous decisions, King Pepi I concludes:

'My Majesty has done this to protect the town adjoining the two pyramids from these abuses so that the ritual can be observed, and monthly ceremonies and all things divine performed for the King Snofru in his pyramid.'[6]

However, even with the king's support, the priests found it no easy matter to defend their privileges. The reason why Pepi I felt obliged to issue a decree maintaining these privileges some two hundred years after Snofru's death, was that officials and laymen alike tended to disregard them. Pepi II, in his first decree concerning the temple of the god Min, threatened severe punishment for all officials, whoever they might be, who disregarded his orders. He refers to certain rumours to the effect that his orders had been cancelled. It has to be noted, however, that the first decree, which was engraved on a stela of hard stone on the gate of the temple of Min, at Coptos, had to be replaced a few years later by a second decree, and that both these charters of immunity were removed sooner or later, since they were found by archaeologists in the foundations of the temple of Coptos which was rebuilt by Tuthmosis III. The state officials were not to be gainsaid, and when they needed men, animals, and other items an estate could provide, they took them where they found them.

The kings tended to favour the priesthood which, by the time of Ramses III, and probably before, had acquired tremendous wealth.[7] First and foremost were the servants of Amun, the god of Thebes. More than 86,000 men and 400,000 beasts lived on the estates of the god, which comprised nearly one-tenth of the whole of Egypt, and included 433 gardens, 46 workshops, and 56 small towns. He had a fleet of 83 ships. The gods of On (Heliopolis) and Memphis, and naturally those of other towns, were far less well provided for. The total value of the property and income of the temples was very impressive, and their owners defended them with great tenacity against the many and various enemies who had designs on them – the destitute in troubled times, soldiers, foreigners and even neighbours. Yet after every period of impoverishment, there was always some pious and clever man who brought his influence to bear, and by dint of cunning and patience, restored the fortunes of his god.

There was, however, a large part of the country which was owned by private individuals. Hapidefai, governor of the Thirteenth Nome of Upper Egypt, specified that the expenses of his funerary rites were to be paid out of the income from his father's household, and not from the household of the prince. In other words, the governor owned an estate which he had inherited from his father and perhaps enlarged through his own efforts. In addition, he was chief steward of another estate, the revenue from which paid for the public works and all the expenses connected with the administrative services of his province. Meten, who has already been referred to and who lived at a much earlier period, was a similar figure: at the time of Snofru, he administered estates on the king's behalf, and at the same time built up a tidy fortune for himself. He had not begun from nothing. His father, a scribe, had not given him a house or land but a few servants and a few head of cattle. From his mother he had inherited an estate of about twelve hectares, and he acquired over fifty more subject to certain liabilities, from the royal household. The steward-ship of an estate was a good profession for an able man. It might well be asked whether it was not in the king's interest to relinquish estates which brought him in so little, since the steward kept the best part of the profits for himself. Privately administered estates, on the other hand, came back to the state in the form of taxes. All transactions were meticulously recorded by the royal scribes, so that the central administrative offices could determine, at any given moment, how much property was privately owned and tax it accordingly. One Old Kingdom inscription records the purchase in the presence of witnesses of a house situated in the vicinity of Chephren's temple, and valued at ten *shat*,[8] the *shat* being an abstract unit of value. Precious metals were brought from the mines in the form of apparently identical rings, but these were not used in payments; it never occurred to any Egyptian official to stamp them so that they could serve as money. When the king wanted to reward one of his servants, he gave him necklaces and gold cups. When he paid for something he had commissioned, he used articles made of gold which had been previously weighed, various other manufactured articles, or provisions. A bed and two lengths of material were accepted as suitable payment for the house mentioned above. It is easy to imagine that this method of conducting business led to endless arguments; often the royal scribes had to intervene and settle the matter.

To sum up, wealth in the form of real estate was divided out in Egypt between the king, the temples, and private individuals. It was subject to constant fluctuations, due to the special needs of the king, to wars and disturbances and, in less troubled times, to circumstances which made the fortunes of some and brought ruin to others.

The central administration

The king in the Old Kingdom had evolved a powerful administrative system, both to keep the people under control and to develop the country's resources. Its various stages can be traced from the Thinite period, when it was still in a rudimentary state, right up to the Sixth Dynasty. With every new reign, the number of official posts increased. It was the king who made the appointments and he chose the nominees preferably from his own family and from the aristocracy. They were known as the Unique Friends of the King, and were far more numerous than this expression might seem to suggest. The king could also promote anyone who had proved himself to be outstandingly zealous or successful.

The Egyptians do not appear to have thought that officials should specialize in one particular field, such as public works, military affairs, book-keeping, the maintenance of law and order or the administration of justice. Uni, one of the best known of the high-ranking officials under the Old Kingdom, practised almost every profession.[9] It is not easy to follow the various stages of his career, because of the impossibility of distinguishing between the honorary titles of which Egyptians were so fond, and those indicating actual duties. Uni did not belong to the *Pat*. He was at various times overseer of a granary, steward of an estate, governor of a town, and a judge. He was entrusted with certain confidential cases and as everyone was very satisfied with what he did he was sent to Tura to supervise the transport of a white stone sarcophagus. At the time he was just an ordinary official; immediately afterwards, however, he was promoted to the rank of Unique Friend and made governor of a town. He distinguished himself as commander of the palace guard which lined the processional routes when great lords were going by. Then he was involved in another legal case, after which he was part of the huge army assembled to beat back attacks by nomadic tribes. All manner of important people took part in the operation but he was responsible for the plan of campaign. Perhaps his account exaggerates the importance of his rôle. Yet he certainly took steps to prevent the soldiers quarrelling among themselves and stealing flour or sandals from the passers-by. He also took part in the census. His duties combined those of a police officer and a civil servant. He acquitted himself well, since on his return from the expedition he was made a chamberlain of the Royal Household and Bearer of the Sandals – probably the king's sandals, because he was given further promotion. He was appointed prince-governor of the south from Elephantine to the extreme limit of Upper Egypt. He was sent to Elephantine and even beyond, to Ibhet, in order to bring back blocks of stone intended for the queen's pyramid; this necessitated the building of barges and other boats, twelve in all. Compared with the hazardous journey to Ibhet, his expedition to Hatnub in Middle Egypt to bring back an offering-table was mere child's play, and took him only seventeen days. Even though the canals had dried up, he carried out the whole undertaking within the time prescribed by the Majesty of his Lord. During a further expedition into southern territory which lasted for a whole year, he dug five canals and, with the help of the local chieftains who provided the necessary timber, he built and fitted out a whole fleet of ships. His was certainly a full and varied career. At some other historical periods, the operations which were successfully carried out by Uni would have required the services of at least four ministers – the ministers of home affairs, justice, public works, and the merchant navy. Officials were under the king's command: he could set them any task he chose if he thought them capable of doing the work efficiently.

Several texts show the king attended by a council, although it is not made clear whether it was a permanent council or one convened only on special occasions. When Kames undertook to drive out the Hyksos, this great decision was not taken by him alone, although, according to the Carnarvon tablet, the members of the council were hesitant and Kames had to force them to agree. Before the attack on Meggido, Tuthmosis III called the principal military commanders together and discussed with them the best route to take. He had already made up his own mind about the road he would follow, yet he took notice of certain of their suggestions. When Ramses II considered that it would be to his advantage to conclude an armistice with the Hittites, his courtiers replied that since such was the king's decision, everything was for the best. It is often stated in official inscriptions that the king was in his palace, engaged on tasks which rejoiced the gods, when an important piece of news was announced to him – usually an act of defiance or an organized attack on the part of his enemies. In every case, the king was given the credit of the decision taken. This is only to be expected in official texts. The king is supposed to have done everything, however modest a part he may have actually played.

The king's councillors are only portrayed as a corporate body on the fragments of the ruined funerary temple of Pepi II.[10] On the base, to the right and the left of the two doors, are depicted groups of ten men bowing deferentially. They are most certainly men of high rank. One of the first groups consists of a noble (*iri-pat*) who was also a prince and a magistrate; a prince and governor of the towns (*hati-â, mu khentesh Per-â*); a prince and governor of the South (the post held by Uni at the end of his career); a clerk of all the works (the post occupied by Imhotep under Zoser); a master of ceremonies; a bearer of the royal seal; and several Unique Friends with no specified functions. Another group, facing the first, contains perhaps less important personages. These are a magistrate who was also a noble and a master of ceremonies; a noble who was a prince with no special function; a seal-bearer; several Unique Friends; and masters of ceremonies. Neither nobles nor princes appear in the third group, in which we find only a few Unique Friends, a superintendent of the two granaries (northern and southern) and an inspector of the wig-makers of the Great House. Practically nothing is left of the fourth group. We may suppose that these men controlled the central administrative system. Each one of them had under his immediate authority a large staff of scribes and technicians, for it was the ambition of every Egyptian who could read and write to become a court official. It is difficult to know whether the four groups represented on Pepi II's monument formed four separate councils, or a single body. They were certainly very powerful, perhaps all-powerful. Information reached the Pharaoh only through them, and reading between the lines, we can conclude that, in most cases, the Pharaoh had little choice but to take the decision on which his council had agreed, but for which he would be given full credit.

Let us take as an example the incident of the gold-mines in Ikaïta (in Nubia), as it is depicted on the stela in the Grenoble Museum.[11] The king was at Memphis, seated on his golden throne and wearing his full regalia, when he was informed of the plight of the miners in the waterless desert. The councillors were summoned and delivered an elaborate eulogy of the king which ended with the words: 'If you command the water to flow on the mountain, the *Nun* (subterranean waters) will instantly rise up . . .' At this point a report from the Royal Son of Kush was read, recalling a previous unsuccessful attempt by Seti I, Ramses's predecessor. 'But,' the councillors went on, 'if you yourself speak to Hapi, your father and the father of the gods (Hapi was a poetic name for the Nile) who loves you more than all your predecessors, he will do anything you ask.' 'That is very true,' replied His Majesty. It is obvious that the council did not want the facts to prove that the king might be wrong. The end of the text is missing, but we may be sure that the well-diggers had already done their work and that their efforts had been crowned with success.

The problem of paying the public officials was undoubtedly a difficult one. The authorities had several means at their disposal;

the least costly consisted in granting honorary titles – such as Mouth of Nekhen or Unique Friend – which were undoubtedly much appreciated. Promotion, when it had been won, provided the recipient with many forms of satisfaction. He had a greater number of scribes under him, and could operate over a wider field. Egyptians certainly believed that the labourer was worthy of his hire. One inscription in the valley of Rohanu states exactly what every member of the expedition, from the most important to the most humble, was to receive – while the work lasted. The officials working within Egypt were not likely to be treated differently. A stela at Karnak states that the office of Prince of Nekhebt (capital of the Second Nome of Upper Egypt), brought with it certain material advantages; bread, beer, meat, provisions, funerary priests, and a house.[12] The family shared in the benefits granted to the official. Stelae of every period contain the following formula: 'If you wish to bequeath your office to your children then say so . . .' In practice, however, the inheritance of offices had sometimes to be ensured by roundabout means. A high-ranking official could not expect his young, and as yet inexperienced, son to succeed him immediately; the boy would be given a junior post to start with. As time went on certain posts were actually considered as being the property of the man who held them. The office of Prince of Nekhebet is a case in point. Its holder, a certain Kebsy, sold it, with all the accruing benefits, to a neighbour, who offered in exchange various articles valued at sixty *deben* (540 g). The interesting point of the story is that the man who sold the office collected the sixty *deben* but did not hand over the post and claimed to have spent the proceeds. An action was brought against him and Kebsy had to admit the facts in a court of law and swear on oath to hand over the governorship.

The stela which relates this curious story dates from the Second Intermediate Period, a time of disturbances and confusion when the king's straitened circumstances forced him to part with certain offices. In some other periods, Kebsy's governorship would have reverted to the king, who would then have appointed a successor.

A final advantage enjoyed by high-ranking officials was that the king undertook to build their tomb, or to procure for them fine stone blocks quarried at Tura, which was royal property. The practice was continued during the New Kingdom. Amenhotep, son of Hapu, the friend and trusted adviser of his king, was entitled to a funerary temple at Thebes, on the left bank of the Nile. To have your statue set up in a temple at the king's command was to be admitted to the table of the gods. If the king wanted his subjects to serve him well he had to be prepared to bear the cost.

The presence of professional magistrates in the king's council proves that it could, on occasions, become a court of justice. Their name, *tati*, was probably connected with the word *tat*, which meant 'door', and more precisely 'monumental door'. According to evidence, which comes, admittedly, only from the later period, the Tribunals did in fact hold their sessions at the temple door.[13] The judges are often shown wearing a picture of *Maat*, the goddess of justice, as a badge of office. Illustrations of what happened during the sessions of the tribunal – at least those dealing with ordinary offences – are frequently found on Old Kingdom *mastabas* (fig. 21). Six or eight judges would sit on the ground, with the records of the case beside them. The accused, usually erring stewards, were ushered in none too gently by the constables (*sa-per* – the sons of the House) who carried cudgels that they were not slow to use, because a good beating was thought to be the only way of finding out the truth. The big landowners and certainly the kings had the right to exercise justice on their estates. Once an oasis dweller who was travelling to the market of Nen-nesu, the present-day Ahnas, was stripped of his possessions and assaulted by an unscrupulous official. Fortunately, he managed to reach Nen-nesu, where he met Meru, son of Rensi, the king's chief steward. Amused by the fellow's eloquence, Meru, with the authorization of the king, had him brought as many as ten times before the judges. Finally the inquiry went in his favour, and a decision worthy of Solomon was arrived at.

Fig. 22. Political prisoner, Karnak, from *Ann. du Serv.*, LIII, Pl. VII. Foreigners, as well as political prisoners, were confined in this uncomfortable cage.

There were no lawyers in ancient Egypt. Each individual stated his own case as best he could, occasionally calling upon witnesses. There was probably no codified system of laws. Ancient Egypt has, however, bequeathed us a wealth of texts carved on stone or written on papyrus which can be said to be legal documents: contracts, inventories, wills, decrees stating the king's will and the punishments that would be the price of disobedience, and also reports of proceedings. So far, no collection of laws has been found, although the neighbouring countries of the Near East abound in legal codes. The absence of an Egyptian code may be a pure accident, so that one day this gap in our knowledge may be remedied. It may well be, however, that justice was administered somewhat empirically. Irrespective of the importance of the case, the accused, once his identity had been established, was subjected to ruthless interrogation by magistrates who, from the outset, regarded him as guilty, and would order him to be beaten if his replies did not conform to their view of the matter. Only rarely was a prisoner released. He was usually condemned without further ado and heavy punishment was inflicted – confiscation of his possessions, further beatings which sometimes caused serious bodily injury, imprisonment (fig. 22), forced labour, the cutting off of nose and ears, exile, and finally death, which was perhaps to be preferred.

The nomes

As a reminder of the days when Egypt formed two kingdoms, the country continued to be divided into two parts, Ta-shema (Upper Egypt) and Ta-meh (the flooded land or Lower Egypt), each with its own separate administrative machinery.[14] During certain periods, the division took on a political significance. Upper and Lower Egypt were in turn divided up into provinces which, following the example of the Greeks, we call nomes. All the available documents agree in putting the number of nomes in Upper Egypt at twenty-two. It should be noted, however, that the Thirteenth and Fourteenth Nomes, then again the Twentieth and Twenty-first, share the same name with the addition respectively of the adjectives 'upper' and 'lower'. It would seem from this that they were found to be too big after their boundaries had been fixed, and were therefore split in two. In Lower Egypt, the number of nomes rose from sixteen during the Twelfth Dynasty to seventeen, then to twenty, and finally, much later, to twenty-two. We have no complete list of nomes for the period of the Old Kingdom.

Each nome was represented by an emblem borne on a standard (fig. 23). If we compare the list of these emblems with the ensigns depicted on Gerzean vases and on the slate palettes of the Chalcolithic period, and again with the list of the great Egyptian gods, we are forced to conclude that the nomes developed from the old clans which, after leading a nomadic existence for countless years, settled in one particular area and retained their emblem. Several of these emblems were subsequently to acquire great fame: the Ibis, which became a nome of Lower Egypt, was connected with the god Thoth; in Upper Egypt, the Belemnite, formerly a clan, became the emblem of the Ninth Nome, and later the embodiment of Min, the chief god of that province; the Cobra, too, was a nome, the Tenth, and a goddess. In Lower Egypt, two crossed arrows referred to two nomes distinguished by the adjectives 'south' and 'north', and to their goddess. Soped, in the Western Delta, was both a god and a nome.

In some other localities, the emblem retained its divine significance, although the god it represented was overshadowed by a more important god. This happened in the Dolphin; the Dolphin goddess became merely the consort of Banebded. In Upper Egypt, in the Crocodile Nome, the animal remained a god, but one of slight importance, who was finally superseded by the goddess Hathor. In the Eleventh Nome, the greyhound, Sha, was supplanted by Khnum.

A good many of the emblems never became the incarnation of a

Fig. 23. Emblems of the Nomes: the Sceptre, the Hare and the Black Dog. Montet, *Géographie de l'Egypte ancienne*, II, 55, 145, 164. These should be compared with the clan-emblems shown in Fig. 8.

divinity, although they still retained their sacred significance. Examples of this in Upper Egypt were the Rural Nome, *Nekhen*, the fetish *Sistrum*, the Oryx, the Hare, the trees of the Thirteenth and Fourteenth Nomes, and those of the Twentieth and Twenty-first Nomes, the scraper, and the sceptres of the Fourth and Nineteenth Nomes; and in Lower Egypt, the Harpoon, several bulls, and the Point of the East.

Finally, three nomes were given names comparable to those frequently applied to provinces in modern states: *Ta-Setet*, the land of the mineral *setet*, the Throne of Horus (the First and Second Nomes of Upper Egypt), and the White Wall (the First Nome of Lower Egypt).

All the nomes, whatever their origin, and whatever changes they underwent, retained, even until Roman times, the right to be personified by men or women bearing the name of the nome on

73

their heads. Forming two long processions, these representatives would bring their produce to the temple deity.

Every nome had a capital where the governor and his administrative staff resided, and which prided itself on possessing a temple revered throughout the entire area. The nome and the capital often had the same name with the exception of the flexional ending and the determinative word meaning city. The Sceptre Nome (the Fourth Nome of Upper Egypt) and its capital were represented by the same sign, *Uast*. Some capitals had two names, one which was related to the name of the nome, and another which was quite independent. The capital of the First Nome of Lower Egypt was originally called The White Wall, occasionally shortened to The Wall. From the Sixth Dynasty onwards it took the name of the palace of Pepi I, *Men nefer*, later transliterated by the Greeks as Memphis. The capital did not always remain in one place; in the Third Nome of Upper Egypt, it was transferred from the ancient city of Nekhen near the Eastern desert to Nekhebt on the opposite bank.

The establishment of the nomes and the disappearance of the weaker clans was a gradual process which was slowly accomplished during the prehistoric period. When the king became master of the two lands, he undoubtedly fixed the administrative divisions of the country, and their boundaries were recorded in the Archives. From the great Beni-Hasan inscription, we learn that the frontier-line between two warring nomes was marked out with fifteen stelae, after the king had consulted the ancient records. In the matter of frontier demarcation nothing was ever final, in spite of an essentially conservative administrative organization. The Throne Nome, to the north of the Delta, seems to have been created only during the New Kingdom. It consisted for the most part of swamps, and for a very long time must just have been a hunting or fishing ground. The Hearty Sovereign, originally the largest nome in the whole of Egypt and which had formerly been a kingdom, was reduced by stages to the average size. The Bast region was separated off from it, and became Upper Royal Child (a Lower Royal Child was created from other nomes), and later it lost the southern region, which included the quarries of Tura and the Red Mountain. During the New Kingdom, the two lands continued to be divided into nomes, although towns which had acquired a certain importance no longer tolerated the idea of being subordinated to the capital of the province, and their representative began to deal directly with the central authority. In the Ta-Setet Nome, the town of Nebi, which lay some thirty miles from Elephantine and was surrounded by a fertile and populated area, was able to realize its ambition to become a minor

74

capital. The same situation arose in the Third Nome, where Esna became the chief town of an independent district, and in other nomes too. In all parts of the country, administrative units appeared and disappeared; one example was the land of Wazet, which King Khaba created along the sea coast.

The governors of the nomes, and even of their subdivisions, were appointed by the king. This fact is officially stated by Qar, the great overlord of the Throne of Horus appointed by Pepi I.[15] Under the Twelfth Dynasty, Khnumhetep was appointed prince in the city of Menat-Khufu by a decree issued by Amenemhat II,[16] exactly as his grandfather had been appointed by a decree issued by Amememhat I. By another royal decree, Khnumhetep's son was installed as regent of the Black Dog. The king therefore chose his governors from among the local bigwigs, although he occasionally appointed an outsider. When Aba, governor of the Mountain of the Serpent, arrived to take up residence there, he kept the title of governor of the Great Land, an area he must have administered previously. In spite of the general rule, there were governors who did not owe their appointment to the king – for instance Ankhtifi, who was by right of birth governor of the Rural Nome, was brought into the neighbouring nome, Throne of Horus, by the god Horus himself, in order to quell disturbances caused by the inefficiency of another governor.[17] This should be taken as meaning that he acted entirely on his own initiative, at a time when the king's authority was not greatly respected in the southern nomes. Each governor had an elaborate titulary. He was a noble, iri-pat, Prince, Great Director of the Soldiers, Great Director of the Prophets and of many other things besides; all authority was concentrated in his hands, just as the supreme authority in the country was concentrated in those of the Pharaoh, the master of the two lands. The governor took up residence in his mansion like a minor sovereign, and had an impressive entourage of courtiers and officials, whose titles recalled those of the king's own officials – scribes, judges and chiefs of works. Just as he was the king's imakhu, so certain members of the provincial nobility enjoyed the privilege of being his imakhu. Ameni, governor of the Oryx nome, reckoned dates according to the years of his governorship, in the same way as the king reckoned by years of his reign; the year 43 of the king corresponded to the year 23 in the Oryx.[18] In spite of this display of vanity, which is the only one of its kind we know of, Ameni remained obedient to the king, since he took part in an expedition to Nubia with four hundred picked men, and in an expedition to the mines with six hundred men.

The responsibilities of the governor were manifold and corresponded, on a smaller scale, to those of the king. They were concerned with public works, law and order, precautions against famine and the levying of taxes.

The Nile and its subsidiary streams provided the main lines of communication from one part of the country to another. Every province had a network of roads and canals. The hieroglyphic sign used sometimes as an ideogram for the word 'nome' and sometimes as a determinative for it was a rectangle divided up into smaller rectangles by intersecting lines. The traveller flying over the Delta today has the same impression of a landscape divided up into small rectangular units by irrigation and transport canals bordered, on one side or both, by roads. Every year, when the canals were cleaned, the dredged up earth could be used to repair the gaps in the roads. A constant stream of pedestrians and animals moved along the roads, while on the canals boats sailing before the wind or propelled along by means of poles, transported people, livestock and harvest produce. In the records, the repair and maintenance of the canals is often referred to. In one instance, the nomadic tribes, who often caused trouble, had thrown blocks of stone into a canal near Aswan, a region where stones were plentiful. When Tuthmosis III was informed of the incident, he had the canal cleared and decreed that it should be the duty of the local inhabitants to keep it in good order.

The governors were responsible for keeping a close guard on the wadis through which nomadic tribes could easily infiltrate into the Nile valley. A tribe of forty-seven Amu, not counting women and children, entered the Oryx Nome through one of these wadis. They had travelled across the desert and wanted to obtain corn in exchange for black and green powders which they had managed to find. They were immediately taken to the governor's residence.[19]

Nomads such as these had no doubt the best of intentions; others, however, came with intent to pillage. Town dwellers and peasants were not at all anxious to meet with soldiers, who would lose no time in robbing them of their provisions, their sandals and even the clothes they were wearing. Sometimes an unscrupulous official would take advantage of some remote spot to rob a passer-by. This is what happened to the oasis-dweller already referred to. A certain Nomarch of Siut maintains that during his governorship, travellers could safely sleep on the road-side with their possessions beside them, because the fear in which the police were held was a sufficient protection against attack. At one point, when there was fighting in the Throne of Horus and squabbles were developing into full-scale battles, Ankhtifi forced the warring parties to make peace and to keep their feelings of animosity in check. This did not prevent him embarking on what amounted to a war against the Fourth and Fifth Nomes. It must be admitted that the Egyptians were much given to fighting; under King Petubastis, there were battles in every nome and every town.

The Egyptians, being conscious of the fact that their country was a gift of the Nile, experienced a feeling of anxiety every year as the summer solstice drew near. If the Nile did not rise to the desired level, there would be a shortage of food, and several years of inadequate inundations meant famine. Lean years, when the inundation was barely sufficient, were not uncommon. A good administrator could minimize the effects of a bad year by wise and cautious distribution of the reserves of food which had been built up after the last good harvest, and by seeing that every field in the province was tilled, so that the following year would be 'mistress of wheat, barley and of all things'. He could also reduce taxes and not insist on repayment of advances made in the previous year.[20] Modern states have recourse to similar devices.

The Nile cannot be held solely responsible for the great famines which wrought havoc in Egypt on more than one occasion. The disturbances, which became fairly general during the First Inter-mediate Period and even more so under the last of the Ramessides, meant that canals and roads were left untended, trade and building operations suspended, and the cultivation of crops brought to a standstill. There was little incentive to sow crops if bandits were likely to make off with the harvest. At the time of the Eleventh Dynasty a man from Thebes wrote to his mother that men and women were being eaten. During a previous period, the inhabitants of Upper Egypt had been reduced to eating their children. During the last years of the Twentieth Dynasty, the price of food continued to rise and people pillaged temples and tombs in order to obtain gold. One year, in particular, was referred to as the year of the hyenas. This was perhaps an exaggeration, yet it may have been literally true. So many people died that there was no time to bury the corpses, which were devoured by hyenas. According to an inscription on the rocks of the island of Sehel, known as the Famine Stela, during the reign of King Zoser the rising of the Nile was late for seven successive years. There was a scarcity of corn, because the crops withered in the fields. There was hardly anything at all to eat, even the courtiers were short of food, and all the temples were shut. The Pharaoh decided to seek the advice of a sage, Imhotep the priest, who, after consulting the holy books promised better things to come.[21] It is no longer believed that the stela dates from the actual reign of Zoser. Maspero considered it to be a pious lie, the purpose of which was to remind the king of the needs of the temple of Khnum. In Sethe's view, it was a new version of a very old document which did, perhaps, date from Zoser's time. According to the most recent editor, it was composed and engraved in Ptolemaic times. None of these hypotheses is completely convincing. The tradition of the seven years' famine also occurs in the Bible story of Joseph, and in other countries. The fact that it was given a literary form in Egypt proves that the spectre of famine was ever present.

The main task entrusted by the Pharaoh to the governors of provinces and towns was the collecting of taxes. Under Tuthmosis III, taxes were paid in the form of cereals, herds, fruit and provisions, gold and silver rings and jewels. During the Old Kingdom, there were two forms of taxation: days or hours of labour were demanded from those whose only asset was their own two hands (or rather their shoulders), cereals and livestock from those who owned estates. The assessment of the amount of cereals payable, perhaps of linen and fruit as well, was based on two factors: the surface area of the nome, and the height of the Nile rising. These two items of information made it possible for the central administrative services to inform each governor of the exact quantities he had to hand over. In order to avoid recriminations, the basis for assessment was made known to the general public. In the chapel of Sesostris III, which has been removed block by block from inside the third pylon at Karnak and rebuilt in the neighbourhood, the information is inscribed on a small monument, placed under the protection of Amon-Ra who, from the Middle Kingdom onwards, was the most powerful of Egyptian gods. Also inscribed on the monument is the surface area of every nome expressed in *atours* (1 *atour* = 110 square kilometres, 250 square metres), in *thousands* (1 *thousand* = 27 square kilometres, 35 square metres) and in *hundreds* (1 *hundred* = 2 square kilometres, 735 square metres). In addition, the monument gives, along with several other useful items of information, the figures for the normal levels of the flood; at Elephantine the level was 21 cubits, $3\frac{1}{3}$ hands, at Per-Hapi, near old Cairo, 12 cubits, 3 hands, 3 fingers, and at Edfu in the extreme North of Egypt, 6 cubits, 3 hands, 3 fingers. When the flood did not reach the above levels, a fact which anyone could check since nilometers had been built for this purpose at Elephantine, Per-Hapi and Edfu, the tax fixed for a normal year was reduced according to a scale that is unknown to us. The information inscribed in the White Chapel was given at great length in the famous Labyrinth which, according to Strabo, delegations from the nomes used as a meeting-place for the discussion of important matters.

Livestock was also taxable. The state carried out a general census of all herds every two years. So important was this operation that it was used for the fixing of dates. On Old Kingdom documents, references to the nth time of the census, or the year after the nth time of the census, can be found.[22] A scene frequently depicted on tombs, bas-reliefs and on sculpture in the round, is the census of livestock on private estates. The owner and the scribes sat in an enclosure while oxen and the smaller animals filed past in a never-ending procession. A nomarch of the Middle Empire called Thothhetep carried out a census of stud animals on the state farms and on his own. Craftsmen certainly had to give the state a proportion of the articles they made in their workshops; however, no mention of this form of taxation occurs before the New Kingdom.

Everyday work

Hesiod described the everyday occupations of his time in verse. The Ancient Egyptians portrayed theirs in pictures on the walls of their tombs. Not content with pictures alone they added explanatory inscriptions, remarks made by masters and servants, the songs they sang and, as if this were not enough, they deposited in their tombs wooden statuettes representing workers and servants, boats, and workshops along with their entire personnel – in short, a kind of concrete encyclopaedia of Egyptian life.[23]

Some description must therefore be given of daily occupations in ancient Egypt, beginning with those of the peasants, the mainstay of the country's wealth. During the season of the inundation, the peasants had comparatively little to do. When the Nile returned to its channel, and the earth – in the words of an Egyptian story-teller – rose up out of the water, they hastened to the fields with the seed and their teams of cows. If the earth had remained submerged for a long time, preliminary work on the soil could be dispensed with. The sower scattered the seeds and the ploughman, using a very elementary form of plough which was only just capable of turning over soft, easily-worked ground, immediately covered them over with soil. The plough was pulled by two cows. The driver of the team had no whip; a stick and persistent shouting were enough to guide its progress. When the ground had the consistency of mud, a flock of sheep was often made to do the work. The shepherd would take a handful of seeds from his basket and throw them in front of the ram, which was obediently followed by the rest of the flock. Servants, armed with long whips, prevented the sheep from straying outside the boundaries of the field. When the ground was already partly dry, a pick was used to cover over the seed after sowing. The universal method was

79

to scatter the seed first and then plough up the ground to cover the seed with soil. According to Herodotus, once these operations were completed, the peasant could sit back at his ease until harvest time. The land had stored sufficient water during the inundation to feed the plants, and to make irrigation unnecessary.

The Egyptians cultivated chiefly barley (*iot*) and emmer-wheat (*boti*), of which there were several varieties. In very early times, barley was wrenched out of the ground by hand, but from the Fourth Dynasty onwards, cereal crops were cut with a sickle. The harvesters formed a line, leaving an appropriate space between each man and the next. A given reaper grasped a bunch of corn, cut it just below the heads, and laid it on the ground to his left; his neighbour did the same, but laid his bunch to his right. In this way the helpers found the sheaves almost complete, so that they had little more to do than bind them. It was strenuous work. In order to forget their weariness, the reapers would organize speed contests either amongst themselves or against a neighbouring team. A flute-player would sometimes take up his position in the centre of the field, and one of the harvesters, breaking off for a moment and tucking his sickle under his arm, would sing and clap his hands. One of the songs was called the 'Song of the Oxen'; another began with the words, 'I started on my way . . .'

The sheaves were packed into huge rope panniers. Then a herd of donkeys would come trotting up, raising clouds of dust. The panniers were loaded on their backs and the herd moved off at a gentle pace towards the village, while the foals trotted on in front.

When the sacks were emptied, the harvest was quickly piled up into a temporary stack. Then the stalks were spread out on the threshing-floor, that was beaten earth, with the tips facing towards the centre, and oxen, donkeys or sheep were driven over it to tread out the grain. Forming a line like the radius of a circle, the animals moved over the threshing-floor, the donkey, cow, or sheep at the centre turning slowly round while the others described wider and wider circles according to their place in the line. When this operation was completed, the threshing-floor was covered with a layer of dust, corn, straw and chaff. The straw was moved to one side with forks and built up into a tightly-packed stack, which was strengthened with papyrus stalks. If the peasants needed straw, they would cut a vertical slice out of the stack, just as peasants do in Italy today. Teams of women cleared the corn with light brooms, winnowing-baskets and sieves, and carried it away to the silos. Throughout the New Kingdom, these various operations were sometimes presided over by an image in the shape of a crescent,[24] very like the human figures which can be seen today on barns to the south of Lake Chad (fig. 24). Offerings were laid before the image. In some localities, thank-offerings were made at the beginning of the summer season to Ernutet, a serpent goddess and lady of the harvest.

When the corn was taken from the silos, it was sieved once more before being ground into flour, a process which called for a large number of workers. First of all the men used heavy pestles to burst open the heads of corn which had been placed in stone mortars. Then the women, perched on troughs consisting of an upper and a

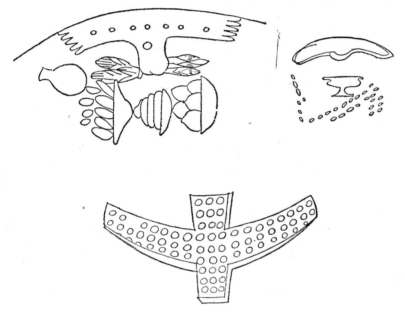

Fig. 24. Rustic idols in Ancient Egypt and in Black Africa. They presided over the cereal harvest.

lower compartment, rolled a heavy stone backwards and forwards over the corn which had been placed in the upper compartment, thus forcing it into the lower one; the process was repeated until the required state of fineness was reached.

Barley flour was used for making beer. Half-cooked loaves were crumbled into, and mixed up with, a sweetened liquid to which yeast had been added. After straining, the beer was kept in jars, which were sealed by means of a plate and a lump of mud plaster. There were several varieties of beer, but none of them could be kept for any length of time.

It never seems to have occurred to Egyptian bakers to build a proper oven. They used earthenware moulds, the insides of which were made very hot; then the women filled the moulds with dough. They were covered over and left until the bread was sufficiently baked to be removed whole. The scribes, who were present at every stage of the operation, measured out the flour and corn in bushels, then counted the loaves of bread which were of various shapes and sizes and sometimes contained fruit. They also counted the jars of beer. Bread and beer formed the staple diet of the Egyptians. There existed what might be called national or municipal bakeries and breweries; others were attached to temples and large estates. There

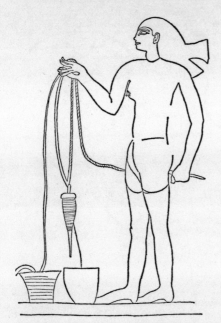

Fig. 25. Woman spinning, from New-berry, *Beni-Hasan*, Vol. IV. Hunters and fishermen also used to take up the spindle between hunting expeditions.

were also perhaps independent bake-houses and breweries whose customers were not maintained by any official organization.

Flax was widely cultivated, especially since the Egyptians hated the woollen materials which were worn by the nomads. The flax ripened at about the same time as the cereal crops. The best quality fibres were obtained by picking it while it was still in flower; but part of the crop was left to produce the seed for sowing or for the making of oil. The stalks were trimmed to the same length, tied into bundles and carried into the villages where they were treated and made into threads of varying thicknesses. The farmers' wives and daughters did the spinning; they had no distaff but were extremely skilful with their spindles (fig. 25).

Fig. 26. Shaduf, from the tomb of Api. In this, and similar, paintings, the shaduf is only being used to water gardens. It seems likely that it was also used to irrigate fields.

When the harvest had been gathered in, the fields were usually allowed to lie untouched until the next sowing season. If they were used for secondary crops, they had to be watered. In any case vegetables and salads, and many annual and biannual plants used for food, dyeing or medicine, needed a lot of water. The gardeners, their two jars slung on a yoke, would go off to the river or the canal, fill up their jars and empty them into the trenches. The operation became much less laborious when the *shaduf* was invented during the New Kingdom (fig. 26). A long pole, with a counter-weight (a stone or a clot of earth) at the thicker end and some sort of receptacle at the thinner end, was fixed to the top of an upright post or a tree with lopped branches. By manipulation of the pole, the receptacle was lowered into the water and, when it had filled up, the counter-weight automatically raised it to the level of the trench. The *saqqieh*, or water-wheel, was much more effective, and its creaking was still a familiar sound in the Egyptian countryside until a few years ago. However, it was invented only during the Late Period, which shows how long it took before human labour was lightened by the use of mechanical devices.

The vine was cultivated in the Delta from the earliest times. The chief vineyards were in the Roads of Horus, at Per-Ramses, and Imet in Lower Royal Child in the east, and the Stronghold of the Cow in the west. The vines of the Lake Mareotis region had the distinc-tion of being mentioned by Virgil and Pliny. There was, in Ta-setet, the most southerly of the nomes, an area known as the wine district, but it is doubtful whether vines could flourish in such latitudes: the name may have come from wine-trading. Vines were also grown in the oases. Landowners in Upper and Middle Egypt all had a few vine plants in their gardens. In Palestine today, the vine is often trained to grow up the fig-tree like a creeper, and to such a height that the picking of the grapes involves real acrobatic feats. The same rudimentary method was used by Meten during the reign of Snofru. A little later, under the Fifth Dynasty, the shoots were held up by forked vine-poles, or allowed to trail along the ground. In either case, they had to be watered. At harvest-time, the grape-pickers carried their baskets on their heads and, forming a single file and singing as they went, emptied the fruit into a vat, which had probably been hollowed out from a huge stone slab. The grapes were immediately crushed by helpers who danced to the clicking of their wooden crotals. The wine was collected in a huge jug. As there was still some juice left in the grapes, the bunches were then put into a sack, which was held over a trough by five men, who twisted it in order to extract the remaining juice (fig. 27). During the Middle Kingdom, the sack was attached at either end to pegs which revolved in a wooden frame (fig. 28).

The wine was allowed to clarify and ferment in jars without stoppers; then it was drawn off into long pointed vessels, which were covered with a plate sealed with mud plaster, and then packed away in store-rooms. The origin and the vintage were sometimes recorded on the sides of the jars. A large number of broken fragments of wine jars have been found at Akhetaton and Thebes.

The fruit harvest, especially the picking of dates and figs, was a form of recreation. Children and monkeys climbed up the trees and

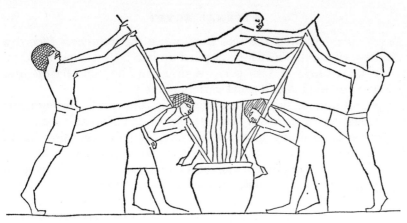

Fig. 27. A primitive method of pressing grapes, from the Tomb of Merruka. The men engaged in this task seem to be performing acrobatic feats. The man stretched out above the bag had to see that it was kept in position above the receptacle.

Fig. 28. Improved method of pressing grapes, from the Tomb of Puimre, with a fixed wine-press. The same result is now obtained more reliably and with less trouble.

Fig. 29. A monkey in a fig-tree, from one of the Beni-Hasan tombs. In Ancient, as in Modern, Egypt, men and animals lived together in close contact.

gorged themselves on the ripe fruit, while the gardeners turned a blind eye (fig. 29). The fruit was piled up into baskets, and was then ready for eating. It was perhaps dried in the sun. Bakers and pastry-cooks used it in a great variety of recipes.

Agricultural methods were gradually improved through the domestication of animals. The people of the Neolithic Age had succeeded in training dogs for hunting, and for guarding herds. During the Old Kingdom, donkeys were used as beasts of burden, cows for pulling the plough, and oxen for dragging sledges laden with heavy blocks of stone; donkeys, oxen and sheep were used for treading out the corn, and sheep, and later pigs, for trampling fields which had been sown with wheat or barley. There were two sorts of oxen. The *ioua*, the *bos africanus*, was not used as a beast of burden; it was fattened and slaughtered. The Egyptians may not have succeeded in breeding them, because they brought boat-loads from Upper Nubia for fattening. Another breed of oxen, the *nega*, still called by this name today in many areas of Africa, had become thoroughly acclimatized in Egypt. The Apis Bull was a *nega*. Both cows and bulls roamed freely over the grasslands. If the bulls fought at mating time, the oxherds would separate them by belabouring them with sticks. They knew where the animals' favourite pasture was to be found, and led them to it. During the hottest periods of the year, they let the herd cool off in deep water and were familiar with the spells for the warding off of the crocodiles which lurked in the clumps of rushes and papyrus plants. When the time came for a calf to be weaned, it was tied to a hoop so as not to interfere with the milk-supply. Neither bulls nor cows objected to being used as beasts of burden. The Egyptians kept other kinds of animals, some destined for the slaughter-house, others for sacrificial purposes; others again provided milk or leather. The main species were goats with magnificent horns, elegant gazelles, addax, and the straight-horned oryx. Whenever they could, estate owners were proud to be able to show examples of rarer species, such as the cream-coloured gazelle, the deer, and the maned moufflon. Some attempts were made to train hyenas for hunting; these detestable animals are shown lying on their backs with their feet tied, while they are forcibly fed with meat and fowls.

Hunting and fishing in the marshes

Although there were no important towns along the coastal strip of the Delta, many people lived near the marshes which were carpeted with lotus flowers and thickly fringed with reeds and papyrus plants.

86

The same type of landscape was to be found in the Fayum, which was called *Ta-she*, the Land of the Lake, or even *wadj-ur*, the 'Great Green', like the sea. The marsh dwellers made regular expeditions to gather papyrus stalks. They tied them in trusses, put them on their backs and, bent double beneath their heavy loads, made their way slowly back to their villages (fig. 30). The papyrus plant was put to many uses. I shall refer later to the paper which was manufactured from it in large quantities. The marsh-dwellers made strong ropes

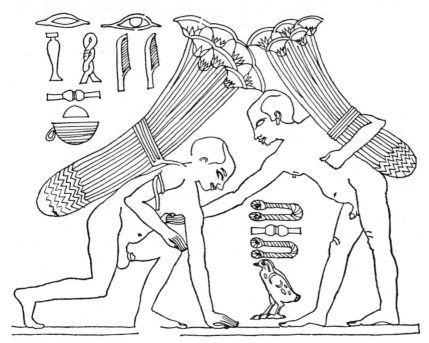

Fig. 30. Harvesting the papyrus plant, Tomb of Ti. The papyrus plant was put to various uses. The stalks had to be periodically harvested and divided out.

from the fibre, and used the stalks for making mats, seats, baskets, bird-cages and huts. Also, the papyrus plant supplied the material for the extremely useful skiffs which enabled the inhabitants to thread their way along the dense thickets, and to catch the birds nesting in the spreading umbels, as well as fishes and aquatic animals. All they needed to build the skiffs were fairly long stalks and rope. After being caulked with a resinous substance, the skiffs were launched and tested. This was made the occasion for amusing contests in which each man tried to overturn his opponent's boat. The douching was not serious, but a heavy knock from one of the steering-poles could leave far more lasting effects.

The fishermen had traps and landing-nets for catching small fish. The fisherman who went out on his own would take up his position in a quiet spot and let his line float; when he felt a tug on his line, he pulled it in carefully and killed the fish with a club.

The seine net was a most efficient instrument for catching fish. It was a huge, rectangular-shaped net fitted with floats along one edge, and weights along the other, and a length of rope at either end. It was stretched across a stream at a likely spot, the fish were driven towards it and when enough had collected the whole contraption was hauled towards the bank. The Nile fish were very lively and quite capable of getting away. If necessary a fisherman, with a band of cloth around his chest as a protection, would follow the net and grab the batensoda which was dangerous because of its bony scales.

It was forbidden to place fish on the offering tables in temples and tombs. In many areas, the eating of certain varieties of fish, and on certain occasions of all varieties, was prohibited. However, even princes did not obey this injunction. The lower classes depended largely on fish for food. Not all Egyptian fish was appetizing, but mullet and other varieties were perfectly edible. When catches were good, the superfluous fish were split open, salted, and left to dry. Mullet-roes were spread out on the ground and salted, then laid in layers between wooden planks and finally hung up to dry. Botargo is still a great delicacy in Egypt today.

The previously mentioned methods of fishing would have been useless for catching very big fish, such as the *lates*, the fat Nile perch, and the *chromis*, which were harpooned. The perch was so large that its tail brushed the ground when the fishermen carried it away slung on a stick passed through its gills. The perch and the chromis were both sacred – the first at Esna, the second at Dendera.

Nobles and princes were fond of fishing with harpoons and also took part in organized hippopotamus hunts. The harpoon used in the latter sport consisted of a single gaff set into, and bound on to, a shaft and attached to reed floats by means of a rope. This harpoon was a sacred object which was adopted as an emblem by two nomes of Lower Egypt, since hippopotamus hunting was considered to be virtually a religious rite. Hunters were not afraid to attack a whole family of hippopotami, even though crocodiles might be dozing close by. When the harpoon was properly thrown, the metal hook embedded itself in the great beast's hide. The animal at once made off; the wooden shaft often broke but thanks to the floats the hippopotamus was caught up with and killed by further harpooning.

Hunting the birds, which nested among the papyrus plants and were invisible from water level, was a much more amusing and far less dangerous sport. It was carried out by means of boomerangs, but first of all the birds had to be forced to reveal their whereabouts. Hunters took along with them cages containing small carnivorous animals – civets, mongooses and wild cats – which would climb up the stalks. When they reached the nests, the parent birds went for them with their beaks and claws, but at the same time became an easy target for the hunters. Once they were struck and dazed, they fell into the water or the skiffs, so that even children could catch them.

A most ingenious device, which was still in use in France and Syria at the beginning of the present century, made it possible to capture large numbers of geese and wild duck during the migration season. It consisted of two nets which were spread on the ground on

Fig. 31. Hunters' huts, Tomb of Ti. It was in these that the inhabitants of the marshlands stowed away their modest treasures.

either side of a pond and big enough to cover it completely. By means of a rope, the two parts of the net could be pulled sharply together, thus trapping a whole flock of birds. The hunters would then rush forward to pull the birds out from underneath the net and put them into cages.

The hunting and fishing community had a different mode of life, even different physical characteristics, from those of the mass of the peasant population (fig. 31). They lived in reed huts, and went about their work either naked or wearing only a belt; they had a flat skull and very little hair over the temples, whereas the majority of Egyptians had round heads and thick hair. They worshipped a meadow goddess and her son Net. The rich nobles liked to join them during the season of the inundation, and, after invoking the goddess Hathor, whose favourite abode was among the papyrus plants, they would take pleasure in both the boomerang and the harpoon.

Quarries and mines

Even after the climate of North Africa became drier, the two deserts which lay on either side of the Nile valley were not entirely the vast, waterless expanses of sand and stone described by some classical authors. As far as Memphis, and even further south, the rainfall was relatively high in winter; grass and shrubs grew in the sand and only withered at the beginning of summer. A certain amount of moisture remained for much longer periods in the wadis where, during the Pharaonic era, clumps of terebinth and tamarisk were to be found. Nor was animal life absent. Artists have left almost idyllic pictures of these areas. In a gently undulating landscape, animals which are destined to fall a prey to hunters with their bows, lassoes and grey-hounds, or will provide a tasty morsel for lions and panthers, are shown serenely pursuing their daily activities. A gazelle is feeding her young, another is lying with neck outstretched on the soft sand; a hedgehog is emerging from its lair and a jerboa is about to return to its hole. Some animals are mating.

On the whole the Egyptians were afraid of the sea and the desert. Yet Egypt could boast a number of sailors and a few men of adventurous spirit, like the seventy-year-old patriarch, the father of seventy children, who all his life zealously hunted game between the Nile and the Red Sea.[25] We have evidence that, under Ramses III, bands of hunters went out to gather the honey of the wild bees, as well as resin from the terebinth, while at the same time they hunted the oryx, which by then had become rare.[26] We can therefore affirm that, at all periods, the Egyptians sought to improve and perfect their knowledge of the desert with its natural tracks and water-holes, its mineral resources, and its mines.

The building of the pyramids and *mastabas* along the borders of the western desert, opposite Memphis, was the cause of constant and extraordinary activity throughout the Old and Middle King-doms. Quays had to be fitted up along the canals for the unloading and storing of blocks of stone of varying dimensions. Then the stones had to be dragged to the building-yards, along with various other goods and movable objects. Vast throngs of people attended the ceremonies which were constantly being held. Towns had to be built to provide administrative services and supplies for the inhabitants since, towards the end of the Twelfth Dynasty, the funerary monu-ments formed one long continuous necropolis from Abu-Roash, opposite Cairo, to the entrance of the Fayum.

During the New Kingdom, a similar outburst of activity took place on the left bank at Thebes. In the capital and in all the towns, the

Egyptians were inspired both by piety, and pride, to erect new sanctuaries, and to make the existing ones more worthy of divine greatness.

In order to satisfy these requirements, a fantastic amount of good building stone had to be hewn out of the two mountain chains bordering the valley. The Egyptians were quick to realize that their labours yielded a double dividend; while they were digging out hypogea in the rock, they obtained blocks of stone of every shape and size with which to build monuments. This explains why the compound word *Kherti-neter*, the worker at the necropolis, was often used as a general term for quarryman.

Fine quality limestone was obtainable almost everywhere, and a belt of solid sandstone was to be found in the southern nomes of Upper Egypt.[27] Particularly valuable deposits were to be found at certain favoured spots. Nature had arranged things extremely well; such sources were not far from the great city of Heliopolis to the east of the Nile, or from the line of pyramids which stretched across the mountain chain on the west bank. There was basalt which provided paving stones for the temples; red or yellow quartzite, which was ideal material for the sculptor, and gave its name to the Red Mountain, still known as Gebel el Ahmar. Stone was quarried here chiefly under the Twelfth Dynasty, and during the New Kingdom at the time of Amenemhat III and Ramses II. The rock was found in the form of horizontal layers from which single blocks as long as an obelisk, and proportionately wide, could be extracted. The two colossi of Memnon were hewn from blocks such as these, as was a gigantic figure said to have been created by the king himself, not to mention a host of other statues which may be fittingly termed colossal. Opposite Memphis the quarries of Roan, later called Ta-Ro-an, the modern Tura, and transliterated by the Greeks in the form of Troya, supplied a very fine white limestone which was frequently used by sculptors and particularly suitable for bas-reliefs. This explains why the walls of temples and *mastabas* built of ordinary limestone were covered over with a layer of Tura limestone, which provided artists with a vast working surface. Stelae and door frames were often made of the same substance. As quarrying was a royal monopoly, it was the king who decided where the quarries should be established. The quarrymen had learned from experience that they had to dig very deep to reach the best stone. Consequently they hollowed out vast caverns, leaving pillars to support the roof.

Alabaster was plentiful in the eastern desert; the main quarry was in Middle Egypt, about twelve miles from Akhetaton. It was called *Hat-nub*, the House of Gold. It supplied the ribbon alabaster, from which were made many of the remarkable plates and dishes which were found in the tombs of the first two dynasties and in the galleries of the Step Pyramid. Occasionally, it was carved into statues thirteen cubits (more than eighteen feet) high.

Aswan was the centre of the granite country. All varieties were found here – red, grey, black, and blue – sometimes in one and the same bed. At Tanis, I noticed a stela with a grey granite base and a top of red granite. Along the road leading to the quarries, you can still see rows of wedge clefts in the cliff face, which enlighten us about the working methods of the Egyptian quarrymen. After removing the upper layer of decomposed granite, they dug into the rock, taking advantage of the faults. Then they drove wooden wedges into the clefts; when the wood was moistened, it swelled and split open the rock. This was quite a rapid method of obtaining huge blocks of stone to be fashioned, as the case might be, into pillars, architraves, doors, small and large statues (some more than sixty feet high), monolithic colossi and obelisks. Monuments such as these were usually carved in the quarry itself. A bas-relief depicting a monolithic column lying on a barge was discovered on the causeway loading to the pyramid of Unas, while a monument in the Thebes area shows an obelisk being transported in the same way. Rough-hewn blocks, sarcophagi and statues were left on the sites. There exists, in a rectangular-shaped cutting, an obelisk over a hundred and thirty feet long which would have been the tallest of all the obelisks if it had been wrenched from its bed; however, the quarry-men left it where it lay, having noticed that it was flawed. It serves to show how difficult was their task. Yet another obelisk, begun under Tuthmosis III, was abandoned, then, after further consideration, was finally completed under Tuthmosis IV and erected, in solitary splendour, along the prolongation of the axis of a building at Karnak. It was transported to Italy under the emperors, and now stands in front of the Lateran Palace. This obelisk is nearly a hundred feet high, and is the tallest of all the obelisks which have been preserved.

Uni, the high official to whom reference has already been made, boasted, as if this were a considerable exploit, of having journeyed as far as Elephantine and Ibhet, on a single expedition. The latter was situated in the Ipsambul (Abu Simbel) area. Beyond Tuskha, on the western bank, diorite, an even harder stone than granite, was to be found, but only after a trek of some thirty-five miles across barren and desolate country. The rock was first quarried in the reign of Cheops. The finest statue of Chephren is made of diorite. King Merenra of the Sixth Dynasty ordered Uni to fetch blocks of granite, a sarcophagus with its lid and a pyramidion, and it was for this reason that he travelled as far as Ibhet. The quarrying of diorite involved such hardships that operations were abandoned after the Twelfth Dynasty.

Large deposits of a black, gritty schist, called *bekhen*,[28] were found in the eastern desert, not admittedly within very easy reach, but at a reasonable distance from the towns. *Bekhen* stone was highly prized by sculptors because it was more easily worked than diorite, and could be given a high polish. The quarrymen and their band of helpers set out from Coptos, and after crossing the eastern half of the Two Falcons Nome and a barren region beyond it, halted at the Lagheila oasis where the water had a somewhat brackish taste. It took them a further two days to reach the valley of Rohanu, half-way between the Nile and the Red Sea. At the junction of the valley and the Wadi Fauakhis, there was a deep well of pure, fresh water. On both sides of the valley, the rocks can be seen to have been cut into blocks of varying shape and size by horizontal and oblique fissures. Some blocks are lying loose, while many others remain attached to the parent mass only by the base. These quarries were worked throughout the whole Pharaonic era. Sometimes when only a limited number of stones were needed, the quarrymen would spread out over the mountain and, with the occasional help of some miraculous happening, would be guided to a stone which corresponded to their needs and it only remained for them to roll it down the mountain-side. The schist being fragile, the stone was often shattered into fragments by the time they got it to the valley below, in which case they patiently repeated the operation over and over again as often as was necessary.

One overseer had the brilliant idea of building a gently sloping road against the mountain-side, and letting the blocks slide down it. The device worked perfectly. The idea of progress was not absolutely foreign to the Egyptian mentality, but it must be admitted that advances took place very slowly.

Under the Twelfth Dynasty, large-scale expeditions, with a personnel as numerous as an army, were organized and achieved outstanding results. In the year 36 of Sesostris I, Ameni, the herald, brought back to the quay at Coptos 150 statues and 60 sphinxes, all of which were hauled by human labour and honoured with the burning of incense throughout the long trek. An official inscription engraved at the close of operations gives a detailed account of the people who took part in the expedition. They were: a staff of administrators 80 strong, 300 notabilities from the court of the Prince of Thebes, 700 people from Coptos whose function is not specified, 520 artisans, 160 caterers, and finally an army of 17,000 men, a considerable proportion of whom apparently travelled backwards and forwards between Coptos and Rohanu in order to carry the provisions necessary for the entire expeditionary force. The same inscription indicates that the monthly rations ranged from 200 loaves and 5 jars of beer for a leader, to 10 loaves and a third of a jar of beer for the ordinary worker. One of Ameni's subordinates is anxious to assure us that not a single man lost heart. A little later, under Amenemhat II, two hundred blocks of stone were brought to Coptos.

The *bekhen* quarries were not worked during the Second Intermediate Period, and the kings of the Eighteenth Dynasty who preferred to quarry granite, quartzite and alabaster, hardly ever attempted to resume operations. An important expedition set out during the reign of Ramses IV but it was on a far smaller scale than the one organized by Ameni.

In the year 1, one of the chief priests of Coptos, Usemarenakht, led a force of 400 men, among whom were sculptors and quarrymen. The statues which he brought back were considered to be o good quality. The following year many skilled technicians visited the Rohanu valley, which was also called the place of truth. In the year 3, an army – for such, in effect, it was – went to fetch the blocks of stone which were waiting to be transported. It was under the command of Ramsesnakht, First Prophet of Amun and Chief of Works, a famous man in his time, who was attended by a staff of ten officials. It also included scribes, grooms (all the exalted personages rode in chariots), police officers, fishermen (who were particularly skilled at packing the blocks of stone into the sledges), quarrymen and master-quarrymen, draughtsmen and engravers who planned, and inscribed on a prominently placed rock, the magnificent stela of the year 3, and finally 5,000 labourers, in other words soldiers, 800 of whom were foreign slaves (Aperu), 3,000 men from the Pharaoh's domains and 900 who were present but who were not mentioned in the official list (in other words 'extras'). The equipment included ox-carts which brought from Coptos the offerings intended for Min, Horus and Isis, the gods of the mountain.

I have dwelt at some length on the Rohanu quarries because the inscriptions carved there are more detailed than those found elsewhere. They show what elaborate preparations were made by those who organized these major expeditions. When they returned, detailed reports were drawn up and kept by the scribes in buildings called 'Houses of Life' (the equivalent of our universities and public archives). They certainly knew how to adapt all the means at their disposal in order to achieve their ends. No effort was too great when it was a question of serving the gods and the dead.

Not only did the desert supply the stones required by architects and sculptors, it also contained the semi-precious stones highly prized by jewellers: amethysts from the Ibhet region, quartz, cornelian and emeralds (found by women slaves in a stone called *benut* from which grindstones were hewn).[29] Prospectors, who were ready to brave hunger, thirst, and the wild beasts of the desert, were chiefly attracted by gold, rich deposits of which could be found in the eastern desert, either in the form of solid veins running through the quartz, or as grains buried in the sand of the wadis. The most important gold-bearing areas were situated to the east of Coptos, quite near the *bekhen* mountain, a little to the east of Edfu, and in Nubia. In the Coptos area abundant evidence of early attempts at gold-mining can be seen in the vicinity of the El Fauakhir well. A somewhat approximate survey of the region, a survey which has been called the oldest map in the world, and which dates from the time of Ramses, is now in Turin Museum.[30] The ancient Egyptian geographer marks the roads, the wells, a stela erected by Seti I, the *bekhen* mountain, the gold-bearing mountain and the village where the gold was worked. Long before the Ramessides, smelters from the Temple of Ptah, the patron of craftsmen, engraved their names and those of the sovereigns of their time – Cheops and his four successors – on a rock. The gold was brought to Coptos in the form of rings and presented to the vizier by officials who had captured or shot ostriches on the way.

To the east of Edfu, a small temple was erected near another gold-bearing region. King Seti I explains at great length in the various inscriptions in this temple how concerned he was about the miners' plight. He himself studied the countryside and succeeded in finding a well. He ordered that all the gold should be conveyed to the temple before going to swell the royal treasury. In Egypt, the treasury never relinquished its rights. The inhabitants of the Mountain of the Serpent Nome were allowed to work silver within their own territory and desert, but they were forbidden to handle gold, which could only be mined by state workers. It has already been mentioned that engineers in the time of Ramses II eventually succeeded, after tremendous efforts, in finding water in the Ikaita desert in Nubia, thus enabling the gold-mining operations to be resumed.

In the matter of mining, quarrying and transporting materials, the Egyptians showed themselves capable, then, of organizing and equipping expeditions which were on a truly lavish scale. The operations were carried out mainly by human labour, beasts of burden playing only a subordinate part. Prospectors made surveys of the ores and minerals found in the desert, discovered where the wells were, dug reservoirs, located the natural tracks and built roads over them. The Egyptians used to say in their own picturesque way: 'I have changed the road into a river and turned the red land into verdant pastures.'

Once the miners and quarrymen had built up adequate stocks, both ore and stones were subjected at the source to some kind of preliminary processing. Near the El Fauakhir well, there were villages where the gold was worked. Workshops for stone-cutters and sculptors were attached to the main quarries, even to the quarry situated in the remote Rohanu valley.

There still remained the task of transporting the precious loads back to Egypt. Both raw materials and finished articles were put on sledges and hauled by well-disciplined teams, until they reached the tributaries and canals of the Nile. After that, it was a fairly easy matter to convey them to the workshops in all the important towns of both Upper and Lower Egypt.

Workshops

At a very early period, the kings took the step of setting up workshops in the capital, and throughout their various estates all over Egypt, for the production of both essential and luxury articles. Meten, for instance, was put in charge of all the king's flax. Under the Fourth Dynasty, a certain Uta was director of the workshops where skins were treated and then made up into trunks, satchels, sandals, and many other articles.

The nomarchs, in imitation of their master, increased the number of workshops in the cities where they resided. The temple personnel included, in addition to the regular priests, scribes, peasants and craftsmen who made the objects which were needed in the religious ceremonies and which varied from one temple to the next. The great priest of Ptah held the title of Overseer of Handicrafts, which is not surprising since Ptah himself was a workman, like the Greek Hephaestus, and his sons, the Cabeiri, were also workmen. Among the personnel serving a powerful god such as Amun representatives of nearly every craft were to be found; even a provincial god such as Min had quite a considerable number of craftsmen in his service. The various craft-guilds whose activities are depicted on Old Kingdom tombs belonged to an organization called *perzet* – the everlasting domain – which was perhaps only an imaginary concept. However, it seems possible that all the great landowners employed craftsmen of their own to deal with the products of their estates, especially everything connected with food and clothing.

In the bazaars of modern oriental towns, the goldsmiths are all grouped along one street, the perfumers in another, and the cloth merchants in yet another. This must have been the case, too, in the cities of Ancient Egypt and explains why the scenes depicting the various arts and crafts are almost always shown in groups on tombs of all periods. Moreover, furniture, vases, and jewellery required the services of several experts, to whose advantage it was to work side by side, sometimes even in the same workshop. Masons, on the other hand, went wherever they were summoned, and the boat-builders set up their workshops along the banks of the Nile or along the navigable canals.

Whereas stone, especially high-grade stone, was used only for religious and funerary monuments, houses, shops, barns and all enclosure walls were built of unbaked brick. How this important building material was made is told in Chapter V of Exodus, as well as in a painting in the tomb of Rekhmire and on the Ptolemaic bas-reliefs. Mud and chaff were mixed with water and trodden out until the right consistency was obtained. The mixture was pressed into a mould, then the mould was removed and the brick was left to dry out. The bricks were cemented together with mud or plaster. Buildings made with bricks proved to be more weather-resistant than those built of stone.[31]

One word, *iqdu*, was used for both the mason and the potter. Both used mud as their basic material. Before the invention of the brick-mould, the mason shaped the walls with his hands; a house could, in fact, be thought of as a large pot, since pottery had also been hand-moulded before the invention of the wheel. Both the brick-mould and the wheel were invented, perhaps simultaneously, at a very early period, in fact during the First Dynasty. Tombs belonging to this period, which were for the most part built of unbaked brick, have yielded a valuable collection of pottery of every shape and size: dishes, plates, bowls, cylindrical, oval or rounded vases, and even chests. The objects had either no decorative pattern or a very simple one. It was during the New Kingdom that the workshops turned out increasing quantities of vessels of glazed composition, which took the place of objects made of hard stone.

During the prehistoric era the Egyptians showed themselves to be outstandingly skilful at making weapons and tools, first out of hard stone, then out of flint. From the First Dynasty onwards, using hard and soft stone, granite, schist, breccia and alabaster, they carved and hollowed out the dishes and plates which amaze and delight visitors to the museum at Saqqara, which was specially built to house the collection. To bore out the central core of the vases, the stonecutter used a sort of forked drill which he rotated with his hands, and the handle of which was fitted with two pads of leather or wood. This tool was used as a hieroglyphic sign, *hemu*, which meant literally vase-maker, but which covered all stone-workers, and even, broadly speaking, all artisans. This proves that the workers in this field acquired their outstanding technical proficiency during those centuries, when they made little else besides vases. Eventually, they felt able to deal more ambitiously with stone, and not only with alabaster and the white limestone from Tura, but with the hardest varieties. Yet their tools remained extremely rudimentary, as can be seen from the bas-reliefs on the tombs of Ti, Abi and Rekhmire, where sculptors are shown at work, and even more clearly from actual tools found inside the Step Pyramid and in the diorite quarries. All tools were made of copper, as bronze did not come into use until later, and were limited in range, comprising only chisels, engravers' points, drills and saws. It is generally accepted that the workers used an abrasive powder. What is more important, they seem to have spared neither time nor trouble in the execution of their work.

Boats played an important part in the economic life of Egypt. Many different types of craft were in existence: pleasure boats for the use of the king and the nobility, boats for transporting troops, barges for carrying huge blocks of stone, and cargo boats for the transport of provisions and animals. Each variety bore a special name for which it is not always possible to find a modern equivalent. There must have been a large number of shipyards, and some were even set up during expeditions outside Egypt. When Uni was sent to the south by the king to bring back blocks of stone for a pyramid, he ordered canals to be dug. Then the local chieftains cut down trees which were made into planks and beams. Three boats, described as broad, and four transport-boats made of acacia wood from the land of Uant, were very quickly constructed. Acacia was the wood generally used in Egypt for ordinary boats; the huge boats used for state occasions were made of cedar (*meru*) or fir (*ash*).[32] Tools used in boat-building included rulers, plumb-lines, axes, saws, chisels, mallets and adzes, and the material included rope.

All the boats built by the Egyptians were flat-bottomed, as can be seen from the numerous small-scale models found in the tombs. There is also a very fine boat which the Egyptians dismantled and hid in a cache near the pyramid of Cheops, and which has been skilfully re-assembled by the *Service des Antiquités*.[33] The planks, the shape and size of which were very carefully calculated, were held together by means of pegs fitting holes that were bored on the slant in the thickness of the wood but without going right through. Cross-pieces supported the two sides and their number was used as an indication of the capacity of the boat, in the way tonnage is in modern times. When the framework was completed, the hull was smoothed down with adzes. Finally, the double mast had to be erected, the rowing and steering oars fixed, and the cabins placed in position.

Boats were probably the earliest products of the carpenter's skill. At a very early period, the Egyptians used wood for building, for making coffins and religious and secular furniture and other objects. The word used to describe all the various activities of the carpenter, *nezer*, is related to *naggar*, the Arabic for carpenter. The tools used by the boat-builders, axes, saws and adzes, were also used by the carpenters. In addition to these the carpenter also needed a bow-drill for piercing holes, and stone or metal polishing-tools. The wood used for ordinary purposes was mainly acacia, and sycamore. For the finer work, ebony was imported from the Sudan, and two kinds of wood from Syria, *sesnezem* (perhaps the carob) and *uan* (possibly the cypress). Other woods used were cedar, pine and fir. Many items of furniture are depicted in the tombs of the Old Kingdom, either singly, or on the bas-reliefs devoted to arts and crafts. The tomb chamber of Queen Hetephras, mother of Cheops, contained an ample collection of objects made of wood and gold. They have been restored by G. Reisner and others, who discovered them. The tombs in the Valley of the Kings which had not been entirely pillaged, such as those of Yuyu and Tuya, and more particularly Tutankhamen's which had remained completely undisturbed, amounted almost to a national furniture repository, containing, in a perfect state of preservation, cupboards, beds, arm-chairs, stools, tables, pedestal tables, coffers and chests, all exquisitely finished and impeccably assembled.

Alongside the carpenters' shops were workshops for the manu-facture of weapons and various ceremonial objects. On monuments and bas-reliefs, gods, kings and dignitaries are shown holding such objects in their hands. From the beginning of the New Kingdom onwards, a new trade – that of chariot-builder – came into being. Just as the horse was brought into Egypt from Asia, so the Egyptian chariots were modelled on those of the Syrians: there is no doubt, however, that the pupils outshone their masters. As regards leather-work, the Egyptians were unacquainted with any tanning process except oiling, now known as chamoising. First of all the skins were stretched, and then placed in an oil-bath. Afterwards they were spread out and hammered to make sure that the oil was completely absorbed into the leather. Finally they were left to dry. During the New Kingdom, the art of embossing leather was discovered, and a quiver from Maherpre's tomb is an outstanding example of such craftsmanship.[34] In the rock tombs of Deir el Bahari, archaeologists discovered a huge bundle of leather which, when unfolded, turned out to be the sort of tent that was put over the sarcophagus during the funeral ceremony.[35] Although only one of its kind has been discovered, many others must have existed.

Both men and women loved finery. Egyptians liked to cover the dead and the gods with jewels, and were also very fond of adorning their own persons. Ceremonial costume, at all periods, included diadems, necklaces, girdles, bracelets and rings, which were naturally subject to the vagaries of fashion. There were certainly many goldsmiths' shops in the capital and the chief towns, as well as in the temples, especially the Temple of Ptah, at Memphis, because he was the special patron of all craftsmen.

As gold-mining was a state monopoly, the metal inevitably found its way into public buildings. Before it was handed over to the foremen of the workshops, it was weighed in the presence of the inevitable scribes. First of all, it had to be purified. The ingots were placed in a crucible and heated over an open fire. In order to make the fire burn more brightly, several men stood round the hearth and blew fiercely down pipes protected at the lower end by a pottery sleeve. It was exhausting work. During the New Kingdom the pipes were attached to two skins (fig. 32). The man using this contraption brought his weight to bear first on one skin, then on the other, so that the air was forced out in alternate bursts. In short, the principle of the bellows had been evolved. When the gold was molten, men able to stand the heat and smoke lifted the crucible off the fire with tongs that were very inferior to the strongly-built instruments in use in present-day workshops. They then broke off a corner and poured the liquid gold off into moulds. Before it was quite cold, the metal was vigorously hammered on an anvil. By this very simple process it was possible to obtain flat plates, bars, strips, and lengths of gold wire which were rendered progressively finer by being drawn through a draw-plate.

Meanwhile, lapidaries and cutters were carrying on the work of boring and engraving the semi-precious stones which had been brought in from the desert, or obtained from abroad. These were lapis lazuli, turquoise, cornelian, quartz, chalcedony and the other opaque stones which were used by the ancient Egyptians at all periods. The stones were finally passed on to the setters, who were less interested in varying their designs than in achieving perfection

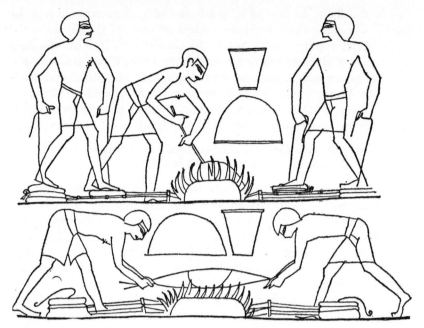

Fig. 32. Bellows from a forge, Tomb of Rekhmare. The workmen blew down a reed protected by a pottery sleeve.

of finish. The skill of the Old Kingdom craftsman has to be appreciated chiefly from the illustrations on the monuments. The museums contain a great variety of jewels belonging to the Middle Kingdom, in particular those found on the necropolises at Dahshur and in the Fayum; examples of the jeweller's craft during the New Kingdom and later periods come chiefly from Thebes, Memphis and Tanis.

The work of setting stones seems to have been carried out, at least at Memphis, by dwarfs with bodies of normal size but stunted arms and legs (fig. 33). Ptah, their patron, was portrayed in the form of a dwarf. When, at Memphis, Cambyses saw a statue representing the

Fig. 33. Dwarf goldsmiths on the tomb of Merruka. These dwarfs, who resembled the Cabieri, or sons of Ptah, seem to have been a special feature of the Memphite workshops.

god in this form, he first of all made fun of it, then ordered it to be burnt. The same thing happened when he entered the shrine of the Cabeiri, who were Ptah's sons and also dwarfs.[36] The so-called 'Ptah-pigmy' statuettes bear a resemblance to the dwarf goldsmiths – a resemblance which is all the more significant since their conversation was interspersed with references to the great god of Memphis and Sokar, the patron of the necropolis. Proof of this can be found in the following dialogue reported as having taken place in a workshop:

'Hurry up with the necklace, it should be finished by now.'
'As Ptah loves me, I want to finish it today.'

The race of pygmies may have been wiped out during the disturbances which occurred in the two intermediate periods. No further mention is made of them in later documents. One pessimistic author laments the fact that native craftsmen could no longer find work and that foreigners were taking their place. It is a fact that Semitic types figure in scenes depicting the arts and crafts on the tomb at Thebes.

All the peasant women living in the provinces where flax was grown had learned to spin. As early as the Old Kingdom, there were workshops for weaving and spinning which belonged to the king. Later, others were set up in the great temples, such as the Temple of Amun, at Thebes. The workshops turned out a very wide range of materials. In 550 Amasis sent garments embroidered with figures to the Temple at Cyrene. These must have been of a similar type to the famous coronation robe found in Tutankhamen's tomb.

We have by no means given an exhaustive list of the arts and crafts which flourished in Ancient Egypt. Mention should be made of the cosmeticians and other beauty experts, whose services were in demand by both men and women; the barbers, wig-makers, chiropodists and manicurists, who every morning prepared their masters for the daily round of receiving and paying calls; the pharmacists and dry-salters who concocted preparations which were said, somewhat ambitiously, to have the power of restoring youth to an old man. The pharmacists, who had chosen Sokar as their patron, were very proud of their professional secrets, which were handed down from father to son. Doctors will be discussed later in the section dealing with Egyptian science. We should, however, draw attention to the existence of a guild, which was peculiar to Ancient Egypt and comprised the vast body of workers employed for the process of mummifying.[37] The rich, the middle classes and the poor, all had to go through the hands of the *ut*. Briefly, the internal organs and viscera were removed from the body and preserved in canopic jars.

The body cavity was filled with aromatic spices, then it was pickled in natron, the two main deposits of which were found to the east of El Kab in Upper Egypt, and north-west of Memphis in Lower Egypt. After seventy days, the body was washed, dried, and wrapped in fine strips of linen which had been soaked in gum. The incision which had been made in the abdomen was covered over with a sheet of gold, engraved with an eye, *udjat*, which had great healing properties. Fingers and toes were bandaged separately. Jewels and amulets were placed in position, and body and limbs were completely swathed in an outer layer of bandages. By the time the whole process of mummifying had been completed the body was nothing but a skeleton covered with yellowish skin. Although it is true that some mummies, such as that of Seti I, still look vaguely like human beings, it is difficult not to conclude that the Egyptians went to a lot of trouble only to achieve very meagre results. However, no one, neither the scholar nor the casual visitor to museums, can remain entirely unmoved at the sight of the remains of the great Pharaohs and their courtiers.

CHAPTER 5

THE EXPANSION OF EGYPT AND THE REACTIONS OF NEIGHBOURING PEOPLES

The Nine Bows

THE Pharaoh was not only the Master of the Two Lands, Upper and Lower Egypt. The Black Land – Kem-t – and the desert were also said to belong to him. In order to develop their country, the Egyptians had to scale the cliffs which hemmed them in on all sides or penetrate up the wadis in order to hunt, keep watch on the nomadic tribes, and investigate and exploit the mineral wealth of the desert. Another more general title of the Pharaoh was Sovereign of the Nine Bows. The Nine Bows was a confederation of peoples and lands over which the Paraoh claimed to have certain rights. On King Scorpion's mace-head, the Bows form a counterpart to the Lapwings; like them they are strung up by the neck from the ensigns of the king's allies. They are mentioned in the Pyramid Texts, where their number is given as seven only,[1] although it was later to become nine. Their names, which are always the same even if the order in which they are presented varies, are recorded in the documents of the New Kingdom and in the Ptolemaic temples.[2]

Upper and Lower Egypt rightly belonged to the confederation, since they constituted the king's most valuable domain. The southerners were represented by the *Iuntiu* of *Ta-setet* which lay just south of Aswan, and by the land of Shat, which was much further south. The bowmen of the 'empty land', *Ta-shu*, and the *Mentiu* lived in the east, while the oasis dwellers of the desert fringe, as well as the *Tehenu*, lived in the west. Finally, the *Haunebu* were sailors whom the north wind had driven towards the Mediterranean coast. In short, the confederation comprised the whole of the Egyptian world – the two lands, and the neighbouring tribes to the east, west, north and south.

It was easy for the Egyptians to maintain communications with the peoples and lands belonging to the confederation, but in order to reach the *Khetiu*, the Marine Terraces – of which there were three types, the Terraces of Fir, the Terraces of Turquoise and the Terraces of Incense – they had to go by sea. It is difficult to imagine the Egyptians venturing eagerly on sea voyages, because during the New Kingdom the sea was held to be a cruel and exacting divinity. However, even at a very early period they were prepared to face the hazards of the Mediterranean.

Temple lists and inscriptions engraved by private individuals mention lands which supplied Egypt with materials. Some of them were situated beyond the regions we have just mentioned.

Egypt's relations with foreign peoples can be considered from two different angles. The foreign peoples were just as strongly drawn towards the valley of the Nile as the Egyptians were to their lands. Egypt was, in fact, accessible from all sides. Under the Old Kingdom, when their civilisation was, as it were, in the first flush of youth, the Egyptians felt secure against any attack by their neighbours. They expressed these feelings in a hymn which is recorded in the Pyramid Texts:

'He (Atum, the demiurge) hath not allowed thee to obey the Westerners
He hath not allowed thee to obey the Easterners
He   ,,   ,,   ,,   ,,   ,,   ,, Southerners
He   ,,   ,,   ,,   ,,   ,,   ,, Northerners
He   ,,   ,,   ,,   ,,   ,,   ,, the Men who are at the Earth's centre
But thou obeyest Horus.
It is he who hath formed thee, built thee, and founded thee.'[3]

In the Temple of Sahura (Fifth Dynasty) the gods themselves are shown leading the conquered peoples, bound and impotent, to the king. Sometimes the vanquished tribes are referred to by a general term, sometimes by their particular names, such as the Iuntiu of Ta-Setet, or the Mentiu, both groups belonging to the Nine Bows as already stated.[4] The sculptures on the walls of Sahura's temple represent the earliest known bas-reliefs. Other kings, however, had preceded Sahura, and he was to have a long line of successors. Following the example of their lord, viziers, like Rekhmire in the time of Tuthmosis III, and Hui in the time of Akhenaten, gave prominence on their tombs to scenes in which they were shown leading foreign delegations to the palace to make their submission and bring gifts as tribute. The old priest of Thebes, who showed Germanicus the monuments of his town, which were unfortunately already in ruins, was still convinced that Egypt's neighbours had only one aim, which was to work for Egypt and offer her the most valuable products of their lands.[5] Since the Egyptians believed in the power of inscriptions and sculptured representations, they depicted more and more scenes like those in Sahura's temple, as if they were trying to force reality to conform to their desires; reality, however, often falls far short of the dream. Towards the end of the poem, the opening lines of which have just been quoted, a note of anxiety creeps in, however reassuring the general tone of the hymn may be:

'The gates (of Egypt) stand fast for thee, like (the god) Inmutef
They will not open for the Westerners
    „   „   „   „   Easterners
    „   „   „   „   Northerners
    „   „   „   „   Southerners
    „   „   „   „   people at the Earth's centre.
But they open for Horus.
He it was who made them, and set them up
It is he who defends them against the evil which Seth has done.'

Unfortunately for the Egyptians, the gates gave way on more than one occasion before the might of barbarian conquerors.

Military resources of the Egyptians

In the following pages I shall try to describe exactly what prompted the Egyptians to embark on expeditions beyond their frontiers, and how the various peoples reacted. First of all, however, some account must be given of the military resources which enabled the Master of the Two Lands and the Sovereign of the Nine Bows to support his claims.

It is probably true that the king did not need a very large army until the end of the Middle Kingdom. Ameni, Governor of the Oryx Nome, supplied four hundred soldiers on one occasion, six hundred on another. If every nome supplied the same number of men, the army may have reached, or even exceeded, a total of twenty thousand men. During the New Kingdom, Egypt was engaged in struggles with other great powers. The army which Ramses II led into Syria consisted of four divisions each of twenty thousand men, not counting the king's own bodyguard. At all periods, foreign soldiers were used. The army which set off to fight the Nomads at the time of Pepi I had been recruited partly from the Upper Egyptian nomes, partly from Lower Egypt, but also from among the southern peoples, and the Timihu, a Libyan tribe. Akhenaton's personal bodyguard included Nubians, Libyans and Syrians (fig. 34): that of Ramses II was chiefly composed of Sherden (Sardinians). Ramses III, when he conquered the Libyans, took a great many prisoners. After Ramses III, the bulk of the army consisted of Meshwesh, who were, in fact, Libyans.

At the time of Herodotus, the warriors (one of the seven classes of the Egyptian population), were divided into *calasiries* and *hermo-tybies*.[6] Although the Greek historian was most certainly using names he had heard in Egypt, we are not able to explain them. Certain nomes were supposed to supply the *hermotybies*, up to a figure of a hundred and sixty thousand, others, a still greater number of *calasiries*. These figures were probably never reached. Herodotus, however, was right in maintaining that the warriors were not allowed to do any manual work, and that they enjoyed great privileges.

Egyptian weapons were not very complicated: the light infantry had bows and arrows, the heavy infantry clubs, pikes and shields. During the New Kingdom, the Egyptians adopted the weapons

Fig. 34. Mercenaries in the service of Akhenaton, from the El Amarna tomb. The Egyptian army was partly recruited from among neighbouring peoples. During the New Kingdom, prisoners of war were pressed into service.

used by their opponents – the triangular bow, helmets and coats of mail, and also imitated them in creating squadrons of chariots.

Inside Egypt and in Nubia, troops were transported by boat. The company which went on a punitive expedition against the Nomads at the time of Pepi I assembled at a spot called the Gate of Imhetep and moved off into the desert, but a little later another company travelled by sea to a place known as The Goat's Nose, at the extreme tip of a mountain chain – presumably Mount Carmel.

The great expeditionary forces sent out during the New Kingdom crossed the bridge over the crocodile-infested lake forming the eastern frontier in the Isthmus of Suez, and after a series of marches across the desert and through Palestine, reached the historic sites of Meggido and Qadesh, where their opponents were entrenched (fig. 3).

It would perhaps be too much to say that the Egyptians evolved any art of war. When the defeated Syrians, Hittites and Libyans took refuge inside their fortified positions, the Egyptians starved them into submission, and when the time was ripe, made an assault on the stronghold by means of ladders, and broke down the gates. In open country, battles would end in hand-to-hand fighting. The victors cut off the head, the penis, or the hands of the vanquished and displayed them to the king's herald. As a general rule, the Egyptians proposed a fixed day for the battle, and postponed it if their opponents were not ready. Surprise attacks were forbidden. Pianhki, who was stricter than the Egyptians themselves in this matter, as he was in the observance of religious commandments, reminded his soldiers of this convention. The Amu did not adopt such noble practices, and the Hittites made a deliberate attempt to trick Ramses II before the battle of Qadesh. They made a surprise attack on the king's camp when the four divisions of his army were still a long way off.

The eastern nations

When the Egyptians ventured across the eastern desert into the Isthmus of Suez, they encountered a tribe called the Setiu (Asiatics, from Setjet, Asia), as well as the Amu, and the Mentiu. During the New Kingdom mention is made of the Shasu. Physically, the Mentiu and the Amu were very much alike; they had the same profile, the same pointed beard, the same long hair, and they wore the same garb. The Mentiu lived in the desert of Sinai, but they had spread into Palestine as far as Shechem at least, and had become so closely intermingled with the Amu that it was impossible to come into conflict with one without becoming involved with the other. Syria was the land of the Amu. The Egyptians made a distinction between the Amu, the 'sand-dwellers', and the Nomads and the city dwellers. During the Middle Kingdom, there were many Syrian cities; one of them, Gubla, became Keben in Egyptian and Kapni in Greek. Byblos occupied a special position in relationship to Egypt. From the time of Khasekhemui, the last king of the Second Dynasty, until the Ptolemaic era, Egypt had trade relations with Byblos; these were only broken off during those periods when Egypt was forced to withdraw within her own frontiers. To borrow an Egyptian expression, it might be said that relations with Byblos went back to 'the time of the god'. A legend was current in Busiris to the effect that the coffin holding the body of Osiris was finally washed ashore at Byblos; here a tree grew round it, and it became incorporated in the trunk.

When Isis went to Byblos, she met the servants of the queen of the land and allowed them to perceive the exquisite perfume emanating from her body. Then she dressed their hair and later obtained permission to bring the sacred tree containing the body of her husband back to Egypt.[7]

Archaeological evidence found at Byblos itself, and the Pyramid Texts, help to explain this charming legend.[8] What the Egyptians went to fetch from Byblos were the coniferous woods with which their own country was poorly supplied: the fir (*ash*) and its by-products, the cedar (*mer*), and also, to a lesser extent, the cypress or juniper tree (*uan*). These trees provided timber for the priests' coffins, the doors of temples and tombs, articles of furniture, and the sacred barges, which were virtually floating temples. The most stately fir trees were shorn of their branches and set up in front of the pylons of the temples. Also, the inhabitants of Byblos sold to the Egyptians boats which were called *Kebenit*, from *Keben*, Byblos. While the Egyptians excelled in the building of flat-bottomed river craft, the people of Byblos had at a very early period perfected a type of sea-going vessel. It was in 'Byblos ships' that the Egyptians made expeditions to the Terraces of Incense, which lay to the south of the Red Sea. The Hyksos king who had his capital at Avaris on the Tanitic arm of the Nile owned a fleet of three hundred boats made of fir wood. When, as a result of some disaster, communications with Byblos were interrupted, the economic life of Egypt was profoundly affected. A sage who lived during the First Intermediate Period expressed his indignation at his country's plight:

'Now that no more ships sail to Byblos, how can we procure for our mummies the fir wood which we need to import in order to bury our priests? Kings as far as the land of the Keftiu (Crete) are embalmed with the resin obtained from the firs.'[9]

The land of forests which the kings of Byblos had turned to good account was called the land of Nega and stretched from the valley of the Adonis to the Homs–Tripoli gap. The sea-pine and the parasol pine were very common in the neighbourhood of Byblos, but firs and cedars had to be brought from the northern slope of the Lebanon.

The travel diary of an official who lived during the joint reign of Smendes and Herihor is by far the most detailed document we possess on the subject of trade with Byblos. Egypt was no longer a great power, but she was nonetheless determined to obtain a load of wood in order to make a new sacred barque for Amen-Re. King Zekerbaal was not very amenable. He nevertheless sent men to cut down the trees and haul them to the water's edge. Finally, towed by Zekerbaal's own boats, they were dispatched to Egypt, after Smendes had sent, in exchange, gold and silver vases, flax, papyrus, ox-hides, rope, lentils and fish. The king was careful to point out that his forebears had supplied Egypt with wood, but that they had received payment for it.[10] This was in fact true, and explains why so many Egyptian *objets d'art* – alabaster vases and jewels, equal in quality to those discovered in Egypt – were found in the temples and royal tombs of Byblos. The Egyptians, for their part, associated

Fig. 35. Unas receives a rudder from Hathor, the Lady of Byblos and Punt, who guided the Pharaoh's ships. Fragment of a vase from Byblos, No. 3867.

the Lady of Byblos with their goddess Hathor (fig. 35), and it seemed quite natural to them to offer her gifts. They had bestowed the rank of Egyptian prince (*hati-a*) on the kings of Byblos which meant that the latter were treated with great respect whenever they visited the Egyptian court, and gained one inestimable advantage; because of the distance between Egypt and Byblos, the royal funerary offering had to take the form of a few but extremely costly objects – golden and obsidian vases and caskets, mirrors, pendants, valuable weapons, rings and bracelets. Shashank I, Osorkon I, and Osorkon II also sent the kings of Byblos of their day statues of themselves (a present which cost them comparatively little), and, in each case, the king had an alphabetical inscription in Phoenician engraved round the cartouches. The relations between the two countries were not of a purely economic nature, but extended also to political and military matters. The Pharaohs of the New Kingdom who sent their armies and messengers into Syria counted on the support of the kings of Byblos. Shashank I, for instance, was helped by the king of Byblos in his Palestinian campaign. Regular contact with the Egyptians brought more than one advantage to the people of Byblos. They learned the language and script of the Egyptians and were inspired by their example to create a form of writing of their own, which was still rather complicated in its initial stage but eventually emerged as the alphabet, the simple and perfect system of writing which spread from the shores of Phoenicia to all other nations. Their art and all their products showed the effects of the Egyptian influence. Having accepted the association between Hathor and the Lady of Byblos, they felt obliged to portray the latter, on their own monuments, with the form and the attributes of the Egyptian goddess.[11]

Meggido was one of several fortresses which barred the road to the fertile plain of Esdraelon. 'To take Meggido,' declared Tuthmosis III, 'is to take a thousand towns.' Under the Twelfth Dynasty, Thothhetep, an Egyptian official, took up residence there. He had been sent to buy oxen and bring them back to Egypt. His mission was so successful that he arranged to have the episode depicted on his tomb in the Hare Nome; the oxen which had made the long trek across the sandy wastes are shown eating their fill of grass.[12]

During the New Kingdom, Beth-Shan, a town in the Jordan valley not far from Meggido, attracted Egyptian officials who were at pains to show respect to Mikal, the Baal of the town. This was considered to be the best way of winning the confidence of the natives.[13] It is impossible to determine whether in this case the Egyptians were prompted by political or economic motives.

Objects dating from the Middle Kingdom have been discovered in Qatna in central Syria,[14] and objects dating from the Middle and New Kingdoms in the very important city of Ugarit.[15] An Egyptian of the Twelfth Dynasty, Sesostris-ankh, placed a statue of himself with his wife and daughter in the temple there. At a much later period another Egyptian paid homage to Baal-Sephon, a divinity who was worshipped at Memphis and in the Isthmus of Suez. A king of Ugarit, Nimgad, married an Egyptian princess and had the nuptial ceremony engraved on an alabaster vase. Yet Ugarit formed part of the great coalition which the Hittite king assembled against Ramses II. Possibly the town had no other choice, since its geographical position laid it open to reprisals; it managed, however, by the exercise of prudence, to remain on friendly terms with Egypt. In the modern world, this is called playing a double game.

From the beginning of the Eighteenth Dynasty until the time of Ramses III, the Egyptians constantly intervened in Syria, and claimed tribute from the vanquished; this took the form of timber, horses, oxen, cereals and metals. The military leaders were also quite willing to accept manufactured goods, such as chariots, valuable weapons and the curious vases or bowls incrustated with precious stones, and used for holding bunches of papyrus or other ornamental plants which were subsequently offered to Amun of Thebes.[16] The Egyptians were very fond of these objects and eventually copied them. During this period the craze for Syrian products introduced a host of Semitic terms into the Egyptian language.

The Terraces of Turquoise were in Sinai.[17] The Egyptians went there by boat. The hero of the Story of the Shipwrecked Sailor, composed under the Twelfth Dynasty, was on his way to Pharaoh's mines in a boat one hundred and twenty cubits long and forty cubits wide when a sudden storm arose. If the crew were heading for the Wadi Maghara or the Serabit-el-Khadim where turquoise was found, it was better that they should land at Ras Abu Zenima. If, however, they had been sent to find copper, he had to enter the Gulf of Akaba. The numerous inscriptions engraved by the Egyptians on the rocks of the Wadi Maghara date from the First Dynasty right up till the Late Period. On the Serabit-el-Khadim, they built a temple dedicated to Astarte, the goddess of the area, after first associating her with Hathor, the Lady of the Land of Mefak, where turquoise (*mefaket*) was found. Other Egyptian gods besides Hathor were patrons of the miners – the gods of Memphis and Heliopolis, Soped, the patron of the Soped Nome, frequently the starting point of mining expeditions, and King Snofru, who, because he was a benevolent king, was proclaimed a god.

The officials in charge of the mining expeditions included princes, the king's seal-bearers, naval captains (naturally enough, since the route lay across the sea), judges, scribes, and interpreters. The workers were either Egyptian or natives, but mainly Mentiu. One contingent was supplied by a sheik from Retenu. The inscriptions contain hardly any references to copper, rather more to malachite, and a great many to turquoise.[18] We owe the most valuable inscription to a certain Horurre, a servant of the king and Chief Treasurer, who was in charge of an expedition. When he reached the mining area, the favourable season for operations was over, the mountains seemed to be red hot and the experienced workers who knew the mine declared: 'There is enough turquoise in the mountain to last for all eternity, but in this season the stones become discoloured.'

However, Horrure energetically set to work and fired his men with such enthusiasm that two months later he had found a far greater quantity of turquoise stones than he had been asked to obtain; what is more, their colour was flawless and they were even more beautiful than those found during the normal season. 'Let us therefore put our trust in Hathor.' In that particular year, after a period of heat during the month of March, the weather must have become cooler, and remained clement throughout the whole of April and part of May. The Tanis expedition was fortunate in experiencing a similar spell of clement weather on more than one occasion.

The Terraces of Turquoise constituted not only a mining area but also a commercial centre and a meeting place for people who came from far and wide to obtain the precious stones. This we learn from a certain Kheti, an engineer and Chief Treasurer, who went to inspect the mines during the Twelfth Dynasty.[19] He worked in several drifts, the names of which he records, and obtained both copper and turquoise. Taking advantage of his prestige as a representative of the king, he was also able to procure several unidentified minerals as well as lapis-lazuli, a frequently mentioned semi-precious stone, which was used by Egyptian jewellers, almost without interruption, from the First Dynasty to the Late Period. There is some doubt as to where lapis-lazuli was found. I would agree with Lucas, the chemist, whose opinion is based on solid evidence and who says that all the lapis-lazuli used by the peoples of antiquity came from one region – Bakhtan (Bactria). It is to be noted that lapis-lazuli was called Khes-bed or Tefrer, and that these words, as was invariably the rule in Egyptian, referred also to the countries from which the semi-precious stone came. In Khes-bed we can recognize the phonetic elements of Badakhchan (Bakhtan) but in a different order, and Tefrer can be identified with the town of Sippar in Mesopotamia. The caravan-masters, whose business it was to dispose of the lapis-lazuli, did not themselves make the long journey from the valley of the Indus to the Mediterranean coast. They went as far as the frontier of their country, and handed their load over to other caravans who then had a long journey to make before they reached Sippar, which was considered as the distribution centre. Kheti makes no mention of having himself gone to Sippar. Although the possibility that he may have done so cannot be ruled out, it seems more likely that he met merchants from Sippar at Sinai and obtained the lapis-lazuli from them. A discovery made in the tomb of Psammeticus during the course of our excavations at Tanis supports this view.[20] This is a ball of very deep blue lapis-lazuli, engraved with an inscription in cuneiform, from which it is clear that the bead, and all the others of the same substance which composed the two necklaces found on the mummy of the king, had belonged to a princess called Napalta, who came from Enlil, a town situated in the neighbourhood of Ashur. Lapis-lazuli, then, reached Egypt by way of Mesopotamia.

Expeditions of this sort involved certain hazards. Tuthmosis I derived great satisfaction from the fact that, during his reign, Egyptian messengers could travel the length and breadth of Syria without being molested. All travellers were not so fortunate. The expedition in which Uni took part was organized under Pepi I in order to put a stop to acts of aggression on the part of the Amu, the 'sand-dwellers'. Similar expeditions were undertaken on five subsequent occasions, but did not solve the problem, since, under Pepi II, a party of Egyptians who were busy caulking a 'Byblos ship', which had just been handed over to them, 'on the mountain of the Amu' (i.e. the Lebanon), were massacred by the Amu. On this occasion, the Egyptians did no more than ensure that the bodies of their dead were carried back to Egypt.

Not all the nomadic tribes were hostile to Egypt. When famine raged in Canaan, the Amu, the Mentiu and later the Shasu came to the frontier posts of the Roads of Horus Nome or of Pithom and asked to be allowed into Egypt. The Egyptians bade them welcome, since this had been the custom ever since 'the time of the god'. Often the nomads were traders, like the tribe who offered green and black powder to the governor of the Oryx Nome. On occasions they would buy and sell slaves. Joseph first came to the Black Land as a slave. Some other Asiatic tribes did nothing but pillage and, in order to check them, Amenemhat I built the Regent's Wall at the beginning of the Twelfth Dynasty. Petty raids such as these were insignificant compared with the invasion of the Hyksos, which began at the time of a king called Didumes, during the Fourteenth Dynasty. The invaders – the Amu and Mentiu whom the soldiers of Pepi I and the various Sesostris had had no difficulty in routing – reached the Delta, took Memphis and were only halted to the north of Thebes. A line of demarcation was finally established between Cusae and Siut.

The Hyksos settled down in the occupied zone and remained there for a long period. They chose Avaris as their capital not only because of its position on the eastern bank of the Bubastite arm of the Nile (at San el Haggar), but because the Lord of Avaris, Seth, was of all the Egyptian gods the one who bore the closest resemblance to their own Baal. They tried to impose their religion on the whole of Upper Egypt. They gave Seth a Canaanite goddess, Anat (Anta in Egyptian texts), as consort. They found an ally in the king of Kush who ruled over the territory to the south of Aswan, which meant that the future liberators of Egypt would have to fight on two fronts. They burdened the Egyptian people with taxes; yet they allowed southern landowners who had estates in the north to go on collecting their dues. They had supporters in all the towns where Seth was worshipped, such as Saka in Middle Egypt. They staffed the workshops with their own people and made determined efforts to buy estates from the Egyptians they were reducing to ruin. They gave the land of Goshen to the sons of Jacob, one of whom became vizier. Yet what the Egyptians resented most of all were the acts of vandalism committed by the Hyksos, who destroyed and pillaged shrines and killed sacred animals. Similar acts of impiety were committed by the Unclean at the end of the Twentieth Dynasty and, at a much later period, by Cambyses.[21]

The princes of Thebes refused to worship Seth and, inspired by the god Amun, undertook to liberate Egypt. Seqeninra died in battle. Kames, his successor, won an initial victory at Neferusi, cut the lines of communication between the king of Avaris and the king of Kush, seized Saka and advanced northwards. Memphis was freed, Avaris besieged and captured and Judea conquered. Fired with war-like fervour, the Egyptians routed their enemies and reached the Euphrates.

During their expeditions across Syria, the Egyptians were soon to encounter adversaries who had been totally unknown to the Pharaohs of the Middle Kingdom. These were first the Mitanni, then the Khatti. The Tell-el-Amarna letters, and the Hittite Annals, provide evidence of intense political activity. Fighting was still resorted to, but negotiation was preferred. Towards the end of the Eighteenth Dynasty, the Pharaohs married foreign princesses; one of the Tell-el-Amarna letters mentions the extraordinary friendship which had sprung up between Amenophis III and the king of Babylon. Later, the widow of Ay asked the Hittite king, Shubbilu-liuma, to send her one of his sons as a husband. A prince was chosen and set out for Egypt but he was murdered on the way, and the queen had to resign herself to marrying Horemhab, whom she referred to, in her royal parlance, as 'her slave'. The conflict which occurred as a result of the above incident was intensified under Seti I and culminated in a full-scale war under Ramses II. The Hittite king had allies throughout the whole of Asia Minor and northern Syria. Ramses led against him four regiments, which had been placed under the patronage of Amun, Pra, Ptah and Seth, and his bodyguard composed chiefly of Sherden. The battle took place in the valley of the Orontes near Qadesh, and was more spectacular than bloody, as if the two kings were anxious to keep their fine armies intact. They lost no time in concluding an armistice.[22] Sporadic fighting continued even after the kings had signed the treaty, both the Hittite and Egyptian versions of which are fortunately in our possession. Hostilities only ceased after Ramses married the daughter of Hattushilish.[23]

Under the Twenty-first Dynasty, the Tanite kings had to adjust themselves to the presence, beyond their borders, of a new kingdom, the kingdom of Judah. There was never any period of stability in the history of their relations with this country. Hadad, an enemy of David, was offered asylum by a Pharaoh, possibly Siamen. Siamen, or his successor, gave his daughter in marriage to Solomon along with a splendid dowry, the town of Gezer. Later Shashank I gave asylum to Jeroboam, Solomon's enemy, and led a major expedition against Jerusalem. Although the list of conquered towns fills a large area of one of the walls at Karnak, the campaign remains less impressive than the spendid expeditions carried out during the Eighteenth Dynasty. Osorkon I allowed the soldiers of Zerah, the Ethiopian, to pass through Egypt, on their way to Palestine where they were defeated. Threatened first of all by the Assyrians, then by the Chaldeans, many Jews disregarded the advice of their prophets, who felt nothing but anger and contempt for the princes of Tanis, and sought refuge in Egypt just as their ancestors had done. After the disasters of the end of the Eighth and the beginning of the Seventh century, Egypt embarked on a new and glorious era. Neko marched through Syria and reached the Euphrates. The defeat at Carchemish deprived him of all his conquests but he soon retrieved his position and one of his successors, Hophra, the Apries of the Greeks, besieged Tyre and Sidon. The last king of the Saïte Dynasty was unable to prevent the Persians, under Cambyses, from turning Egypt into a satrapy. It was as if the Hyksos, under another name, had returned to spread devastation throughout the two lands.

The southern countries

To the south, the Aswan cataract formed the natural, and often the political, frontier of Egypt. It is interesting to note that the same name *Ta-setet* – the land of the mineral seti – was given to the first nome of Upper Egypt, and to a fairly long stretch of the Nile valley above the cataract. Here lived the Nehesiu, swarthy-skinned Nubians who supplied soldiers for the army and labour for working mines and quarries. The diorite and amethyst, highly-prized by sculptors and lapidaries, was found in the region of Ibhet, in the same latitude as Toshka, a little to the north of Abu Simbel. The Egyptians were therefore most anxious to see that peace was maintained in this area. During the Sixth Dynasty, Hirkhuf forced the chieftain of the land of Yam to give up fighting against the Timihu, who lived in the oases and in other regions from which the Egyptians obtained valued products. Hirkhuf brought back from Yam asses loaded with *sonter*, terebinth, a product essential for religious ceremonies, as well as ebony, ivory, herds of oxen and smaller livestock.

He brought back something even more valuable, at least in the opinion of his young sovereign – a *deng* dwarf who danced a sacred dance, literally 'who danced the god', and who probably came from the basin of the Upper Nile. Previously, a traveller called Baurded had brought back a dancing dwarf from the land of Punt which lay along the two shores of the straits of Babel Mandeb.[24]

It was the avowed aim of many kings to extend Egypt's frontiers. Sesostris I probably annexed the whole of *Ta-Setet*. One of his successors built a fort and a temple at Semneh above the Second Cataract, and erected two boundary stelae which are now in the Berlin Museum. One of the stelae bears an inscription forbidding the Nubians to go beyond the boundary mark except for trading purposes. A passage from the other stela, in which the king bluntly expresses his warlike doctrine, has already been quoted. It also reveals his lofty scorn for the Nehesiu: 'When you attack him (the Nubian) he turns his back; but if you retreat then he starts attacking you. They are not brave men, they are feeble and broken of spirit. My Majesty has seen it: it is no lie. I have seized their women. I have brought back their servants when they lingered too long at the wells. I herded all their beasts together, pulled up their corn and set fire to it.'[25]

After the decline of the Middle Kingdom, the Nubians who had been so harshly treated broke away and set up their own Kingdom which quite naturally became the ally of the Hyksos, when the latter took up residence at Avaris. Kames was able to cut their lines of communication, and after the expulsion and destruction of the Hyksos, his successors brought the southerners once more under Egyptian control. In order to forestall any rebellion and to ensure possession of the valuable products of their land, the Pharaohs created 'the royal sons of Kush' governors whose authority extended from the town of Nekhen, in Upper Egypt, to the farthest point reached by their armies, which was beyond Gebel Barkal, in an area situated between the Fourth and Fifth Cataract where traces of

Tuthmosis' expeditions into Nubia can still be found. It seems that the Egyptians never reached the confluence of the two Niles, since no document mentions the fact. Under the leadership of the 'royal sons of Kush' and their officials, huge and impressive edifices were either hewn out of the rock or built at the foot of the cliffs – Bet-el-Wali, Garf Husein, where the colossal statues have such a frightening expression that even today the natives of the area believe them capable of destroying anyone who offends them; Wadi Sebua, Amada, which makes up for its small dimensions by the elegance of its design and ornamentation; Deir; the two shrines of Ipsambul (Abu Simbel), the larger of which represents perhaps the most ambitious achievement ever accomplished by Egyptian architects, and the Temple of Soleb, which is in no way inferior to the other monuments erected by that enthusiastic builder, Amenophis III.

The Nubians appeared to have resigned themselves to being a colony of Egypt. A few small-scale revolts were soon quelled. The Viceroy Hui received a delegation (of Nubians) and their picturesque appearance made a strong impression on the artists in his retinue.[26] Such receptions were part of the governor's duties; but of all the royal sons of Kush, Hui is the one who has supplied the fullest documentary accounts.

At the head of the procession, magnificent black kings wearing panther-skins and fine loin-cloths, with ostrich-feathers stuck in their hair, and adorned with ear-rings, necklaces and bracelets, bow down before the Egyptian. After them come a group of princes, dressed in Egyptian style, some of them completely black, others with swarthy skins and more or less indistinguishable from the young people who lived north of Aswan; then a queen on a chariot drawn by two oxen, protected from the sun by a parasol (fig. 36). The porters have spread out on the ground, or are offering, golden rings, cornelian, ostrich-feathers and skins. Others are leading giraffes and oxen. At the end of the procession come prisoners, with ropes round their necks, and women carrying children. As well as unworked materials, the natives are offering manufactured goods, bows, shields, pieces of furniture and purely decorative articles – for instance, stands bearing models of miniature negro villages (conical huts are set in the middle of palm plantations peopled by wandering giraffes and natives making obeisance) (fig. 37). It would seem, then, that the Egyptian governors encouraged native arts and crafts; the Nubians had their own artistic traditions and at the same time borrowed from the Egyptians.

But the attitude of resignation already referred to was only on the surface. The kings of Kush had once before taken advantage of

Egypt's decline under the Thirteenth and Fourteenth Dynasties to break away from their Egyptian masters. Kames, a prince of Thebes who controlled only a very restricted area, felt hemmed in between the king of Avaris and the king of Kush, who had established lines of communication through the western oases. After the fall of the Ramessides, the institution of the royal sons of Kush managed to survive more or less under the Bubastite kings, but from the Eighth century onwards there existed a Kingdom of Napata which, under

Fig. 36. The Queen of Kush on the Tomb of Hui, *Th. T.S.*, Vol. 4, Pl. XXVIII. Of all the processions accompanying foreign dignitaries, that of the Queen of Kush is undoubtedly the most picturesque.

Piankhi, became powerful enough to subdue the whole of Upper Egypt, and the southern half of Lower Egypt. Tirhakah achieved even greater success. The kings of Napata behaved exactly like Pharaohs. They had a court ceremonial and their official stelae were drawn up and engraved in due and proper form. They had almost more respect for the gods and traditions of the country than the Egyptians of their day. Their dynasty was short-lived; Tirhakah's successor was forced back into Ethiopia, and an attempt to reconquer Egypt under Psammeticus II was very quickly suppressed.

From then onwards the Ethiopian kings devoted all their energies to developing their native country. Their capital was transferred to Meroe in the south, and relations with Egypt proper were to all intents and purposes broken off. Yet the Kingdom of Meroe can be given credit for having carried Egyptian civilisation further south than the Pharaohs themselves had ever succeeded in doing.

The Terraces of Incense

The Terraces of Incense (*Khetiu anti*) were also called *Ta-neter*, the land of the God, or even the two lands of the God. These were periphrastic expressions; the real name of the land of incense, as given in the Annals of the Old Kingdom, in the section on Sahura, was Punt.[27] This, at least, is how it has been transliterated. As the pronunciation of the word is very uncertain, a connection has been suggested between Punt and the colony known as Οπωνη, which is thought to have been situated in the Bay of Hafun, to the south of Cape Guardafui. This may be a valid suggestion.[28] The name Punt perhaps referred to a much vaster area than that frequented by the Egyptians. It is rather unlikely that the Egyptians ever sailed round Cape Guardafui and down the African coast as far as the Bay of Hafnun. Whether they did or not, the land of Punt was certainly in African territory because, according to a stela of the Saïte period, if it rained on the mountain of Punt, the region of the Nile was affected; the area also extended into Asia because Punt of Asia was a geographical expression, the only (and as yet unpublished) example of which is to be found at Soleb. In the light of these two indications, we can identify the two shores of the land of the God with the two banks of the straits of Bab el Mandeb. Further proof is supplied by the fact that the incense-bearing tree grew equally well in Arabia felix and in Africa.

The Egyptians seem to have adopted the same policy with regard to Punt as they did with regard to Byblos. They themselves did not handle the various products; they left this to local labour and paid regular visits to a central point where the negotiations could conveniently be carried on. Just as they had erected a shrine at Byblos to Hathor, the Lady of Byblos, and another at Sinai to Hathor, the Lady of the Turquoise, so they must inevitably have set up a shrine in hard stone to Hathor, the Lady of Punt, and placed stelae and statues in it, according to their usual practice. A well-equipped expedition which made a thorough investigation along the shores of the straits of Bab el Mandeb might perhaps be fortunate enough to discover the remains of such a shrine. If so, this would solve a

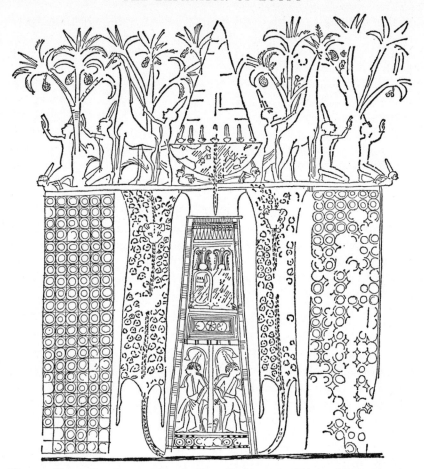

Fig. 37. Examples of arts and crafts from Kush on the Tomb of Hui, *Th. TS.*, Vol. IV, Pl. XXVI. These were greatly valued in Egypt throughout the whole of the New Kingdom.

problem of historical geography that has long puzzled Egyptologists. In the case of Punt, as in that of Byblos and Sinai, documentary evidence found on the site itself would supplement that afforded by texts and bas-reliefs.

The earliest known expedition goes back to the Fifth Dynasty. However, it is not beyond the bounds of possibility that the first navigator to reach the Terraces of Incense was a contemporary of those who left a vase inscribed with the name of Khasekhemui in the temple at Byblos. Byblos and Punt are found together on two Old Kingdom inscriptions. In the first, a man from Aswan says: 'Having set off with my masters, the princes and chief treasurers,

Teti and Khui, to Byblos and Punt, I travelled through these lands eleven times.'[29] Another man from Aswan, Pepinakt, was sent to the mountain of the Amu (the Lebanon) in order to bring back the bodies of two Egyptians whom the Amu – the sand-dwellers – had massacred, along with the escort of soldiers accompanying them, while they were caulking their 'Byblos ship', prior to an expedition to Punt.[30]

It should be noted that Khumhetep and his commanders went just as often to Byblos as they did to Punt. They appear to have taken the following route: first they went to Byblos, then came back into Egypt and, after sailing up the Tanitic arm of the Nile as far as Bubastis, proceeded by canal to the Wadi Tumilat, crossed the Bitter Lakes and reached the Gulf of Suez. Such was the intended route of the unfortunate Egyptians, who were attacked by Nomads before they had even left the Syrian shore. In conjunction with their friends, the people of Byblos, the Egyptians had, in fact, established a shipping-route between Byblos and Punt, via Egypt; the boats which plied along this route were 'Byblos ships', and were probably manned by mixed Syrian and Egyptian crews. These voyages were no doubt temporarily suspended after the reign of Pepi II, but were resumed as soon as possible. Fir-wood and incense were both equally necessary. Under one of the Mentuheteps, Henu, the treasurer, was told to fit out a 'Byblos ship' and sail to Punt in order to procure fresh incense. He left Coptos with a large force – three thousand men, he says, but he was perhaps exaggerating a little – and, after marching from one water-hole to the next, he reached the Red Sea at a point on the coast which was later to become the port of Berenice. There he found the ship, the *kebenit* already referred to, and fitted it out with all the necessary equipment. After a voyage about which he gives no details, he returned with the various products he had obtained on the shores of the land of the God. During this, or some other, expedition, he paid a visit to the valley of Rohanu and brought back a cargo of stone. This achievement is commemorated in a fine stela which, as is so often the case, leaves a good deal unexplained.[31]

The Pharaohs of the Eighteenth Dynasty had far more elaborate means at their disposal. The expedition undertaken during Queen Hatsheput's reign was probably on a much larger scale than previous ventures. It is certainly the best known, because the artist who decorated the temple of Deir el Bahari depicted its various episodes.[32] The queen had been told by her father, Amun, to include Punt in her domains, and to send for trees from the land of the God in order to plant them along both sides of his Temple. A council was convened. Its members had no doubt already studied the question and planned and prepared the great expedition which was placed under the command of a Unique Friend, Nehesi, the Chief Treasurer. A fleet of five ships, called *kebenit* as in former times, was fitted out. They were long boats, typical Byblos craft, with sharply pointed bows, and sterns decorated with the papyrus design. They were sailing boats, but were also fitted with oars. The men went on board and the ships were loaded with provisions and gifts. After an uneventful voyage, the Egyptians sighted the conical huts which stood on piles among palm, ebony and incense-bearing trees, which were the object of their expedition. They went ashore – having taken the precaution of being armed – and were welcomed by the queen of Punt, a mountain of quivering flesh (fig. 38), and her daughter, who showed every sign of having inherited her mother's tendency to obesity. These ladies were accompanied by a party of natives who, in their general appearance and attire, bore a close resemblance

Fig. 38. The Queen of Punt, from a bas-relief in the Temple of Hatshep-ut, Naville, *Deir-el-Bahari*, III. Egyptian artists were obviously intrigued by this ill-favoured creature.

to the Egyptians themselves. Their chief feature was a long, pointed and plaited beard. The artificial beard worn by the Pharaohs and the Egyptian gods is an imitation of the natural one worn by the men of Punt. It may be wondered whether, at some point, the latter did not leave the country of the god and settle in Egypt, introducing some of their own customs, and perhaps their gods.

Greetings were exchanged, then presents, which consisted of the various products of each country. The Egyptians loaded their ships with incense-bearing trees, complete with roots and soil, just as a careful nurseryman would pack them today, dry incense, ebony, several varieties of perfume, and panther-skins. They also took on board natives and their children, animals, baboons, monkeys and greyhounds. Although such a motley cargo cannot have been easy to transport, it eventually arrived in Thebes. The trees were replanted, the incense was measured out in bushels and everything else carefully recorded. Delegations of men from Punt are referred to on other documents of the Eighteenth Dynasty; it is, however, impossible to say whether they made their own way into Egypt or were carried there in Egyptian boats. On a bas-relief of Horemheb's time, the artist is careful to portray the visitors from Punt with their characteristic plaited beards.

The great Harris Papyrus provides a very interesting account of an expedition to Punt under Ramses III. The fleet, composed of heavy transport ships, *menesh*, and escort vessels, sailed from the 'sea of Mu Qedi', the Euphrates, in other words the Persian Gulf. Some commentators have thought it impossible that the Egyptians could have followed this route. According to them, the Egyptians must have supposed that the Euphrates flowed into the Red Sea. By this gratuitous attribution of a gross error to the Egyptian chronicler, they have obscured the importance of a magnificent expedition organized by one of the last great Pharaohs.[33] Before the time of Ramses III, Tuthmosis III had employed oxen to haul fir-trees from the land of Nega to Carchemish, and with these trees had built boats to cross the Euphrates. Ramses III repeated this exploit. The ships were constructed and launched in Chaldea, sailed down the Euphrates to the Persian Gulf, went round the enormous Arabian peninsula and eventually reached the land of Punt. In order for them to do this, Ramses had to have the good will of the people living along the shores of the Euphrates, but it was well within the Pharaoh's power to ensure this. When the boats were fully loaded with incense, they headed back to Egypt preceded by the children of the chieftains of Punt. The latter landed without incident opposite the mountain of Coptos, the present-day Qosseir, crossed the desert and boarded river craft at the quay of Coptos and sailed downstream to the Pharaoh's northern capital, Per-Ramses. The large cargo vessels probably waited in the shelter of one of the Red Sea ports until the time came for the next expedition. Their crews had made the longest voyage mentioned in Egyptian history before the circum-navigation of Africa, which, according to Herodotus, was undertaken at the instigation of King Neko of the Twenty-sixth Dynasty.[34]

The western nations

To the west of the Nile, between the latitude of Aswan and that of Athribis, stretched a long line of oases whose inhabitants were called *Sekhetui ges*, the oasis dwellers on the fringe. Their territories were referred to by the word *sekhet*, meadow, or by the word *uhat*, which gave the Greek οασις and the English oasis. During the Sixth Dynasty, a Nubian chieftain tried to gain possession of Kenem, the great oasis inhabited by the Timihu. Hirkhuf from Elephantine re-established peace. At that period all the oases were controlled by the Egyptians who recruited soldiers there. A great many tracks linked them with the chief cities of Ta-shema. The god Seth was very popular in the oasis of Dakhleh, also called Zeszes, and perhaps in all the oases which supported the King of Avaris at the time of the Second Intermediate Period. Kames, prince of Thebes, took military action against Zeszes to avoid being attacked on the flank during his attempt to reconquer the valley of the Nile. The gods Min, lord of the sands, and Ha, who threw the harpoon, had extended their sphere of influence to the northern oases. At Hibis, capital of Kenem, the temple, the building of which was begun by Amasis, was dedicated to Amun who was also the lord of the oasis of Siwah where Alexander the Great consulted the oracle. The old name of Farafrah, *Ta-ihet*, the land of the Cow, can be explained either by the fact that the oasis provided pasture for herds of cows, or by the worship of a cow-goddess who was honoured throughout the whole of the western Delta. Vines were cultivated in the southern oases and the wine of Kenem and Zeszes was a favourite drink of the gods. The account of the peasant from the Salt oasis on his way to the market at Nen-nesu with a variety of products is proof of the fact that life cannot have been too difficult there. Yet, during one period, undesirables were banished to the oases.

Immediately beyond the oases lay the land of Tehenu, already mentioned by name on the palette depicting the tribute offered by the Libyan people, before the time of Menes. Trees grew there although they are not represented in sufficient detail to be identified. They are perhaps olive trees – but they could also be either carobs or junipers. The natives obtained from them a substance called 'essence of Tehenu', which was used in Egypt as early as the first dynasties. Throughout the Old Kingdom the Tehenu supplied Egypt with asses, oxen, sheep and goats. A magnificent bas-relief in the temple of Sahura shows herds of livestock and also a great many natives arriving in Egypt.[35] The men are tall and muscular, with thick heads of hair, aquiline noses and pointed beards. They are wearing a small uraeus on their foreheads, necklaces, pendants, bands of material crossing over the chest, and belts with leather pudendal sheaths. The women are in more or less the same attire, with the addition of loin-cloths and bracelets; the children are wearing necklaces, pendants and crossed-over bands of material (fig. 39). One woman, who could be a queen, bears an Egyptian name, *Khut-it-es*, 'her father's favourite', and one at least of her two sons, Usa and Uni, has a name which is common in Egypt. They may, however, have been given Egyptian names when they arrived in the valley of the Nile. The chiefs have the title of prince, *hati-a*

Fig. 39. Tehenu warrior and woman from the Temple of Sahura. The Tehenu dressed quite differently from other neighbouring peoples.

Tehenu, exactly like the Kings of Byblos, who called themselves *Melek Gebel* when they wrote in Phoenician, and *hati-a en keben* if they used the Egyptian language. The Tehenu can therefore be looked upon as permanent allies of the Egyptians. The army of the Prince of Saïs, Tefnakht, included a contingent of Libyans, a fact of which Piankhi, his opponent, was well aware, since he ordered his troops not to engage battle until Tefnakht's allies had taken up their position. Heredotus provides further evidence on the subject. Anxious to be rid of the Greeks, the Cyrenians asked the Pharaoh to come to their aid. Convinced that his soldiers would easily get the better of the Greeks, Apries, the Pharaoh, sent an army off to Cyrene; it was completely destroyed at Irasa, and the defeat cost Apries his throne.

That, however, is another story; for the moment, it is important to remember that the Libyans were bound to Egypt by an offensive and defensive alliance, which like all alliances, operated with varying success. At the beginning of the Twelfth Dynasty, an Egyptian army occupied the land of the Timihu – the region of the oases – and captured several Tehenu who had invaded it. The Egyptian army was still feared in this area during the Late Period. Ash, the Lord of the Tehenu, was given a place in the Egyptian Pantheon, and Horus is sometimes called Horus Tehenu. It has been asserted that Neith, the Lady of Saïs, was of Libyan origin.

During the New Kingdom, the Timihu and the Tehenu were outnumbered by newcomers, the Libu, who gave their name to Libya, and the Meshwesh, whose physical characteristics and attire are depicted on the painted bas-reliefs in the temple of Medinet Habu, and on the glazed composition plaquettes in the palace adjoining the temple. Like the early Tehenu they had aquiline noses and pointed beards. Their hair was cropped short over their foreheads and along the nape of the neck; however, a long, plaited tress was allowed to hang down one cheek and they had two feathers set on the tops of their heads. Over their loin-cloths the Libyans wore a sleeveless coat, open at the front and revealing tattooed arms and legs. The Timihu were quick to adopt the attire of the Libyans, as well as the practice of tattooing the body (fig. 12).

Once they became masters of this area where the Egyptians had been wont to circulate freely, the Libyan hordes constituted a real danger for Egypt. Ramses II realized this, and built fortifications along the coast as far as Marsa Matruh, but his efforts did not prevent the Libyans from bringing Egypt to the verge of disaster under his successors. Merneptah succeeded in halting the Libyan invasion, just in time to prevent a general rising of the Canaanites. The sons of Israel, who until then had been confined within the land of Goshen, took advantage of the situation and made a mass exodus out of Egypt. By the time of Ramses III, the Libyans had advanced into the region of the Delta situated between the Canopic branch of the Nile and the desert, and were masters of the area. They soon felt strong enough to attack, but their onslaught was defeated. Hordes of prisoners were branded and incorporated into the Egyptian army, and later defended their new masters against the Peoples of the Sea.

Under the Twenty-first Dynasty, the bulk of the Egyptian army consisted of mercenaries, and their chief, who was given the shortened title of 'Great Chief of the Me' (Meshwesh), proved to be a very aggressive character. Some members of the Tehenu tribe still figured among the mercenaries; one of them, a certain Buyuwawa, was to found a princely line.[36] His descendant in the fourth generation, a prince called Sheshank, married an Egyptian princess, became 'Great Chief of the Me', and transmitted his title to his son Nemrod, who in turn passed it on to his son who was called Sheshank, like his grandfather. Whether or not the throne of Horus was unoccupied at the time or the last ruler had proved himself to be inadequate, the fact is that Sheshank seized the throne and founded the Twenty-second Dynasty. The Libyan dynasty produced an initial spurt of triumphant energy, but it was unable to prevent the country from falling victim to partitions and invasions which persisted until the establishment of the Saïte Dynasty.

Herodotus tells the following curious story. Weary of complying with the dictates of the Egyptian religion, the inhabitants of Marea and Apis, two towns in the Western Delta, asked the oracle of Amun to declare them to be Libyan; the oracle refused. The incident proves that an important Libyan element had become established along the western side of the valley. The Egyptians may have invaded Tehenu territory, but the Libyans certainly paid them back in their own coin.

Primitive Greeks and Cretans

The Mediterranean shore was very sparsely populated until the time of Alexander. Edfu, which the Egyptians considered as their most northerly town, was some twenty miles from the coast. A region of swamps lay between Lake Mareotis and Lake Menzala and separated the coast from the fertile soil of the Delta. The marshes were a hunter's and fisherman's paradise. The only people who lived along the coast were the soldiers stationed there by Pharaoh to guard the various arms of the Nile. The water of Avaris, later called by Plutarch the Tanitic arm, was used by the ships which plied between Egypt and Byblos. The Damietta arm seems to have been used only for internal navigation. During the Late Period, the sea at Alexandria was called the sea of the *Hau-nebu* (Hellenes). The boats which crossed the sea of the *Hau-nebu* sailed up the Canopic arm of the Nile to the town of Naucratis, where the ruins of several Greek temples have been found. Psammeticus enlisted in his service Ionian and Carian pirates who had been forced to put into port on the Egyptian coast. After gaining control of the whole of Egypt, with their support, he provided them with a settlement along the banks of the Pelusaic arm, at Daphnae, below Bubastis, where Flinders Petrie discovered fragments of Greek vases. Amasis later created a colony of them at

Memphis and continued to enlist them in the Egyptian army. Such is the account given by Herodotus.[37] At the same time, the Egyptian texts reveal that foreign mercenaries formed a proportion of the army of Psammeticus, and the name given to them is generally read as *Hau-nebu*. They were somewhat unruly, and caused their leader a great deal of trouble. Amasis allowed them to settle in the district of Anu, in the vicinity of Naucratis. However, to the great annoyance of the native population, they did not remain within the prescribed limits, and spread as far as Terenutis, a distance of about forty-five miles.[38]

These Hau-nebu correspond, then, exactly to the Hellenes. Further proof is provided by the bilingual decrees of Canopus, Rosetta and Philae:[39] in the paragraph which is concerned with their promulgation, the writing (*sech*) of the Hau-nebu is the equivalent of the Greek, Ελληνικα γραμματα.

There is nothing in this to surprise Greek scholars. However, there is evidence to prove that the Hau-nebu were found in Egypt at all periods, and not only from the time of Psammeticus I and II onwards. There is even mention of them during the Old Kingdom. In the Pyramid Texts, 'the circle of water which girdles the Hau-nebu' was a way of referring to the Mediterranean.[40] Hau-nebu were brought before King Sahura (Fifth Dynasty) along with other foreign tribes, Iiuntiu from the south, and Mentiu from the north-east. A bas-relief dating from the Fourth Dynasty,[41] photographs of which have recently been published, provides even more precise evidence; on it, the name Hau-nebu figures most unexpectedly in the name of an ox: 'that which surrounds the Hau-nebu belongs to Cheops'. They can be found at a still earlier period in Egyptian history for they formed part of the Nine Bows, the confederation to which we have already referred, and which was in existence before the time of Menes, under old King Scorpion. We may conclude that the Hau-nebu who were referred to explicitly at the time of Cheops, can by implication be assumed to have been present in Egypt from the time of the predecessors of Menes. Although Greek scholars are generally unwilling to admit that Hellenes made their appearance in the eastern world before the Eighteenth Dynasty, two pieces of evidence must be taken into account.

The general opinion among Egyptologists is that the first element of Hau-nebu is a *nisbé* formed on the word *ha*: those who are behind, beyond. Some people consider that the second phonetic element, *nebu*, which means 'basket' in Egyptian, was a way of referring to the islands of the Aegean Sea; others that it referred to some unspecified region.[42] I myself have put forward an entirely different explanation,[43] based on the phonetic value of the sign which is invariably used for the first part of the word. It is a papyrus thicket, and corresponds to a name for the papyrus-plant which occurred not only in Egyptian, but in other Oriental languages too – hely, helu. It can be found in the name of Lake Huleh in Palestine which certainly deserves to be called the Papyrus Lake. Consequently, I suggest replacing the reading hau by helu, which contains the root on the basis of which the Greek words Ελλας Ελλην, and Ελλοί were formed. It follows that the Egyptians did not use a more or less incorrect circumlocution to describe their foreign visitors; according to the usual practice, they simply found a phonetic equivalent for their original name.

The second piece of evidence is the fact that Hellenes are known to have been present at all periods of Egyptian history; there were Greek sailors, traders, mercenaries and pirates at the time of Psammeticus and Nectanebo, just as there had been in earlier times. They were an essentially seafaring people and the sea on which they sailed was originally called 'the circle which girdles the Hau-nebu', then the 'Great Green of the Hau-neby'. Probably the Egyptians did not know where they came from. They only knew that the north wind drove them towards the Egyptian shores; this fact was expressed in a popular song, 'The Song of the Four Winds', which will be quoted later.[44]

The Helu-nebu were traders as well as sailors, and it was in order to trade that they penetrated so far inland. Under the Saïte Kings, they settled at Naucratis and even beyond. At the time of Cheops a distinction was made between the 'Helu of the baskets', which I interpret as sailors, and 'the inland Helu', traders who had sailed up the arms of the Nile and gone ashore in order to make contact with the Egyptians. A herald (uhemu) acted as interpreter. During the Middle Kingdom, a scribe wrote that his 'reed pen caught the Helu-nebu'; in other words, he was acting as an interpreter.

Before Psammeticus I, one Pharaoh employed the Helu-nebu as mercenaries; this was Amasis, the liberator, who urged his subjects to acclaim his wife, the Lady of the Helu-nebu, probably a Greek; the Helu-nebu unanimously declared: 'We serve with him.'[45] The word 'serve' is used here in a military sense. On the basis of the above declaration, which is confirmed by the fact that the Helu-nebu are put on an equal footing with the Pat, the Henemmt and the Rekhetu on the triumphal stela, it can be confidently affirmed that they fought alongside the Egyptians to achieve the liberation of the country.

In spite of their civil dispositions, the Helu-nebu were feared and even hated. Amasis treated them most generously, yet they were quick to take advantage of his kindness. Under the Eighteenth Dynasty, several decades after Ahmosis, Queen Hatsheput, and Tuthmosis III threatened them with punishment. One of the Karnak bas-reliefs[46] depicts a group of Helu-nebu being brought, bound, before Horemheb, along with a party of Syrians. This particular group of Helu-nebu had certainly not been picked up by the Egyptians along the shores of Greece; they were pirates who had come, like Ulysses' companions in the story of the false Cretans,[47] to pillage the Delta farmlands. They were arrested by Egyptian soldiers and forced to throw themselves on the Pharaoh's mercy.

For the various reasons I have just listed, I believe that the Helu-nebu who made recurrent appearances on Egyptian soil from the earliest times onwards were in fact primitive Greeks. The decipherment of Mycenian Linear B provides initial confirmation of this theory. Perhaps one day we shall discover who the inhabitants of the Greek mainland were at the beginning of the third millennium.

The Greek poets were fully aware that their legendary heroes had visited Egypt. Helen and Menelaus put into port on the Mediterranean coast. Perseus went through Chemmis in Upper Egypt on his way to Libya to cut off the Gorgon's head. He stayed there long enough to introduce games in the Greek manner.[48] An Egyptian woman who had been carried off by the Phoenicians, then sold in Greece, is supposed to have founded the oracle of Dodona; the early inhabitants of this place, incidentally, were called the Selles, or Helles.[49] Io is said to have landed in Egypt in order to escape from persecution by Juno. She changed herself into a cow and gave birth to Epaphos, whose name is a version of Apis. His descendants were to remain in Egypt until the Danaïdes, with the support of Zeus, ceased to sing their homage to the Nile and the mouths of the Nile.[50] Greek scholars have maintained that, in all probability, the legends were created during the Seventh Century when there was closer contact between the Greeks and the Egyptians. I believe, however, that the two peoples had been in contact ever since 'the time of the god', to use a favourite Egyptian expression. The Egyptians were a people of habit and they must have maintained relations with the Greeks just as they did with Byblos, Punt, and Libya.

The Egyptians were always careful to differentiate between the Helu-nebu and the Keftiu. The latter are referred to for the first time in a text belonging to the First Intermediate Period. At a time when the Egyptians were no longer able to import fir-trees from Syria to make coffins for their priests, the kings of Keftiu (totally insignificant personages in the eyes of the Egyptian sage, although he does not say so openly) were embalmed in the resin extracted from the fir. Most of the texts and illustrated monuments which refer to the Keftiu and the products of their country, date from the Eighteenth Dynasty.

Tuthmosis III, who was anxious to instil a salutary fear into all the peoples of his day, attributes the following lines to Amun: 'I have caused you to smite the lands of the West. Keftiu and Isi cower with fear. I have caused them to see Your Majesty as a young and powerful bull, sharp-horned and impossible to attack.'

Keftiu was Crete, or perhaps only a part of Crete, and Isi was the

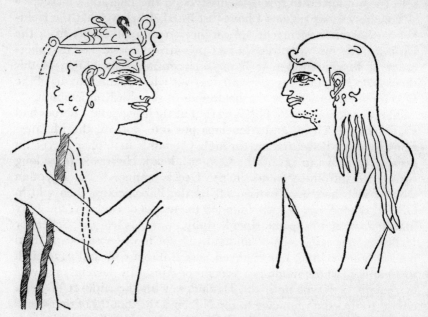

Fig. 40. Keftiu emissaries on the Tombs of Senmut and Puimre.

other large island, Cyprus. In his Hymn of Victory, Tuthmosis appears before each foreign people in turn, in the form of their principal god. For the Cretans and Cypriots he became a bull, because he knew that the bull was extensively worshipped in both islands. When his victorious Syrian campaign brought him enormous quantities of booty, in all the ports under his control he requisitioned Cretan and Byblos ships, and *sekut* made of fir-wood. These were loaded with beams, posts and other large pieces of timber to be used in His Majesty's great building operations. It seems likely that the embassy, or embassies, that the Keftiu sent to Egypt, during his reign, came with the express purpose of demanding the return of their boats. They did not arrive empty-handed, and in order to predispose their hosts in their favour, they laid out an array of valuable gifts. The procession of Keftiu bearing offerings thus became a common theme on several tombs of the period, and chiefly on those of Senmut, Puimre, Usermare, Rekhmara, and Menkheperreseneb. Whether the artists made their drawings from life, or whether they copied original sketches commissioned by the king, it is impossible to say. The fact remains that the tombs provide valuable information about the inhabitants of Keftiu, the clothes they wore, and the gifts they brought.[51] We can distinguish cups closely resembling Mycenian goblets, rhytons, jugs, jars, bowls, statuettes of animals and ingots. The shape and ornamentation of the various objects, like the details of the features and attire of the bearers, are typically Aegean, although the artists were occasionally guilty of mistakes and inconsistencies which some archaeologists have found shocking.

Were the Keftiu successful in their mission? It seems likely that they did not leave empty-handed. A magnificent alabaster vase, engraved with the cartouches of Tuthmosis III, was found a few years ago at Candia and may well be one of the gifts received in exchange for the Cretan offerings.

Relations between the Cretans and the Egyptians had begun before the accession of Tuthmosis III and continued after his reign, but only for a short time. No mention is made of any such relations during the Ramesside era.

In some Egyptian texts, from the time of Tuthmosis III onwards, the inhabitants of the islands of the sea are associated either with Asia, or with the Helu-nebu, or with the Keftiu. Under the Nineteenth Dynasty, frequent references were made to the islands from whose shores powerful and aggressive hordes were later to set sail. As the aggressors were at first few in number, they were easily captured; Ramses II included in his army, and even in his own bodyguard, 'Sherden captured by His Majesty which he had taken by the strength of his sword.'[52] The Sherden in the Pharaoh's service retained their own distinctive weapons and equipment. The attacks became more frequent under Merneptah, and at the time of Ramses III, the Sherden were sufficiently numerous and powerful to land along the Egyptian coast, advance southwards *en masse* and sail up the arms of the Nile. The invading hordes included, in addition to the contingents of Sherden, Philistines, Tjakarai, Danai, Shekelesh and Weshesh. Ramses III launched attacks against them both by land and sea; their armies were beaten back with enormous loss, and many prisoners were taken.[53] An account of this great victory which, together with the defeat Ramses III had already inflicted on the Libyans, was to give Egypt a ten-year respite, fills one immense wall of the pylon at Medinet-Habu. The Barbarians made up for their defeat by occupying Palestine, and certain islands in the Western Mediterranean such as Sicily and Sardinia, which have preserved their names.

The Egyptians were right when, even as early as the Old Kingdom, they asked their gods to erect, along each of the four horizons, impregnable gates which would open only for Horus, in other words for the King and his followers. Hordes of greedy and treacherous barbarians, most of whom came only to plunder, were massing beyond the gates. Yet the Egyptians, in spite of the hazards they had to face, realized from the earliest times that they could never develop their country as they wished if they remained confined within their natural frontiers. Both the eastern and western deserts were always considered as appendages of the Black Land; so too was the stretch of the Nile valley which lay to the south of the Aswan cataract. These regions were a source of auxiliary man-power. The Egyptians were irresistibly attracted by the mines of Sinai and the forests of the Lebanon. These were within their reach, whereas they felt they were not good enough sailors to venture as far as Crete and Europe. Contact with these latter regions was ensured by the Helu-nebu, and for a relatively short period by the Keftiu, who drifted with the north wind towards the Egyptian shores.

Thus the Egyptian world is seen to be far from confined within that stretch of the Nile valley which lay between Aswan and the sea. To the south, it extended as far as Gebel Barkal and even a good way beyond. Pharaoh's armies, engineers and traders visited the whole of the eastern desert as far as the Red Sea, the western desert as far as the oases, the Mediterranean coast as far as Cyrenaica, the peninsula of Sinai and the whole of Syria as far as the Euphrates. And at one special point of the Syrian coast, the population was always ready to sell timber at an extremely reasonable price, and even *kebenit* ships which enabled the Egyptians to reach the Terraces of Turquoise and the Terraces of Incense, lying at the southern tip of the Red Sea.

Important expeditions of this kind were successfully carried out in very early times, under the Fourth Dynasty and even before. Satisfied with their achievements in this field, and with advantages gained at relatively little cost, the Egyptians felt no desire to explore new lands. They probably never knew, except perhaps by hearsay, that the two Niles met at Khartum and helped to swell the beneficent flood. Traditional habits were extremely powerful in all departments

of Egyptian life. There were, however, men who cast tradition aside –
like the sailors in Ramses' time who chose a hazardous route in order
to reach the land of incense. Although the only evidence we have
for the circumnavigation of Africa during the reign of Neko is found
in Herodotus, we may suppose that this expedition at least was
prompted by an almost scientific curiosity.

The inhabitants of the regions visited by the Egyptians reacted in
various ways, according to temperament and their different attitudes
to Pharaonic authority. The Egyptians were not always well received.
Yet up till the end of the Twelfth Dynasty, neither the Nubians, the
Libyans, nor the northern peoples constituted a serious threat to
Egypt. Less than a century after Amenemhat IV, dissension among
the princes had so weakened the country's defences that the Hyksos,
whose numbers were entirely made up of tribes who until then had
been easily held in check, made their way into the Delta without
meeting with any resistance, and took Memphis and half of Upper
Egypt, pillaging the temples and towns as they went, and massacring
the sacred animals as a crowning insult. The Eighteenth Dynasty
certainly marked a recovery, but things were no longer the same.
Henceforth, Egypt had to deal with powerful states and learn the
art of international politics. In this she was brilliantly successful.
Neither the Hittites nor the Libyans nor the Sea peoples could
undermine her power. A day came, however, when, subject to
attacks from all sides, she was again invaded. Her only means of
escaping from the abhorred Persians was to welcome with open arms
the invincible conqueror who seemed to have descended from
Olympus to found, on the coast where the Helu-nebu had so often
landed in the past, a new metropolis which was to bear his name:
Alexandria.

CHAPTER 6

ON THE NATURE OF GODS AND PIETY

In the opinion of Herodotus, the Egyptians were the most strictly religious of all men.[1] Probably no other people has ever created such a host of gods, goddesses, sacred beings and sacred objects. No other people ever built such magnificent temples for its deities, or placed at their service such an elaborate personnel of priests, cantors and musicians, or invented such a diversity of rites and ceremonies. The periodic, ceremonial progresses of local gods through their particular towns caused much astonishment among Greek travellers in Egypt.

Number and diversity of the gods

The first point to be stressed is the number and diversity of the Egyptian divinities. Each one of the forty-two nomes had its official god, although the same deity might be shared by two or more provinces. Hathor was the goddess of both the Sixth and Twenty-second Nomes of Upper Egypt; Neith ruled over two neighbouring nomes of Lower Egypt; Thoth was the patron of the Ibis Nome in Lower Egypt, and the Hare Nome in Upper Egypt. Seth presided over the Heseb Bull in Lower Egypt and the Sceptre Nome in the south. The reduction thus achieved was, however, to a large extent offset by the fact that Hathor, Neith, Thoth and Seth and other gods were associated with companion deities both in their nomes, and even in their capitals. Thebes, the 'city of a hundred gates', honoured a large number of gods in addition to the triad of divinities normally associated with the city, and those of Memphis were perhaps even more numerous still. Even the smallest town had its local god, and most divinities had more than one cult centre. Hathor had so many it would be impossible to enumerate them all. Nekhebt, the capital of the Third Nome of Upper Egypt, worshipped a goddess called by this name. Opposite Nekhebt, on the other bank of the Nile, was Nekhen, one of the towns which worshipped Horus. Further north, but still within the Third Nome, the town of Esna worshipped two divinities of high repute: Khnum and Neith, and several others

besides. To come back to the right bank: Hefat had as its patron a
god, Hemen, who was little known throughout the rest of the country.
The towns under the patronage of Horus were very numerous, yet
the Horus of Edfu was so different both in appearance and in the
rôle assigned to him from the Horus of other towns, such as Nekhen,
Hebenu, or Khem, in the Thigh Nome, that we may well wonder
if the name refers to one and the same god. It follows that to give a
complete list of all the Egyptian gods is a well-nigh impossible task.
The figure arrived at can always be disputed, and any newly-
discovered stela might well add to it.

Fig. 41. The cat associated with Mut and the goose associated with Amun.
Usually, Amun is represented in human form and Mut in the form of a woman
with the head of a lioness.

The diversity of forms taken by the deities is equally astonishing.
Olympus had no lack of inhabitants, but its great gods were human
in form. They were mature men, adolescent youths and maidens,
children and finally women who vied with each other in beauty and
charm. The forms in which the Egyptian gods were represented
amazed the Greeks but horrified the Romans: 'Who does not know,
Volusius, what monsters are revered by demented Egypt? One part
worships the crocodile; another goes in awe of the ibis that feeds on
serpents. Elsewhere there shines the golden effigy of the sacred long-
tailed monkey.'[2] Juvenal was far short of the truth. Almost all living
creatures, whatever their habitat, land, air or water, and even

137

inanimate objects, became the embodiment of some divinity: the lion, the ox, the ram, the wolf, the dog, the cat, the ibis, the vulture, the falcon, the hippopotamus (fig. 42), the crocodile, the cobra, the dolphin, several varieties of fish, trees, a harpoon, and small animals such as the frog, the scarab and the locust and others, were worshipped in various places. There were also anthropomorphic gods, men in the prime of life, like Amun, Atum, Onuris, or on occasions, Seth; or an older man such as Anzti, who had a distinctive garb, head-dress and physical characteristics. All those just mentioned are shown with two separate legs; other anthropomorphic gods are

Fig. 42. Seth in the form of a hippopotamus among the marshes, Brunton, Qua and Badari, III, Pl. 32. The hippopotamus was hunted in most of the Horus towns.

represented with their legs imprisoned in a sheath – these were Min, Osiris, Ptah, Khonsu. Male children were also found, and goddesses clad like Egyptian women in a simple shift held up by straps. It would be impossible to distinguish between them if they did not have the appropriate hieroglyphic signs on their heads. This is true of Isis and Nephthys, Neith and Selkit, who can be seen on the corners of one of Tutankhamen's sarcophagi.

Some of the anthropomorphic deities had close affinities with the animal kingdom. On a stela from Thebes (fig. 41), the Nile goose and a cat are facing each other.[3] This could pass for a domestic scene, because both creatures were allowed into Egyptian homes; here, however, the goose represents Amun, and the cat, Mut, who had her temple at Karnak not far from the temple of the king of the gods. Amun it was too who, according to Herodotus, had a liking for small snakes,[4] and welcomed visitors to Karnak in the form of a ram. On a certain feast day in the year (but not before the New Kingdom), the statue of Amun was covered with a ram's skin, which was subsequently buried in a sacred chest. The two sisters, Isis and Nephthys, turned into kites when they watched over a sarcophagus; there was a period at Byblos when Isis became a swallow.[5] Even the great sun god of Heliopolis, Atum, could take the form of an ichneumon, a small carnivorous animal who attacked the nests hidden among the papyrus flowers. These metamorphoses were of varying duration. Sometimes a deity took a certain species under his or her protection; for instance, Neith, the elegant warlike goddess, took a special interest in the *lates*, the largest fish to be found in the Nile; Hathor protected the *chromis*, a slightly smaller fish; Khonsu protected the baboon, and in so doing overlapped with Thoth. The reasons for the various metamorphoses and affinities remain for the most part unexplained. In the case of Amun, the resemblance between his name and the name of the Nile goose, *smon*, may have facilitated the process of identification. Perhaps there was a general belief that the *smon* had laid the divine egg from which the world sprang. The Egyptians themselves were always very ready to account for the various metamorphoses, but it is unlikely that the legends they invented for this purpose furnish the true explanations. The *smon* was perhaps a local god whose territory had been included in Amun's ever-expanding domain. At the same time, the iconography of the great god was enriched by certain features adopted from the god who had been absorbed. Perhaps this is too facile a supposition, but could it be that Neith, who was generally considered to be the mother of Sebek, the crocodile god, and who lived on fish, did not eat the *lates* because it was too large and pugnacious?

By the reverse process, gods who normally assumed the form of some animal frequently took on a human aspect. The god Thoth was just as often represented as an ibis-headed man as he was as an ibis. Horus and Montu were falcon-headed. Wadjet was a woman with a serpent's head. Seth was represented as a quadruped, whom naturalists have been unable to identify, with a long curved muzzle, squared ears and an upright tail; he was also frequently portrayed with only the head of the animal. He sometimes took the form of a man with a human head who could only be distinguished from the other anthropomorphic gods by his garb and head-dress.[6] Hathor, whom the Thebans on the left bank worshipped in the form of a cow who suckled the king, appeared in the Twelfth Nome of Upper

Egypt as a woman with the head of a cow. The goddess's son was said to have cut off his mother's head in a fit of anger, so that it was replaced by that of a cow.[7] In other towns, Hathor was a woman, but her head was adorned with the two horns of a cow with the sun disc between them. The same tendency accounts for the fact that the cat-goddess, Bast, became a woman with a cat's head, and the lioness Sekhmet a woman with a lioness's head.

In places where an animal god was worshipped, the cult had a dual aspect. Nowhere is this more clearly illustrated than in Mendes, a town in the central Delta, whose god Banebded (Mendes in Greek) took the form of a ram. The ruins of his temple still stand at Tell Amdid where the outer walls and a rectangular pond are clearly visible.[8] On what remains of the foundations of the temple stands a shrine of the Saïte period, still in an excellent state of preservation. Banebded had a consort, the goddess Dolphin, who gave her name to the province. Not far from the settlement which had grown up round the temple, another town *Ta-hut-Bau*, the stronghold of the Rams, Thmuis in Greek, enjoyed the privilege of having within its precincts the live ram which was the incarnation of the god. During the reign of Ptolemy Philadelphos, the sacred animal would appear exactly in the place where its presence had first been revealed. The scribes of the House of Life and the priests of the nomes would go to the place, recognize the divine nature of the animal by certain signs and draw up a titulary, while a pen was prepared for it. Followed by an impressive procession, the god would then make his official entry and there would be great celebrations lasting four days. To some extent, ordinary rams enjoyed the privileges bestowed on the chosen one. This happened wherever the god took the form of an animal. At Sumenu (the modern Rizzeigat) in the Thebes area, and in the central district of the Fayum, the god Sebek took the form of a crocodile.[9] He was worshipped in his temple where his statue was erected, and venerated as a sacred animal as he splashed about in his pool. A lady of high rank would kneel down and, without the slightest trace of disgust, would drink from the pool in which the crocodile wallowed. Ordinary crocodiles were mummified throughout the whole of Egypt and placed in underground caverns, like the one called the cavern of the Crocodiles in Middle Egypt. At Khmun (Hermopolis), the town of Thoth, the sacred ibis had its abode no doubt next to the temple. No trace of it has been found, but the vast necropolis which housed the mummified bodies of ibises brought from every part of Egypt has been discovered. The Egyptians mummified falcons in the towns of Horus, cats at Bubastis, and dogs in the Seventeenth Nome of Upper Egypt.

A large number of bulls and cows were held to be sacred. In the central area of the Delta, four provinces chose as their emblems various types of bulls or cows: the Black Bull, the Heseb Bull, the Foreign Bull, the Cow and the Bull-Calf. A necropolis of sacred bulls has recently been discovered near Horbeit. Especially privileged animals were interred in huge granite sarcophagi; those revered less deeply were buried just under the surface of the sand. The town of the great solar god was also the town of the Phoenix, in which Herodotus was interested, and also the town of the bull Merwer (Mnevis). At Saïs, Neith tolerated the presence of a sacred cow. These various cults were, however, eclipsed by the veneration in which the Apis Bull was held in the old capital of Egypt. At any one time there was only one Apis Bull. But as soon as it died, another was chosen to take its place. The foremost learned men gave their advice, and when they had decided which was to be the new Apis, the bull was led into his sacred enclosure near the temple of Ptah, where he was fed on delicacies and given as many heifers as he wanted. The public could come and admire him. Bullfights were held in his honour. The people mourned his death just as they had rejoiced at his enthronement. His mummified body, adorned like that of a prince, was placed in a huge sarcophagus alongside those of his predecessors. His date of birth was recorded, as well as the dates of his recognition as a god, his enthronement, death and interment. The Serapeum discovered by Mariette contains in its vaults the whole succession of the Apis Bulls from the time of Ramses II to the Late Period. It is clear from the inscriptions that the bull had been worshipped ever since the Old Kingdom.[10] The priests of Ptah took part in the ceremonies connected with the Apis Bull, which was often called Herald or even son of Ptah, 'he who reveals fair-faced truth'. The bull enjoyed amicable relations with Atum and Horus and he became an Osiris after his death. The priests of the great gods no doubt considered that it was in their interest to be connected with such a popular cult, although the worshippers themselves may have insisted on the various cross-references.

We are far less well-informed about the cult of trees and inanimate objects. The tree which was the emblem of the Twentieth and Twenty-first Nomes of Upper Egypt was given a human arm holding out the sign of protection,[11] but did not retain its significance as a cult object for very long. It is impossible to say whether the sycamore tree, near which the souls of the dead came to quench their thirst, actually concealed a goddess who sprinkled water from her ewer, or whether it was the material form assumed by the goddess. The harpoon which was the emblem of two Lower Egyptian nomes

141

was a sacred, and perhaps even a divine, object; it was mounted on a stand which was placed inside a boat of very archaic design.[12] The town which was the chief centre of the Osiris cult, Zedu, took its name from a fetish which it is not easy to define. It looks like several sheaves placed one above the other. Osiris eventually adopted it, but it does not seem to have been associated with him in the beginning; just as the knot, *tit*, had not always been a symbol of Isis. The object which bears the name *neteret*, and was used as the symbol for the word *neter*, god, appears to be the stand on which the ancestors of the Egyptians placed the emblem of their clan in the days when they still led a nomadic existence. Illustrations of a whole series of such emblems have been preserved on vases dating from the Gerzean period and on pre-dynastic stone palettes: the elephant, the falcon, the ibis, the wolf, the sun, a falcon in a basket, a mountain, a harpoon, two crossed arrows, a thunderbolt and the beast of Seth (fig. 8). The emblems did not disappear when the clans settled in fixed localities or when towns were founded; however, they met with varying fates. The Elephant clan, as can be seen from Gerzean vases, founded the town of Iebo, Elephantine, on the island of the same name. An elephant god may have existed, but nothing was heard of such a god after the animal finally disappeared from the Aswan region and even from Nubia. Most of the other emblems survived in some form or other. The solar disc became the god Ra, while the harpoon became the emblem of a nome and a sacred object. The thunderbolt became the great god Min, gave its name to a nome and was held to be a sacred object. The two crossed arrows were at once the emblem of a province, which was subsequently divided into two parts, and the insignia of the goddess Neith. The ibis was the ensign of a nome, a town and the god Thoth. The falcon was identified with Horus, who was worshipped in many localities, the dog with Anubis, and also with the Seventeenth Nome of Upper Egypt. The wolf represented the god Upuant, the bird in a basket, Andjti and the Eighteenth Nome, a greyhound, the god Sha and the Eleventh Nome. It should be added that the emblems of all the nomes were carried on stands and that the signs of the gods, not only those already named but many others besides, were also carried on stands, as is stated in the famous geographical text of Edfu.[13] Whatever importance they acquired during the historic period, whether they were installed in luxurious temples or in humble shrines, served by an elaborate staff of priests or by a modest keeper, all the national gods stemmed from the nome ensigns of the wandering clans. They existed long before Menes, and if Egypt added to the number of gods she had inherited from prehistoric times it was through the adoption, at various periods, of foreign deities, such as Anat, Astarte, Reshep, Dedun and Baal who, however, seem never to have been granted the honour of being carried on a stand. Egypt herself added no new deities to her existing pantheon.

Temples and priests, festivals and prohibitions

One fundamental difference between the Greek and Egyptian religions was that the Egyptians did not imagine their gods as having a special abode like the Olympus of the Greeks. The Land of Punt was sometimes called *Ta-neter*, the land of the God, or the divine land, but this was because, in the very remote past, the god Min had come from Punt, and with him other gods too perhaps; but it was never stated that Punt was even a temporary residence of the gods. On one occasion, several great gods assembled in 'the island in the middle', in order to judge and settle the dispute between Horus and Seth.[14] However, they chose the spot in order not to be disturbed. The gods remained in possession of the territory in which they had originally settled, and their ownership was recognized at all periods. Seth was master of Avaris, Sebek of Sumenu, the obscure god Hemen of the little town of Hefat. Even the cosmic deities had a locality attributed to them. Amun-Ra was Lord of Ipet-Esut, 'the chosen place', a small part of Karnak; Ra was Lord of the two lands of On (Heliopolis); the first pair of gods to be born of Atum, Shu and Tefnut, had their domain at This near Abydos. The Great Harris Papyrus, in which Ramses III recorded all the gifts he had offered the gods, invariably puts the name of the residence after that of the god. No doubt certain gods bore epithets which conveyed either their function or their character. Their chief attribute, however, was invariably the one which indicated their geographical domain. Sometimes they had several domains, and often several gods were lords of the same domain, because they liked to travel round and were extremely hospitable.

The property owned by the gods shared the same fate as that owned by men. It changed hands on more than one occasion. In the Crocodile Nome, the Sixth of Upper Egypt, the eponymous god Iqu, who was a crocodile, gave way to Hathor, who owned innumerable domains. A little to the south of Siut, a greyhound called Sha, who gave his name and image to the Eleventh Nome, still retained a few faithful followers during the Middle Kingdom, but the majority favoured Khnum, the god of the cataract. Osiris is perhaps the best example of a conquering god. According to certain stelae, he was generally supposed to have two domains, Zedu in the Delta and Abydos in Upper Egypt. Yet he was not originally associated with either of these localities. Zedu was first of all the property of a god called Andjti, who was represented as an old man, holding a crooked sceptre in one hand and a whip in the other, and with two feathers on his head. At a very early period, although it is impossible to ascertain exactly when, Osiris completely absorbed all the attributes of Andjti, whose name became a mere adjunct of his own. The name Horus-Andjti figures in the dedicatory inscription of the magnificent temple of Hebit, in the central Delta.[15] For a long time, and even as late as the Thirteenth Dynasty, Abydos worshipped a god Khenti-Amentiu, 'Foremost of the Westerners', who is represented with folded arms, entirely swathed in wrappings and with the crown of the south on his head. The Osiris who was referred to as Osiris-Khenti-Amentiu was perhaps represented in the same way.[16] Thus Osiris, who had no province of his own, ousted and supplanted two older gods, divesting them not only of their attributes, but probably of their functions.

When we read that a god was lord of a certain domain or town we can assume that he had a temple there. This fact, which is confirmed both by the ancient texts and by archaeological evidence is a reliable guide in all archaeological research. The temple was the castle of the god, *hut neter*, and its design was based on that of the palaces of the Pharaoh. Egyptians had such a strong sense of property, coupled with such an urge to make records of even the smallest domains, that every temple and even the main divisions of each temple were given special names. The temple stood inside a walled, rectangular enclosure built of unbaked bricks, which was sometimes more than three hundred, even five hundred yards long, over fifteen yards thick and proportionately high. As the walled enclosures are now more or less in ruins, it is impossible to say whether the Egyptians were able to walk along the top of the walls, but it seems extremely likely that they could. A gateway led into an inner court. This gateway was a monument in its own right, being covered with inscriptions and bas-reliefs extolling the power of the god, and its dimensions were in keeping with those of the walled enclosure. During the Late Period, the monumental doors provided a summary of the personality of the god.[17] Behind the door lay a spacious forecourt which was often as crowded with sculptures as a modern museum gallery. The central avenue was lined with obelisks and led between the two tall towers of the pylon first into a courtyard with colonnades on one or more sides, then into the hypostyle hall, beyond which was the sanctuary of the god. Round the shrine containing his most revered image ran a passage from which opened chambers containing the sacred apparatus, or sometimes chapels dedicated to friendly gods. The space between the temple buildings and the enclosure wall was usually occupied by shops, dwellings, schools, gardens, and a sacred lake. The general plan varied from one temple to another. The dwelling of the god Min included such original features as a conical hut before which stood a pole crowned by a pair of horns. Sebek welcomed his devotees in front of a hut with a circular roof and a tall post bearing a bucranium. Two stands, of the type used for carrying the emblems of the gods, stood on either side of the temple of Neith, while the emblem of the goddess and a shrine could be glimpsed at the far end of an avenue. These examples were no doubt survivals from more primitive times (fig. 43). The early temples conformed less rigorously to a pattern than those built during the classical periods.

Fig. 43. Primitive shrines of Min, Neith and Sobek, from Jéquier, *Bull. Inst. fr.*, VI. The shrines still retained their primitive appearance even during the Late Period.

In addition to his temple, every important god had altars, either in the town or in some other place, a sacred orchard and a sacred barque, capable of sailing on the Nile. The vessels of the great gods were virtually floating temples, some of them being a hundred cubits in length. They were built of wood imported from the Lebanon and all magnificently gilded. The sacred barques were frequently renewed. During the New Kingdom every Pharaoh wanted to associate his name with the building of a new barque for Amun. Herihor, at a time when Egypt was emerging from a period of disturbances and confusion, was anxious to do likewise.

A considerable temple staff was employed to look after, repair and increase the possessions of the gods.[18] The chief of these was the *hem neter*, the servant of the god. Amun, being king of the gods, had four such servants; other gods had two or three, the majority no more than one. The *hem neter* was much more an administrative official than a priest. He had full authority over all the manual workers, he conducted the temple business, undertook building operations, and solicited contributions from the faithful. The daily rites were performed by priests who had been specially trained for this function; these were the *uab*, or pure ones. Theirs was a physical rather than a spiritual purity. They were circumcised, shaved the hair from their heads and bodies, washed frequently, were dressed in linen robes and, if they had had intercourse with a woman had to wash before entering the sanctuary. They were not obliged to be celibate, or to lead a life of austerity. An inscription on a stela runs as follows: 'O priest of Ptah, do not refrain from eating and drinking, from getting drunk or making love, from spending days in joyous celebrations, or following the dictates of your heart day and night. After all, what are the years we spend on earth, however numerous?'

It would seem that the priests were not given to proselytizing. They had their particular believers and, provided the numbers did not decline and the temple possessions and privileges were not reduced, they accepted the fact that the priests of other gods should exist side by side with them. They did not preach any particular moral code, and ancient Egypt offers no example of a priest reproaching a Pharaoh with having committed an injustice, in the way the High Priest rebuked David. A possible exception is a story relating to King Pepi II, of which we possess only a few fragments. Someone, either priest or layman, is said to have had the intention of rebuking the king. Perhaps the god eventually did intervene to force the king to renounce certain practices.

Priests were nearly always the sons of priests, and simply respected the tradition according to which sons followed in their fathers' footsteps. The priesthood was not an easy profession. The incumbents had to know everything concerning the god they served: what he looked like, what he wore, what his attributes were, his history, the various metamorphoses he had undergone, which things pleased him, and which displeased him. They had to be able to recite hymns, prayers and magic formulae and, as far as possible, they had to model their behaviour on that of the god. This is made clear by the list of priestly titles, only some of which, however, can be explained. The priest of Khnum was called 'he who shapes bodies', because, before each birth, Khnum fashioned the child and the child's protective genius on his potter's wheel. Of the two priests of Thoth, one was called 'the bald', because the ibis was bald, while the other was 'he who separates the two companions', because that was the part played by Thoth in the dispute between Horus and Seth. The priest of Horus at Edfu was a 'harpooner', because his god hurled a harpoon at Seth when the latter took the form of a hippopotamus. The priest of Ptah was known as 'the chief artist', because Ptah himself was an artist and a demiurge. Alternatively, the function of the priest was closely allied to the requirements of his particular god; for instance, at Coptos, the priest of Min was a chemist who could concoct a black dye called 'the divine substance' and which was painted on the statue of the god.[19] Other priests of Min kept bees and produced honey, because the god was very fond of honey. In the Thigh Nome, the priests of Sekhmet were called *sunu*, doctors, because their lion-headed goddess had the power of both creating epidemics and bringing them to an end.

In many cases, it is not clear what the link was between the priest and his god, because we lack adequate documentary evidence. Only when we are able to translate the word *hesek*, shall we understand why this word was used to designate the priest of Osiris at Abydos. One day, no doubt, we shall understand why the priest of Thoth at Khmun was referred to as 'the Great One of Five', and why the priest of Banebded, in the Dolphin Nome, was called the 'Chief of the soldiers', or why the priest of Herishef at Nen-Nesu was known as 'the son who loves him'.

Not only the priests but also the female sistrum players who contributed to the splendour of the ceremonies were referred to by particular names. Some simply took the name of a particular divinity; at Athribis, this was the name of the local goddess Khetutet or Khuit, at Elephantine, Satet. Others were known by an attribute of the divinity; for instance, in the Western Nome, the goddess of which was a cow, Sekat, 'she who suckles', and at Saïs, Weret, 'the Great One'. Others again took over one of the functions of the goddess; in the Dolphin Nome the name was Waza-es-Ba, 'she who satisfies the Ba', the Ram, and in the domain of Bastet, the 'Lady with the red clothes' was both the name of the priestess and one of the epithets denoting the goddess.[20]

Whatever special services priest and musician might render to their particular god, since the temple was held to be a palace, and the god a prince, certain duties were the same everywhere. Every morning the priest entered the holy of holies and made sure that the door was bolted. He would then open the door, and see the god who was supposed to have slept. He would wake him up, present him with his various garments, head-dresses and insignia, and proceed to dress him. After the god had been dressed, he ate his first meal; he would have two or three more during the day, like human beings. In the evening, his insignia and garments were removed and he was put back into his shrine. Meanwhile, hymns had been recited, songs sung,[21] and dances performed before the god. The ritual was the same from temple to temple with slight variations.

These ceremonies were performed, for the most part, silently and out of the view of the public, by a few appointed priests. This does not mean that the public had no access to the god. The very design of the temple buildings, with the forecourt in front of the pylon and a series of courts between the pylon and the hypostyle hall, indicates that the public were admitted. In the large cities, the royal palace was often next to the temple and its front elevation overlooked the main court. The king would appear on the balcony and distribute rewards in the presence of the people. The main-gates were probably not opened every day, but only when the people had to be allowed in to attend the ceremonies ordained by the king, and the special festivals. These were called, literally, 'the coming forth' of the god, and one was known as the 'great coming forth'. Although they differed in length and in certain details, the festivals all had one feature in common. A huge crowd of townspeople formed a procession behind the official personages and took part in the proceedings. Others gathered in the streets so as to miss no detail of the scene. Sometimes the procession took place within the temple enclosure, and halted at the sacred lake in the gardens. On the other hand, the god frequently left his abode in order to visit other temples, gardens or hamlets, or in order to meet other deities. Throughout the town and the province in which the particular god was worshipped, as well as in all the neighbouring provinces, the festival was an eagerly awaited event which helped the people to forget the harshness and monotony of their daily lives.

Classical authors provide evidence of this fact. When the festival of Bubastis drew near, the villagers gathered from far and wide, crowded into boats, and rounded up passers-by who soon became as excited as the rest of the mob. Women joined in the general jollity, brazenly lifting up their skirts and unaware that the goddess Neith had done likewise in the presence of her august father. More wine was drunk during the week of the festival than during all the rest of the year.[22] At Papremis, the statue of the god was carried out of the temple and placed in a chapel. Priests mounted guard over it and on the following day set it on a four-wheeled carriage. The worshippers then formed themselves into two teams; one tried to enter the sanctuary while the other barred the entrance. In the ensuing scuffle many skulls were cracked, although the local inhabitants were unwilling to admit the fact.[23] At Ombos, according to reliable witnesses, supporters of Seth and devotees of Hathor used to engage in bloody battle. Egyptians were proud and happy to have taken part in the most famous festivals. At Abydos, it was the custom to re-enact the mourning into which Seth's heinous crime plunged the whole of Egypt. A procession making its way to the tomb was stopped by the enemies of Osiris. However, the latter were put to flight, the god was restored to life and returned to his palace in his sacred barge.[24] At the time of the New Kingdom, the festival of the king of the gods lasted for twenty-one days during the period when the flood water was at its height. The sacred barges of Amun, Mut and Khonsu were released from their moorings and, escorted by a flotilla of boats, made their way to Luxor, where they remained for some time before returning to their starting point. A huge procession walked along the roads, keeping abreast of the boats, and the crowds which composed it made the most of the festive occasion.[25] It must be admitted, however, that while we can determine the dates of the festivals, and describe some of their episodes, we cannot always grasp their exact significance.

One last feature of the Egyptian gods should be mentioned: the prohibitions they imposed.[26] Certain actions were forbidden by every god, and always with good reason. For instance, it was forbidden to harm certain species; in some places, it was the crane, elsewhere the gazelle, the cow or the hippopotamus, or a certain fish or even all fish, because the god could take under his protection the entire species of the creature of which he was a temporary or permanent embodiment; or again, the reason might be that he reserved the right to kill those animals himself, at leisure. In the Tenth Nome of Upper Egypt, the hippopotamus was sacred and no one was allowed to harm it. At Edfu, only Horus or his priest were allowed to hunt it with the harpoon. Sometimes only a certain part of the animal's body could not be harmed – the head, for instance, or a fore-limb. Certain forms of human behaviour, some of which might strike us as being of slight importance, were forbidden; for instance, no one was allowed to eat honey in an area where the local god was particularly fond of honey, and it is understandable, indeed only elementary good manners, that the king should not hunt the lion on the festivals of the lion-headed goddesses. Sometimes the prohibitions imposed by the gods corresponded to universal moral principles or certain rules of hygiene. We cannot assume, however, that the god was concerned with such matters when he forbade pederasty at Memphis and the frequenting of certain types of infected people at Thebes. In these particular cases, the mere mention of the vice or the disease in the presence of the god would have been tantamount to talking of rope in the house of a man who has been hanged.

Some prohibitions existed only in one particular town, or in one particular province; others were valid throughout the country—that is, they applied to all the devotees of the god in whatever area they happened to reside.[27] The public authorities saw to it that the various prohibitions were respected, and even the people were anxious that they should be obeyed. For instance, when the inhabitants of Cynopolis found themselves faced with people from neighbouring provinces who worshipped the oxyrhynchus fish and killed dogs, they became extremely violent.[28] This behaviour was a result of the strong local patriotism characteristic of the Egyptian people, and it intensified that patriotism, since one quarrel led to another; fights undertaken on behalf of the god also strengthened the bond between the god and his devotees.

Work of the gods. The creation

The god of the clan had probably no specialized function – or rather, he had to fulfil all functions. He protected his devotees against illness, against their enemies and other external forces, and he was responsible for the success of their various undertakings. After becoming localized, he still retained his universal powers. However, the classical authors were convinced that the Egyptian gods, like their own, had specialized functions. It was for this reason that they tended to give them Greek names instead of simply adding a Greek flexional ending to the Egyptian name. Almost the only exceptions are Osiris and his two sisters Isis and Nephthys. The Greeks were fully aware that Min was the god of Coptos, Thoth the god of the Fourteenth Nome and Ôros (Horus) the Son of Isis, but they preferred to call them Pan, Hermes and Apollo. The associations established by the Greeks were not based on any physical resemblance; Amun did not look like Zeus, nor Horus, with his falcon's head, like Apollo. Thoth was even less like Hermes, and Hathor, the cow-goddess, very different from Aphrodite. Nevertheless, certain affinities were thought to exist between Greek and Egyptian gods.

Not all the Egyptian gods had the power to create; this was the special function of the gods, Atum and Ptah, whose temples lay quite close to each other at Heliopolis and Memphis, although separated by the width of the Nile. Their methods of creation were different. Atum lived alone and brought forth the first divine pair of children from his own semen or sputum, whereas Ptah made use of all the organs of the body: the heart which is the seat of knowledge, the tongue which repeats everything which has been thought by the heart, and the limbs which execute all actions. Khnum fashioned men and their protective geniuses on his potter's wheel, while Hekat, his wife in Middle Egypt, helped women in childbirth.

Thoth was the lord of all the secret writings, indeed of all writing. He was the patron of scribes, and they called upon him for inspiration. With the help of Seshat, he inscribed the name of the reigning king on the leaves of the sacred tree of Heliopolis. Whenever the building of a temple was decided upon, he helped the king to determine in which direction it should face. He made an inventory of the booty brought back from the land of Tehenu, or from Punt.

Several gods had a warlike disposition, in particular Seth, the harbinger of battles, and Montu, Lord of Thebes. Both loved horses. Next come Horus and Amun, the opponents of Seth, Onuris god of This, and Ha, who always carried a harpoon. These were not, however, gods of war in the same way as Mars and Ares. It is impossible to say whom Herodotus had in mind when he referred to Ares of Papremis because the Egyptian equivalent of the name remains unknown.

Hunters frequently invoked a meadow goddess, Sekhet, who occasionally took the form of a peasant woman carrying game. Both she and her son, the god Net, were friends and allies of the hunters.[29]

Some gods represented the elements: Shu, the air, Geb, the earth, Nut, the sky, and Hâpi, the Nile. During the Old Kingdom the Egyptians sometimes worshipped a water god, and a corn god in the shape of a man full of water or seeds.[30]

The goddess Ernutet was a harvest goddess and her festival was held on the first day of the first month of the harvest season, or summer (shemu). Maat was more than the goddess of justice; she was a personification of justice.

It must be remembered that several of these gods possessed domains, a fact which brought them into line with the majority. As for the most popular gods, Amon-Ra, Ra-Harakte, Osiris, Min, Isis and Hathor, who had shrines throughout the whole country and attracted worshippers from far and wide, they were called upon to take action in so many matters that it would be difficult to assign to them any one specialized function. It must be admitted that, on the whole, the Egyptians did not think in terms of a god having one specialized function, and that the Greeks were mistaken in assuming that the forms and names of their own gods had earlier parallels in the Nile valley. It has already been mentioned that towns of some importance worshipped two or more gods. The citizens of a given town, or of two neighbouring towns, who thus found themselves attracted to more than one deity, hit upon the idea of creating divine families, through the linking together of gods who had been associated by the accidents of history or geography. Ptah was undeniably the great god of Memphis and of the White Wall Nome.

To the north-west of Memphis, Sekhmet reigned over the Thigh Nome. On the outskirts of Memphis, there was Nefertum, a pleasant figure with his lotus flower and the two plumes on his head. Here was a family ready to hand. In the Elephantine area, Khnum was lord of the main islands, while two goddesses reigned over two other islands of the archipelago. Khnum took one of them, Satet, as his wife, while the other, Anuket, became his daughter.[31] At Thebes, the triad consisted of the Lord of Karnak, Mut, the Lady of Ioshrew, and Khonsu of Thebes. Under Ramses III the town of the Sun had two pairs of divinities, Harakhte-Insas and Atum-Nebthotep, who were later joined by two others, Sepa-Isis, Shu and Tefnut. At this period and even before the town had two great sanctuaries, one dedicated to Harakhte, the other to Atum, Nebthotep, or to give her her rightful name, Hathor, owned in her own right both the Red Mountain with its magnificent quarries of red quartzite, and the fertile plain next to it. To the north of Heliopolis was a district called Insas. The other two pairs were also known in the region. Consequently, theologians and worshippers did not have to make great efforts in order to establish family relationships between the gods. The process may not have begun very early because the White Chapel, on which can be found a summary of the religious geography of Egypt at the beginning of the Twelfth Dynasty, makes no mention of it. It will be noted that Montu did not figure in the Theban trinity, although his claim to the Theban domain dated from very early times. At Memphis, one would have expected Ptah to prefer Hathor, the Lady of the Sycamore, to the lion-headed goddess. Perhaps, however, Hathor had already chosen the solar god. We do not possess any texts which might throw light on these various family relationships.

On the other hand, certain literary texts show how worshippers pictured the conflicts between the gods of the same town, or between neighbouring gods. In the Seventeenth Nome of Upper Egypt, Anupu, the god of the chief town, had for his immediate neighbour Bata, Lord of Saka. According to a story, the manuscript of which dates from the time of Ramses II, Anupu and Bata were brothers and lived happily together, cultivating their lands. Anupu, however, was married and they eventually quarrelled because of his wife. Bata decided to live abroad and settled down in the valley of the Ash, in the Lebanon, perhaps because men from Saka had already gone there to seek their fortunes. His brother went to find him; they were reconciled and returned home. Bata, the younger of the two, became king first and then was succeeded by his brother. Horus and Seth were another pair of companions or brothers, according to certain authorities. Almost everywhere throughout the country, their cult centres were side by side. This explains why they inevitably became rivals, each one claiming for himself the inheritance of Osiris, their father. They argued their case before the gods, fought, were reconciled, then started fighting once more. Finally, Horus got the better of his opponent. The gods, not all of whom had been his supporters, proclaimed him master of the whole of Egypt. Thoth asked what should be done with Seth. Harakhte replied that he would take Seth with him into the sky and place thunder in his hand so that men might fear him.[32]

In Lower Egypt, Osiris was firmly established at Zedu, a town in the central Delta known to the Greeks as Busiris. Seth had his domain at Avaris on the Tanitic arm. Isis reigned at Hebet, a little below Busiris, and Nephthys held sway over the semi-desert land which lay to the east of the Tanitic arm. Pe, situated a little further to the west, was a Horus town. As can be seen, the Osirian family was composed of gods who had been established for a very long time in neighbouring localities. In Upper Egypt, the same gods were found within a fairly limited area – Osiris at Abydos, Isis at Coptos, Seth on the opposite bank of the Nile, Horus at Edfu, and Nephthys in the nome which was later to be called the Sistrum Nome. From the close contact between worshippers and from the fantasies they wove around their gods sprang the most famous Egyptian myth which was known before the birth of Egyptology through Plutarch's account of it and, subsequently, from the Pyramid Texts and a large number of stelae.[33] There is no doubt that every town had its own version of the story, and the same god did not always play the most prominent part. The Pyramid Texts, on the whole, give the Abydos version. Osiris and Seth were brothers. Seth killed Osiris at Nedit and threw his body into the water. The two sisters of Osiris found it and Nut, his mother, re-assembled its various parts. According to a scene depicted on the sarcophagus found to the east of Abydos in King Zoser's cenotaph, Isis changed into a bird and placed herself on her husband. She became pregnant and Horus, after avenging his father's death, succeeded to his throne.

Although Plutarch makes no mention of the fact that he found the material for his narrative in the Delta area, it seems obvious from the main episodes of his version that he must have. Zedu was not far from Avaris – the two nomes even had a short stretch of boundary-line in common. Seth invited Osiris to visit him, and persuaded him to get into a coffin, which he had had made with perfidious intent. His accomplices immediately flung themselves on the coffin, sealed it with lead and threw it into the Tanitic arm, the part of the Nile on which stood Avaris, where Seth had his residence. The coffin floated down to the sea and a mysterious force drove it as far as Byblos, where so many Egyptians landed in historic times. Here a tree grew round it, and it became incorporated in the trunk. The king of Byblos had the tree cut down and taken to his palace. Isis, having learnt by supernatural means of the whereabouts of her husband, set off for Byblos. She met the maidservants of the queen near a spring, dressed their hair, and they recognized the exquisite perfume emanating from her person. The king and queen could not refuse to give her the sacred tree. However, after she had given birth to her son among the swamps at Chemmis, Seth stole the body of Osiris, cut it up into fourteen pieces and scattered them throughout the land. Finally right triumphed. The body of Osiris was found and restored to life and Horus defeated Seth.

Among the legends which can be pieced together from references found in religious writings, especially deserving of mention are those which claim to explain the creation of the world.[34] Ancient Egypt has bequeathed us no single message comparable to the Babylonian poems or the Book of Genesis. The Egyptians were too attached to their local legends for a uniform account of the creation of the world to be current throughout the country. In every important sanctuary we can expect to find an original presentation of the story of the creation.

A phrase found in the Pyramid Texts refers to a time when there was no sky, when neither the earth, nor men nor gods existed, and when even death did not exist. All of this was the creation of the Demiurge, but something already existed when he first appeared; this was the primeval ocean called Nun, the existence of which seems to have been generally accepted. The Egyptian conception of Nun was not the result of abstract speculation; it went back to the long years during which the men of the paleolithic era looked down from the barren tops of the cliffs and saw the vast unruly river carving its way through the African continent. With the annual inundation, the valley reverted to its original appearance, which was that of a vast sea out of which rose hamlets and dikes. The primeval ocean, Nun, did not create the world, it played only a passive rôle as the medium in which the first manifestations of the divine force were to occur.

At Memphis, it was naturally thought that Ptah was the first to emerge from Nun. He was therefore called *Ta-Tenen*, 'the land which rises up'. He created the gods, built the towns, arranged for offerings to be made, founded sanctuaries, and fashioned their bodies to the satisfaction of their hearts. In this way, the gods entered into their bodies in every sort of plant, every sort of stone, every sort of clay and every substance which grew on the surface of Ptah, and through which they could manifest themselves.

According to the Memphite conception, the sun was only one of the elements created by the Demiurge. In the rival town of Helio-polis, on the other side of the Nile almost opposite Memphis, the sun, under the name of Atum, was the creator. Although he lived alone, he brought forth – either by masturbation or, according to a different version, from his sputum – the first divine pair of children – Shu (the air) and Tefnut (moisture), whose children were Geb (the earth) and Nut (the sky). They were closely bound together at birth, but Shu, their father, tore them apart; standing with one foot on Geb he held Nut above him in his uplifted arms. In this way, the sky and the earth were separated by air. Geb and Nut gave birth to Osiris, Hor-Mekhenti-irty, Seth, Isis and Nephthys, all of whom in turn created a multitude of beings and inanimate objects.

Khmun, in Middle Egypt, was known as the town of Thoth, but the scribe of the gods was a late-comer to the town, the name of which meant 'the town of the Eight', the eight primeval gods – four male frog-headed gods, and four serpent-headed goddesses, who personified respectively the primeval water, infinity, darkness and that which is hidden. In their time, nothing evil existed on the earth. Everywhere abundance reigned.

Why should famines occur, in spite of hard work? Why wars? Why epidemics? It may be that the Egyptians did not formulate the problem of evil until a later stage. According to a tradition, which grew up at Per-Soped, a town influenced by the Heliopolitan cosmogony, the revolt against Atum occurred at the time when the air had become cooler and the earth drier, and when gods, men, towns and nomes had been created and recorded in writing. Shu, the son of Atum, defeated the rebels, but after he had created the sanctuary of Per-Soped, the same rebels, the sons of Apophis, returned to the attack.[35] However, Apophis never assumed the same importance in Egyptian theology as the spirit of evil in certain other religions.

Judging by the Per-Soped legend, we can suppose that the inhabitants of most cities must have believed that their local god occupied a prominent position in the divine family tree, and that he had played an honourable part in the creation of the world, by founding, for instance, the temple in his town.

It follows that the creator assumed very different guises, according to the locality concerned. He could be a single figure, or a group of figures. Sometimes he created everything at once, sometimes in successive stages. One belief, however, was prevalent throughout the whole country. The 'first occurrence' was the emergence of the order of the world from chaos, and this order was by no means secure and final. Its existence was threatened every time the sun went down. No one could be sure that the sun would ever rise again. Nor was it certain that the Nile, as the summer solstice drew near, would overflow and refresh the sun-baked banks. Some Egyptians imagined that the sun had issued from the womb of Nut, and was received by two divinities, just as the newly-born child is delivered by midwives. But it then slipped through their hands, pursued its course underneath the belly of Nut and in the evening vanished into the goddess's mouth. It passed through her body during the night and was re-born the following morning. In this way the miracle of 'the first occurrence' was renewed.

The kings' duties to the gods

The essential duty of the kings was to build temples, see to their upkeep, and provide the means whereby the offering tables could be constantly replenished. This duty was enjoined upon all kings and was in no way a matter of choice. The building of a new temple gave the king a fresh opportunity of co-operating with the gods. This is the subject of an ornamental motif, the most comprehensive examples of which are to be seen at Edfu and Denderah, although it must in fact have existed at a very early period.[36] Like all such motifs, it consisted of numerous episodes. The king is shown coming out of his palace, and directed by the gods, goes to the site on which it is proposed to build a temple. When darkness falls, he takes up his position in relation to the Great Bear, the constellation seen in the northern sky, and then seeks out one particular star, the one associated with the deity to whom the future temple will be dedicated. Once the orientation of the temple has been established, the king, with the help of the goddess Seshat, drives in four stakes, one at each corner of the site, and runs a line along the four sides. Subsequent operations called for a great labour force, but convention decreed that they should be supposed to have been accomplished by the king alone. The ground was dug along the line between the four stakes until the subterranean water-level was reached. A foundation wall of unbaked bricks was built along each side. The inside was filled with sand; there were buried under the corner stones objects which commemorated the founding of the temple, including seventeen stone slabs of which at least a few bore the name of the king responsible for the building as well as those of the temple divinities. When the temple was finished, and after the performance of the purification rites, which varied in number from one temple to another, the house was handed over to its master. The god took possession of the temple, and the ritual of worship could begin.

When King Zoser founded the Third Dynasty, most of the gods had only very simple sanctuaries made of wood or reeds. His architect, Imhotep, started replacing them by stone buildings. If our interpretation of the stelae found in the subterranean chambers is correct, the first beneficiaries were the god of Memphis, Thoth of Shmun and Horus of Edfu.

King Snofru, who established a great many sacred estates in all the nomes, did not fail to provide each one with a sanctuary, and this no doubt accounts to a very large extent for his reputation as a beneficent king. It is certainly impossible to believe Herodotus' story, according to which the builders of the great pyramids were guilty of impiety. Egyptologists have shown these allegations to be obviously biased. If the Annals of the Old Kingdom, of which we possess only fragments, had been complete, we should know much more about the activities of the kings who built the pyramids, from Aswan to the cities of the North. The kings of the Fifth Dynasty did much to enhance the fame of the Heliopolitan gods, and created estates for them throughout the country. When Merenra visited the region of the cataract, he took the opportunity of winning the favour of the local god, Khnum. Pepi I, who, in his cartouche, proclaims himself son of Hathor, Lady of Iuni, enlarged and embellished her sanctuary at Denderah.

The kings of the Old Kingdom were, then, supporters of polytheism, which they encouraged by building temples to the local gods throughout the land and by declaring themselves sons of the god of every city.

The kings of Ithy-taui were more in favour of a policy of religious centralization. This is clear from the White Chapel built at Thebes in honour of Amonrasonter (Amon, king of the gods). The latter is named fifty-nine times, whereas the neighbouring god, Montu, although Lord of Thebes and Atum and Ptah, gods of the famous cities of the north, are mentioned only very occasionally. In the geographical section of the White Chapel, the chief god of every nome is carefully recorded.

The general tendency at this particular period seems to have been to worship only the most important deities, the chief of whom was the king of the gods. A special place in the pantheon was also allotted to the Lord of Abydos, who had a greater popular appeal than any other Egyptian god, as well as to Sebek, especially after the start of the major undertakings in the Fayum, such as regulating the outflow of the waters of Lake Moeris for the purposes of irrigation, and the building of the Labyrinth which, according to the Greeks, was more impressive than the Pyramids. Seth who, under the Old Kingdom, was revered no less than the other gods, seems later to have been neglected, or even persecuted.

When the Hyksos controlled Lower Egypt as far south as Cusae, their leader chose as his city of residence, Avaris, an old theological centre, where Typhon, i.e. Seth, was worshipped. The Hyksos chief came to realize, if he had not already been aware of the fact beforehand, that Seth had much in common with the various Baals of his own country. He not only adopted him as his own god but, unlike the Pharaohs, regarded him as the only god and even attempted to impose the cult of Seth on the rest of Egypt which had retained its independence. There was a vigorous reaction from Amun, who inspired Kames with the desire to liberate Egypt.[37] Once the Hyksos had been driven out, Amun thus became chief of all the other gods; nevertheless, they too benefited in no small measure from the king's generosity, a fact which seems to have redounded to the general good of the country. However, during the reign of Amenophis III, there occurred one of those phenomena which are both common and uncommon – revolution. The king turned against Amun; his son went much further and set about persecuting Amun, Mut and Khonsu, and completely disregarded all the other gods. He moved his capital some two hundred and fifty miles to the north, and changed his name from Amenophis, which signified 'Amun is satisfied', to Akhenaton, meaning 'Glory of the Aton'. For a period of twenty years or so, Aton was to be the only officially recognized god. He was represented in the form of a sun disc, from which rays spread out fan-wise, terminating in hands. This did not signify, as might at first appear, that the god of Heliopolis had triumphed over the god of Thebes. The new god rejected all the former names of the solar god, as well as the crown, the sceptres, the barques and the solemn processions up and down the Nile by day and by night. Egypt thus made a complete break with the past, so much so that the Hymn to Aton would seem more appropriate in the mouth of a foreigner than in that of an Egyptian. It declares the sun to be the creative principle of all life; it is the father of all men, gave them different coloured skins and different languages, and established them in diverse regions. To some it gave the Nile, to others rain.[38]

For a few years, the court resided in the new city created by Akhenaton, impervious to everything other than its religious doctrine, unconcerned by the loss of Egypt's far-flung empire, and completely cut off from the rest of the country. However, Akhenaton died, and as he had daughters but no son, the throne went to the husband of his eldest daughter, then to Tutankhaten, who soon made his peace with the god of Thebes, changed his name to Tutankhamen, and brought the court back to Thebes. He set about restoring the old order of things, reinstituted the famous Festival of Opet, built new sacred barques, and erected statues. Ai, his successor, who had held high office under Akhenaton, made no attempt to defend Akhenaton's innovations and Horemheb, the last ruler of the Eighteenth Dynasty, destroyed all remaining evidence of them. Nevertheless, Amun was again about to find himself in a situation every bit as serious as the one he had faced at the time of the Hyksos rule, or during the years when Akhenaton was destroying his name and images throughout the land. As Horemheb left no male heir, a new dynasty was founded by a general almost as old as Horemheb himself, and who is known to Egyptologists as Ramses I. He came from a family which had worshipped Seth for four hundred years, and not only had he to fight enemies from without, he had also to combat the feeling of dread which the name of the Lord of Avaris inspired in the majority of Egyptians. The dynasty was consolidated by his son Seti I. The third king, Ramses II, did not consider it necessary to proceed as cautiously as his two predecessors. He did not care for Thebes, partly because of the climate, but mostly because of Amun, whose ambitious and dictatorial rule he found most distasteful. Following the example of Amenophis IV, during the early part of his reign he sailed northwards, but with far more than three boats, and built at Avaris, the locality his family had haled from, a new town which he called after himself, Per-Ramses.[39] This was to be his principal residence. He was not so rash as to put forward Seth as the only or even the chief god. He created a company of gods in which no individual deity held first place, and which included the patrons of his army regiments – Amun, Ra, Ptah and Seth, then Atum, the goddess Wazet, whom his father had served and who was greatly revered in the central and western Delta, and foreign gods such as Hurun, who had become known at Memphis through the presence of Asiatic workers, Anat who became the consort of Seth, and Astarte. At the same time, Ramses II completed Seti I's temple at Abydos, the hypostyle hall at Karnak, and created Egypt's most magnificent monument at Abu Simbel, in honour of Amun and Harakhte. And so everybody was happy.

Under Ramses III, Amun was undoubtedly the wealthiest of all the gods. Atum and Ptah were still richly endowed, and lesser gods such as Seth of Nubit, Seth of Per-Ramses, the gods of Siut and

Abydos and twenty or so others also benefited from the king's bounty.[40] Amun could not tolerate the establishing of the comparative equality between the gods, or perhaps he was afraid of a fresh offensive on the part of Seth. Whatever the reason, he was responsible for plunging Egypt into the tragic upheavals known as the War of the Unclean, which we are told about by Josephus (who took Manetho as his source), and of which there is evidence at Tanis and in other localities. With the help of the Palestinians who had so often suffered at the hands of the Egyptians, the supporters of Seth defied the Thebans and forced them to take refuge in Nubia. The Sethians spread over the whole country, committing acts of violence which far exceeded those perpetrated at the time of the Hyksos invasion, and pillaging both temples and tombs and killing sacred animals. It was a time of appalling hardship. Some years later the people of Thebes reassembled their armies, and as Kames had done on a former occasion, defeated or drove out their enemies. Ramses' palace was destroyed, a disaster from which Seth never recovered. From that time onwards, he was worshipped only in the oases.[41]

Apart from Seth, the gods of Egypt were just as numerous after the War of the Unclean as they had been before. In spite of the destruction and humiliation brought about by the various invaders of Egypt – the Assyrians, the Ethiopians, and the Persians – the Egyptians remained staunchly faithful to their gods, and, if anything, became even more devout. As soon as the invaders relaxed their vigilance, the kings of the Saïte Dynasty and, after them, the two Nectanebos made great efforts to rebuild the sanctuaries, and restore the splendour of the religious ceremonies. If the throne of Horus happened to be unoccupied, private individuals were ready to take the necessary steps; for instance, Petosiris in the town of Thoth, and Zedher, the saviour, at Athribis. Thwarted in her rightful ambitions, and oppressed by barbarian invaders, Egypt, during the last years of her civilization, withdrew within herself. Her gods, her sacred animals, and her religious rites, which were incomprehensible to foreigners, continued to provide support and comfort during those troubled times.

Whenever the gods seemed to have turned away from men, whenever the Nile did not rise to a sufficient height, or the harvest was ruined by the south wind or locusts, or disease took a heavy toll of both beasts and men, or enemy hordes crossed the frontiers bringing desolation and death in their wake, the sages who undertook to discover the causes of such disasters, did not hesitate to ascribe them all to one thing – ungodliness, and to add that only by a return to piety would happiness be restored. Ramses III, in particular, was profoundly convinced of this and he expressed his feelings with great vigour in the opening lines of the historical summary which ends the Great Harris Papyrus.[42]

'The land of Egypt was topsy-turvy. Each man being his own judge, there was no master, for many years before until other times. The land of Egypt was divided up into nobles and chieftains. Every man, rich or poor, killed his brother. Other times succeeded these, and they were barren years. Irsu, a Syrian, brought the whole land under his control, and every man killed his companion in order to rob him. They treated the gods in the same way as they treated men. No more offerings were brought to the sanctuaries. But the gods changed all this to peace and restored the country to normal. They established their son born of their flesh as sovereign, Life – Health – Strength of every land in their place . . .'

At the end of the Ptolemaic period, the author of the Jumilhac Papyrus expressed much the same thoughts, in referring to his fellow-citizens of the Eighteenth Nome of Upper Egypt. They were valid, however, for all Egyptians.[43]

'If there are very few offerings on the altars, the same is true of the whole country and life is wretched for all living beings. If, however, gifts abound on the offering tables, there is food throughout the land, and all living beings are filled with the tree of life, for Anubis brings forth the wheat and makes the Two Lands live . . . But when this place is deprived of its libations and of the offerings for the divinities which are there . . . the inundation is small, the mouth of the tortoise is shut and there is a year of famine throughout the entire land . . . If people fail to observe the ceremonies of Osiris in this region at the appointed times, and all the feast-days marked on the civil calendar, this land will be without laws, the common people will abandon their lord, and there will be no rules for the populace . . . Continue, therefore, to do that which is seemly in the presence of the god, so that the god is satisfied because of this. Osiris beheld the writings of Ra. And just as these writings are of value to Osiris, they are of value to all those who read them, to all those who act on earth in accordance with them; they are of value to them in the necropolis.'

Thus the people were held collectively responsible not only for their own ungodliness, negligence and greed, but for those of the royal authorities too.

The gods as patrons

In moments of distress, whether or not they felt guilty as individuals, people would turn towards their favourite god and direct their prayers to him. This was what Ramses II did at Qadesh, when he suddenly realized that he was surrounded by his enemies.[44] In the same way Bata called upon Harakhte who could distinguish truth from falsehood when his brother, blinded by anger and jealousy, was about to strike him. The peasants in the fields did not forget to thank the gods for the harvest. At the close of the grape harvest, rustic offerings were piled up before the images of Ernutet, who took the form of a serpent.[45] During the process of winnowing, a sort of idol, rather like figures that are still found today on barns in the Tchad area, was fixed to the silos.[46] Every guild had its own patron. The metal-casters and goldsmiths used to appeal to Ptah or Sokar whenever they were parched with thirst. Thoth was the patron of the scribes. Statuettes dating from the New Kingdom portray a scribe apparently writing at the dictation of the baboon, who sits perched on a small pedestal. The scribe asks Thoth to receive him in Shmun where life is so pleasant, and for once he invents a rather subtle image – that of 'a coconut-bearing palm-tree sixty cubits high. Inside the shell is a delicious liquid, but it is far off'. True enough, the coconut palm was quite rare in Egypt. The worshipper who is also a silent man knows that the rare liquid is sealed away from the garrulous and the excitable, but available to the silent.[47]

Humble prayers were addressed to Amun: 'I love you and I hold you in my heart.' Sometimes the great god turned into a vizier and administered justice in favour of the poor.

The guilty man who was stricken with blindness or with some disease believed that he was being justly punished for his sins. The Friend of Silence, a goddess on the left bank at Thebes, heard his prayer and pardoned him. On another occasion, Ptah punished a liar by plunging him into darkness in broad daylight, and later cancelled the punishment. Anxious fishermen could hardly ask the mighty gods of the great sanctuaries to forgive their sins; they would appeal for forgiveness in humble shrines, sometimes inhabited by quite insignificant gods who, for some inexplicable reason, had acquired a certain popularity. For instance, in Sahure's funerary temple, there is a representation in relief of the goddess Sekhmet who at one period was credited with miraculous powers both by humble folk and by high-ranking dignitaries. Among the protectors of the poor can be found deceased kings, officials who had enjoyed a high reputation during their lifetime (such as Imhotep, Zoser's minister, who became a son of Ptah), and lesser gods whose very ugliness gave them a certain appeal, for instance, Tueris, the female hippopotamus, and Bes, the grinning dwarf.[48] About fifty years ago, the statue of a temple official who had been a snake-charmer, was found at Athribis. Even after his death, the worthy man seems to have been able still to be of service. He is represented in a sitting position with his arms crossed over his knees and a Horus stela dealing with crocodiles propped up against his legs, while the god holds snakes in his hands, and is wearing a Bes head above his own. Apart from the face, hands and feet, the whole statue is closely covered with formulae which were thought to be very helpful against bites and stings. The base of the statue is hollowed out in front to form two basins. When a little water was poured over the statue, it absorbed the healing properties inherent in the formulae. Whoever drank of the water would be neither bitten nor stung, or if he was already suffering from bites he would be cured. In return he would pray that the healer would want for nothing in the next world.[49]

This statue and others of the same type belonged to the Late Period, but it is quite probable that devout Egyptians of all periods found obliging intermediaries between their modest persons and the god who was master of all things.

Monotheism

On several occasions, the Pharaohs behaved as if they considered their gods to be too numerous by far, and were anxious to create some sort of order within the Egyptian pantheon. The first step was obviously to reduce the number of gods; no one was more zealous than Akhenaton in this respect. He persecuted Amun and his triad, and repudiated the other gods. In his domain he worshipped only one god, the solar disc with the human-handed rays. He was the prophet of a new religion which might be termed monotheistic. However, the new religion was practised only by the king, his family and court, and the inhabitants of Akhetaton. It is well known that the Egyptian people were immensely relieved when they heard that the court had returned to Thebes and reopened the temples.

The people were not yet ready to accept a doctrine of this sort. We have absolutely no information about the reasons for its emergence and development in the mind of Akhenaton. He may have invented it or come upon it in the course of his reading, but again we do not know what books he had read. Perhaps it occurred to him during conversations with wise men, either Egyptian or foreign.

These questions are, I think, unanswerable. However, I feel that I cannot conclude a chapter on Egyptian religion without discussing a question which has troubled a great number of Egyptologists in the past, and still does so today.

According to certain scholars, monotheism is clearly expressed in the old Egyptian books of wisdom, from the Old Kingdom to the Late Period, in which the word god is used in the singular, in the same way as it might be by a modern preacher. 'God is all-powerful. He knows our thoughts. He rewards and punishes. We must tread in the paths of righteousness.' Canon Drioton has collected a number of similar maxims.[50]

'Beware of being inexorable.'
'We do not know what measures God resorts to when he punishes us.'
'God knows the ungodly.'
'God punishes the sins of the ungodly until he draws blood.'
'Man is clay and straw, and it is God who forms him.'
(Amenemope 24, 13–14)

However, it should be pointed out in the first place that none of the sages, whether they belonged to an early or a later period ever wrote the words 'God is a single being' or 'There is only one god'. How could they possibly have done so, since, for instance, Ptathotep, a vizier at the time of King Isesi, was a divine father and served Ptah and probably other Memphite gods as well, and it never occurred to him to repudiate them. A prince of Abydos who died during the reign of Amenemhat II, called upon at least twenty-five divinities when commending his soul to the supreme powers.[51] Amenemope who arranged to be buried in the Nome of Min, lived in the Nome of the Great Land, married a singer in the service of Shu and Tefnut, and finally had a son who became a priest of Min. There are no grounds for thinking that the sages adhered to the doctrine of monotheism and ignored it in their daily behaviour by serving gods whom in their heart of hearts they thought purely illusory.

In actual fact, the impression of monotheism comes from modern translations. Egyptologists, however, do not associate the word *neter* with monotheism, because they know that it refers, not to an essentially single being but to a whole category of beings, who were the chief creations of the Demiurge. In the section dealing with created beings, the Onomasticon records: *Neter*, god; *Neteret*, goddess; *Akhit*, spirit; *Nesu*, king; and *Nesut*, queen. All these words refer to a class of beings comprising a greater or a lesser number of individuals. When Ptahhotep wrote, 'It is God who gives promotion', he was expressing exactly the same idea as Ani, who was to write several centuries later, 'Your god (Neter-ek) bestows good fortune'. This same Ani, having urged that the feast of his god be celebrated, goes on to generalize by saying that God is angry with anyone who fails in this duty. His injunctions could have applied equally well to the citizens of Memphis who were about to worship Ptah in his temple, to the worshippers of Osiris at Zedu and Abydos and to the devotees of Thoth at Khmun. Similarly, the author of the Ebers Papyrus concludes his introduction with the words, 'God gives life to the man who loves him. I am a man who loves God, he gives me life.' Yet a few lines earlier he points out that he has acquired his knowledge from the lord of Heliopolis and the divine mothers of Saïs. There is no trace here, even by implication, of any monotheistic doctrine.

Conclusion

In the field of religion, as in all other fields, Ancient Egypt started off from very primitive notions. At the beginning of the Old Kingdom artists embodied the old clan ensigns in forms and images which were often magnificent. Theologians, scholars, and the Egyptian people themselves, wove sagas around them, endowed them with special functions and emotions which were to give them a compelling quality of realism, which it is impossible to ignore. In spite of a few premature attempts to break away from tradition, and even though the sages, for the sake of convenience rather than through any deliberate policy, express themselves in terms of which monotheists would not disapprove, both the educated class and the common people remained faithful to their gods. The curious figures, the ritual of worship, the offerings, prohibitions and public festivals, the magnificence of the temples, the miracles which occurred from time to time – all these things formed a whole which the Egyptians valued more highly than life itself.

CHAPTER 7

HUMAN DESTINY AND CARING FOR THE DEAD

The elements of personality

THE Egyptians did as much for their dead as they did for their gods, perhaps even more. Visitors admire such buildings as the Temple of Deir-el-Bahari, the hypostyle hall at Karnak, the colonnade at Luxor, or the two cliff temples at Abu Simbel, but they are no less impressed by the magnificence of the great pyramids, the private tombs of the Old Kingdom, the tombs in the Valley of Kings or the treasures found inside the tombs and preserved in the Jewellery Room and Tutankhamen's gallery in Cairo Museum. Along the edge of the two deserts, from Kom el Hisn and the Red Mountain to Aswan, the necropolises dating from all periods stretch in an almost unbroken line. Neolithic and Chalcolithic tombs have been found in the El Badari region and at many places in Middle Egypt. Tombs of the Thinite period are found at Abydos, Saqqara, Abu-Roash and Helwan. The inhabitants of Memphis, during the period when the town was the capital of Egypt, were buried along the fringe of the western desert from Abu-Roash as far as Medum; the kings of the Middle Kingdom at Dahshur and in the Fayum; during the Middle Kingdom private individuals hollowed out tombs for themselves at Beni-Hasan, Cusae, Siut and Aswan. The Theban kings chose the Valley of the Kings, while queens, princes and private individuals built their tombs in the mountain-side, opposite Thebes, but closer to the inhabited areas. Tombs of the Twenty-first and Twenty-second Dynasties have been discovered at Tanis, those of the Ethiopian Dynasty at Thebes; Late Period tombs have been found at Tunah el Gebel not far from Khmunu. These represent only a fraction of the necropolises or sets of tombs which archaeologists have brought to light during the past one hundred and sixty years, and everything points to the fact that the list is not yet complete. The worship of the dead, and the importance given to tombs, represent one of those permanent features of Ancient Egypt which we are trying to define.

Although the Egyptian conception of life after death was still rather uncertain at the time when they first laid their dead in graves along with a few provisions and weapons, by the time of the First and Second Dynasties it had become much more clearly defined. During this period they started building brick mastabas which, even at this early date, were of monumental proportions, and contained an ornate and varied selection of furniture. Also at this period, the human personality seems to have been thought of as consisting of four elements: *Khet*, the body, especially the dead body; *Shut*, the Shadow; and two elements which were not perceptible to the senses – the *Ba* and the *Ka*. The old hieroglyphic sign for *Ba* was a bird, the stork, perhaps simply because it had the required sound, or perhaps because it seemed legitimate to compare the immaterial element to a bird. From the Eighteenth Dynasty onwards, the *Ba* took the form of a human-headed bird which flew round the passages in the tomb and was even thought of as soaring to the upper air.[1] It quenched its thirst in the little trough which the Sycamore goddess filled with water from her ewer (fig. 44). The *Bau* of Pe, Nekhen and Heliopolis who appear

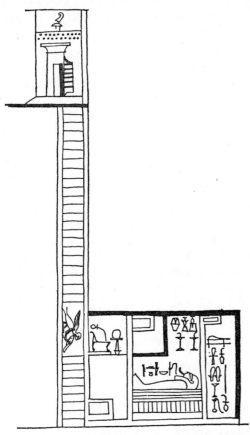

Fig. 44. The *Ba* flying round the tomb. Ned-Qad Papyrus, Maspero, *Hist.*, I, 198. No early representation of the *Ba* exists.

in very early texts were the spirits of the kings who ruled before Menes. Perhaps originally the *Ba* was the exclusive possession of the king.

It is clear, on the other hand, that every man possessed a *Ka*. Khnum fashioned it on his wheel at the same time as he modelled the newly-born child. It was represented by two arms bent vertically upright at the elbow, the fore-arms and hands pointing towards the sky. This was an attitude of prayer, perhaps also an expression of admiration at the pile of offerings, for *Ka* had in fact the meaning of food. With a suitable determinative, the phallus, it designated the bull, and this has been taken as evidence of the fact that the *Ka*

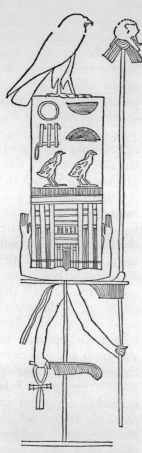

personified the creative force. Sometimes it corresponded to conscience. An accused man says: 'My *Ka* is good, what have I done?' A sage writes: 'The *Ka* is forbidden to tell a lie.' In the case of the king, the *Ka* surrounding the serekh is fixed on a pole which is provided with arms supporting a staff set in a tiny human head (fig. 45).[2] Certain proper names such as *Ka-i em hat-i*, 'My *Ka* is before me', 'My *Ka* is my staff', 'My *Ka* is my guide', are perfectly in keeping with this little picture.

Such were the functions of the *Ka* during a man's lifetime. After death, it left the corpse, although it liked to remain in the tomb with the body. In the tomb built for King Hor, in the pyramid of Amenemhat III, a wooden statue of the king was found in a shrine near the sarcophagus. The king is shown naked as on the day he was born, without any of his royal insignia, but wearing a plaited beard like those worn by male gods, and with a huge wooden *Ka* fixed to his head.[3] The expression *hut Ka*, the castle or house of the *Ka*, meant strictly speaking, the tomb, but it also had the more general meaning of the domain which supplied the provisions offered to the deceased. The *Ka*, in fact, needed both food and drink. A hunter declares, as he puts the birds he has just caught into a cage: 'These are for the *Ka* of Ti.'[4] Stelae of the Middle and New Kingdoms which promise thousands of loaves of bread, jugs of beer, oxen, fowls, and occasionally lengths of rope and material or ointments and perfumes, specify that all these pure and good things which the god creates and which are brought by the Nile or brought forth by the earth, are for the *Ka* of the deceased.[5]

Fig. 45. The royal Ka and its guide in the Temple of Sahura.

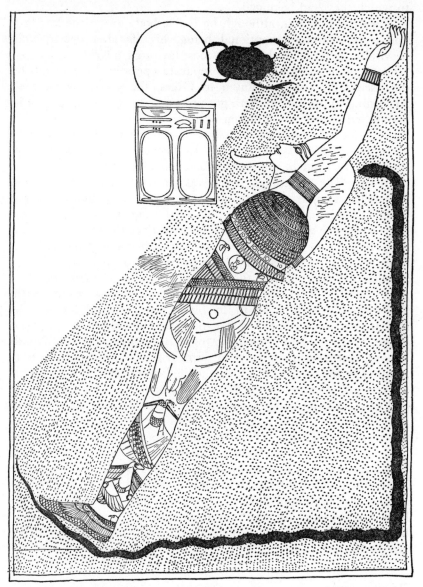

Fig. 46. The ascension of the dead King, on the Tomb of Ramses IX, from Guilmant. Riding on a serpent, the king travels through infinite space.

At all periods, the tomb was built in such a way that the *Ba* and the *Ka* would have no difficulty in becoming reunited with the body to which they had belonged.

Since the Pharaoh, although he had a body and a shadow, a *ba* and a *ka*, was an exceptional being, his life after death would inevitably differ from that of his most favoured subjects. The king's after-life was made up of three separate episodes. First of all, the deceased king was assimilated to Osiris, the god slain by Seth. According to the legend, Seth got possession of the dead body of his enemy, cut it up into fourteen or more pieces and scattered them throughout the land of Egypt. Isis set out to look for them, and found all but one – it is easy to guess which – because it had been devoured by fishes. She put her husband's body together again and restored it to life. The Pharaoh's body was probably not dismembered. Nevertheless each part of it had to be put into its tomb or sarcophagus, symbolizing the royal palace, through a special door, and there in silence and in darkness, the mystery of the resurrection was supposed to take place.[6] His limbs were fitted together again; his head was joined to his bones and his bones to his head. Nut, the mother of Osiris, played the chief part in the resurrection. 'She gives thee thy head, she brings thee thy bones, she assembles thy limbs, she places thy heart in thy body. His spirit, his strength, his soul are restored to him and the gods assembled around him shout, "Rise, rise!" '[7] The Pharaoh, however, did not remain in the tomb. Ra and Horus set up a ladder for him. If the king thought this to be a rather prosaic way of reaching the life beyond, he could fly off like a falcon, or a crane, or the Nile goose, or leap like a grasshopper or locust, or even cling to the hands of Nut who would pull him towards her, so that he might become an imperishable star and enter the heavens (fig. 46). The gates were opened for him, the huge bolts were drawn back. He was ushered into the palace of the gods by Ra himself, and greeted by Isis, Nephthys and the glorified ones. He could take up his abode in the north-eastern part of the sky among the circumpolar stars; he could also be invited by Ra himself to join his company[8] and travel through the night sky in the boat called *mesketet* and through the day sky in the boat called *manzet* (fig. 47).

Primitive tombs

The tombs of the first two dynasties were large rectangles built of unbaked brick, adorned on the outside with projections, and niches which can be regarded as the precursors of the false doors to which

The Egyptian Landscape

1

The temple of King Mentuhetep (Eleventh Dynasty) and the temple of Queen Hatshepsut (Eighteenth Dynasty) at the foot of the Libyan Mountains.

2
The ancients used the 'shaduf' for raising water to irrigate their fields, and the device is still in use in modern Egypt.

3
The Nile during the inundation. The fresh mud brought down by the river provides new soil in which the crops are planted.

4
The oasis of Pharan in Sinai, where date palms, pomegranates and tamarisks grow
abundantly.

5
Some of the most famous Pharaohs of the New Kingdom were buried here in the Valley of the Kings at Thebes. The burial place is marked by the Quorn, or horn, which surmounts it.

Monuments

6
The famous Imhotep was the designer of the Step Pyramid of Zoser at Saqqara, which was built in the Third Dynasty.

7
The three great pyramids at Giza – in the foreground, Mycerinus; in the centre,
Chephren; at the back, Cheops.

8

The Bent Pyramid at Dahshur probably had to be finished in a hurry, so that the angle was changed to reduce the height. The pyramid is one of the three ascribed to Snofru (Fourth Dynasty).

9

The pyramid of Snofru at Medum, which may have been begun by Huni, the last king of the Third Dynasty. It was constructed in seven steps and faced with limestone, and is therefore the first true pyramid.

10

Papyrus columns in Zoser's funerary monument.

11

Proto-Doric columns of Ameni's tomb at Beni-Hasan (Twelfth Dynasty).

12

Primitive architectural supports made of the stems of plants are represented in stone in these columns in the entrance hall of the Step Pyramid enclosure.

13

Palm columns hewn during the Old Kingdom at the Temple of the East at Tanis

14

The papyrus columns stand in the Temple of Amun at Karnak, which was built by Tuthmosis III.

15
Ramses II built the Great Hypostyle Hall at Karnak. This photograph shows capitals and a clerestory window.

16

The cartouches of Ramses II form an important part of the decoration of these columns of the Hypostyle Hall.

17

Obelisk bearing the cartouches of
Ramses II in position at the Temple at
Luxor.

18

(*right*) The tallest obelisk in the world is
that of Tuthmosis III and IV. It stands
outside St John Lateran in Rome.

19
The four enormous statues representing Ramses II dominate the façade of the Great Grotto of Abu Simbel in Nubia.

Sculpture

20
The Great Sphinx of Giza showing the stela recording the dream of Tuthmosis IV who
was instructed by the sphinx to clear away the sand from its flanks.

23

(*right*) Menkaura is seen striding forward, while the Queen, slightly smaller in stature, treads more delicately.

21

Alabaster statue of Chephren from Memphis.

22

This statue of Chephren from Tanis shows him in the form of a sphinx.

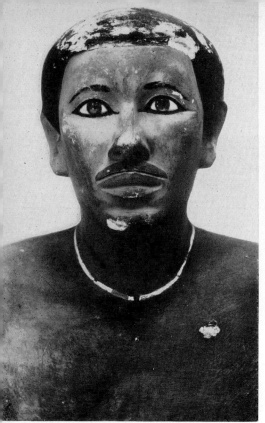

24
(*above*) The eyes in this statue of
Rahotep are inlaid with quartz
and rock crystal, which gives the
face its very lively expression.

25
(*above, right*) Nofret, the wife of
Rahotep, is wearing a diadem of
silver – a metal rare in the Old
Kingdom. Both this and the
previous statue are from Medum.

26
(*right*) This head of King Userkef
is part of a colossal statue of the
King in the Temple attached to
the King's Pyramid at Saqqara.

28

(*right*) Hemiunu, Vizir and Overseer of all the King's Works of Cheops. His prosperity and importance are indicated by the representation of his heavy body and fleshy chin.

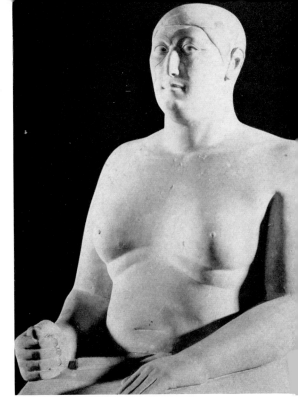

27

(*below, left*) The workmen who found this wooden statue of Ka-aper called it the 'Sheikh el-Beled' because of its resemblance to their own village headman, and it is still known under this name.

29

(*below, right*) This reserve head of a princess with strongly negroid features was probably made in the royal workshops for a member of Cheops' family. The statue is from Giza.

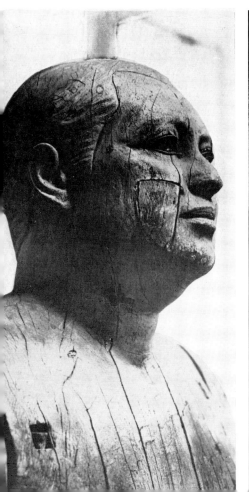

30 to 33

These reserve heads from Giza are portraits of the deceased and were placed in the burial chamber, perhaps to serve as substitute heads of the bodies which were destroyed.

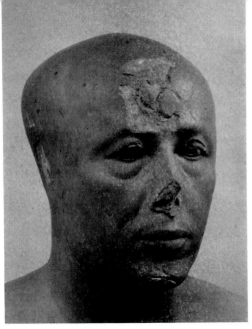

34
Prince Ankh-haf, a son of Cheops,
sculpted in limestone, the stone
core being covered by a thin layer
of painted plaster.

35
This portrait of an unknown man
is known as 'The Salt Head'.

36 and 37

There are several representations of men of importance in the Old Kingdom in a cross-legged attitude, but this work, the Squatting Scribe from Saqqara, is certainly the finest example.

38 and 39

Two heads of Ranefer from Saqqara.

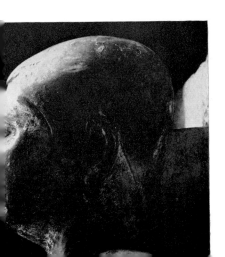

40

Amenemhat III, seen here as a
young man, was the legendary
builder of the Labyrinth. One of
his two pyramids was at Hawara,
where the temples and buildings
probably formed a walled town,
the view of which suggested to
the Greek writers the idea of 'a
labyrinth'.

41

Head of the same statue.

42
Head of Amenemhat III.

43
Amenemhat III as an old man.

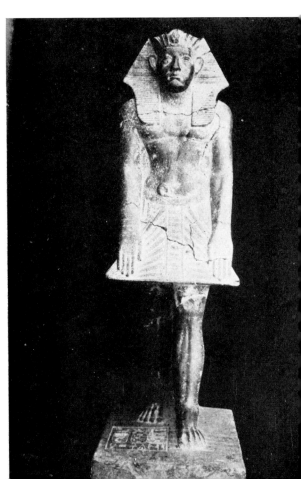

44
The child sitting on his mother's knee is Pepi II, who reigned in the Sixth Dynasty for possibly 94 years – the longest reign recorded in history.

45

The wooden statue of King Hor (Thirteenth Dynasty) is surmounted by the Ka in a shrine and was found at Dashur.

46
A black granite statue from Tanis, showing a human-headed lion.

47
Another human-headed lion from Tanis.

48
The two offering-bearers are bringing fishes and birds. The statue dates from the Middle Kingdom but was later usurped by Psusennes, and was found at Tanis.

49
During the reign of Amenophis III, shown here, Egypt was probably at the zenith of her power abroad and of luxury at the royal court.

50

(*left*) The new artistic trends introduced by Akhenaton (Amenophis IV) are exemplified in this limestone statue of the king.

52

(*below*) Detail of the head of a standing granite statue of Tuthmosis III, from Karnak.

51

Something of a return to the old artistic ideals can be seen in this statue of Tutankhamon, although the sculptor is still influenced by the Amarna style favoured by Akhenaton.

53

A painted limestone sculpture of Nefertiti, the wife of Tutankhamen.

54

The same head full face.

55
(*above*) An unfinished
head of Nefertiti made
of quartzite from
Akhetaton.

56
A quartzite head of a
princess found at
Akhetaton.

57
A nude female figure in
crystalline sandstone from
Akhetaton.

58
The bust of a young girl in
painted limestone from
Akhetaton. The girl has
the side-lock of youth
added to her wig instead of
hanging from a shaven
head.

59
(*opposite*) A painted
limestone statue of a
husband and wife.

61

A grey granite statue from Tanis of Ramses II protected by the goddess Anta.

60

(*opposite*) Ramses II was perhaps the last great warrior king of Egypt who was able to boast with any truth of his foreign conquests. This black granite statue of the king is probably from Tanis.

62

Ramses II kneeling to present an offering. This sculpture in schist is from the Karnak cachette, a collection of sculptures dating from the Twelfth Dynasty to the Hellenistic period.

63
A wooden standing figure of the
Lady Tui.

64
Queen Karomama, the wife of Osorkon II
(Twenty-Second Dynasty). The statue is
bronze, inlaid with precious metals.

65

The sky goddess Nut stretched across the curved lid of a sarcophagus as a protection for the mummy (Tanis, Nineteenth Dynasty)

A black granite statue from Tanis of the priest Panemerit. The head is in the Cairo Museum, the body in the Louvre.

6₇

A falcon's head in gold, from Hieraconopolis.

68

A gold mummy mask of Shashank II, as it was found at Tanis.

69

The Apis bull was an incarnation of the god Ptah of Memphis. This statue is from the Serapeum at Saqqara.

71

Dog-headed baboons worshipping the sun, from the foot of the Luxor obelisk, dating from the time of Ramses II. The baboons were believed to greet the sun with their cries and chattering at its rising and setting.

72

The sacred cow of Hathor protecting Tuthmosis III. The statue is of painted limestone and comes from the temple at Deir el Bahari.

70

(*opposite, below*) This pink granite lion once guarded the entrance to a temple at Tanis, and now stands in a public garden in Cairo.

73
A pendant representing the ram of Amon in front of its stall. The figure is made of gold and lapis lazuli, and is intended to be placed in the shrine. It comes from the tomb of Psusennes at Tanis.

74
A bright blue glazed composition figure of a hippopotamus decorated with aquatic plants.

Bas-Reliefs
and Paintings

75
Ti watches his
men armed with
harpoons and
ropes engaged in
a hippopotamus
hunt in front of
a papyrus thicket.
(From Ti,
Saqqara – Fifth
Dynasty).

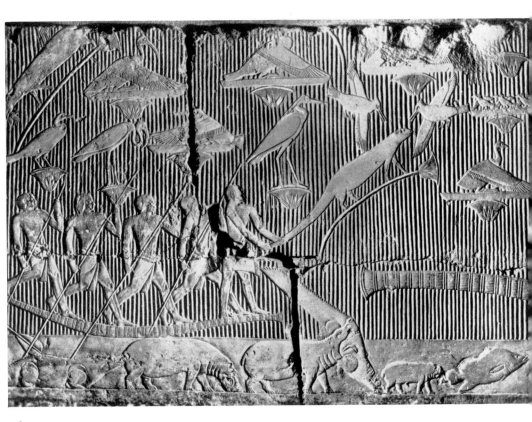

76
This marsh scene shows hunters and marsh-dwellers. Hippopotamus and crocodile can
be seen in the water, and in the papyrus thicket an ichneumon is stalking birds. (From
Merruka, Saqqara, Fifth Dynasty).

77
Reaping and gathering in the harvest, from Ti, Saqqara (Sixth Dynasty).

78
Herdsman carrying a calf across a canal, watched by the worried mother. (Ti, Saqqara, Fifth Dynasty).

79
An agricultural scene, showing cattle being led and various birds. (Ptah-hotep, Saqqara, Sixth Dynasty).

80
Prisoners being brought into the presence of the scribes. (Merruka, Saqqara, Fifth Dynasty).

81

Representations of various sports and pastimes. At the top boys are wrestling, in the centre section men are seen returning from the hunt, and at the bottom various types of desert game are depicted. (Ptah-hotep, Saqqara, Sixth Dynasty).

82

Carpenters building boats. (Ti, Saqqara, Fifth Dynasty).

83

Metalworkers weighing, smelting and pouring the metal. At the bottom of the illustration dwarves are shown holding up a collar they have made. (Merruka, Saqqara, Sixth Dynasty).

84

Stela of Ahmosis, the founder of the Eighteenth Dynasty, and his wife Queen Tetisheri.
The text records that Ahmose is telling his wife of his determination to do further honour
to the memory of his ancestors.

85

The Rosetta Stone, with the decree of Ptolemy Epiphanes in three different versions. By means of this tri-lingual text Champollion was able to decipher the hieroglyphic writing.

86

The Judging of the Dead. The heart of the deceased is being weighed against the feather of Truth. Anubis holds the balance and Thoth records the result. This and the next illustration are from the Papyrus of Ani in the British Museum.

87

Occupations of the dead in the fields of Ialu.

88

Cattle census, a New Kingdom Theban painting.

89

(*right*) Nebamun is hunting with the boomerang, and his cat is acting as retriever – a New Kingdom Theban painting.

Furniture and Precious Objects

90

The bed of Queen Hetepheres (Fourth Dynasty), the mother of Cheops.

91

A wooden carrying chair overlaid with gold, belonging to Queen Hetepheres. The original burial site of the queen was plundered soon after her death, and Cheops ordered the remainder of her funerary furniture to be removed to a secret hiding place not far from his pyramid.

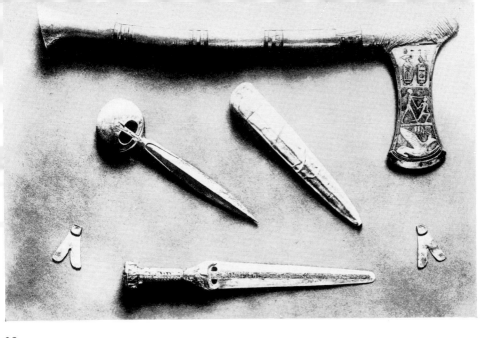

92

Costly weapons from the tomb of Queen Iah-hetep.

93

The axe-blade of Queen Iah-hetep bears the cartouches of Ahmose and a scene of the king smiting his enemy. Beneath this group is a winged gryphon and the inscription 'Beloved of Mont' – the Theban war god.

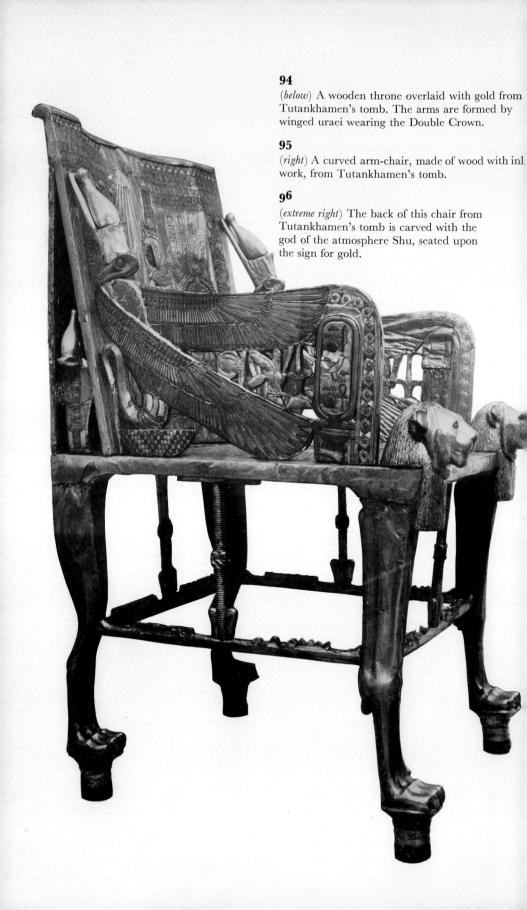

94

(*below*) A wooden throne overlaid with gold from Tutankhamen's tomb. The arms are formed by winged uraei wearing the Double Crown.

95

(*right*) A curved arm-chair, made of wood with inl work, from Tutankhamen's tomb.

96

(*extreme right*) The back of this chair from Tutankhamen's tomb is carved with the god of the atmosphere Shu, seated upon the sign for gold.

97
Chair from the tomb of Tutankhamen. The seat is painted in imitation of hide and the back is inlaid with glass and semi-precious stones.

99
Girls swim among fish and water lilies in this silver dish from Psusennes' tomb at Tanis.

98
(*left*) The queen is seen offering her husband a bouquet in this scene on the lid of a casket from Tutankhamen's tomb.

100
A silver jug with a gold handle in the form of a goat, and various other objects from the treasure found at Bubastis.

101 and 102

Two dishes from a set of gold plate used by the king when travelling. From Psusennes' tomb, Tanis.

103

The crown of the Princess Khnemit, from Dashur. The wire is of gold, and the flowers strung on it are inlaid with lapis lazuli and carnelian.

104

Amenemhat III is shown smiting foreign enemies, while the vulture goddess spreads her wings over him, in this pectoral found at Dashur.

105

Pectoral belonging to Shashank II, from Tanis. The scarab beetle in the centre is flanked by uraei wearing the crowns of Upper Egypt.

106

The name of Shashank I is inscribed on the inside of this bracelet of gold inlaid with coloured glass.

107

Wooden and ivory spoon in the shape of a swimming girl (New Kingdom).

108

Gold jug inscribed with the name of Psusennes, from his burial at Tanis.

109

A pectoral of gold, inlaid with glass and semi-precious stones, from the burial of Shashank I at Tanis. The sun-boat, protected by Maat, sails across the primordial waters; the star-studded sky is held up by the plants symbolic of the North and the South of Egypt.

110

The reverse side of the pectoral.

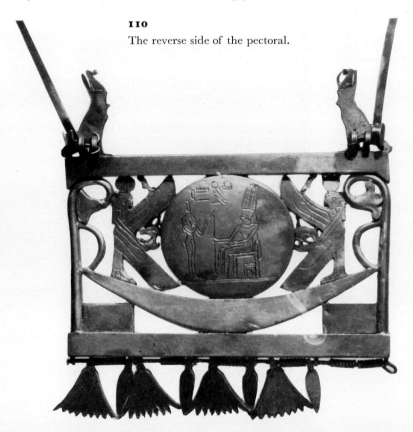

reference has already been made. The coffin, a simple wooden chest, and part of the funerary furniture, were placed in an underground vault, while provisions were stored in cells. The deceased had at his disposal food and drink, an amazingly abundant and varied selection of earthenware dishes, weapons, pottery, various games which were early forms of the game of goose, draughts and chess, toilet requisites, and even an oar.

The tomb of Hesire, which belongs to a somewhat later period, was decorated with wooden panels carved with magnificent portraits of the deceased, the list of his official titles, and pictures of food and drink, and articles of clothing (fig. 48). On the rough-cast walls, various useful or valuable objects were represented such as ointment jars and toilet boxes.[9] The requirements of the deceased were still very modest.

The great monument of Zoser

At the beginning of the Third Dynasty, there occurred a revolution in funerary architecture. Stone took the place of brick. Zoser's tomb was a huge monument built entirely in stone and, thanks to the efforts and publications of the *Service des Antiquités*,[10] we are familiar with the details of the lay-out, in spite of the damage it has suffered at various periods.

The king's tomb chamber was built of granite at the bottom of a wide shaft nearly a hundred feet deep. An opening was left in the ceiling to allow the mummy to be put through, and was afterwards blocked by a granite plug. Smaller shafts led to more vaults which were intended for the queen and the princes. The long corridor leading down to the vault was intersected by the famous blue chambers, the walls of which were lined with turquoise blue tiles all impeccably fitted together. Three stelae were inserted into the tiles, each one surrounded by a frame, and all exquisitely engraved. The king is shown consecrating monuments and performing other ritual actions.

Other corridors were piled with vases made of alabaster, schist, breccia and other stone, almost all of which had been broken by parts of the ceiling falling on them. They date not from Zoser's reign but from the first two dynasties, the kings of which must have deposited them in temples or in their own tombs. Perhaps Zoser had assembled them and stored them in the corridors of his own pyramid in order to get the benefit of offerings which belonged by rights to former kings.

The Step Pyramid was built over the underground chambers;

it was the first of its kind and was not designed as such at the beginning. It started off as a simple mastaba, then became a four-step pyramid nearly two hundred feet high. It finally became a six-step pyramid. It was literally the staircase by which the king would leave the earth to become united with Nut, his mother.

The sacred area, in the centre of which stood the pyramid, is enclosed by a stone wall, in itself an admirable achievement. In the style of the old brick mastabas, it has fourteen false doors, framed by alternating recesses and projections, carved along the outside. A single real door gives access to the interior. The wall spans a second shaft as wide and as deep as the first, and at the foot of which is a tomb vault exactly like the king's, only smaller. This leads to a chamber lined with blue tiles, and containing three stelae which, like the others, commemorate royal foundations. This second tomb has greatly puzzled archaeologists, because there is no indication of its purpose. It was not built for the queen, nor for the royal children, since they occupied small tombs near the royal vault. Snofru and Amenemhat III, who built two pyramids, face us with a similar problem.

After entering by the single real door, the visitor would walk along a covered gallery at the end of which was an imitation half-open door carved in stone. This led into the huge rectangle on which stood the pyramid, a ruined temple and several dummy buildings, solid masses of masonry, faced with fine limestone and adorned with extraordinary engaged columns, which are, if I am not mistaken, replicas of the buildings the consecration of which is depicted on the stelae in the underground chambers: temples to Nekhebet, Horus of Edfu, and Thoth of Khnum, which the architect Imhotep had constructed in fine white stone. To the north of the pyramid lay another temple, where the cult of the dead king was celebrated. His statue could watch the performance of the religious ceremonies through two openings in the stone screen of the recess in which it was set.

Thus Zoser's great pyramid, and staircase to heaven, was planned and built in order to ensure the preservation of his mummy and of the royal mummies, against all possible dangers. It immortalized the memory of his worthiest achievements and housed the superb plates and dishes which had been made for former kings. The cult of the deceased king was celebrated here – and perhaps posthumous jubilees too. We cannot claim to have entirely understood the intentions of the builders. Whatever they were, Egypt had by now resolutely embarked on a certain course from which she would never deviate. The Egyptians were indefatigable in the services they rendered to the dead, and in the first place to the deceased kings. It was no longer enough to preserve their bodies: the memory of their deeds must also be immortalized, and they must be allowed to fulfil the destiny imagined for them. Even at this early period, the gods and the dead claimed the major part of Egypt's resources. A whole people was to toil for them in the mines and quarries, and precious materials were to be sent for from distant lands. This may have been a mad extravagance, but it won for Egypt her place among the great civilisations of the world.

The pyramids of Snofru and of his successors

The Third Dynasty remained faithful to the step pyramid. The last of its kings, Huni, was probably buried in the pyramid at Medum, which stands on a mound of sand and rubble a little to the north of the Fayum. Initially this splendid monument was a step pyramid, like Zoser's, with seven steps. It was turned into a true pyramid by Snofru, the founder of the Fourth Dynasty, who added a temple of welcome and an ascending causeway. This explains why the scribes who visited Medum throughout the ages recorded only the name of Snofru.[11]

An official decree issued by Pepi I formally ascribed to Snofru two other pyramids both situated near the village of Dahshur, and now referred to as the Dahshur pyramids.[12] The Southern Pyramid is unique of its kind.[13] Its angle of incline changes just over half-way up, it has two separate entrances, two galleries and two chambers with fantastically high ceilings. The name of Snofru was inscribed on the stones in red ink by quarrymen, and can be read on some of the door-posts. It was to Snofru that the domains represented on the small temple were offering gifts, although it is not certain that the king's body was ever housed in either of the two chambers. Architects hold the view that it was for reasons of economy that the angle of its slope was changed half-way up, although the chiefs of works at this period were not normally given to worrying about such considerations. Architects also believe that the chambers were rebuilt because there was some anxiety about the solidity of the first series. Finally they believe that the Bent Pyramid served no useful purpose, a fact which has not been proved.[14] We can only hope that if one day we are able to explain the double shaft in Zoser's pyramid, we shall also be in a position to solve the problem of Snofru's funerary monument.

The Northern Pyramid is over three hundred feet high and by common consent is attributed to Snofru. The interior is in a bad state of repair and we do not know if anyone was ever buried in the sarcophagus. Less care and attention have been devoted to the study of the surroundings of this pyramid than is the case with most others.

Proceeding in chronological order, we now come to the great Pyramid of Cheops at Giza, Dedefra's Pyramid at Abu-Roash, which was robbed of its stones down to the base during the Middle Ages, the Pyramid of Chephren which was almost as large as that of Cheops, and the much smaller Pyramid of Mycerinus, both these last being situated at Giza. For reasons which have never been explained, Shepseskaf abandoned the pyramidal form and built his tomb in the shape of a huge sarcophagus. However, no one else followed his example.[15] At Abusir, a little to the south of Giza, three kings of the Fifth Dynasty built pyramids which were replicas on a smaller scale of the monuments erected by their famous ancestors. Isesi came back to Saqqara, and Unas, his successor, as well as the kings of the Sixth Dynasty, in the main followed the plan of the Step Pyramid.

From the time of Snofru onwards, the complex of buildings which comprised the royal tomb ceased to be confined within the enclosure wall. It began at the edge of the desert, where the building which we call the Valley Building or the Temple of Welcome was erected. From there an ascending causeway led to the Mortuary Temple which was built against one face of the pyramid but without any communicating door between the two.

All these monuments have been severely damaged. Of the Valley Buildings the one built by Chephren is in the best state of preservation; its granite pillars seem to defy the centuries. We possess, however, a few magnificent bas-reliefs from the causeway of Unas. The Mortuary Temples which, from the Fifth Dynasty onwards, were built of limestone, were used to feed the lime kilns. Thanks to the pious devotion of Egyptians to the lion-headed goddess, part of the upper temple of Sahure has been preserved. Many fine statues have been rescued from the temples of Dedefra, Chephren, Mycerinus and Userkaf. Some bas-reliefs emphasize the divine nature of the king. Others recall glorious episodes of his reign, such as the receiving of booty from Libya, or the launching of a fleet, perhaps setting out for Byblos to bring back a new royal spouse. Supplies are being sent to a tribe of Bedouin who are in the grip of a terrible famine. A picture of the conveying of a palm-column by ship suggests that all the operations which the building of the pyramids entailed were probably recorded in frescoes and bas-reliefs. The king is shown firing his arrows at antelopes, which have been lured into a narrow pass in the desert. Representatives from estates founded by the king offer him gifts. Peasants and craftsmen pursue their daily tasks.

Cattle are being slaughtered for the daily repast. In this respect the king's needs were no different from those of the rest of humanity.

When the king died, his body was taken to the Valley Building and there the ritual ceremonies of purification and embalmment were carried out. These took at least seventy days, after which the mummy was dressed and adorned, swathed in bandages and laid inside the sarcophagus. The protective portcullises were lowered into position and the entrance closed. A new life was about to begin for the deceased king. Architects had either hollowed out, or built, a number of additional structures to help the king in the next life, but it is not always possible to establish what their purpose was. For instance, small secondary pyramids have been found inside the main enclosure, against the wall; these were from fifty to sixty feet high and contained a gallery and a chamber which was, however, too small to house the body of an adult. Nothing has ever been found inside the small pyramids which might enlighten us as to their purpose.[16]

In 1954, the *Service des Antiquités d'Egypte*, while engaged in clearing away the loose rubble from the south side of the Pyramid of Cheops, unearthed two rectangular caches covered over with huge slabs of limestone. When the roofing slabs were removed from the first cache, which lay to the west, a pit containing a huge boat made of cedarwood was disclosed. The boat had been dismantled and the various parts placed in the pit side by side. After several years of hard work, it was reassembled and could, if necessary, be launched on the river. It is more than one hundred feet long and the prow is shaped like a papyrus head. The planks of the hull are held together by rope. It has cross-beams with bosses at each end to help it to withstand the pressure of the water. A cabin of elegant design stands on the deck. The fittings include oars for rowing as well as steering oars.[17]

However great one's admiration for Egyptian achievements may already be, one cannot but be astounded by this superb example of the boat-builder's art. It would be interesting to know why it was buried so close to the pyramid; the answer can only be given when the contents of the second pit have been examined with the same care and attention as were devoted to the first. It seems very probable that another boat lies concealed inside the second pit. Pictures of boats making pilgrimages to sacred towns, such as Pe, Dep, Zedu and Abydos, occur frequently on tombs of all periods. The barque bearing the deceased king was towed by a tug. This probably explains the significance of the boat we have just described; the king had the power to leave his house of stone, to reassemble or order the reassembling of the various parts of his boat and journey by magical

Fig. 47. The awakening and ascension of the King, on the Tomb of Shashank III at Tanis. After being awakened, the king is pushed and pulled towards the day-boat, which is waiting on the left, and the night-boat, which is waiting on the right.

means to the sacred regions, then return to his pyramid without anyone suspecting that he had ever left it. The dismantled boat could, indeed, only be used through the intervention of magic.

In the immediate vicinity of the pyramids of the Fourth Dynasty, varying numbers of boat-shaped pits have been discovered. The fragments of objects found inside would seem to have collected there by chance, and do not explain for what purpose the pits were intended. If I am not mistaken, they were dummies like the buildings in Zoser's pyramid enclosure. The solar barqes, the *manzet* required for the daily journey across the heavens, and the *mesketet* for the nightly journey, were no doubt supposed to alight in them when fetching the king or taking him back (fig. 47). These pits disappeared at the beginning of the Fifth Dynasty when sun-temples began to be built in the vicinity of the later pyramids. The sun-temples were vast courtyards with porticos, and in the centre of which rose a huge obelisk built of dressed blocks of stone. Outside the courtyard, and a short distance from it, lay a huge barque built of unbaked brick which was obviously waiting to receive the *manzet* and the *mesketet* and which fulfilled, but more conveniently, the same purpose as the boat-shaped pits.[18]

Inscriptions on the pyramids

With Unas, the last king of the Fifth Dynasty, an important change occurred. Until now the pyramid walls had been completely bare. The red ink inscriptions found on some of the stone blocks were made by the quarrymen and were not intended to be visible once building operations had been completed. The names of the kings were inscribed only in the two temples and along the causeway. But from the time of Unas onwards, the various chapters of what was virtually an entire book were engraved on the walls of the corridors and chambers. The same texts, with variations, additions or omissions, are also found in the Sixth Dynasty pyramids of Teti, Pepi I, Merenra and Pepi II, in the pyramids of Pepi II's queens, and in the pyramid of a later king called Ibi.[19]

These writings cannot be compared either to the Bible, or to the Koran. They consist of a collection of spells designed to provide the king with everything he might need, to help him to overcome hostile forces and to make life easier for him in the other world. Although the movement from one idea to the next often appears disconcerting to the modern mind, several episodes emerge clearly and vividly. The Pyramid Texts provide us with an account of the creation of the world according to the Heliopolitan cosmogony, a list of divine dynasties, the story of Seth's quarrel with Osiris, then with Horus, as well as a mass of information about local deities and even about neighbouring countries. Since their discovery in 1880, the Pyramid Texts have been of absorbing interest to Egyptologists and have proved to be well worth all the efforts expended on them. The sacred quality which theologians and worshippers alike had attributed to the pyramids from the very first[20] was considerably heightened by the addition of the religious texts. From this time onwards, the mothers, wives and daughters of the king started to include in their titulary, instead of the name of the reigning king as had been their usual practice, the name of the pyramid. The pyramid was held to be the king himself, not the man of flesh and blood who was doomed to die, but a being destined to live eternally and who could ensure that they too would live for ever.[21]

Tombs of the queens and courtiers

The chief royal spouse was entitled to a smaller pyramid which contained a vault and a funerary temple. Recent excavations have made it possible to attribute the small pyramids next to the pyramid of the king at Saqqara to the three queens of Pepi II. The small pyramids situated in the vicinity of the Pyramids of Cheops, Chephren and Mycerinus undoubtedly contained the tombs of queens. A remarkable discovery made in this area was that of a shaft, with a most skilfully camouflaged entrance, and leading to a chamber containing the magnificent funerary equipment of Queen Hetephras, the wife of Snofru and mother of Cheops.[22] Hetephras probably outlived her husband and spent the last years of her life with her son, who no doubt saw to his mother's burial. However, we do not know where she was buried because no mummy was found in the alabaster sarcophagus.

Low, solid buildings which, since the time of Mariette's excavations have been called mastabas, were grouped round every pyramid like houses round a village church. They were the tombs of princes, courtiers, and high-ranking officials who had died during the king's reign. They themselves did not choose the sites. It was the king who decided where they should be buried; he would often make known his decision to the person concerned when inspecting the work in progress on his own pyramid, and at the same time grant the favoured subject blocks of fine white stone from Tura. Inside the mastabas were vertical shafts – usually two in number – which terminated in a tomb-chamber containing a huge sarcophagus. Even as early as the Fourth Dynasty, the sarcophagus was often adorned with false doors which served the same purpose as those on the royal monuments. On his death, a prince also became an Osiris; his limbs were supposed to pass through the doors in order to be reassembled inside. Valuable objects like the beautiful gold belt recently found at Saqqara were placed on the mummy or laid inside the tomb-chamber.[23] At ground level, a door leads into a single room, or more often into a succession of rooms, where the master, either modelled in the round or depicted in low-relief, is shown welcoming his visitors. The walls are divided up into huge panels on which scenes of every-day life are portrayed – the cultivation of crops, hunting, fishing, every aspect of the marsh-dweller's existence, cattle-breeding, hunt-ing in the desert, the making of beer and bread, and the work of various craftsmen. Scribes are keeping a check on all these operations. We are shown boats being built and launched immediately they are finished; we even see children at play, musical and dancing enter-tainments, and water-tournaments. The visitor would imagine himself to be in the fine mansion of some nobleman rather than in a tomb, if he did not, sooner or later, come across scenes which show the slaughtering and cutting-up of animals as butcher-meat, and series of men carrying these pieces of meat and accompanied by others laden with loaves of bread, jugs and baskets. The procession leads to a table. The first group of men have already put down their load. The dead man, who is seated in front of the table, can choose from the bill of fare, a long list of viands and drinks. Scholars have put forward the idea that the scenes depicting the various arts and crafts were merely preparatory to the presentation of the offerings which preceded the dead man's repast. It should be noted, however, that the provisions piled up in front of the table do not correspond exactly to those inscribed on the bill of fare, nor indeed does the whole series of scenes correspond to the requirements of the dead man. For instance, great prominence is given to fishing, and the dead men did not eat fish. Similarly, prominence is given to hunting in the desert, yet the slaughtered cattle provided the required amount of meat. Why was the master of the tomb not shown carrying out the official duties, often very important, which he performed during his lifetime? The answer is, no doubt, that the artists drew their subject-matter from stock themes which had been created and prudently embellished throughout the whole of the Old Kingdom, and which aimed at giving the spectator a vision of what was known as the *per-zet*, the everlasting domain. In the narrower sense, the expression referred to the tomb itself, but more generally, it was the name of the ideal region imagined by the Egyptians. Their ideal world was based on observation of the world of reality, but it was a paradise from which all forms of disaster – such as hail, locusts, epidemics, and robberies – had been banished. In short, the *per-zet* was Egypt without the plagues. The individual lived there in the prime of life, along with his ever-young and beautiful wife and surrounded by his children (fig. 49), and his staff of scribes, valets, stewards and craftsmen who remained in his service. The middle-

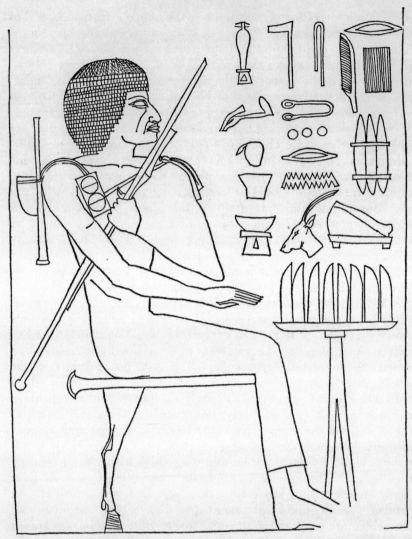

Fig. 48. The funerary repast, from a panel on the Tomb of Hasire. At all periods, this was the main theme depicted on tombs.

classes were buried in modest tombs, like those found at Saqqara and at Beni-Hasan. For the poor, there was only the communal pit. As for those unfortunate wretches who were overcome by the intense heat as they hauled the granite blocks, or who died on the road-side as the result of a butt or a kick from an animal, they were either left lying where they had fallen or thrown into the Nile, where the fish soon gobbled them up. The appalling inequality between those who possessed a tomb, however small, and the poorer classes who did not, was, however, offset by one factor. It has already been mentioned that those who belonged to what we call the official or higher civil servant class had both their names and their offices inscribed on the walls of their masters' tombs. Their subordinates were only referred to by the name of their trade or craft. But they could at least be sure of having a place in the 'perpetual domain' similar to that which had been theirs during their lifetime.

In the days of the Old Kingdom, the Egyptians did their utmost to ensure that after death each man retained the rank to which he had risen: the Pharaoh was considered as a god, the princes and courtiers as great lords; the various officials were treated in accordance with the posts they had held, and so on, down the line. As yet, there was no thought of rewarding the meek in the hereafter, or of punishing the wicked.

When the king made his plans for the building of his pyramid, he always appointed a certain number of persons to attend to the ritual of worship after his burial. To be a member of the personnel in charge of a king's pyramid was a coveted honour. The ritual of worship also involved expenses for which the king had to make provision. The Dahshur stela proves that Pepi I brought back into force certain rules concerning the privileges enjoyed by, and the obligations imposed upon, the town that Snofru founded for the building and upkeep of his two pyramids and the perpetual celebration of his funerary rites. Near certain pyramids a number of stelae have been found, proving that the cult of some monarch of the Old Kingdom was still practised under the Twelfth Dynasty.[24]

Following the king's example, the owner of a fine tomb, although he knew that all his needs would be provided for, was anxious that the provisions laid in his tomb on the day of his burial should be periodically renewed. Part of his estate was set aside for this purpose, and any of his heirs who failed to respect his wishes were threatened with severe penalties.[25]

The heirs of the dead man used to visit the tomb on the first day of the new year and on all the prescribed feast-days of the particular burial-ground. In the wall dividing the public rooms from the recess holding the statue of the deceased, or perhaps the statues of both him and his wife, there was a slit. The perfume of the terebinth or incense that the descendants of the dead burned in front of this slit was thought to reach the nostrils of the departed. Provisions were laid on an offering table, which was either placed in front of a statue, as in Merruka's tomb, or, as was the more general practice, in front of the stela.

During the Middle Kingdom, the performance of the funerary rites underwent certain changes. The *Ka* had now only one servant, as a rule the eldest son, who acted more or less as his father's executor. During his lifetime, a man of importance would set aside a considerable portion of the wealth he derived from the dues paid him as governor of a province and chief of the local priesthood, or from possessions left him by his father, in order to provide remuneration for the priests, whose task it would be to associate his memory with all the temple ceremonies. They would light candles in the temple and let them slowly burn away in front of statues of the dead man, and they would sing as they walked in procession from the temples to the tomb in order to leave bread and beer there. In short, the family depended on the professional priests for the accomplishment of the many duties entailed by the funerary cult.[26]

Hapidefai, when he made arrangements which were to prove very costly for his descendants, declared that if any of his royal successors made the slightest alteration in them he would be most distressed. Yet, in spite of threats, in spite of contracts drawn up in due form in government offices and inscribed on the tombs, the funerary monuments were exposed to the same dangers as all other property. Carelessness and the destructive instinct are common to all times and all countries. Among the visitors to the tombs there were always some people who were capable of damaging the statues, the inscriptions or the offering tables, either out of spite or stupidity; who raised their voices inside the tomb, or entered without observing the purification ritual which all women and sick people were supposed to perform, or after partaking of food forbidden by the spirits – fish, for instance. The deceased was thought to be able to punish the culprits, either by wringing their necks as if they were chickens, or by rousing the anger of the serpent or the crocodile against them. He could even bring an action against them, before the Great God. This threat, frequently expressed in inscriptions, establishes the existence of the idea of a supraterrestrial court, whose purpose was not perhaps simply to see that people respected the funerary monuments.

The dead often appealed to the living, earnestly requesting some charitable word or deed: 'O you who are on earth and who pass by this tomb, pour me out some water. Let my funerary repast appear, made up of all the things which you are bringing with you.'[27] In order to strengthen his appeal, the deceased may point out that it is to the advantage of passers-by to comply with his requests: 'O you who are on earth, whether chief of the servants of the god, or dressers or lamp-tenders in the temple of The Majesty of my master, may the king live for you if you pronounce, on my behalf, the *pert-kheru* ("that which is created by the voice").'[28] If the deceased were a scholarly man, he might introduce some variety into the expressions. Such a man was Nebpusesotris, who addressed the priesthood of the temple of Abydos, and the priests of the royal chapels in the following terms:

'The king shall be rejuvenated in your life. The monuments of your city gods shall stand fast for you. Ye shall be in the favour of your sovereign, ye shall hand on your offices to your children, ye shall not hunger, ye shall not thirst . . . according as ye shall say: "An offering which the king gives to Osiris, Lord of Abydos, even the great god Onnophris (Unnefer), a thousand loaves of bread, beer, oxen and fowl, invocation offerings at every feast to the spirit of the keeper of the diadem, and attendant of the great house of Nebpusesotris".'[29]

The Egyptians were fond of thinking in terms of contrasting ideas. Hapidefai of Siut, in his appeal, underlines the difference between the well-behaved visitors and the more unruly ones. The latter, who raise their voices inside his tomb, damage his inscriptions and wreck his statue, will be smitten by the anger of Thoth. The good visitors who pronounce the divine formula: 'May the king present a royal offering . . . etc.' will live to be old men in their towns and become *imakus* in their nomes.[30]

The judgment of the dead and the negative statements

Another way the deceased had of influencing the passer-by was to express a very high opinion of himself:

'I am beloved of people. Never since my birth, have I ever been chastised in front of any magistrate. Never have I taken anything from anyone by violence.'
'I am beloved of my father, my mother's favourite. I love my brothers and sisters. I have given bread to the hungry, water to the thirsty, clothes to the naked and I have ferried those who had no boat across the water.'

These self-laudatory declarations would have much more weight if they were pronounced by some tribunal, or by the Great God who protects the dead in their tombs. And, in fact, the ancient Egyptians must be given credit for having conceived the idea of the judging of the dead before they are allowed entry into the next world. The terms of judgment after death were codified, once and for all, at the beginning of the New Kingdom, but before then theologians had given much thought to this difficult problem.

Timid references to the subject can be found as early as those passages of the Pyramid Texts which relate to the judging of the

deceased king: 'King N wishes to be justified through his actions.'
It was, after all, in the interests of the gods, who were preparing to
welcome the dead king, not to allow a wolf to slip into the fold.
However, it is not until the First Intermediate Period that we find
an unmistakable reference to judgment in the other world; it occurs
in the moral testament which King Kheti drew up for Merikara, his
son and heir.

'Go with quiet step towards the Other World . . . Thou knowest that
the court which judges transgressors is not lenient at the hour when it
passes sentence on the wretched and carries out its function. Woe to the
sinner, if the accuser is well informed. Do not trust in length of years,
for they look upon a life's span as but an hour. When man remains after
death, his deeds are heaped beside him. What is there is there for all
eternity. He who practises that which is condemned is a madman. But
he who reaches the other world without wrong-doing shall exist there
like a god.'[31]

Thus an infallible and incorruptible court awaited the Egyptians,
and on its verdict depended eternal happiness or unhappiness. An
episode of a tale composed at a late period, and rightly compared
to the tale of the rich man in the New Testament, shows beyond all
doubt that the belief in judgment after death was perfectly in keeping
with Egyptian views.

According to the story, the father of the little boy, Setna, saw two
funeral processions moving towards the necropolis, one being that
of a rich man, the other that of a poor man, and he looked with
envy on the first. However, his son, who knew the secrets of the Other
World, revealed the horrible punishment that would be meted out
to the rich man and the favoured treatment the poor but virtuous
man would enjoy. He explained that those called to judgment are
divided into three groups: those whose misdeeds outweighed their
good actions are handed over to the Devouress; the good are led
before the council of the gods; finally those whose good and bad
deeds were equally balanced are covered with Sokar-Osiris amulets[32]
and have to act as servants.

It is significant that the earlier of these two texts was written by
a king for another king. The attributes of Osiris were initially
bestowed only on the deceased king, then later extended to the mass
of the people. The idea of heavenly judgment appears to have
followed a similar pattern. At any rate, between the warnings issued
to Merikara and the explanations of Setna's son occurs what is
perhaps the most famous piece of religious imagery handed down by
the ancient world: the weighing of the actions, and the text which

provides a commentary for it, chapter 125 of the *Book of the Dead*.[33]
Between the Eighteenth Dynasty, and the Late Period, both texts
and the illustrations underwent only very minor changes.

After being ushered into a hall called the Hall of the Two Truths,
the deceased, who has already become Osiris N, salutes the Great
God and his forty-two assistants. Then, after declaring that he has,
generally speaking, shunned iniquity, he proceeds to utter thirty-six
negative statements – the number never varied – statements such
as: 'I have not acted sinfully towards men.' After the final statement:
'I have not obstructed the god in his comings forth', he repeats four
times: 'I am purified', and concludes with the statement that no
evil can happen to him in this land because he knows the names
of the forty-two gods. He then utters his declarations of innocence
again, addressing the forty-two gods one after the other, and being
careful in each case to state the divinity's place of origin: 'On
Broad-Stride-that-comes-out-of-Heliopolis, I have committed no sin.'

When he has finished doing this, he abandons the negative form
and declares that he has done what men have told him to do, and
that which pleases the gods. 'I have satisfied the god with that which
he desires. I have given bread to the hungry, water to the thirsty,
clothing to the naked and a ferry to him who had no boat.' His
mouth is pure, and so are his hands. He has even heard the ass and
the cat conversing (the text of this dialogue has unfortunately not
come down to us) in the temple of him who opens the mouth
(Sobek?) He feels that he has already been granted remission of his
sins, because he has taken the precaution of calling upon his heart
not to undo him because it, perhaps, is better acquainted with his
innocence than are the gods.

'Heart of my mother, heart of my various forms, rise not up against me
as a witness. Oppose me not in the court of justice. Send not the balance
down against me before the Guardian of the Scales. For thou art the Ka
which is in my body, thou art Khnum who strengtheneth my limbs.
Mayest thou attain to that good whereto I aspire. Let not my name be in
bad odour with the court. Speak no lie against me.'

His heart, then, remains silent. Anubis steadies the scales and notes
that the two sides balance each other perfectly. Thoth records the
result and declares the deceased *maa-kheru*, 'true of voice'.

Few texts have been commented upon as fully as chapter 125,[34]
but certain problems remain unsolved. It is difficult to explain why
there should be two sets of confessions, which overlap to a certain
extent. Several sins which are denied in the first set are also denied
in the second, and in almost identical terms. The deceased then

twice protests that he has not stolen, killed, lied or done anything which might offend public morality. Certain differences, however, can be detected. The first text accords great importance to respect for sacred property, horned animals, sacred birds and fish, the weights and measures used in business transactions (but also by the tax-collectors) and the regulations relating to irrigation. Statement A27 is rather touching: 'I have not snatched away milk from the mouths of sucklings.' The author, whoever he may have been, certainly merits the epithet positivistic which has been applied to him. The author of the second confession, on the other hand, was something of a moralist, because he makes the deceased protest that he has never been envious, or told lies, or pried into other people's affairs, or talked too much, or acted deceitfully; another of his assertions is that he has never reviled the king, whereas the first set of confessions makes no reference to this subject.

It should be noted that the first list of confessions is shorter than the second since it consists of thirty-six negative statements, as opposed to forty-two. These figures were probably not arrived at by chance. There were thirty-six Decans (units of time). Perhaps this was meant to suggest that the deceased had committed no sin from one year's end to the next. There were certainly forty-two nomes, but this figure was reached only at a relatively late period. When the first *Book of the Dead* appeared, there were still only thirty-eight nomes. Text B, however, reveals a certain interest in geographical considerations, because the deceased, when calling upon the forty-two gods in turn, is careful to start each statement by announcing the place of origin of each god: a town, a nome, a shrine or necro-polis, or a grotto; or again, some geographical entity such as the West, the sky, darkness, dawn or the primeval waters. In Text A, the deceased speaks in the first person: 'I have not acted sinfully towards people.' In Text B he prefers to use the third person: 'Oh Breaker-of-Bones-that-came-out-of-Nen-nesu (Heracleopolis), N has not uttered falsehoods.'

It is possible that the two texts, which were composed separately, at different periods and in different places, were combined when chapter 125 was given its final form. In other countries, some attempt would no doubt have been made to cut out the verbal repetitions; the Egyptians, however, had a respect for the written word; 'Neither add nor strike out a single word,' was the advice given by the sage Ptah-hotep.

Whether there were initially two or more authors, they all adopted the negative form which gives both sets of confessions their striking originality, and which would have been difficult to explain if the gods had not expressly and clearly forbidden all those actions which the deceased denies having committed. The statement A10 is a formal admission of this: 'I have not done that which the gods forbid.' In the preceding chapter, we stressed the fact that the god of each locality prohibited a certain action, often several actions. Prohibitions of this sort were not – at least in the beginning – concerned with either morality or public health. The god forbade people to harm certain animal species, which he had placed under his protection, or which he reserved for his own use. Similarly, he prohibited certain actions either because they were considered contrary to universal morality, or because they had unpleasant associations for him. If we compare some of the negative statements with certain prohibitions, the connexion between the two becomes immediately obvious.

'O Iremibef-coming-out-from-Tebu, I have not fouled water' (B 36). The god of Tebu, capital of the Tenth Nome of Upper Egypt, was a hippopotamus who lived in the swamps and was unlikely to allow anyone to muddy his chosen element.

'O Harbinger-of-Battles-coming-out-of-Unes (a town of Seth in the Nineteenth Nome), N has caused neither trouble nor strife' (B 25). Seth was essentially a quarrelsome god and did not want people to imitate his behaviour. In other words, this is a case similar to the previous one.

'O Thou-who-comest-out-of-Tepeh-Zat (a suburb of Memphis), N has not committed sodomy' (B 36). Sodomy was considered to be a vice, and was forbidden at Memphis and in two other nomes.

We certainly do not possess anything like a complete list of the things which were forbidden. Although some of the negative declarations do not correspond to an officially recognized prohibition, they at least echo what might be called an implied prohibition, in so far as it was in keeping with the nature of the god. Min, for instance, who was noted for his amorous exploits, could not approve of masturbation, which explains why we find in B 20: 'O Thou-who-comest-from-the-Temple-of-Min, N has not been guilty of self-pollution.'

Many declarations in the first confession, in particular those referring to temple property, the sacred animals, the pasture-lands, the diverting of the waters of the irrigation canals and the falsification of weights and measures, can be explained quite simply by the fact that several gods had placed a certain animal species under their protection, or had made a rule that it should not be harmed in any way, or had condemned the use of false weights and measures (as Amenemopet, the author of a famous piece of wisdom literature, was later to do).

It would even seem that the double confession did not entirely satisfy those whose consciences were more exacting. Some Egyptians had their own private confession inscribed on their funerary stela; for instance, the Vizier User, who attained a very high rank in the hierarchy of the priests of Amun at the time of the Eighteenth Dynasty.[35] In his capacity as officiating priest he took part in many ceremonies, and recalls the fact with considerable self-satisfaction. It does not take him long, however, to begin expressing himself in negative declarations:

'I did not raise my shoulder in the Temple of the Master of the Bowed. I did not hold my arm high in the Temple of Him who holds his Arm High. I did not raise my voice in the Temple of the Master of Silence. I did not utter falsehoods in the Temple of the Master of Truth. I did not . . . in the chapel of my god. I did not covet his offerings.'

Actions such as these might, with some justification, have been considered offensive by the god of the temple, Min, Osiris or Thoth, and they were in all probability forbidden by certain rules about which we have no information.

Ramses IV also introduced a personal note into the habitual confessional pattern.[36]

'I have not eaten that which is forbidden
I have not fished in the Lake of the god
I have not hunted the lion during the feast-days of Bastet
I have not pronounced the name of Tatenen' . . .

Fishing was generally allowed, but not, however, in the sacred pool. Lion-hunting was a favourite sport of the Pharaohs, but to indulge in it during the festivals of Bastet who, at this period, was represented with a lion's head, was held to be an improper, even perhaps an impious, action which the goddess would not forgive.

All this explains why chapter 125 contains two similar, yet not identical, confessions.

Plutarch, who was familiar with all the episodes of the Osirian Drama, relates that Isis, anxious lest her efforts and devotion might be forgotten, instituted certain very sacred mysteries to be both an example and a source of comfort to humanity.[37] Chapter 18 of the *Book of the Dead* gives a list of the privileged towns where the mysteries were enacted: Heliopolis, Zedu, Imet, Khem, Pe and Dep in the Delta; Ro-setau in the Memphite region; Naref near the Fayum; and Abydos in Upper Egypt. Several stelae at Abydos, and especially the stela of Ikhernofret, now in the Berlin Museum, give some idea of the mysteries which were performed in the town of Abydos.[38] They included a representation of the valiant battle waged by the supporters of Osiris round the god murdered by Seth. The supporters of Osiris would win and would move off towards his tomb, while Horus continued to fight the Sethites. Osiris, having been restored to life, would return to his temple and take his place on the throne surrounded by his divine court.

Certain references in the texts to legal charges brought by Seth against his victim, and which demonstrated his duplicity, indicate that the judgment scene was enacted in one of the above-mentioned towns.[39]

The assembled crowds derived great comfort from these performances, as several inscriptions testify:

'My sins are wiped out, my transgressions are swept away, my iniquities have been destroyed.'[40]

'You lay down your sins at Nen-Nesu . . .'[41]

'The great enchantress purifies you. You confess your sin, and it is destroyed for you.'[42]

'Homage to thee, Osiris, who art at Zedu. Thou hearest his words and thou wipest out his sin. Thou makest his voice just against his enemies, and he is strong against his tribunal on earth.'[43]

'The evil said against you does not exist.'[44]

A certain Zed-her, on whom was conferred the noble title of Saviour, says to his god:

'Thou hast established my house with my children. No fault was found in them when they appeared before the Lord of the Gods. Thou hast made me great in my town, and revered in my nome.'[45]

The worshippers felt comforted because they saw a parallel between themselves and the virtuous god; like him, they had been first accused, and then proclaimed innocent.

The mechanism of the process seems quite clear. Osiris proved his innocence, and his total obedience to the demands of all the gods. Following his example, the worshippers with one accord rid themselves of the burden of their sins. The first confession was made by Osiris; his was the confession of the 'first occurrence', because in Egypt there was always a 'first occurrence'. Then came the second confession, made by the worshippers. They were able to recite it without any feeling of hypocrisy, because they had become identified with the god.

So great were the changes which had occurred since the time

when the Egyptians were interested only in keeping the dead supplied with food and drink and various material possessions, that it might almost be said that a new religion had come into being. Osiris was not only, like all the other Egyptian gods, the lord of one or of several domains, or temples. He was not to be defined simply in terms of his temples, his priests, or his functions. He was a beneficent deity who revealed useful ideas to men, and so had incurred the hatred of Seth, who murdered him, dismembered his body, and scattered the various parts throughout the land. Isis brought him back to life and Horus, his son, avenged him. Alone of all the gods, Osiris deserved to be called Unnefer, the Good Being, because he provided the entire Egyptian people with the means of salvation.

By making the dead undergo the ordeal of the Judgment before entering the other world, the Egyptians, more emphatically than any other of the peoples of antiquity, proclaimed their faith in the perspicacity and impartiality of the judges whose task it was to reward virtue and punish transgression. At the same time, they asserted their belief that good works and pious deeds could obtain remission of sins.

Tombs of the Middle and New Kingdoms

We must now go back to our account of the development of the tombs, which was interrupted by the discussion of the Judgment of the Dead.

The kings of the Twelfth Dynasty, who resided chiefly at Ithytaui, situated a little to the south of Memphis, built pyramids inspired by those of the Old Kingdom at Dahshur, Lisht and the entrance to the Fayum. They rise to about two hundred feet and are not in a very good state of preservation. Several of them were brick pyramids. Their chief interest lies in the adjacent tombs built inside the enclosure wall. Amenemhat II granted tombs to several people. Those of the two princesses, Khnumet and Ita, which escaped the molesting hand of the robber, contained jewels so exquisitely wrought that they might have been made by fairies. The Egyptians, indeed, attributed them to the sons of Ptah. Amenemhat III, following the example set by Snofru, built two pyramids, one at Hawara, near the Labyrinth, which was his main achievement, and in which he was buried; the other at Dahshur, which was found to contain the violated sarcophagus, wooden statue and canopic chest of King Hor, who was ten years or so younger than Amenemhat.

The first Theban kings hollowed out deep caverns at Drah Abul Nega in the northern sector of the vast Theban necropolis. From the time of Tuthmosis I onwards, most of them chose their burial ground in the two valleys which lay behind the last spur of the Libyan mountains. At the same time, they constructed, along the fringe of the cultivated plain, a row of temples, where they themselves were worshipped alongside the Theban gods. Of these temples, the largest was that of Amenophis III, and its site is still marked by the Colossi of Memnon. Those in the best state of preservation are the temple of Queen Hatsheput at Deir-el-Bahari, the Ramesseum of Ramses II, and the temple of Ramses III at Medinet Habu. They all contain extremely valuable large-scale bas-reliefs depicting historical scenes – the expedition to Punt, episodes in the Syrian wars, and the victories over the Sea Peoples and the Libyans. Religious themes, such as the divine birth of Queen Hatsheput and the festival of Min, are also present. These palace-temples of the New Kingdom took the place of the Old Kingdom temples which had been built against the pyramids. Some of them underwent strange transformations. After his return to Thebes, Tutankhamen began building a temple, and its construction was soon sufficiently advanced for him to set up his own statues in it. Ai, who had acquired the wife and the throne of Tutankhamen, had no scruples about appropriating the statues as well. Finally, Horemheb took possession of both the temple and the statues. Occasionally, the temple of a private individual took its place alongside the royal buildings. For instance, Amenhotep, son of Hapu, had this extraordinary honour conferred on him as a reward for his devotion to his king, Amenophis III.

The hypogea were a series of passages and chambers hewn out of the living rock. Most of them were dug in the western slopes of a mountain, called the Horn, which might be compared to a gigantic pyramid, placed there by nature for the use of the Pharaohs.

Weird creatures peopled the passages and chambers. Although it is reassuring to see statues of the king alongside those of familiar deities, such as Osiris, Hathor, Horus, and Anubis, how are we to explain the huge serpents, some with wings, others with three heads, the headless or armless men and the various personages seated in the void?

The images and accompanying texts were not all evolved during one and the same period. Under the Eighteenth Dynasty, the Book of What is in the Underworld described Ra's journey through the dark realm of night which ended at the twelfth hour when the boat bearing the scarab beetle, the symbol of the birth of the sun, passed through the body of a serpent to emerge from its mouth as the barque of the sun at daybreak.

The two compositions which we call the Book of the Coming-Forth by Day and the Book of the Coming-Forth by Night are found only from the time of Seti I onwards.[46] First of all, the king, lying in his sarcophagus, is awakened by Horus, and with the help of the gods who follow Osiris and the gods who follow the *Ba*, he grasps the hands of Nut, the Goddess of the Sky. Waiting for him are the two boats of the sun, *manzet*, the one which does the day-journey, and

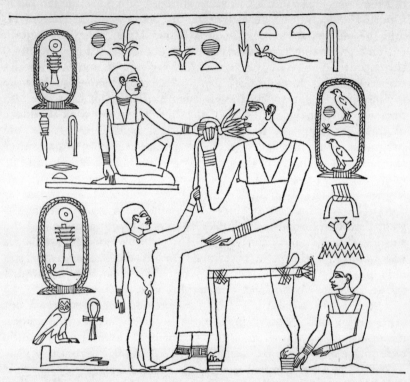

Fig. 49. A united family, from Junker, *Giza*, V, 91. Egyptian women were usually very affectionate mothers.

mesketet, the night-boat. He then takes his place by the side of the god (fig. 47). The Ocean across which the *manzet* boat travels follows the under-belly of Nut, whose body forms an arch above the earth. The barque enters the Fields of Ialu, an archipelago protected from intruders by walls of bronze, and where the corn grows as high as a man. During the final hour, the sun is swallowed up by the goddess, and during the night, passes from the West to the East. The realm of darkness is divided into twelve sections, and entered by a gate, the guardian of which acts as guide. Towed by the seventeen imperishable stars, the barque and its crew sail up the subterranean river between two banks, one of which is inhabited by friendly beings, the other by outcasts. Of particular interest is the hour – sometimes the sixth, sometimes the seventh – during which the crew meet with human beings, men (i.e. Egyptians), red-skinned men, negroes, Semites and Libyans, all grouped together under the authority of Horus, who smites them because they rebelled against Osiris, his father. The ship pursues its course until the hour of Ra, 'the hour which sees the beauty of its Master', when the god infuses life into men. However, the dead king lying inside his sarcophagus was not required to undertake the tedious journey we have just described; he could perceive in a flash, on the domed roof of the hall, the entire sky with the northern and southern constellations.[47]

The discovery of the tomb of Tutankhamen, which had been left undisturbed, gives us some idea of the fabulously valuable objects which were buried together with the king during the period when the glory of Thebes was at its height. The mummy, covered with amulets and jewels and swathed in linen bands, was laid in a coffin made of solid gold, placed inside a second coffin, which in turn fitted inside a third. The stone sarcophagus holding the three protective coffins was itself contained within four catafalques placed one over the other and made of stuccoed and gilded wood.

The other rooms in the funerary apartments were piled high with a haphazard assortment of objects – ceremonial beds, ordinary beds, arm-chairs, stools, chests, boats and chariots, and statues of the gods. There were also several objects which had come from the royal palace, souvenirs of family life, toys, even a lock of His Majesty's hair when he was a child. In short, there were so many of them that one entire gallery of the Cairo Museum, half of another and one room had to be cleared, in order to allow them a minimum amount of space.[48]

As early as the Twelfth Dynasty, the artists who decorated the tombs of the governors of provinces included, alongside the stock funerary scenes, or scenes of everyday life, others illustrating the public life of their client. This trend became much more marked after the beginning of the New Kingdom. The old stock themes took second place and more and more importance was given to the various activities of the deceased during his lifetime; he is shown introducing foreign emissaries to the king, receiving taxes, going off on pilgrimages, attending banquets, or taking part in religious ceremonies. This vast range of subject-matter is an admirable complement to the material found in the mastabas of the Old Kingdom. We are thus given a picture of both the private and the political and social life of the Theban aristocracy.

In Lower Egypt, where the towns were often situated a long way from the desert, the necropolises, being built among the houses and occasionally, as Herodotus rightly noted, inside the enclosure walls of the temples, were not able to develop as freely as those in the south. The inhabitants of Lower Egypt were just as anxious to protect their dead and to ensure that they were provided with everything they needed. The tombs in the royal necropolis at Tanis were low-ceilinged constructions, neither as wide nor as high as the great mastabas lying close to the pyramids, and they could be safely ensconced between ground level and the underground water-line.[49] They were family tombs. The tomb of Psusennes was intended for four people: the king, his mother, and two of his comrades-in-arms. Two of the above-mentioned were, in fact, replaced by two others. Two kings, Amenemopet, the second successor of Psusennes, and one of the Shashanks of the Twenty-second Dynasty, and two persons whose names are unknown, were buried alongside Psusennes. The tomb of Osorkon II was intended only for the king, but subsequently a royal prince, Homekhti, King Takelot and several unknown persons were housed in it too. The tomb of Shashank III contained a second sarcophagus, which appears to have been intended for Shashank I, the founder of the Bubastite Dynasty, whose original tomb had apparently been broken into by robbers. Such disorder and confusion bear witness to the disturbances which were widespread in Lower Egypt, now that Egypt was no longer a united country. Another proof of the weakness of the Tanite and Bubastite kings was the fact that the huge stone sarcophagi no longer came directly from the sculptor's workshop. Some were hastily cut out from some former monument, others were taken from one of the necropolises pillaged under the last of the Ramessides. However, the funerary furniture and the ornaments and jewels were made in the royal workshops, and bore the names of the personages for whom they were intended. They compare favourably with the finest examples of Egyptian art. The intense humidity which prevailed in the tombs was detrimental to silver and bronze, and caused wood to rot, leather and fabrics to perish. Nevertheless a good many of the objects found in Psusennes' tomb and a number of those from Osorkon's are more or less intact. Together with the sacred and non-sacred vases, the masks, necklaces, pectorals, rings, bracelets and amulets are a host of souvenirs of family life, objects brought from the royal palace, and even a number of exotic items such as an Akkadian cylinder and a ball of lapis-lazuli engraved with a cuneiform inscription, all of which give the collection its unique character.[49]

In other necropolises, small limestone buildings, surrounded by four walls of unbaked bricks, contained a single chamber just big enough to hold a sarcophagus. The descendants of the deceased were able to identify the monument with which they were concerned by a lintel of fine limestone, on which were engraved a representation and the official titles of the deceased, along with one or two scenes taken from stock themes. The means were modest but the essential purpose was achieved. Southerners were more exacting in their demands. Theban officials such as Mentemhat, a mayor of the town, Peta-menophis and Aba, built for themselves funerary palaces worthy of a king. In a provincial town, a humble priest of Thoth, Petosiris, built his 'house of eternity' in the form of a temple and arranged for the decoration to be carried out by the town's most skilled engravers.

Attitudes to ancestral respect

When allowance has been made for certain temporal and geo-graphical divergencies, it can be seen that Egypt never deviated from the course on which she had embarked at the beginning of her history and which was the inevitable consequence of her conception of human destiny. A stela of Ahmosis discovered at Abydos and which is, perhaps, the most beautiful of all the stelae preserved in the museums, provides touching evidence of the piety shown by the Egyptian people towards their ancestors.[50] The king and his wife are in a hall and both are asking how best, during the feasts of heaven and earth, they may minister to those who are no more. 'Why do you have such thoughts?' the Queen is saying. 'Why do you speak thus? What emotions fill your heart?' The King replies: 'I am thinking of my mother's mother and my father's mother, the Great Royal Spouse, Tetisheri, the true of voice, whose tomb and funerary monument now lie in the lands of Thebes and Abydos. This is what I say: My Majesty wishes to build for her a pyramid and a castle in the sublime land, near to My Majesty's own royal monument. A pool will be dug, an orchard planted, offerings will be established along with the men to make them, there will be estates, herds, servants, and trained priests to perform the ceremonies, each man knowing what he has to do.'

He adds that former kings never did so much; this was a common boast. Ahmosis, who adored his grandmother, then stretches out his arm and opens his hand as he pronounces the formula for the funerary offering. Such was the behaviour of a pious king during a period of happiness, but very different times were to follow under the inefficient rule of the last of the Ramessides. Not only did the most securely guaranteed funerary arrangements fall into disuse, but also organized bands desecrated the ancestral tombs in order to secure possession of the gold they contained. The first outbreak of tomb robberies occurred under Ramses IX, and it was only half-heartedly dealt with by the magistrates, who allowed themselves to be bribed.[51] By the time the government decided to arrest and punish the thieves, appalling havoc had been wrought. Most of the tombs had been rifled; the mummies of the most famous kings had been stripped of all their jewels and ornaments. The officers of the law hid the mummies as best they could and, when order had again been restored, they were laid inside simple wooden coffins, on which were recorded the different transfers which had taken place.[52] The coffins were assembled in various hiding-places, along with a few other salvaged objects. The severe punishment meted out to the robbers did not discourage subsequent generations, for the tombs were again pillaged during the Saïte Dynasties, during the reigns of Nectanebo I and II, and during the Ptolemaic period.

Although the Egyptians were on the whole a docile people, naively respectful of established authorities, inclined to flatter those in high places, and humbly grateful for any word of praise bestowed on them by their superiors, there was no lack among them of adventurers who were only waiting for an opportunity to overthrow the divine monarch of the throne of Horus and become king in his place. Priests were not above selling the sacred animals, appropriating the sealed treasures and contents of the warehouses, and bribing the magistrates, and those thieves, professional and otherwise, who knew where gold was to be found.

The social unrest prevalent under the last Ramesside kings was no new experience for the Egyptians. A similar period of turmoil had occurred as a result of the Hyksos invasion, and even during the First Intermediate Period many valuable objects had changed hands and the magnificent tombs of the Old Kingdom had not escaped desecration. These sad events were echoed in certain pessimistic writings, the most remarkable of which is called The Dialogue of a Man-who-is-tired-of-Life with his own Soul (*Ba*). The text is not easy to understand, because certain fragments are missing at the beginning and the language used is obscure.[53] However, the passage dealing with the futility of burial arrangements is startlingly clear:

'My soul opened its mouth towards me, replying to what I had said: "If thou thinkest of burial, it is a grief for the heart. Those who have built in granite, constructed chambers within the pyramid, and achieved great works, have become gods, yet their offering-tables are as empty as are the tables of those who died on the river-bank without survivors to maintain their cult. They are destroyed both by the waves and the heat of the sun. The fish along the shore speak to them. Hearken to me, for it is good for men to hearken – pursue the pleasures of each day and forget care . . ." '

The soul justifies its advice by means of two fables, the moral of which is that too much should not be expected of life. The man, however, protests angrily that his name is abhorred, that there is no one to whom he can talk, and that he is surrounded by wickedness. Fortunately, death is there to offer him a glad release, and the celestial barque will be waiting to receive him. The soul finally states that, whatever the circumstances, it will remain united with its body.

The author of the Dialogue was not the only one to express feelings of despair. A papyrus dating from the New Kingdom has preserved a song copied from the tomb of King Antef of the Eleventh Dynasty in which the same melancholy reflections occur:

'The gods who once lived and who rest in their pyramids, the nobles, and the glorious departed likewise are buried in their tombs.

'They built houses the sites of which no longer exist. What has become of them? I have heard the words of Imhotep and Hordedef, whose sayings are repeated as proverbs and have survived everywhere. What has happened to their places now? Their walls have crumbled, their places no longer exist; it is as if they had never been.

'No one returns from those distant regions to tell us how they fare, or what their needs are.

'Therefore follow the happy day (i.e. enjoy yourself) and be not weary therein. See, no one takes his goods with him. Behold, no one returns who has once departed.'[54]

A tradition had been established. On the tomb of Neferhotep, another harpist was to sing of the transience of life. 'The houses of our ancestors have crumbled. They are as if they had never been. Therefore follow the happy day.'[55]

The advice was addressed to a dead man, but the living who listened to the harpist's song most certainly took it to heart. Herodotus was no doubt present at assemblies held in the houses of rich Egyptians, during which the statue of a mummy was paraded at the end of the meal: 'Look on this mummy, then drink and be merry, for when death claims you, you will be like him.'[56]

In this way the Egyptians remained faithful to what might be termed an epicurean tradition without relinquishing their age-old aspirations. They realized that even the most solidly constructed and securely protected of funerary monuments would eventually fall into ruin or neglect, and that in the long run the privileged classes fared no better than the poorer members of the community, yet this did not lead them to ease the burden they had imposed upon themselves in their efforts to combat death. The people of the Delta may perhaps, at times, have been tempted to do so ; yet the fact that their tombs are less impressive and less ornate than those of the south can no doubt be explained by purely geographical factors.

Written evidence of what the Egyptians really thought on this score is to be found in a tale composed during the Ramesside era and sometimes referred to as the Tale of the Ghost.[57] This ghost appears to one of the first prophets of Amun Khonsuemheb and complains that his tomb has been taken away from him. Some eight centuries earlier, his king made him a gift of an alabaster sarcophagus and four canopic jars, but for a long time the tomb has been in ruins and exposed to the elements. He has been promised four times that it would be repaired and the promises have not been kept. The prophet of Amun proposes that an offering of a libation of water and a sack of wheat be instituted for his benefit. The ghost, however, is not satisfied with such a niggardly offer. What he wants is the restoration of his tomb. We do not possess the end of the story and we cannot be sure that his wish is fulfilled, but the fact that he expressed such a wish is in itself significant.

Conclusion

Ever since 'the time of the god', the Egyptian people had felt the need to preserve the bodies of their dead by means of mummification, and to provide them with suitable burial-places. A glorious destiny awaited the deceased king, although even he was to a certain extent bound by the limitations imposed on humanity as a whole in so far as he had to be supplied with food, and have his offering-table constantly replenished. The nobles and officials imagined that in their 'everlasting domain' they would relive the happiest moments of their lives, surrounded by the members of their family and their full complement of servants, each one of whom would pursue the task for which he was fitted. However, a doctrine was eventually evolved according to which the dead must have deserved the care and attention lavished on them by their descendants, and must have proved themselves worthy of the prayers offered up on their behalf by visitors to their tombs. The court, whose function it was to prevent the violation of funerary property, was also entrusted with the task of weighing human actions in the balance and of subsequently determining the fate of every individual. No doubt people resorted to magical formulae in an attempt to force the judges to absolve everyone. The judges, however, were not blinded by such precautionary measures. Even the kings had to undergo a similar trial before they could step into the sun boat; they could not have done without the tomb and its valuable contents.

It is chiefly in their views on death and the dead that we can see how little concerned the Egyptians were about the various contradictions which can be discerned in their behaviour. Being unable to relinquish any part of the past, they finally lapsed into extreme confusion, but never lost sight of their essential aim, which was to ensure indefinite prolongation of the life which they held so dear.

CHAPTER 8

INTELLECTUAL ACHIEVEMENTS

Language and writing

IT is generally agreed today that Ancient Egyptian can be defined as a semiticized African language. Or to be more exact, Egyptian, the westerly (Kushite) group of African languages, the easterly, Libyan-Berber, group, and the Semitic languages, all sprang from a common source. They are characterized by certain common features, such as the predominance of consonants over vowels, the importance of the roots, elements of which are retained in the derivatives, the large number of guttural sounds, the most characteristic being the sound *aîn*, and the formation of the parts of the verb by doubling the second root and by the use of prefixes. The indirect genitive was common to Egyptian and the African languages; the nisbé (adjective of relationship) and the pseudo-participle are found in both Egyptian and the Semitic languages. Although it is a fact that certain roots and words are common to Egyptian and the African languages, and a still greater number common to both Egyptian and the Semitic languages, the greater part of the Egyptian vocabulary is original and the conjugation of the verbs is peculiar to the language. So complete was the fusion between native and borrowed elements that even as early as the first dynasties Egyptian gave the impression of being a homogeneous language. This is linked with the racial factors referred to in previous chapters. The Egyptian people consisted, on the whole, of native types; however, since the country was exposed on all fronts, immigrants converged upon the Nile valley from every direction during the prehistoric era and during Pharaonic times and were soon integrated with the mass of the people.

The Egyptians had a copious and varied vocabulary for everything connected with rural activities, the various arts and crafts, hunting, fishing and war. However, it contained very few abstract terms. In order to convey some emotional or intellectual quality, the Egyptians had to resort to circumlocutions consisting of an adjective or participle, and the name of a certain part of the body. A shrewd man is defined as being sharp of feature; a brave man as being strong of arm; a stubborn man as being stout of leg. It was only as the result of a somewhat laborious process that the majority of abstract terms came into being. A loaf of bread on a piece of rush matting initially expressed the idea of 'offering', *hetep*, and later took on the meaning of tranquillity or contentment.

The king *nesu* meant originally he who possesses a clan ensign, the reed, then the king of Upper Egypt, and finally king of the whole of Egypt. Foreign kings were called the 'great' and some, such as the Hittite king, the king of the Persians, and the Ptolemaic kings were referred to as the 'very great'.

Speech usually consisted of a succession of short independent sentences which could be either descriptive or active. The relationship between them may have been indicated by means of intonation. In Sinuhe's story, the sentences: 'I set out in the evening. Brightness flooded the land. I reached Peten.' can be interpreted as follows: 'Having set out in the evening, I reached Peten as dawn broke.' The Egyptian language had a range of particles to indicate the relative importance of the various clauses. So we find on an Old Kingdom tomb: 'His eldest son did this for him when he was buried in the good land of the West in accordance with what he had said on this matter when he was alive and on his feet.' Continuous prose of this type was rare. Usually writers were content to express themselves in a succession of juxtaposed sentences.

The Egyptian language has a very long history, since Coptic was merely a more recent form of Egyptian written by means of the Greek alphabet. Egyptian is in fact the only language whose evolution can be traced back over a period of nearly 5,000 years. It was influenced for better or for worse by all the events which left their mark on the nation. It was under the Twelfth Dynasty that court officials and scholars were responsible for bringing it to its most highly developed form. The invasion of the Hyksos and the wars which took place during the Eighteenth Dynasty, brought in their wake a whole series of changes which have been compared, rather exaggeratedly perhaps, with those which caused the emergence of the Romance languages from Latin. The Egyptian vocabulary was invaded by foreign terms. The relationships between the various words, which in classical Egyptian had been conveyed by intonation, were expressed by particles, and articles came into use to express gender and number. Possessives were used pronominally and the conjugation of verbs was helped out by periphrastic expressions.

In the seventh century BC, at a time when artists were looking to the Old Kingdom for inspiration rather than to the reigns of the various Tuthmoses or to the Ramesside era, the scribes too showed a tendency to hark back to the language of the Old Kingdom, although everyday speech continued to evolve independently. In this respect, the history of the language closely followed the history of society.

Among the general public, hieroglyphic writing is rightly held to be as essential a feature of Ancient Egyptian civilisation as the pyramids, the Sphinx, the obelisks and the mummies. Other peoples have had forms of picture writing but they moved on to non-pictorial alphabets. Right up to the Roman conquest the Egyptians continued to use drawings of human beings, parts of the body, plants and objects, and although they had evolved a cursive form of writing at a very early stage, they went on adding to the number of hiero-glyphs and actively endeavoured to make them more difficult to read. We have here an instance of how tremendously powerful tradition can be, when it is allied to national pride. The Egyptians were proud of having created a form of writing not only beautiful but so powerful in its effect that, in the funerary texts, the scribes thought it necessary to remove or deface the hieroglyphic signs denoting soldiers, wild beasts and even unarmed men, in case they might harm the deceased.

Hieroglyphic signs were invented as early as the Chalcolithic period. There is no trace of sign writing on either the Neolithic or Amratian tombs, but the clan ensigns traced on the Gerzean vases can be called a primitive form of writing. The schist and ivory palettes dating from the days of the predecessors of Menes give titles, names of people and names of communities in hieroglyphs. Their number was to increase steadily during the first two dynasties. On Zoser's magnificent monument and on the ruins of a temple to the Ennead of Heliopolis are preserved, in very beautiful hieroglyphics, the titulary of the king, the titulary of his chief adviser Imhotep, and short sentences recording the consecration or the erection of a monument, and the promises made by the gods. This was only a beginning, but it marked a decisive step forward. Memorable events could now be recorded and ideas expressed, since the above-mentioned Imhotep, who built Zoser's Pyramid, is reputedly the author of the oldest known book of moral instruction.

For the sake of convenience, Egyptologists have divided the signs into several categories: men, women, parts of the human body, gods, mammals, birds, reptiles and their various parts, plants, the sky, earth, water, as well as all the products of human skill, so that the list drawn up by Egyptologists is at the same time an inventory of everything found in Ancient Egypt.[1] The most complete list gives each sign its name, its Egyptian definition and its reading, which is never arbitrary since it was based on the name. Each hieroglyph is, as a general rule, an ideogram. As such it means what it represents: a hand, an eye or a tool. However, it also refers to the various actions performed by the hand or the eye and all the uses to which the tool can be put, and even to the people using it. Thus the names of the crafts are generally represented by the tool associated with the particular profession.

A purely ideographic form of writing would have remained limited in scope. But since the signs had both sound and shape, the meaning could be disregarded and the sound only retained: in this way, the signs became phonetic symbols. Conversely, the sound could be disregarded and the meaning only retained; this gave a series of determinatives, which could be used to form a large number of words. For instance, legs can indicate everything connected with walking, a roll of papyrus everything used in writing, and everything that can be written down. It would be wrong to imagine that the inventors of the hieroglyphic system carefully drew up a complete list of ideograms, from which they then evolved phonetic symbols and determinatives. They may well have invented the phonetic symbols they needed, by using the ideogram at the outset for its phonetic value. For instance, to write the word *nib*, lord, they used the sign *nebet*, meaning basket, which was easy to draw. This did not prevent *nebet* also having the meaning of basket. By using a phonetic symbol which derived from a true ideogram, or from what was virtually an ideogram, the scribes were unconsciously conforming to the laws of language, in virtue of which consonants are more important than vowels, and roots more important than derivatives. It was of no great account that the vowel in *nebet*, basket, was not the same as the vowel in *nib*, lord, or that the first of these two words had a flexional ending not present in the second.

Among the signs thus evolved, triliterals such as *nfr* are in the minority, and biliterals such as *mn*, and uniliterals, are in the majority. With the number of consonantal groups exceeding twenty, the scribes had at their disposal an alphabet which students of Egyptology learn at the beginning of their course.[2] It is not quite complete, as there is no sign for the sound *l* which nevertheless did occur in the language. There was nothing to prevent the Egyptians realizing that the alphabetical signs were in themselves adequate for the expression of their language, and indeed all languages. But they used them mainly for grammatical terms, pronouns, propositions and particles, and to serve as reminders when employed in conjunction with the various consonantal groups. The scribe who momentarily forgot that the chessboard had to be read as *mn* was reminded of the fact when he saw the letter *n*, water, below the chessboard. In this field as in all others, the Egyptians, as the eminent Egyptologist, Adolf Erman, has pointed out, were cursed with an inability to forget. They were incapable of carrying their most ingenious inventions to a logical conclusion. They never discarded any old belief when adopting a new one, or abandoned any old method in favour of one more recent. They evolved an efficient way of distinguishing between the two uses of a hieroglyphic sign. If it was an ideogram, they added a small vertical stroke; a *t* and a small stroke, if the word was feminine. It was not long before this simple and practical rule was applied indiscriminately. The Egyptians were justifiably fond of their writing, which not only was beautiful and picturesque but also gave scholars the opportunity of inventing new ways of writing familiar words. This possibility led to the creation of secret writing, evolved by shrewd scribes who wanted to force the reader to decipher texts which, had they been drawn up in the current style, would have attracted no attention at all. Later, under the Greek and Roman occupations, it gave the Egyptians great satisfaction to concoct unintelligible documents, of which their foreign masters could make nothing.

Hieroglyphic writing was an ideal medium for artists, since every sign was a drawing or, more accurately, a painting. It was rather elaborate for such tasks as inscribing the name of the owner or the nature of the contents on the rounded sides of vases; the signs were therefore reduced to outline, and often traced with the calamus rather than the brush. In this way there grew up a form of writing, erroneously called hieratic, which was used chiefly in secular documents: notes, lists of works and products or details of official writs. In it, the signs were greatly simplified, and, as time went on, they became linked together.[3] It was this cursive form of writing which should have led to the creation of an alphabet. Its range was more limited than that of the hieroglyphs. Certain signs, clearly differentiated in the hieroglyphic form of writing, were given a single, identical form in the cursive script. General determinatives took precedence over special determinatives, although the use of the latter remained optional, according to the preferences of the scribe. The final step towards the creation of an alphabet was never taken, nor even attempted.

Scribes and literary genres

For the Egyptians, to be a scribe was the finest of all professions. It was certainly a much sought after office. A landowner such as Ti had half a dozen scribes at his service, who were constantly employed in recording, weighing and measuring; scribes were employed in the temples, in the main administrative departments, and in the prisons. Governors and magistrates in the capital and in the provinces all had their own staffs of scribes. Not all of these can have been well paid. The cross-legged scribe in the Cairo Museum arouses pity rather than envy, but the scribe in the Louvre, with his acutely penetrating gaze, was undoubtedly the sort of man who enjoyed living on terms of intimacy with the great and having to deal with important and confidential matters. Even the best-paid scribes, however, were not to be compared with the scholarly scribes, who considered that the quality of their writings was an even greater guarantee of immortality than the pyramids.

'Set your heart on being a scribe . . .
A book is of greater value than a house, than the tombs in the West.
It is more beautiful than a castle, or than a stela in a temple.
Is there anyone among us to equal Zedefra?
Is there anyone here to equal Imhotep?
There is no man in our time like Nefri and Akhte, who is the greatest of all. I also mention the names of Ptahzehuti and Khakheperresenb. Is there a man to equal Ptahhotep, or even Kaïres?'[4]

The personages referred to are not unknown to history. Zedefra and Imhotep are mentioned in the poem known as the 'Song of the Harper'.[5] There is no doubt about the fact that Imhotep was Zoser's adviser and architect, or that Zedefra was one of the sons of Cheops. Ptahhotep lived during the reign of King Isesi, and Kaïres' name has been found elsewhere. We can consider these men as being the first professional writers ever mentioned in history. It is obvious from this that literary works were highly esteemed in Ancient Egypt. We know too that several works which can be classified as literary reached us in the form of manuscripts written on papyrus and, in their day, must have been part of the temple libraries or the libraries of the nobility. Cases in point are the story of Sinuhe, the tale of the peasant from the salt oasis, the Hymn to the Nile and various books of 'moral instructions'. On the other hand, in those cases such as the Tale of the Shipwrecked Sailor, the Dialogue of a Man-Weary-of-Life-with-his-Soul, the Tale of the Two Brothers and the Maxims of Ani, where there is only one manuscript, we must suppose that they have been destroyed by the accidents of history. It is an established fact that literary works were to be found in the schools, where the children learnt them and copied them, not on papyrus or parchment, which were too costly to be used for scholastic exercises, but on pieces of limestone incorrectly referred to as ostraca. Sinuhe, the Instructions of Amenemhat, the Hymn to the Nile, and the Satire of the Trades were some of the works copied out most often.

In certain works, we find quotations from some earlier writer, in the same way as lines from Homer keep turning up in Greek texts. All this material is still being actively investigated today, and Egyptologists are always publishing their findings so that the state of Egyptian literary studies may be kept constantly up to date.[6]

Those Ancient Egyptians interested in fine language only had to walk into the temples to see, transcribed in beautiful hieroglyphs on the walls or on stelae, the exploits of the Pharaohs as presented by the court poets – the liberation of Egypt by Kames, the victories of Tuthmosis III, and Ramses II's struggle against the Hittite coalitions. Ramses II was not content to have his victory at Qadesh commemorated on a single monument. It can be found at Ipsambul (Abu Simbel), at Karnak, Luxor and Abydos and it would certainly have been found at Per-Ramses as well, if Ramses' northern residence had not been pillaged.[7] Egypt, therefore, enjoyed all the conditions necessary for the creation of a literature, since she possessed writers who were encouraged by both the king and the court, an audience, buildings where the texts could be preserved, and schools where they could be taught.

Collections of 'instructions' appear to have been the first literary genre practised by the Egyptians. The famous Imhotep, who was the first of the professional writers, wrote a book of 'instructions', now lost, but the Prisse Papyrus has preserved the end of another composed for Kagemni who was appointed vizier, when the Majesty of King Huni having passed away, the Majesty of King Snofru rose like a beneficent effulgence over the whole land; this fact appears to prove beyond all doubt that the teaching given to Kagemni had been excellent.

The Maxims of Ptahhotep have come down to us in their entirety.[8] They were composed by a vizier of King Isesi whom the king ordered to choose a young disciple and teach him the sayings of the sages and the maxims of the Ancients, those uttered in the hearing of the gods. It must be admitted that these sayings, which were supposed to be so precious for the obedient listener, and so disastrous to the transgressor, which are rarer than the emeralds found by slaves in sandstone, hardly seem to merit such high praise. Their burden is that tradition should be respected. The son who listens does well to listen. Understanding enters into the listener, and the listener becomes in turn one to whom other people listen, because he who is a good listener is a good talker. Secondly, moderation should be the rule in all things. If a man meets with an arguer, three possibilities may present themselves. The opponent may be taller, smaller or of the same size, but he must on no account be resisted. The tall man will not tolerate opposition and the small man will feel humiliated; with the man of the same size, silence is the best course to follow. The wise man should found a household, take a wife and keep her happy as long as she is alive, for she is a profitable field for her lord.

We may find it surprising that platitudes such as these could ever have been considered as the essence of wisdom, yet in all fairness we should remember that it was an advantage in the age of the pyramids to express the rules of good behaviour in the form of maxims which could be easily memorized. From this same period date certain texts which show that the Egyptians were capable of expressing themselves vividly and lyrically, especially when they were not aiming deliberately at such effects. They did, in fact, create a genre which is still popular today: the picture with a caption. Any number of examples can be found in the scenes of everyday life, including one or more characters and drawn on the walls of the mastabas.[9] The scene is set briefly and explicitly, and occasionally snatches of conversations are given, so that the general effect is that of a fable. For instance, a herd of oxen is shown standing in a pool in which crocodiles are lurking. 'Thy hand on the water,' says a witness who remains on the river bank. 'Do not talk so much,' replies another cowherd while the first pronounces a spell: 'Oh cowherd, may thy face live against this plant which is on the water. May he (the crocodile) go off as if he were blind.' A knife-sharpener answers an impatient butcher with the words: 'I'm making you an edge as fine as a hair so that it'll cut of its own accord.' The following conversation is overheard in a goldsmith's workshop: 'Hurry up and finish that necklace. It should be finished.' 'As Ptah (the patron of goldsmiths) loves me, it will be finished this very day.'

The vine-growers, harvesters, and craftsmen had a varied repertoire of songs and sayings, of which we possess only a few fragments. However, on the tombs of Ti and Mereruka, we can read the lament of the shepherd as he drives his sheep on to the land which has been sown with seed, or on to the threshing-floor where the corn has been laid out:

> 'The shepherd is in the water among the fishes,
> He is talking to the silurus,
> He is exchanging greetings with the oxyrhyncus,
> Oh West! Where is the shepherd? the shepherd of the West!'

If the shepherd met with an accident, he could not expect to be buried in a tomb. His body was thrown into the water – that was the West as far as he was concerned. We have here, no doubt, the initial treatment of a theme, which was to be taken up subsequently by professional writers.

The coffin texts were, of course, written to help the deceased in the other world, but sometimes a jovial ditty found its way unexpectedly into their vast and confused mass. Such, for instance, is the 'Song of the Four Winds', whose beneficent effects are described in neatly-turned verses:[10]

> 'These winds have been given to me, say these young girls,
> Here is the north wind, who brings the Helu-nebu (the Greeks)
> His arms stretch to the far ends of the earth.
> He retires to rest having cheered his friend every day.
> The north wind is a life-giving wind.
> He has been given to me, and from him I derive life.'

The east wind opens the windows of the sky and guides the sun. The west wind is the brother of Ha (god of the Sahara). He is in a single body, yet there are two beings (Horus and Seth) in this land. The south wind is the negro from the southern regions who brings the water which makes all things spring into life.

It may be asked whether the Egyptians ever had anything that can be called historical writing. In the early days, they were in the habit of inscribing the chief event of any year on a wooden or ivory palette pierced with a hole. At the close of a given reign, the palettes could be strung together, thus providing, in convenient form, a résumé of all that had taken place under that particular monarch. Occasionally, the record was transferred to a beautiful stone slab. Fragments of one such stone slab are to be seen today in the Palermo Museum and the Cairo Museum.[11] But all this was no more than material out of which an historical narrative might have been made. The biographical inscriptions on the tombs sometimes took the form of a narrative. However, the writer, although ready to note some strange occurrence or picturesque detail, was usually concerned only with the part he himself had played and which he presented as being far more important than anything that had happened before his time. Uni, who was proud of having taken part in a large-scale expedition against the Nomads, introduces a sort of war-song into his narrative:

> 'This army returned in peace,
> It had laid waste the land of the Nomads.
> This army returned in peace,

It had crushed the land of the Nomads.
This army returned in peace,
It had dismantled their strongholds.
This army returned in peace,
It had cut down their fig trees and their vines.
This army returned in peace,
It had set fire to their encampments.
This army returned in peace,
It had slaughtered their hordes which were swarming there.
This army returned in peace,
It brought back the hordes as prisoners.'[12]

Officials who had been sent on special missions would send back reports to their chief, sometimes to the king, and later would have the king's reply inscribed on their tomb. Several letters of this type have been very severely damaged, but there is one which has come down to us intact; it is the one addressed to Harkhuf by the youthful Pepi II:

'I know the contents of thy letter, which thou has written for the royal archives, whereby thou informest me that thou returnest in peace from the land of Yemaim with thy escort of soldiers. In thy letter, thou sayest that thou bringest back all the great and beautiful produce which Hathor, had given to King Neferkara, may he live everywhere and forever. In this letter, thou sayest that thou bringest back a dwarf, who danceth the god (a religious dance) in the land of the Akhetiu, like the dwarf which Chancellor Baurded brought from Punt during the reign of King Isesi.

'Thou informest My Majesty that no other man who hath previously made the journey to Yemaim, hath ever brought back his equal. But surely it is thy duty to do that which thy master loveth and praiseth. Surely thou art ever vigilant in my service, doing that which thy master loveth, praiseth, and commandeth? My Majesty will grant thy wishes for the well-being of thy son, and thy son's son for ever and ever, so that all men can say that they know what My Majesty has done for thee on thy return from Yemaim, because of the zeal thou hast shown in doing that which thy master loveth, praiseth and commandeth.

'Come immediately to the court.

'When he sails downstream with thee, appoint special guards over him along both sides of the boat to prevent his falling into the water. When he sleeps at night appoint trusted guards to sleep near him in his cabin, and inspect them ten times a night.

'My Majesty desireth to see this dwarf more than all the produce of the mines of Punt.

'If thou arrivest at court, the dwarf being with thee alive and well, My Majesty will do for thee a thing greater than that which was done for the Chancellor of the god Baurded, at the time of Isesi . . .'[13]

The letter is extremely revealing and well phrased. The boy king expresses his desires most explicitly, and shows that he is ready to pay the necessary price to satisfy them. In short, we have here the first outstanding example of epistolary art.

The Intermediate Period between the end of Pepi II's reign and the accession of Amenemhat I, under the Twelfth Dynasty, was marked by a decline in all forms of artistic expression, by divisions within the country, and the weakening of Pharaonic authority, accompanied by disorder and confusion, invasion by foreign powers, and famine. The general state of collapse was reflected in the literature of the period.

The story of Cheops and the magicians may well have been written during this period.[14] It relates how the king used to get his sons to tell him tales about magicians who were always cleverer than the king. The king would call upon them to provide him with a diversion. One magician organized a charming entertainment which banished the memory of a disturbing incident. Another terrified the Pharaoh by producing a crocodile which, at his command, would either shrink and become harmless or swell to a great size and carry off its prey. A third performed a series of marvellous feats in the presence of the king, and told him that in the third generation his children would be superseded by another family born of Ra. Perhaps the accusations of impiety levelled by Herodotus against Cheops go back to the period during which this story was written. Another story, which has come down to us in a very fragmentary state, accuses Pepi II of dissolute behaviour.[15]

The sages who lived during these times of social upheaval were extremely pessimistic, and they were not content merely to advocate the adoption of a certain pattern of behaviour. They also cast a disillusioned eye on all the great changes which had taken place. Ipuwer who lived during the reign of a very old king – perhaps Pepi II – compares the present state of chaos to the happy days of yore, by which he meant, according to certain interpretations, the golden age when Ra reigned on earth.[16] Carried away by his subject, in a series of stanzas he contrasts the undeserved favours enjoyed by upstarts, and the misfortunes suffered by the true élite. Since boats no longer sailed to Byblos, no one could get pine wood to make the priests' coffins, yet foreign kings, even as far afield as the land of the Keftiu (by which he meant insignificant kings) were embalmed with the resin which is obtained from the pines which provide wood for the coffins.

The author of the Dialogue of a Man-Weary-of-Life-with-his-Soul seems to us to stand out both from the professional writers of the preceding age and from his contemporaries.[17] The idea of making a man converse with his own soul was, in itself, novel and interesting. As far as we can judge from the text, which is defective in its earlier part, and obscure in several places, the interest of the work increases steadily right up to the end. We can, of course, find traces of the wearisome reiteration which mars so many works, but on the whole the ideas are powerful and clearly expressed. It is a pleasure to find such a resolutely nonconformist attitude in a tradition-loving country and at such an early period in its history.

Controlled literature

The Twelfth Dynasty is presented by historians as a period of peaceful reorganization. A sound administrative policy guaranteed peace within the country, prevented the recurrence of famine, and made possible impressive building operations. As the result of vigorous action abroad, the frontiers were pushed back, and the various warlike tribes forced to keep the peace. The literature of the period was to be devoted, for the most part, to extolling the virtues of the monarchy, thereby helping to consolidate its successful achievements.[18]

The first outstanding composition is a prophetic work attributed to a sage called Neferrehu whom Snofru is supposed to have summoned to his court in order to have the future revealed to him. The most immediate threats to Egypt's safety and prosperity were the raiding Asiatic tribes, and the variations in the flow of the Nile. Fortunately Ameni, in whom we can recognize Amenemhat I, a native of Ta-setet, the most southerly district of Egypt, restored order and built the Wall of the Prince, which halted the advance of the invading tribes from the East.

Then a scholar, Kheti, was to associate his name with a work which was considered as a classic during the whole of the New Kingdom: The Satire on Occupations. It gives a vivid picture of the poor, or even appalling, conditions in which the manual workers lived. It mentions neither the soldiers nor the priests, but stresses the advantages of the profession of royal scribe. Even before this, the author of a book called Kemit had praised the profession of scribe, the reason being – as has been pointed out – that the State was lacking in civil servants, since the former administrative officials had disappeared during the First Intermediate Period and during the wars between the southern princes.

Glorification of the king provides the subject-matter of two didactic works. One was written by a certain Sehetepibra, who stressed that the cult of the king should consist of personal piety and the observance of religious rites; the king combined in his person the god Sa, Knowledge, Ra, Ha, Hu (eloquence), Atum as on the Beni-Hassan stela, Khnum (the marker-out of land) and the goddesses Bast and Sekhmet who created and cured epidemics.

The other didactic work is a moral testament from a father to his son and describes the general improvements in the human lot and, like the previously mentioned work, is monarchist in inspiration.

A similar royalist spirit prevails in the accounts of proceedings within the Great Council. The king puts forward a certain plan; the high officials agree with him unreservedly; events then prove the king to have been right. This panegyrical style of writing appeared for the first time during the Middle Kingdom after Sesostris I decided to found the Temple of Atum at Heliopolis. Thereafter, it was to enjoy great popularity for many years; the stela of Kames, the dedicatory inscription at Abydos and the Kuban stela, all belong to this style of writing.

The poets, too, extolled the king. The Hymn to Sesostris III consists of a series of stanzas, the first of which praises the martial qualities of the king; the second describes the great joy he inspired in the gods, as well as in his ancestors and his subjects; the third presents the king as a shade, a parasol, a cool place during the two warm seasons, and a warm dry corner in winter-time. The hymn concludes with a reminder that it is the king who has brought unity and order to Egypt. The work, which is more distinguished by its artistry than its sincerity, was probably read out to Sesostris when he made his official entry into his capital.

The Sesostris legend proves that the whole period of this dynasty was remembered by succeeding generations as a golden age. It quite unjustly caused people to forget the task of organization and expansion carried out by the Old Kingdom. It was as if the people had not forgiven their former kings for inflicting on them the tremendous labour that the building of the pyramids had involved.

The Twelfth Dynasty was also famous for its literary achievements. It was during this period that the Egyptian language reached the height of perfection, and it is to this same period that we owe several imaginative works which are among the best Egypt ever produced.[19] The Story of the Eloquent Peasant (or Oasis-dweller), although its action is presented as taking place under the Heracleopolitan kings, is considered to be a Middle Kingdom work. The oasis-dweller's adventure provides a framework for nine supplications containing a number of statements distinguished by common sense:

'The inflicting of punishment is quickly done. The evil that has been committed is of long duration.'

'Do not dispose of the morrow before the morrow is here, for no one knows what evils it will bring with it.'

'It is natural that he who has nothing should steal. We should not be angry with the thief. He is merely trying to keep himself alive.'

However, the rhetorical eloquence of the plaintiff soon becomes monotonous and strained. The modern reader will find the narrative which introduces the appeals more interesting than the appeals themselves. It tells how an inhabitant of the Wadi Natiur was making his way to the Valley where he intended to sell his produce and buy provisions. A wicked man barred the way with his linen raiment, from which one of the peasant's donkeys took a large bite. The rogue then gave the poor man a sound beating, and seized both donkey and produce. The notabilities of the area sided with the thief because he was one of them, but the king's chief steward was amused by the oasis-dweller's speech and finally saw that justice was done to him.

The Story of Sinuhe was aimed at encouraging loyal feelings towards the king but at the same time it must have had an appeal for anyone who liked adventure stories. Sinuhe was fighting in the Libyan army when he heard a piece of news which was not intended for his ears. Panic-stricken, he fled across the desert and the Delta, crossed the Nile and finally reached the eastern desert, after joining up with a group of men working in the sandstone quarries near Onu. Travelling under cover of night and following the Wall of the Ruler, he reached the Ismailia area. By this time, however, he was in a state of collapse and would have died of thirst and exhaustion if a group of Bedouin had not offered him hospitality. They took him into Syria where he prospered, and overcame a rival chieftain. However, as old age approached, he grew weary of his exile and asked the king's pardon. Letters were exchanged. The outlaw returned to his own country and obtained an audience of His Majesty. He then settled down in his home and spent his last years in preparing his tomb.

Sinuhe's story unfolds smoothly and naturally, and it delighted cultured Egyptians because it extolled the part played by the king, in particular his clemency, and stressed the superiority of the Egyptians over the Asiatics. There were good Asiatics, like the Sheik of Retenu who recognized Egyptian supremacy, and envious elements, whose arrogance would be justly punished.

Another adventure story deals with a sea voyage. A boat is ship-wrecked on its way to the Royal Mines, and the only survivor lands on an island where he finds a profusion of everything. This island is ruled over by a kindly serpent who loads him with gifts and sends him back home. A ship takes him off from the shore, and after a voyage lasting two months he arrives back in Egypt.

New Kingdom literature

During the New Kingdom, we find an increasing number of hymns to the various divinities, for instance, the hymn to Amen-Re, then later the hymn to the Aton, the disc with the human-handed rays. The old hymns had been little more than an inventory of the contents of the temples of the gods, of their possessions and their functions, with here and there a few ingenious phrases expressing their power and their goodness.[20] In the hymn to the Aton, inscribed on the tomb of Aï, we are immediately struck by the absence of the usual temple paraphernalia. The long lists of names, the crowns, sceptres, boats and the sacred domain – everything in fact which formed the basic subject-matter of former hymns, and which was to be revived after the failure of Akhenaton's reform – was carefully omitted. Instead, we have a lyrical poem describing the effect of the disc on the natural world:

'The birds leave their nests, and lift their wings in adoration of thee. All the beasts leap to their feet, all winged creatures who fly, live when thou hast shone upon them.'

The artists illustrated this stanza by showing ostriches dancing and cynocephalus apes galloping to greet the rising sun.[21] The same poem declares that all men are children of the god who gives to some the Nile, to others rain from heaven, that they may live.

Egyptian artists of the Old Kingdom have left a very attractive picture of family life. The wife was always shown with her husband and children (fig. 49), because for Egyptians the greatest happiness was to be in the company of one's family. The kindly serpent foretells that the shipwrecked sailor will soon be able to clasp his children in his arms, embrace his wife and see his home again. This quiet happiness was taken to be the aim of all sensible men, and to judge by the best female statues of the period, the women who acted as models were neither capable of, nor consumed by, passion. Yet, during the New Kingdom, even before – but especially after – the Armarnian period, Egyptian artists portrayed the female face and form in such a way as to make one think that the Egyptians no longer shared their ancestors' simple view of women and young girls. About this time too a new literary genre made its appearance – the love song, the chief examples of which are to be found in the Harris Papyrus 500 and on the back of the Chester Beatty Papyrus, I, as well as on a Turin papyrus.[22]

The first theme dealt with in these poems is feminine beauty, which the poets define in the same way as they defined the beauty of the gods, by comparing it to everything the Egyptians considered to be most beautiful – gold, lapis-lazuli, the lotus flower, and the star Sirius:

'Sweet in love, Mut-ir-dis, priestess of Hathor,
Sweet in love, says King N,
Sweet in love, say the men,
Sweet in love, say the women.
The daughter of the king, sweet in love, is the most beautiful of women.
A young girl whose equal has never been seen
Her hair is blacker than the night,
Blacker than grapes, than the fruit of the fig-tree,
Her teeth are more neatly set than grains of corn,
Her breasts are firmly planted on her chest.'

Another theme was the feeling aroused in a young girl's heart by the sight of a handsome young man, and that experienced by a young man at the sight of a beautiful girl. Love's uneasiness provided a third theme. The boy and girl experienced it in turn:
The boy says:

'I have not seen my beloved for seven days,
I am a prey to listlessness,
My heart has become heavy.
I am forgetful even of my own life.
When the physicians come to me,
Their remedies do not satisfy me,
The magicians are helpless.
My sickness cannot be discovered.
But if they say to me, "Look, there she is", then I am restored to life.'

The girl speaks:

'Is it necessary to send me a messenger, fleet of foot as he comes and goes,
To tell me that he is unfaithful?
Speak therefore and say that I am no longer the same.'

The poems are interspersed with allusions to the charms of the Egyptian countryside and to gardens and gods, since the whole of nature naturally shares in the joys and sorrows of the lovers.

The exploits of the Egyptian warriors during the war of liberation,

215

the conquest of Syria, the struggle against the powerful foreign coalitions, and the defensive war against the barbarians, inevitably gave rise to a form of heroic poetry. It has already been mentioned that Uni was so exhilarated after taking part in an important action that his inscription has a poetic quality. On the triumphal stelae of Kames and Ahmosis, the narration of events is interspersed with violent invective and shouts of triumph which undoubtedly have an epic and a rhythmic quality. There is one monument the mere appearance of which proclaims its poetic nature: this is the black granite stela in which the god expresses his immense joy at the great services rendered to him by his son, Tuthmosis.[23] The god begins his speech with a series of strophes which are somewhat irregular in form, but from line 13 onwards the rhythm becomes more marked. Each strophe, which is divided up into two hemistiches, comprises a single line and opens with the same words:

'I have come, I granted thee to trample the Kings of Zahi,
I spread them beneath thy feet along their mountains . . .
I granted that they saw Thy Majesty as a Lord of the Rays.
Thou didst shine in their faces in the image of a god . . .'

After the kings of Zahi (Phoenicia), the Asiatics, the Easterners, the Westerners, the Sea-Peoples, the Peoples of the Islands, the Tehenu, the People of the End of the Earth and the People of the Beginning and, finally, the Barbarians from the south, were all to be crushed in turn. To each people the Pharaoh would appear in the shape of their own gods, or in the form of an avenging hero; the People of the Islands saw him as a bull, the Tehenu as a lion.

After his campaign against the Hittite coalition, Ramses II commissioned one of the royal scribes to compose a poem which deserves to be classed as an epic, since its aim was to extol heroic deeds and the victory it describes was due in part to supernatural intervention.[24]

Although this poem cannot be compared to the *Iliad*, it should nevertheless be emphasized that the two epics have certain points in common.

Details of the armed strength of each of the opposing forces are given. On the Egyptian side are four regiments placed under the protection of Amun, Harakte, Ptah and Seth, along with the king's own bodyguard of Sherden and native auxiliaries; the opposing army consists of a coalition of seventeen towns or districts including, in addition to the Hittites, men from the large Syrian towns of Qadesh, Ugarit, and Carchemish on the Euphrates and from several parts of Asia Minor. The text, which was incorrectly interpreted during the Late Period, accounts for the tradition according to which Ramses – or Sesostris – controlled an empire as vast as Alexander's. The first remarkable feat consisted in getting the Egyptian army as far as the Syrian coast, to a point between Beirut and Tripoli, and then in scaling the slopes of the Lebanon. Finally the army reassembled in the Orontes valley; the advance-guard was not far from Qadesh, the regiment of Ra was crossing the ford at Shabtuna, the regiment of Ptah had remained at Irnam, and the regiment of Seth was still a long way in the rear; the army was, in fact, spread out over a large area.

There were two major incidents. Spies gave misleading informa-tion and the Egyptians were lulled into a false sense of security. However, the two captives revealed the true facts just in time. The enemy, who was thought to be a long way off, was in fact close at hand – close enough to launch an attack, which routed the regiment of Ra.

The king seized his armour and his weapons, and then realized that he was alone. He appealed to his father, Amun, and took care to recall all the pious deeds he had performed for him, the sacrifices he had made, the obelisks, pylons and ships he had built. Surely Amun was worth more than millions of soldiers or hundreds of thousands of chariots. The king's cry for help was heard in the Heliopolis of the south (Hermonthis), and a miracle took place. The enemy was defeated. The king heaped reproaches upon his army, who replied by extolling the bravery of Ramses. An armistice was signed and the king returned to his residence at Per-Ramses.

Ramses was so delighted with the poem, which comprised 343 verses, that he had it engraved in beautiful hieroglyphs on his temples at Abu Simbel, Karnak, Luxor, the Ramesseum, and Abydos. Copies were made on papyrus. Bas-reliefs were carved depicting the attack on the camp and the routing of the enemy, and another text was composed which would appear to be more histori-cally accurate; this was the official report which gave a more objective account of the battle.

The Annals of the Old Kingdom and certain stelae of kings and private individuals provide material for history, but can hardly be called history proper. The Turin Papyrus, even if it had been intact, would have contained nothing more than a succession of names of kings, with the lengths of their reigns, interspersed with a few brief summaries. Apart from the beginning, the Annals of Tuthmosis III are merely a dry and monotonous catalogue of booty. Much more interesting is the stela of Tuthmosis found at Napata. As a general rule, the official stelae are divided into two parts: a scene in the upper part shows the king and the gods exchanging gifts, and below is the text, in which the titulary and eulogy of the king occupy far more space than the account of events and their explanation. The official report of the battle of Qadesh is more satisfactory, and so also, up to a point, is the marriage stela of Ramses II. After the inevitable eulogy of the king, it goes on to describe how the Hittite king, terror-stricken by the successes and ambitious plans of his rival, decided, after all his attempts at reconciliation had been spurned, to offer his daughter to the king along with costly gifts. Ramses accepted the offer and, foreseeing the difficulties of the Princess's journey to Egypt in mid-winter, he prevailed upon Sutekh to create a succession of summer days, so that the princess and her escort travelled in comfort. The king was charmed by her beauty, and the marriage marked the beginning of an era of friendly relations between the two countries.

The papyrus texts are nearer to the classical conception of history. In the Great Harris Papyrus, after a long list of facts which are more clearly classified than usual, we find the outline of a philosophy of history.[25] A king who understands the nature of his duties towards the gods and their priests can heal the evils caused by ungodliness and prevent their recurrence. No doubt the Houses of Life contained similar documents, or detailed reports made by high-ranking officials on some important branch of national activity, or summaries of the events of various reigns.

The story of Wenamun, which dates from the beginning of the Twenty-first Dynasty and which we possess almost in its entirety, is an excellent report on the journey undertaken by the above-mentioned personage, who was sent to Byblos by Herihor with the permission of Smendes, Prince of Tanis, to buy the wood needed to build a sacred barque for Amun. Although excavations at Byblos have not yet confirmed the existence of King Zekerbaal, we have no reason to doubt his authenticity since we have evidence of the existence of a succession of kings whose names were also formed from the name Baal with the addition of an adjective. The geographical setting is described with great accuracy and the atmosphere in which the preliminary negotiations took place is skilfully conveyed. The situation at the beginning of the eleventh century BC was no longer the same as it had been in the days when the Egyptian emissary had only to speak for his request to be instantly granted. The wily king was quite ready to hand over the wood but only at a price. It may even be wondered whether he was not in league with the pirates who were waiting for Wenamun and his cargo of wood off the coast of Byblos.[26]

The stela of Piankhi, which is much later in date, is so interesting that it makes us wish we had many more like it.[27] It is not so enlightening about actual events as about the haughty character of Piankhi himself. His instructions to his soldiers, the reproaches he heaped upon them, and his outburst of anger when he saw the sorry state to which the prolonged siege had reduced the enemy's horses, could provide inspiration for any writer of colourful historical novels in the style of Flaubert's *Salammbô*.

From the period of the New Kingdom we have a few anecdotal accounts with a historical setting, such as the quarrel of the Hyksos king, Apepi, with Sekenenre, Prince of Thebes, and the capture of Joppa under Tuthmosis III. The kings of antiquity occasionally sent riddles to each other. We do not know the end of this particular story, so we cannot tell how the hippopotamuses in the Lake of Thebes came to disturb the sleep of the king at Avaris, which was nearly six hundred miles away. The story of King Petubastis, the manuscripts of which are written in demotic, describes the great war between the two halves of Lower Egypt, which was caused not by the abduction of some beautiful princess, but by the stealing of a breast-plate which should not have been removed from Heliopolis.

The art of straightforward story-telling continued to be practised from the time of Ramses II up to the Late Period. The monotony of style and a certain lack of inventiveness which characterize most of these works, are occasionally redeemed by some amusing episode. The beginning of the Story of the Two Brothers gives a charming picture of the Egyptian countryside during the ploughing season. Many of the themes can also be found in the popular literature of other countries – the virtuous young man who resists the advances of a loose woman, the prince whom the seven Hathors threaten at birth with three equally alarming fates, the young stranger who, all on his own, succeeds in reaching the top of a tower inhabited by a beautiful princess, the magic statue which refuses to let go of the person who has benefited from its miraculous powers – but they were first written down in Egypt. While giving the Egyptians full credit on this score, we must nevertheless admit that we owe the best story – that of Rhampsinitus – to Herodotus.[28] No doubt the Greek traveller heard it during the course of his journeyings through Egypt, but in the retelling he added a pinch of Attic salt. The adventure of Setna with the mummies and the true story of Setna Khamonwas, both of which we know from manuscripts written in demotic, consist of a somewhat wearisome succession of metamorphoses and magical operations. It should be noted, however, that the first of these tales contains the story of the wicked rich man and the poor man who is justly rewarded in the next world. Thus, after an interval of many centuries, Egyptian literature produced an illustration of the hope expressed by the father of Merikara.

We possess two almost contemporary works which belong to the category of moral and didactic literature – the Maxims of the scribe Ani,[29] whose touching remark about the love each man owes his mother is often quoted, and the Moral Treatise of Amenemopet in thirty chapters,[30] which won instant fame, as soon as it was published, because it was almost unanimously recognized as having served as a model for the Proverbs of Solomon.

A moral treatise which was probably written during the Saïte period, and is therefore still later in date, came to light only a short time ago.[31] The beginning and the end are missing. The maxims and precepts deal with the relations between people of different ranks, with the functions and duties of persons in authority, and the advantages of agricultural work. (An earlier author had spent much of his time stressing the disadvantages of this situation.) There follows a parable describing a place which is very difficult of access; this is comparable to the passage in the Sallier Papyrus I in which a learned botanist speaks enthusiastically of the water in the nuts hanging high up on the coconut tree.

The question of whether or not the Egyptians ever had anything in the nature of a theatre has been much discussed during recent years.[32] They certainly had troupes of jugglers and acrobats who attracted crowds of interested onlookers. Children invented games in which two camps fought each other. Whenever a god made his public appearance, episodes of his legend were mimed – such as the slaying of Osiris, the defeat of Seth, Ares separated from her mother, and probably many others. We know that the Egyptians were not averse to reporting dialogue. This may perhaps indicate that they came very close to creating a true theatre. If, however, we mean by theatre a performance independent of the ritual of worship, given by professional actors before a public which has come either to listen, boo, or applaud, or if we mean first and foremost a dramatic text, then we must admit that the theatre did not exist in Egypt. Or perhaps it would be more accurate to say that no proof of its existence has as yet come to light.

It is clear from the foregoing that the Egyptians had a literature both in verse and in prose, which they appreciated at its true value; and that its value is undeniable. What remains of it should not be made to appear insignificant through being compared to Greek literature. Egypt had no writers to equal Homer, Pindar, Sophocles, or Herodotus. There is no flow of inspiration, the narrative is almost always perfunctory and the style bare. Just as shrewd critics found beauties in the sterile wastes of Ennius' writing, so those who are fond of Ancient Egypt can enjoy a few songs, certain pithy sayings, and some well-constructed stories. It should not be forgotten, moreover, that the various literary texts to which we have referred delighted a people of very high antiquity, who lived centuries before the Trojan War, and long before the Bible stories were put into writing.

The exact sciences

In the opinion of the Greeks, the Ancient Egyptians were well-versed in mathematics, astronomy and medicine.[33] Even more eloquent than this tradition are the buildings constructed by the Egyptians – the pyramids, obelisks, and rock-tombs – which suppose carefully drawn-up plans, accuracy of measurement, and efficient devices for the transport of materials, and the raising and setting into position of extremely heavy stone blocks. The chiefs of works were in daily contact with difficult problems; so too were the land-surveyors who measured out both the royal domains and private estates and assessed taxes; so again were the scribes in charge of food supplies whose task it was to divide out the various commodities between thousands of individuals who did not all have equal rights.

The Egyptian system of counting was decimal. The units were indicated by strokes; tens, hundreds and thousands by phonetic signs; the finger represented 10,000, the tadpole 100,000; a god holding up the sky with his raised arms, was equal to 1,000,000. The units of long measure were the finger, the palm, and the cubit (·523 metres). It has been claimed that the last mentioned measurement could not have been arrived at as a result of observation, because, in the case of the majority of men, the cubit is in fact much smaller than that. However, there are, in the Nile valley, men whose arms are longer than the average. 7 palms corresponded exactly to one cubit; and 100 cubits made a *khet*. For long distances, surveyors and geographers used the *atour* which consisted of 20,000 cubits. It was common knowledge that Upper Egypt was 86 *atours* in length, Lower Egypt 20 *atours*. These figures are approximately accurate; if we knew the itinerary followed by the geometrician, we might perhaps discover that they were absolutely accurate.

Area measures were the *setat*, 100 square cubits, the land mile (thousand) or 1,000 square cubits and the *atour*, a square with sides each of one lineal *atour*. Geographers had worked out the surface area of each nome by marking out, theoretically, as many *atours* or half-*atours* as was possible, and measuring the area left over in 'thousands' and in *setat*. So that all those concerned should know exactly what they were, the figures were engraved on various monuments, such as the White Chapel of Sesostris I and the Labyrinth which Strabo was able to visit but of which nothing is left today.

Units of capacity were the *hekat* consisting of 4·54 litres and its divisions, $\frac{1}{2}$, $\frac{1}{4}$, $\frac{1}{8}$, $\frac{1}{16}$, $\frac{1}{32}$, $\frac{1}{64}$, which gave $\frac{63}{64}$ when added together; the difference of $\frac{1}{64}$ had been claimed by Thoth. The standard weights were the *deben*, 91 grams, and the *kite* which was equal to a tenth of the *deben*. Usually only metals were weighed. Cereals were measured out in bushels.

One of the paintings at Beni-Hasan depicts an arithmetic lesson.[34] It included two stages: counting on fingers, and mental arithmetic. The Egyptians were good at adding and subtracting. Sometimes, as can be seen from the Great Harris Papyrus, they added together an assortment of objects or animals of different species. They had no multiplication tables, but their method of picture-writing made it easy for them to multiply or divide by ten. When this was not possible, a series of operations whereby they multiplied or divided by two provided a solution. Division by three is found in a few examples. In fractions, they hardly ever used any numerator beyond 1. The fraction $\frac{2}{3}$ occurs occasionally, but $\frac{3}{4}$ hardly ever. All fractions could be reduced to the numerators 1 or 2. All these mathematical calculations were empirical rather than theoretical. The devices the Egyptians employed were clumsy, but they handled them with ease, and obtained results the accuracy of which has been confirmed by later mathematicians. They could also calculate the area of the square, the rectangle, the triangle and even the circle, having to recourse to the number π by constructing a square the sides of which were equal to $\frac{8}{9}$ of the diameter. They were also able to determine the angle of a pyramid and pass the information on to the quarrymen who were busy hewing the blocks for the outer layer.

The way in which the Egyptians organized their knowledge proves that it was undeniably scientific in character; they began with elementary conceptions, went on to increasingly complicated arithmetical problems, then to operations with fractions, and finally to geometrical problems. The Egyptians can, therefore, be said to have evolved an organized system of mathematical knowledge. They did not try to discover the properties of numbers, but they succeeded in solving relatively simple problems in which experience, rather than reasoning, played the predominant part. This at least is what can be deduced from the mathematical papyri: the measurements which have been taken of the great pyramids have shown that the men who built them fixed the dimensions with the help of the sacred triangle, the sides of which were in the ratio 3 :4 :5. The relationship between the height and half of the perimeter of the base is of the order of $\frac{22}{7}$. Those who are best qualified to judge do not believe that the Egyptians arrived at these results through theorizing. They think rather that architects after the time of Cheops, then the Greeks when analysing the Great Pyramids which were one of the wonders of the world, succeeded in discovering in them qualities which had not been consciously planned.[35]

The calendar was drawn up by and for the agricultural workers. As the inundation lasted for one-third of the year, the remainder consisted of two more or less equal periods, the 'emergence' (of the cereals) and the harvest. This gave three seasons of one hundred and twenty days, divided up into four months of thirty days, and which were known by their place in the natural cycle : *akhit*, the inundation, *perit*, the emergence and sowing, and *shemu*, the harvest (fig. 54). At a period which it is impossible to determine exactly, certainly before the Fourth Dynasty, five extra days were added, to bring the annual total to 365 days.

Since the inundation never occurred at an absolutely fixed date, the Egyptians tried to find some regular phenomenon which could be easily observed and which would mark the beginning of each year. The event by which they fixed the calendar was the appearance, or the rising, of the dog-star, Sirius, in Egyptian *Sopdet*, in Greek Sothis. A love song refers to the fact that Sirius rose at the beginning of the perfect year.[36] The star, which had remained invisible for a considerable period made a brief appearance every year at dawn, at the same time, along a certain latitude. The Sothic year corresponded more or less to the true year; the discrepancy between them is so slight that observations would have had to be carried out at regular intervals over a great number of years for its existence to become obvious.

On the other hand, after four successive years the men who had fixed the calendar must have realized that a year of 365 days was too short. In the fifth year of this way of counting, they must have noted that the star appeared only on the second day, and in the ninth year, on the third day. The solution to the problem was not far to seek; they merely had to do what Ptolemy III in fact eventually decreed should be done, that is, add an extra day every four years.[37] They do not appear to have chosen this solution, preferring to follow the discrepancies of the irregular appearances of Sirius in what they called their 'lame' or 'wandering year'. We can find several instances of the use of the 'wandering' year, in both early and later periods. The earliest instance is provided by a papyrus from Kahun[38] in which those following the 'wandering' year are requested to note that in the year 7 of Sesostris III (Twelfth Dynasty) the rising of Sirius should take place in the fourth month of *perit*, on the 16th day, that is to say on the 226th day of the year. In the year 9 of Amenophis I, the second king of the Eighteenth Dynasty, the rising of Sirius was observed on the 9th day of the third month of *shemu*, that is to say the 309th day of the year.[39] An inscription at Elephantine records that in one year (which is not specified) of the long reign of Tuthmosis III, the event took place on the 29th of the same month, that is to say the 328th day of the year.[40] As time went on, the rising of Sirius occurred increasingly late. Finally its appearance coincided with the first day of the New Year as it had done 1,460 years previously. This happened to be the year 1 of Ramses I, founder of the Nineteenth Dynasty. It also marked the beginning of an epoch called the 'era of Menophres', which was to end 1,460 years later in the year AD 139.[41]

This somewhat unusual method of calculating time presented many advantages. It should not be forgotten that the Egyptians counted the years from the beginning of each reign. It was difficult for them especially in times of trouble and confusion which were characterized by a rapid succession of reigns, some of them even overlapping, to calculate how much time had elapsed. Supposing someone living at the time of Amenophis I had wanted to find out how many years had elapsed since the reign of Sesostris III, he had only to compare the Sothic dates, and having noted that the rising of Sirius was 83 days late, multiply the number by 4, which would give a total of 332 years.

What was much more important and what concerned an infinitely greater number of people, was the possibility of being able to determine at any given moment the connexion between the civil year and the natural year. For as well as the wandering year, the Egyptians went by the natural year in which months and seasons followed a regularly recurring cycle. Everyone whose livelihood depended upon the natural course of the seasons – doctors and veterinary surgeons, hunters, fishermen and agricultural workers – all observed a seasonal calendar. This explains why a scribe who was writing out medical prescriptions was careful to give a table of concordance at the top of his papyrus (known to us as the Ebers Papyrus). It was well known that certain diseases or complaints recurred some in *perit* others in *shemu*. One form of treatment was prescribed during the first two months of *perit*, and another during the last two months. On the other hand, certain preparations could be used in *akhit*, *perit* and *shemu*, in other words, the whole year round.[42]

In the temple of Medinet-Habu (Ramses III) is a calendar listing the principal annual festivals with the corresponding date in a Sothic year. If people knew the date in the civil year on which the rising of Sirius took place, it was not difficult for them to calculate the dates of all the festivals.

Thus, an analysis of the Egyptian calendar, while confirming the strength of the Egyptian belief in tradition, also reveals the ingeniousness of their methods, which were often very far removed from ours.

The Egyptians were keen astronomers. They made a distinction between the imperishable stars, which are the circumpolar stars, and the indefatigable stars, that is to say the planets and stars which were not visible at all hours of the night. From the latter they chose thirty-six stars which presided in turn over the ten-day periods (decans) of the annual celestial cycle. During the Middle Kingdom they drew up tables which were divided into thirty-six vertical columns and 12 horizontal registers. This made it possible to note the position of each decan at every hour of the night during which it operated, and consequently to ascertain the time during the night, at least approximately.

The Egyptians were also able to determine true north by stellar observation. The Memphite pyramids, especially the Great Pyramid, were all orientated with astonishing accuracy, the margin of error being only 2′ 30″. Such a high degree of accuracy could not have been achieved by observation of the course of the Nile, which flows more or less due north, nor even from the observation of the rising and setting of the sun on the two equinoctial days of each year; it can, in fact, only have been achieved by astronomical observation. The materials used were extremely simple and consisted of two separate instruments: one was a right-angled measuring rod marked in cubits, to which a plumb-line was attached, and the other was a rod with a slit. Through the slit the observer tried to sight both the plumb-line, which was held by a second person, and a certain star. According to the ritual of the temple foundation ceremonies, the observer turned towards the Great Bear, which was the constellation characteristic of the northern sky. This was only one stage of the operation. The observer had then to seek out a polar star, which during the Old Kingdom must have been the α of the Dragon. Once this star was located it was an easy matter to mark on the ground a line running due north and south.

Although the pyramids were orientated towards the north, the New Kingdom temples were not given an exact orientation. They were probably directed towards the star with which the divinity of the temple in question was associated. This called for a second operation, after which the four angles of the building were marked out on the site.

Yet the development of this quite remarkable technique in no way proves that the Egyptians had realized, or even guessed, that the earth was round; nor does it mean that they had any idea of the earth's movements. They believed that the earth was flat, that the sky was a table held up by four pillars, and that the imperishable stars revolved in the sky round the celestial pole.

The hieroglyph, V 9, in the Gardiner list, gives a very schematic representation of the world. It consists of a fairly thick circumference representing the limit of the area lit by the sun and which is firmly attached to a bar, slightly broader in the middle, representing the earth. The sign is often held by the divine falcon, or the divine vulture, and the Sphinx, the symbol of Harakhte, places its claws over it.

The natural sciences

In discussing history as a literary genre, I pointed out that particularly important events, such as the laying of the foundations of a temple or trading and military expeditions, were most carefully recorded by the archivists and stored in the Houses of Life. The Egyptians were historians in their own way and, within certain narrow limits, they were always interested in geography and anxious to get to know their own, as well as neighbouring, countries. This explains why they recorded important data concerning each nome in special administrative offices, and in inscriptions on temple walls: first of all the name, then the chief town, a secondary cult centre, the river or canal, the agricultural land, the *pehu* (borders) within which the flood water collected, and the surface area. These details were followed by information regarding priests and priestesses, the sacred boat, the local feasts, the ritual prohibitions, and the protective genius. No mention is made, however, of the economic factors which must have caused the prosperity of towns such as Aswan or Coptos. Geography was, really, nothing more than a list of names and titles. As far as foreign countries were concerned, the Egyptians were anxious mainly to know their names and chief products. They were also interested in whether they obtained their supply of water from natural springs, from the Nile, or from rain. The magnificent bas-reliefs on the Punt colonnade at Deir-el-Bahari, and the Libyan bas-reliefs on the temple of Sahure provide evidence of the fact that the Egyptians were perfectly well acquainted with the physical types, and the dress of the inhabitants of these countries, as well as with the flora and fauna. We know that, before leaving for the turquoise mines, engineers were aware of the fact that it was advisable to start operations before the heat of the summer set in. The documentary evidence in our possession makes no mention of the geographical position of foreign countries, nor of the best routes to follow in order to reach them. Information on these matters must, however, have been available for those who needed it, from the time of the Old Kingdom onwards. Satisfied with what they already knew, although aware that the world stretched a long way beyond the farthermost points that they could hope to reach, the Egyptians did not, generally speaking, feel the urge to push their journeys of explorations any further. There is no evidence to prove that they ever reached the confluence of the White Nile and the Blue Nile. It was common knowledge during the Saïte Period that rain on the mountain of Punt caused a rise in the level of the Nile.[43] Even the Greeks, who were curious about the causes of the inundation, were unable to explain the phenomenon.[44]

However, it must not be forgotten that under Ramses III, sailors went to Punt by a route other than the usual one. Herodotus records an expedition which might be said to have been inspired by scientific curiosity.[45] Neko, when he had finished repairing the Red Sea canal, wanted to know whether Libya (in other words, Africa) was surrounded on all sides by sea. He instructed his sailors, who were Phoenicians, to go beyond the strait of Bab-el-Mandeb and to come back by the Mediterranean. The journey lasted three years and there was a time during which the navigators found themselves to the left of the rising sun. This voyage cannot be compared with the accomplishments of Christopher Columbus and Marco Polo. However, there should be a place in the history of exploration for Henu and all the other sailors 'who had seen the sky and had seen the earth'.

Natural history did not go beyond the process of naming, which, however, was very extensive. It should be noted that *mat* is used for all types of granite found at Aswan irrespective of colour. It follows that colour cannot have been the only distinctive feature. It may be that *bekhen* referred to several kinds of rock including, amongst others, the black sandstone schist of the Wadi Hammamat. The use of *nehet* (sycamore) as a generic term, in the expressions 'fig *nehet*' and 'incense *nehet*', shows some attempt to bring trees of very different appearance into the same category. Egyptian artists showed themselves able to depict both native and foreign animals, with an accuracy in the rendering of their specific characteristics that has aroused the admiration of naturalists, although, as Keimer has shown, their powers of observation were limited in some respects.[46] The fact of the matter seems to be that when the tomb decorators depicted cattle-breeding, hunting and shooting, they drew from models that other artists had made from real life, and did not always copy those models with absolute fidelity.

Egyptian doctors had a very high reputation throughout the whole of the ancient world.[47] Medical science was practised at Memphis at a very early period. An inscription, unfortunately in a very poor state of preservation, notes the fact that when the architect of Neferkara's Pyramid succumbed to the heat while the king was visiting the site, doctors were called and medical documents were sent for. Doctors were often priests of Sekhmet, who was the goddess of epidemics. One of Sahure's doctors was called 'Living for Sekhmet'. At a much later period, a doctor from Saïs found great favour with Cambyses.

Our knowledge of Egyptian medicine is derived from various papyri – the Edwin Smith Surgical Papyrus, the Ebers Papyrus, the Hearst Papyrus and others.[48]

It is clear, from the outset, that the Egyptians made a distinction between injuries caused by a blow, a fall, or an accident of some sort, and disease, the causes of which were almost always unknown.

The treatise on surgery, which is partly preserved in the Edwin Smith Papyrus, reveals an obvious attempt to classify medical knowledge. The human body is examined from the head to the spine in a methodical manner, in striking contrast to the usual hotchpotch of medical recipes. Each observation includes the name of the case, its examination and a diagnosis, followed by the verdict, favourable, doubtful, or hopeless, and finally the treatment and other relevant remarks. Modern surgeons find the definiteness of the prognosis surprising. There is no mention at all of divine intervention. Ambroise Paré used to say: 'I dressed his wounds, God cured him.' His Egyptian predecessor, in a country known for its piety, makes no such affirmation. The description of the various ailments is extraordinarily clear, although the suggested treatment may seem inadequate. The Egyptian surgeon believed that time was a great healer and often did no more than prescribe a special diet, which at that time was the best thing he could do; severe cases were treated by means of a surgical operation, not by medicine. The whole method was that of scientific empiricism. The first scholars who commented on this remarkable document believed that the chapter entitled 'How to turn an old man into a youth', and written on the back of the papyrus in a different hand, was out of keeping with the rest of the treatise; as the text was rather obscure, it was thought to be a magical charm. In actual fact, it is the formula for a very costly beauty preparation which was supposed to remove wrinkles and pimples and all other ugly blemishes. The title is no more surprising, after all, than the claims made for similar beauty creams today.[49]

Orderliness and method are singularly lacking in the different medical papyri. The doctor was capable of naming illnesses but when it came to the causes of sickness, he could only suppose that some god or goddess was responsible, or the influence of some dead person. The Egyptians had, however, discovered that dirt encourages epidemics, because personal cleanliness, and cleanliness in the house, were often advocated. However, once an epidemic had broken out, remedies were for the most part ineffective. There are a few exceptions; for instance, castor-oil was a valuable medicine and the treatise on its healing properties in the Ebers Papyrus, which derived from an earlier document on things useful to man, can be compared with the best chapters in the surgical papyrus. The disorders and their treatment are classified: how to cure headaches, how to cure colic, how to make hair grow, how to cure festering wounds, etc. It would appear, if we can judge by this extract in the Ebers Papyrus, that the document on things useful to man was perhaps a work similar to Dioscorides' medical manual, or Ibn Baïthar's treatise on herbs. Doctors must have been able to cure diseases of the eye, gastric fevers and women's complaints, yet the fact remains that there was a high rate of mortality in Ancient Egypt and that all types of epidemics took a heavy toll of the population.

Even before the end of the Old Kingdom, the Egyptians had amassed a prodigious amount of knowledge to which, perhaps, they never subsequently made any important additions. This knowledge was divided up into categories according to subject-matter, in such a way as to provide a classification of the sciences: astronomy, mathematics, natural history, geography, medicine, chemistry and surgery. In every branch of science, specialists recorded a vast number of facts, not so much to satisfy a thirst for knowledge, as to achieve some practical aim, such as to supply information to administrative officials, travellers and technicians, or to relieve the sufferings of the sick and the wounded. These were very worthy aims, and in modern times too the desire to ease the sufferings of the sick has been responsible, and still is, for many new scientific discoveries. What prevented the Egyptians being genuinely scientific in any field was their blind respect for tradition (this too has not entirely disappeared from the modern world), a kind of religious awe which inhibited their natural curiosity, rather confused habits of thought and, above all, a false conception of causality. Not only did Egypt never give birth to any great poet, she did not produce either an Archimedes or an Hippocrates, yet the store of Egyptian knowledge was sufficiently impressive to inspire the Greeks to imitation and emulation.

CHAPTER 9

ART

Royal and provincial art

I T would be impossible to embark on a study of Egyptian art without reflecting on the tremendous span of time during which it flourished; it existed before, and persisted after, the period of the Pharaonic dynasties. Before the two lands were united in a single kingdom, the men who cut broad blades from flint and made them perfectly curved through exploiting the lines of cleavage in the stone, and who at the same time carved hunting and battle scenes on ivory, with great mastery and precision, deserve to be called artists. When Egypt lost her independence, the Ptolemies, carrying out plans made by the Nectanebo, undertook or completed the construction of grandiose buildings, at Behbeit in the Delta, at Edfu and Philae, at Denderah and in many other places. The decoration of these buildings, although inspired by archaic models, was so markedly different from them that it seemed as if a new artistic style had come into being. The quarries, and the workshops of the sculptors and the goldsmiths were all still working at full capacity when Egypt became a Roman province. Denderah, Esna, and Erment were all finished under the emperors. On the island of Philae, the pearl of Egypt, the 'kiosk' of Trajan added the final touch to an architectural complex which was without parallel.

Egypt which, as Herodotus noticed, was like no other country, was to demonstrate her originality in the realm of art. Visitors to the Egyptian galleries in London and Paris have no need to consult the explanatory captions to know that they are in the presence of the Pharaohs. So recognizable, indeed, is Egyptian art that it is open to the criticism, frequently expressed, of being too uniform. Surely, it is said, all those seated kings, or all those men standing against pillars are exactly the same. True, many of them do look alike, but for the moment it need only be pointed out that some are unforgettable. It might be said that when we have seen one temple door, with its jambs covered with hieroglyphs and gods, its lintel adorned with the winged disc, and crowned with a cornice decorated with palms, we

231

have seen the doors of all the other temples. Actually, no two temples in Egypt were quite alike, just as no two are alike in Greece or Italy. Architecture, sculpture, drawing and design continued to evolve from the time of Imhotep, the earliest known artist. Students of Egyptian art have gone to a great deal of trouble to work out the chronological sequence of works whose original inscriptions have been destroyed, often by the Egyptians themselves, and to establish subdivisions which are, in some cases, as numerous as the various reigns. Working from this system of classification, which is constantly being modified, critics have tried to determine whether several artistic centres flourished simultaneously, or whether there was one single centre in which artists tried to outshine, or to break away from, their masters or rivals.

Egyptian art was undeniably a royal art. The periods during which Pharaonic power was most firmly established were also those of greatest artistic activity. Proof of this is to be seen at Memphis throughout the whole of the Old Kingdom. Immediately after the long reign of Pepi II, and even during his lifetime, the quantity and quality of art declined at the same time as the power of the Pharaohs diminished. The restoration of Pharaonic authority by Amenemhat and his successors brought about a general artistic revival. However, the arts again fell into decline under the Thirteenth Dynasty, and the decadence became even more marked during the Hyksos domination, when destruction rather than construction was the order of the day. The rulers of the New Kingdom, chiefly Queen Hatsheput, Amenophis III, Akhenaton, Seti I, and Ramses the Great were all enthusiastic patrons of the arts. When Egypt ceased to be a first-class power, Psusennes and the Bubastite kings struggled to emulate their illustrious predecessors. Later, the kings of the Saïte Dynasty actually achieved this ambition.

Since the capital was not always in the same place, the artistic centres too moved from one locality to another – Memphis, Ithytaui, the Fayum, and Akhetaton – after which Thebes and the cities of the eastern and western Delta again became the leading centres. Yet the capital was never at any time the only artistic centre. The workshops in towns like Memphis and Thebes continued to flourish even when the cities themselves had been abandoned by the king and his court. Provincial governors, anxious to imitate the king, assembled a staff of scribes in their residence city, as well as judges, chiefs of works, painters and sculptors. Khnumhotep, who was a comparatively unimportant personage, since his authority extended only over the eastern region of the Oryx Nome, added embellishments to his town, built chapels, erected statues, and set up schools in all the arts, to counteract the general decline. He did all this, not from disinterested motives, but to ensure that his name would be remembered.[1] Every provincial town, however small, possessed a temple which was a sort of museum, both in respect of its structural design, its ornamentation, and its fittings. Sphinxes and statues lined the avenue leading to the monumental door; others were placed between the pillars and columns, and precious objects were stored in the various apartments. In spite of acts of pillage and vandalism, and the greed which prompted tomb-robbers to ransack funerary monuments for anything that would sell at a price, the inventory of all that is to be found in twenty or so of the larger museums and in many of lesser importance beggars the imagination. To this we should add the catalogues which the Egyptians themselves drew up of the valuable objects stored in some of their temples.[2] It was the ambition of the provincial nobility to be laid to rest in tombs as perfect both in ornamentation and furniture as those intended for the court nobility; evidence of the success of their efforts is to be found all along the Nile Valley.

The question arises whether regional artists drew their inspiration from the capital, or were able to avoid slavish imitation and create their own traditions and technique; or again whether they managed to combine foreign influences with those reaching them from the royal city. G. Maspero was perhaps the first to put forward the idea that regional schools of art flourished alongside the official schools. This is a very attractive theory but in practice it raises a good many problems. Many kings had several cities of residence; Middle Kingdom Pharaohs divided their time between Ithy-taui, the Fayum and Thebes; Ramses II moved between Thebes, Memphis and Per-Ramses. When the Pharaohs travelled from one palace to another, they took with them their chief advisers, and perhaps their favourite artists too. Quarrying operations were almost exclusively a royal monopoly. The work consisted not only in hewing stone blocks of every shape and size to be sent to the workshops, and in trimming them down so that they could be transported more easily; it was also almost always the case that a workshop for sculptors was set up near the quarry and the finished objects were sent from there to the temples. This explains the presence of a large number of sculptors in the Rohanu valley. The royal herald who was in charge of the most important expedition known to us had one chief sculptor and a hundred stone cutters under his command. Sixty sphinxes and one hundred and fifty statues were hauled as far as Coptos and incense was burnt before them throughout the journey. In the same way the statue of Thutyhotep was transported from the alabaster quarries to the temple of his town by four teams of enthusiastic and well-disciplined young men, while a priest stood on the base of the statue brandishing aloft his censer, which had been lit in order to ward off evil influences (fig. 50). Similarly, there is to be seen on the floor of a rectangular quarry site at Aswan an obelisk still attached to the parent mass[3]; close by are a sarcophagus and two abandoned statues. On the Red Mountain, the domain of Hathor, a statue higher than an obelisk was uncovered in the presence of Ramses II, and everyone proclaimed that the king had created it by his omnipotence.[4] Not long afterwards, other statues were sent from the quarry to the temples at Heliopolis and Per-Ramses. A century earlier the famous Colossi of Memnon had been carved out on the quarry floor and subsequently transported from Heliopolis in the north to Heliopolis in the south, or more exactly from the Red Mountain to the left bank at Thebes, where they still stand today for all to admire.[5]

At the same time, the quarrymen dispatched rough-hewn blocks to the temples of Upper and Lower Egypt, most of which had workshops for sculptors, potters and goldsmiths. At Memphis, Tanis, and in many other places, excavators have found furnaces used by metal-workers and potters, as well as pieces of sculpture and samples of engraving which bear witness to the work that was carried on there. But we are faced with the same problem in considering the art of most of the provincial towns. The statues found there may have been sent to the particular town as a result of an order from above. If so, they were part of the official art, and it is natural that the same features should occur in all the statues. This being so, we might be inclined to attribute to the regional schools any works which seem more unorthodox in inspiration and technique. It is difficult, however, to make a distinction of this nature. When Ramses II decided to build a palace on the site of Avaris, being anxious to establish a sculpture gallery as quickly as possible, he called upon all the sculptors in Egypt at once. We know from the stela of year 8 that the Red Mountain group of sculptors sent a colossal statue made of sandstone as their contribution to the embellishment of Per-Ramses: they sent in addition a group of four statues, and two other single statues of impressive size, also of sandstone. These last two had an insect, which was a sort of trade mark, on their shoulders, and a long, upright stake against the calves of their legs instead of the line of the muscle. These features indicate that they came from the same workshop, which was under the patronage of Hathor, the Lady of the Red Mountain. Two granite giants about sixty feet high were the pride of the royal residence. They were given names and were worshipped like gods. However, it is difficult for us to appreciate

Fig. 50. Transporting a colossus, from Newberry, El Bercheh, Vol. 1. The statue
is dragged along a rocky road towards the temple, from the workshop near the
quarry, by enthusiastic teams of workmen

their true quality, because they were probably altered and used again on more than one occasion. They would seem to have been dispatched, in their finished form, from a workshop situated in the Aswan region, along with other granite colossi, in particular the one found in the Ramesseum. Other granite statues again, closer to the human form in size, have been found at Sân and it is reasonable to suppose that they came from the workshops at Per-Ramses. One is a statue of Ramses II; one or two others are deities associated with the western region of the Delta – Anta, Hurun, who came originally from Syria, and Ptah, because he was the lord of the jubilees and Ramses celebrated his jubilees at Per-Ramses. Most of the statues were half-way between sculpture in the round, as practised by the Egyptians, and low relief. The figures, and the stela against which they are standing, are sculptured in one block. The sculptors have made the shoulders of the goddesses too wide and their arms too long. The same is true of the figure of Nut on Merneptah's sarcophagus (later appropriated by Psusennes) which was also the work of a local craftsman. In the various groups, and also on the two statues representing the king in a sitting position which guarded the entrance to the temple of Anta, Ramses' face is shown as being disproportionately wide and almost triangular in shape. The two statues are not of equal artistic merit. The better of the two appears to have been taken as a model for the less successful; in the latter, the sculptor has not quite been able to convey the king's majestic, yet slightly ironical, expression. If I am not mistaken, the artists living near the court, who were partly natives of the area, and partly men from different artistic centres, combined their talents and techniques and created an original style. As far as the reign of Ramses II is concerned, there are good grounds for supposing the existence of an official art, examples of which were fairly widely distributed throughout the country, and also the existence of a more emancipated school which flourished in the Delta, at Per-Ramses, the official residence of the king.[6]

Anonymity in art

Dedicatory inscriptions on the temples mention only the place, the divinity and the king concerned: 'King N has built as his own monument a temple of granite (or sandstone, or limestone) to his father, the god X, in the town of Y.' No reference whatever is made to the architect who drew up the plans and supervised the building operations. On the statues of kings and divinities, only the names of the king and god are given, and quite often the name of the town in which the temple of the god was situated. There is no signature, just as there is none on the statues of private individuals. There is, however, an exception to every rule; in this case the exception is particularly remarkable in that it occurs at a very early period in Egyptian history. The statue of Zoser, which, according to the present state of our knowledge, is the first outstanding example of sculpture in the round, not only bears the name and titles of the sovereign, Horus Neterkhet, followed by the words, 'brother of the king', which can be interpreted as a guarantee of true likeness, but also the names and titles of the royal treasurer, Imhotep, who was also 'first under the king', great lord, steward of the great castle, great seer, carpenter, sculptor and engraver. An inscription such as this is tantamount to a signature.[7]

The sculptors who carved statues of Chephren and Mycerinus, and of other kings and private individuals, did not follow Imhotep's example. They may have been anxious to do so, but finally decided against it as if they considered the action taken by Imhotep, which appears perfectly natural to us, to be improper.

Puimre, who was the second prophet of Amun under Tuthmosis III, caused to be depicted on his tomb a scene in which he is shown receiving three leading craftsmen, and three chiefs of works from the temple of Amun.[8] The first had supervised the making of the furniture, vases and cult objects, the others had been working on a pair of obelisks, and all expressed their joy at having successfully completed their various tasks. There is no mention of Puimre congratulating the six men, and their names were not recorded. Anonymity was, then, a characteristic feature of Egyptian art, apart from the case of Imhotep and a few others who will be discussed later. The anonymity can to a certain extent be explained by the fact that the artists worked in teams. On the tombs of the Old Kingdom, we can see sculptors, drillers of stone vases, goldsmiths, jewellers, carpenters, makers of sticks and canes, and cobblers, all plying their trades in the workshops of the 'everlasting domain'. We find similar scenes on the tombs of the New Kingdom, a period when the workshops were for the most part attached to the temple of Amun. There is no separation between the various groups. In the Old Kingdom scenes, the owner of the tomb can see at a glance all that is going on. On the New Kingdom tombs, a high-ranking official supervises the whole range of activities.

The different trades each had a specific name, but there was one word which included them all: this was the word *hemut*, which can be interpreted, according to circumstances, either as art or arts and crafts. The word belongs to the same family as the verb *hemu*, meaning to work, *hemuu*, later *hemuti*, the worker, and *hemut*, the collective noun. All these words were represented by the same ideogram – the instrument which was used to drill stone vases. It consisted of a metal rod forked at one end and fitting into a handle provided with two leather pads. The craftsman held the drill by the handle, applied it to the appropriate place and rotated it with his left hand (fig. 51). With this instrument alone the Egyptians hollowed out the countless vases of alabaster, schist and breccia which were preserved in the tombs of the first two dynasties, and in the galleries of the Step Pyramid. For a period of two hundred years the manufacture of stone vases and bowls provided Egypt's main industry. In this way the Egyptians acquired the art of working stone and learnt to excel

Fig. 51. A workman hollowing out a vase, Tomb of Ti. The Egyptian artist failed to indicate how the vase was kept in position.

in the field of sculpture proper. The artist was a development of the artisan. The ideogram and the word which referred to one specified craft, that of drilling stone vases, gradually took on a broader meaning, as the range of activities was extended.

A statue usually passed through several hands. The sculptor, armed with chisel and mallet, trimmed the stone block, shaping it in such a way as to give some hint of the form it would finally take – that of a man or a woman, in a sitting or standing position, or perhaps that of an animal. His colleagues cut into the stone with a sort of hook, rather like the tip of a harpoon. As their work progressed, the features of the face, the lines of the body, the limbs, attire and insignia began to emerge.

Two or more craftsmen worked on the same statue and at certain moments their metal tools must have clashed one against another.

The eyes of statues were usually added later by a goldsmith, while an engraver was entrusted with the hieroglyphic inscriptions on the base and supporting pillar. The polishers started work almost before their colleagues had finished; finally the painters took over, if the statue happened to be made of limestone or sandstone (fig. 52). This was the general procedure for a statue which was hewn out of a single block, but more complex works were also produced: groups, figures wearing finery and metal ornaments, stone and metal vases, and ceremonial furniture, certain parts of which were carved like pieces of sculpture. Such a wide range of objects called for the services of several experts. The various parts were finished separately and then assembled, and a whole swarm of craftsmen crowded around to add the finishing touches. This, at any rate, was how work

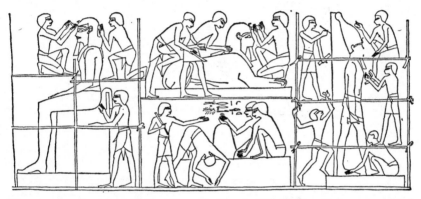

Fig. 52. A sculptor's workshop, from the Tomb of Rekhmire. A fine example of team-work.

proceeded in the studio of a sculptor called Api.[9] At least a dozen craftsmen, joiners, engravers, and stone-carvers, are busy finishing a catafalque in several tiers; one of the workers has fallen asleep on the roof and has to be wakened up because the supervisor is on his way, and another, a practical joker, is slapping paint on his neighbour's head (fig. 53). Obviously, none of these men could claim to be solely responsible for the work they were busy on. Someone, however, must have evolved the general plan and decided on the sizes of the different parts, since each craftsman set to work without having any model to guide him, and without bothering about what his neighbour was doing. Yet, by some miracle, the work eventually came together as a whole and was so skilfully assembled that hardly any adjustments were necessary. Qenamun, who was active in many fields during the Eighteenth Dynasty, is shown presenting the king with New Year gifts which had been made in his workshops.[10] Among them are

Fig. 53. Workmen completing a catafalque, Tomb of Api. The catafalque called :

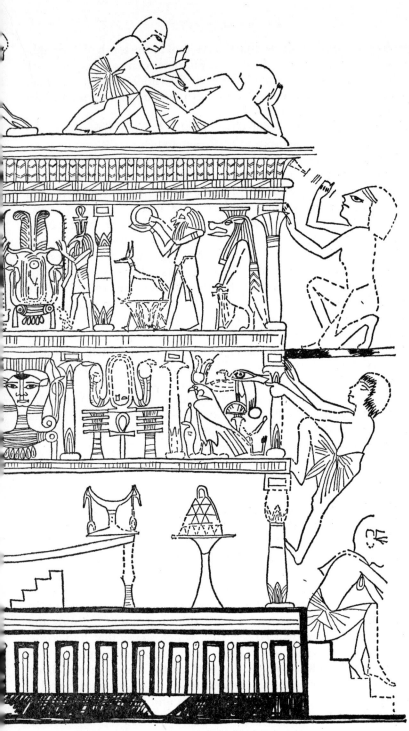

ed efforts of experts – cabinet-makers, assemblers, sculptors, painters and gilders.

exquisitely beautiful objects, like those found in the tomb of Tutankh-amen – statues, articles of furniture, chariots, chairs, weapons and utensils of various sorts, the chief credit for which went to the man who was in charge of the workshops, although he himself may never have held either a chisel or a brush.

Modesty was not the chief virtue of the Ancient Egyptians. We can hardly expect the artists and craftsmen to behave differently from the scribes and officials whose self-satisfaction was so often and so naively expressed on various stelae. On stela C 14 in the Louvre, a certain craftsman draws up a list of his talents. He is well versed in liturgical and mythological subjects. He can execute whatever statue he is asked to do – whether of a god or a king – without having recourse to a model. Merira, a scribe of the divine books used to say that his inspiration came from his heart. This craftsman has every-thing within his head. 'I know,' he continues, 'the proper stance for a male statue, the way a woman holds herself and the attitude of the harpoon-thrower; I know how to catch the expression of a fleeting glance, the bewildered stare of the man who has been roused from sleep, the raised arm of the spearman and the crouching position of the runner.' He can make inlays which fire cannot melt, or water dissolve. He is equally successful with precious stones, gold and silver, ivory and ebony. Here we have an instance of the complete artist who, in attempting to analyse his particular qualities, stresses his respect for tradition and his technical skill, since tradition and technique were the twin poles of Egyptian art. This explains why team-work was so outstandingly successful.

Various artists

It is cheering to discover that certain artists won the esteem and confidence of those who employed them.[11] The chief sculptor, Niankhptah ('may Ptah live for me'), was able to depict himself on one wall of Ptahhotep's tomb which, apart from the tomb of Ti, is perhaps the most picturesque of all the Old Kingdom mastabas. Seated in a papyrus skiff, with a plentiful supply of food and drink, Niankhptah is ideally placed for observing the various activities in progress among the marshes. To his title and name he adds the words 'his *imakhu* and trusted servant', which shows that he was on good terms with Ptahhotep. This is not an isolated instance. The sculptor Neferihi also depicted himself on the tomb he had been commissioned to decorate. He is standing by a basket of fruit, and is being entertained by a group of musicians and a troupe of dancing girls. In another tomb, the sculptor is shown taking part in a hunting expedition, along with the owner of the tomb and his sons. Accompanied by a doctor, he also takes his place in the long procession of offering-bearers. These various scenes help us to understand the import of an inscription which can be read on a Fourth Dynasty tomb. 'No man who has done this (the tomb and the decoration of the tomb) for me, will ever have cause for complaint. Whether he be an artist (*hemu*) or a quarryman, I have rewarded him.[12] No doubt

Fig. 54. An artist painting the seasons, from the Tomb of Merruka. The easel he is using is not very different from the type used today.

the finest recompense of all for the craftsmen who had built and decorated the tomb was to be depicted on it, with their names and official titles.

A noteworthy instance of this can be found at the entrance to Merruka's tomb. A painter is sitting on a stool, with his brush in his right hand and his mixing bowl in his left; he is busy painting a picture on an easel (fig. 54). His small son, Khenu, is standing in front of him, ready to help him. The subject of the picture is the three seasons of the year: *akhit* the inundation, *perit* the emergence and sowing, and *shemu* the harvest, symbolizing everyday life which is depicted in great detail in the halls of the tomb.

Unfortunately, this bas-relief is not intact. The upper section, which might have given us the name and official titles of the artist, is missing. Although several Egyptologists have claimed that the man painting the picture is none other than Merruka himself;[13] it seems more probable that we have here another instance of the tomb-artist trying to make sure that his work will not be forgotten.[14]

Fig. 55. The painter Hui, a bas-relief from Deir el Medineh. The portrait is signed by the artist.

Others were to do the same later. Under Ramses III, a painter called Hui painted a portrait of himself on a tomb at Deir el Medineh, after he had completed a succession of deified kings and queens (fig. 55). He is dressed quite differently from everyone else and, while he paints, he allows his long hair to fall loosely over his shoulders. Perhaps it was customary, even at this early period, for artists to wear their hair long? It is interesting to note that someone, maybe the painter himself or one of his disciples, copied this portrait of Hui on an ostracon.[15]

Higher up in the Egyptian hierarchy than the artists were the men who bore the title of chief of works, which covered many and various activities, today divided between the engineers and the architects.

At the beginning of the Eighteenth Dynasty, the famous steward, Senmut, was chief of all the works of the king at Epit-Esut (Karnak), in the Heliopolis of the south (Erment), in the Temple of Mut, and in the 'Sublime of Sublimes' (Deir-el-Bahari).[16] He did not consider it beneath his dignity to organize the transport of a pair of obelisks from Aswan to Thebes. Furthermore, he played an important part in all the works undertaken during the reign of Queen Hatsheput, particularly her funerary temple. Credit must go to him for having chosen the magnificent basin of Deir el Bahari and adapted the ramps and terraces of the building to the nature of the ground, and also for having designed the impressive lines of the colonnade.

The portrait he engraved behind the door of the grotto and the objects buried in the foundations of the building can be considered as a sort of signature. Not content with the tomb he had prepared for himself in the necropolis, he set up a cenotaph underneath the temple and some unknown artist engraved his profile on it. Two other chiefs of works, Thuty and Hapusenb, deserve to be mentioned after Senmut. Hapusenb built the sacred vessel of Amun as well as a temple which has never been discovered. Thuty's achievements were extremely varied – two obelisks each one hundred and six cubits high (although he was perhaps exaggerating a little), a granite sanctuary, several temples, gates, an ebony shrine, various ornaments, offering tables and even garments. In each case, the inscriptions repeat, with refrain-like insistence, that Hapusenb has directed the artists and craftsmen who have carried out the work.[17]

Under Amenophis III, one of the king's favourites was also an eminent engineer and a great architect. He was called Amenhetep, like the king, and in order to distinguish him from his numerous namesakes, he added to his name that of his father, Hapu, and a surname Hui. He came from Athribis, which lay north of Memphis. It was Amenhetep who brought the two Colossi of Memnon from the northern to the southern Heliopolis, or to be more exact from the Red Mountain to the left bank at Thebes. He obtained permission to build his own funerary temple behind the king's great monument.[18] He certainly played an important part in the work of embellishment which was undertaken at Thebes at this time. The two brothers, Suti and Hori, were responsible for the additions to the Temple of Luxor, the great colonnade, the porticoes and the hypostyle hall; this, at any rate, is clearly stated on the stela shared by the two architects.[19]

It can be concluded, then, that a few artists succeeded in extracting a grateful response from the Pharaohs and in breaking through the indifference of the public. Incidentally, we know that there existed in the workshops lists and family-trees of the famous chiefs of works, accompanied perhaps by explanatory comments. A chief of works, called Khnemibre, who lived at the time of Darius, must have seen such documents, because he had an inscription engraved on the rocks of the *bekhen* mountain, in which he states that he comes from a line of architects.[20] However fanciful his genealogical table may be, it is not without interest. It begins with a chief of works called Kanefer who is otherwise unknown. Next comes his son, Imhotep, already referred to, who was an architect and sculptor at the time of Zoser. The third person mentioned, Rahotep, was reputedly even more famous than Imhotep, although we know of no monument with which his name is associated or when exactly he lived. The official titles ascribed to him do not appear until the Middle Kingdom.

After jumping from the Third Dynasty to the Twelfth, Khnemibre moves straight on to the Nineteenth, because he refers to Rahotep's successor as being Bakenkhonsu, the chief priest of Amun, who did in fact undertake several large-scale building operations under Ramses II. Unfortunately, history makes no mention whatever of the fourteen names which follow. As research progresses, we shall be able to make out a fuller list of Egyptians who distinguished themselves in the various arts, and we may be able to tell what their special talents were. Even so, any future list will always fall far short of the facts and far short, too, of what we know about the Greek artists.

Architecture

The art of building in Egypt began in a very modest way. Clay was used for the walls, tree trunks for the uprights, and bundles of reeds for the roofs. The invention of unbaked brick, which was easy to manufacture and transport, marked a tremendous step forward. The Egyptians were soon able to build solidly constructed walls set at right angles and relieved by niches and pilasters. The royal tomb of Negada, the mastabas of Abu-Roash and Saqqara – especially the latter – provide evidence of a great advance in technique, and a more ambitious approach. The front of the royal palaces, which consisted of three solid masses of masonry into which were set two deeply recessed doors, was adorned with horizontal and vertical beams, and with ornamental motifs which were to occur on later palaces: twin papyrus stalks joined at the top, diamond-shaped insets, and *chevaux de frise*.

At the beginning of the Third Dynasty, at the instigation of King Zoser, and under the skilful direction of Imhotep and his disciples, the Egyptians started to build monuments entirely of stone. The capital was surrounded by a stone enclosure wall – the White Wall, after which both the city and the nome were called. The temples erected in honour of the great gods have been destroyed, but we can get some idea of what they were like from the stelae and the models of Zoser's great funerary monument.[21] For the first time the position of the royal tomb-chamber was indicated by a step pyramid, instead of being concealed beneath a low, flat building. The pyramid was about a hundred feet high, and was a sort of staircase leading to heaven which corresponded to the theories of the theologians. The enclosure wall was in itself an admirable piece of architecture, not only because of its massive proportions, its ornamentation, the skill with which the stones had been cut and fitted together, but also because of certain unexpectedly sophisticated features, such as carved imitation closed doors, and rectangular recesses occurring at regular intervals along the upper part of the wall which was inlaid with tiles. Inside are *chevaux de frise*, sculptured representations of gates and doors in an open position, friezes of cobras and *zed* pillars, which were to remain stock decorative motifs in later centuries.

It was, however, in the use of supports that the Egyptian architect showed his inventiveness most clearly. After passing through the single doorway, the visitor walked down a long colonnade, the ribbed columns of which were some fifteen feet high. They were sculptured representations of bundles of reeds, the upper part being enclosed in a hollow cornice. All were placed against the end of a low wall, as if the Egyptian builders did not trust the free-standing column to support the weight with which it would be loaded. Columns of the same type, but even taller, were used in one of the buildings inside the enclosure wall. Even more impressive are the ribbed columns forty-five feet high, which are part of the dummy buildings known as the northern house and the southern house. They were not erected at the end of a wall, but half engaged in the façade. The capital was formed by making the top of the stems hang downwards from the abacus. Zoser's monument is the only one we know of, to date, which possessed columns of this type. Probably Imhotep and his contemporaries, perhaps his immediate successors, used them in other buildings which did not survive for any length of time. Another type of column, which was invented during this same period, was to enjoy great and prolonged popularity. This was the papyrus-column, three small-sized examples of which are found in what is known as the northern building. It had a single shaft and an open capital and exactly resembled the amulets in the form of the papyrus plant which are to be seen in all museums. Like the other columns in Zoser's monument, the three papyrus columns, too, were half engaged in the façade. Perhaps the southern building also possessed three floral columns, representing the southern plant, the lily.

During the reign of Zoser and his immediate successors, monuments in which the recent advances in architecture were applied and perfected gave new beauty to the capital and the chief towns. These monuments have been destroyed. We must never forget that our knowledge of Ancient Egypt is incomplete; we know the country chiefly through its tombs, and even these have suffered considerable damage.

One of Zoser's successors, Neferkare, planned a funerary monument on a very large scale, but it remained unfinished. Building operations got no further than the laying of three rows of granite blocks, the size of which contrasted sharply with the smallness of the stones of the Step Pyramid.[22]

During the Fourth Dynasty, true pyramids were constructed, of a height never before equalled. The chiefs of works and their workmen were able to undertake such large-scale monuments because they had acquired extraordinary mastery in the art of stone-cutting and the handling of heavy stone blocks. Not only their contemporaries in the ancient world but also modern students have wondered how the pyramids were built. The Egyptians had no apparatus for lifting stones, but they were able to construct ramps of unbaked brick which sloped upwards from the level of the ground to the required height. All archaeologists agree on this point, although the form of the ramps is still a subject of debate. Some people claim that they were built around all four faces of the pyramid; others that they were at right angles to one of its sides. Then the coffin was no longer let down into a well inside the pyramid. It was placed in a relatively large chamber (in Cheops' pyramid, this measured more than 30 feet by 15 feet), a chamber set inside the pyramid, at a height which varied from one pyramid to the next. The chamber was reached by a long corridor, the entrance of which was usually in the north face. The chiefs of works being afraid that the ceiling might not withstand the pressure of the heavy blocks resting on it, had recourse, in the first place, to a corbelled roof, an architectural device already employed during the First Dynasty, although only in small brick tombs. The two chambers in Snofru's Bent Pyramid were over 55 feet high and most impressive. The corbel vault was soon abandoned; even in Snofru's time, it was not considered to be absolutely safe, since cedar-wood poles were used to prop up the upper chamber.

It was still used in the pyramid of Cheops, but only for the Grand Gallery which was 28 feet high and unanimously held to be a magnificent piece of workmanship. The ceiling of the chamber consists of nine enormous granite slabs. Above the great slabs of the roof were five relieving chambers, although one would have been quite adequate. Later, pointed roofs were used and this was no doubt the best solution.

The architects eventually abandoned the ribbed columns made up of small drums, because they were afraid they would collapse, unless given some sort of support. At this early stage, the Egyptian builder was afraid to trust a free-standing column, and systematically adopted square pillars both as supports and architraves. The Valley temple of Chephren,[23] in which the pillars are without any form of ornamentation, has a sort of impressive simplicity. The architects continued to use the square pillar, but from the Fifth Dynasty onwards, they were unwilling to leave such magnificent surfaces unadorned. They engraved on them first of all inscriptions and single figures, then scenes.

Since the discovery of the huge barque of Cheops, it has been known that the palm-column existed at this time. Three extremely elegant columns of this type support the roof of the large cabin. They are, however, made of wood and we have no proof that similar stone columns were in use at this period.

On the other hand, it is clear that by the time of the Fifth Dynasty, the three types of column – the papyrus, lotus, and palm – which are among the glories of Ancient Egypt, were in current use, and the correct proportions (diameter to height as 1 to 7) had been worked out.[24] The lotus-column and the papyrus-column consisted of seven stalks rising vertically together in a fasciculated shaft held together, below the capital, with a five-fold band, curved over on the side facing the entrance to the monument. Plants of smaller size nestled in the grooves; the capitals consisted of a cluster of closed lotus or papyrus flowers. Illustrated texts prove that, at this period, there was a preference for the open capital in non-religious buildings.

The palm-column had a cylindrical shaft ending in a cluster of nine palm leaves which, like the lotus and papyrus stems, were held together by a five-fold band supporting a square abacus. With great sureness of instinct, the architects combined the cluster of palm leaves, uneven in number, with a four-sided abacus. Later, the Egyptians made capitals with eight palm leaves, two under each side of the abacus, which gave the column a somewhat dull appearance.

In the temple at Tanis, three clusters of palm-columns are to be seen; some are giant columns thirty-five feet high, others rather less than twenty-five feet, and their capitals resemble those found in the monuments of Sahure and Unas. The original inscriptions, which consisted of the name of the king and the god, framed by the sky, the earth and the two sceptres, have been effaced and replaced by the much lengthier inscriptions of Ramses II and other usurpers.

After the Old Kingdom, the papyrus-column was perhaps the type most often used, although it differed from its original model in that it resembled less and less closely the actual plant from which the architects had drawn their inspiration. Behind the pylon in the temple of Luxor, a group of monolithic granite papyrus-columns is still standing.[25] The grooves in the capital are no longer filled in with smaller plants, but with truncated stems, devoid of flowers. The same development is evident on the columns in the peristyle and the hypostyle hall designed by the brothers Suti and Hori.[26] Under the Nineteenth Dynasty, it was decided to eliminate the grooves and to cover the entire shaft of the column with hieroglyphs and figures. A little later, the capital was reduced to insignificance by the superstructure, and a period of decadence set in. The architects of the Saïte period could think of no better course than to return to the old forms. Then their successors during the Ptolemaic and Roman periods initiated a new style in which the capitals became sheaves of lotus, papyrus, irises and other plants, including, of course, the palm. The shaft remained cylindrical in form, and continued to be covered with inscriptions and small-scale figures, the effect of which was to make the columns look even taller.

The flower-columns were not the only forms invented by Egyptian architects. We should mention the columns with 'Hathor' capitals, and those used in the Festival Hall of Tuthmosis III at Karnak, which were rather clumsy stone representations of what had been a more graceful wooden model. Lastly, there were the columns which for a long time were called proto-Doric, and of which good examples are to be seen in the Beni Hasan tombs and in Hatsheput's temple at Thebes.[27] These were a rather more rigid type of the ribbed or fluted column found in Zoser's monument; they no longer needed any form of support and the number of ribs remained fixed at sixteen.

The funerary monuments of Giza and Saqqara show how the Old Kingdom architects combined the various elements that have just been described. We are less well-informed about the temples of the gods. Although columns, architraves and some fragments of bas-reliefs have been preserved, the plan cannot be ascertained with any certainty. For this reason, the reconstitution of the chapel of Sesostris I at Karnak, by means of fragments drawn from the third pylon where they were buried by Amenophis III, represents a vitally important discovery.[28] Sixteen pillars, eight square and eight rectangular, were erected on a rectangular base. The pillars were joined at the bottom by a solid stone balustrade broken only at the doorways, and at the top by architraves supporting the roof, the stone slabs of which projected slightly to provide room for the traditional cornice. The base level was reached by two gently-sloping staircases, set at right-angles to the narrow sides. The simplicity of the plan and the perfect execution of the whole make this building comparable to the Valley Temple of Chephren. Sesostris' chapel was certainly not the only one of its kind: similar monuments, now reduced to fragments, existed at Sân, and others were built during the New Kingdom.

The temple of Ptah at Memphis, and the temple of Ra at Heliopolis were certainly on a larger scale and had a more complex plan. Evidence of this can still be found at Heliopolis, although the original site is now below the underground water level. The magnificent obelisk of Sesostris I, seventy feet high, is still standing, and encourages us to suppose that the classical obelisks, pylon, open court with portico, hypostyle hall, and halls closed on all sides had already been established by the time of the Middle Kingdom and perhaps even during the pyramid era. The architects whose task it was to draw up the temple plans felt the same urge to reach ever higher into the sky as did the builders of the Step Pyramid, the great pyramids and the sun-temples. They satisfied it by erecting obelisks and pylons.

We do not know exactly when the idea of the obelisk was invented. Votive obelisks dating from the Fifth Dynasty are preserved in certain museums.[29] Three fragments of an obelisk which would have reached a height of twenty-five feet and which dates from the time of Pepi II have been discovered at Sân. It should be noted that under the Fifth Dynasty the Egyptians began to erect buildings generally referred to as sun-temples on the fringe of the desert alongside the pyramids. They were open to the sky and their principal feature was a podium built to support a squat obelisk and standing inside a spacious enclosure. The fashion died out even before the end of the Fifth Dynasty. Perhaps the introduction of obelisks rendered the sun-temples unnecessary, although the obelisks were very different from their so-called prototypes. The latter were heavy constructions with no ornamentation of any sort. The obelisks were slender monoliths covered with figures and hieroglyphs. However, obelisks and sun-temples had a common aim, which was to glorify the sun. Figures of cynocephalus apes were carved in granite on the base of both the obelisks in the Temple of Luxor. Portrayed in a standing position, they greeted the rising and the setting sun. Being acute observers of animal behaviour, the Egyptians had noted how joyfully certain creatures greet the break of day. The choice of this particular motif is a clear indication of the significance these magnificent tapering pillars had for the Egyptians. It should be added that the apex of the pyramidion was often crowned by a metal cap, which formed a dazzling point of light in the Egyptian sky.

Although obelisks were generally erected in pairs in front of the temple entrance, we know of at least one single obelisk which Tuthmosis III set up at Karnak in the building known as the axial building.[30] This is the Lateran obelisk, more than a hundred feet high and the tallest extant. Eighteenth Dynasty records mention obelisks one hundred cubits high, but this seems an obvious exaggeration, because the obelisks which have been preserved, whether intact or in a fragmentary state, and which belonged to extremely important buildings, are far below this figure. We can, however, have nothing but praise for the skill of the engineers and stone-cutters who, in the space of seven months, managed to quarry, shape, engrave and erect one of Hatsheput's obelisks at Karnak. They were not always so successful. The Lateran obelisk, which was begun by Tuthmosis III, had to be abandoned and was only erected thirty-five years later by Tuthmosis IV. The obelisk left lying in a quarry at Aswan was no doubt one of those which had to be abandoned. Yet another abandoned obelisk can be seen at Tanis in the middle of the temple, where it was used as the threshold of a door. The Romans, who were well qualified to have an opinion on the matter, were certainly impressed by the difficulties that the erection of obelisks involved, and during their period of domination in Egypt they transported several obelisks to their own capitals.

The pylon was an almost indispensable complement to the obelisks. It consisted of a monumental door flanked by two huge rectangular towers with sloping walls, and whose cornices rose high above the level of the building proper. The name for the pylon, *bekhen*, also signified a fortress and an observation post. The pylons had a dual purpose: they provided artists with the vast surfaces they needed in order to extol the power of the kings and the goodness of the gods, and formed a background for the flag-staffs, obelisks and statues of various sizes.

From the New Kingdom onwards, or perhaps even earlier, the Egyptians also worshipped their gods in subterranean temples.[31] For a long time the dead had lain in tombs hewn out of the desert cliffs. It occurred to the Egyptians that what was fitting for the dead would please the gods. Wherever the site lent itself to such an arrangement, there was a subterranean part, and another part built in front of it and sometimes open to the sky. This is the case at Amada. If the cliff rose sheer from the river, the whole temple was hollowed out of the rock. The most famous example, as regards size and brilliance of achievement – and also because of the threat to which it is exposed as a result of present-day schemes – is to be found at Abu Simbel, where Ramses II had two grottoes hewn out of the rock, one large and one small, although in any other setting the smaller one would appear large. Set in front of the larger of the two rock temples, are four seated colossi which, like the temple itself, were hewn out of the living rock, and which gaze towards the tracks leading to the gold-mines. The cluster of small statues at their feet make them appear even larger. In the centre of the façade is a somewhat narrow door through which the rising sun streams every morning, lighting up for a brief moment the statues of Osiris within. In the whole of Egyptian art, there is no more magnificent representation of the function of Ra, who gives life to the creatures of earth and to the works of men.

An essential quality of Egyptian monuments was that they were completely in harmony with the surrounding landscape. The pyramids and the Sphinx, in spite of their present extremely dilapidated state, still form a magnificently harmonious pattern on the Giza plateau. Similarly at Thebes, the temple of Hatsheput is built on a series of terraces hewn out of the sheer cliff-face, while the temple of Luxor is built in a long, horizontal line parallel to the Nile. Anyone looking towards the west at the time of the greatest glory of Thebes, must have seen, against the background of the Libyan cliffs, the line of the great royal temples; he then had only to turn towards the east to gaze upon the no less impressive sight of the temple of Amun, with its pylons and obelisks. In the less important towns, the temple of the local god was set among palm-trees and sycamores. By the beginning of the nineteenth century, all that remained of the splendours of the past was ruined walls and broken statues. The ruins, themselves, have been further ruined, but only a slight effort of imagination is needed to conjure up the achievements of the chiefs of works from Imhotep onwards, in all their original beauty and grandeur.

Sculpture

The stone-cutters, who learnt their trade by hollowing out vases and bowls, at a very early period tried to carve figures of men and animals and achieved some success. From the time of the creation of the first outstanding piece of work by Imhotep's craftsmen, Egyptian sculptors were kept almost constantly busy. The works which have survived, numerous though they are, represent only a minute part of the output of two and a half thousand years. Statues adorned the palaces of the kings and the mansions of the nobility. Even quite humble folk probably possessed small statues of the various divinities. Practically nothing remains of the works of sculpture owned by private individuals. Examples of Old Kingdom statuary come from the funerary temples of the kings, the mastabas, and the temples of the gods. For knowledge of Middle Kingdom statuary we depend more on the temples, and this is even more true in the case of New Kingdom works. The favissa (cachette) at Karnak is a museum in itself. Akhenaton's short-lived capital has provided us with a precious collection of statues executed in the workshops there. Statuettes made of wood or metal, as well as pieces of furniture decorated with figures, have been found in the tombs, particularly in that of Tutankhamen. There is scarcely any Egyptian town which has not made some contribution to the great store of Egyptian sculpture.

Historians have been at great pains to define the distinctive characteristics of the various periods and schools, and their efforts have been most praiseworthy. Keeping to what has been my general purpose throughout this work, I should prefer on the whole to disregard the chronological approach and to concentrate on the most striking features of Egyptian sculpture. As you walk through the Cairo Museum or any of the great museums in Europe or America, within the space of a few minutes you are faced with works belonging to widely separated periods – the two Ranefers, for instance, which belong to the Fifth Dynasty, or the statue of Tuthmosis III and the statue of Mentuemhat from the favissa. Their facial expressions are very different and clearly reveal their personalities, yet they are all represented in the same attitude, standing against a pillar, with their left leg advanced and their arms hanging by their sides.

This brings us at once to the limitations and restrictions of Egyptian sculpture. The attitudes are stiff and show little variety. Only wood and metal statues, or small-scale stone statues, did not require a back pillar; under the Old Kingdom the width of this pillar exceeded that of the shoulders. In the case of figures in a sitting position, either the supporting slab of stone reached to the shoulders or, if it were lower than the shoulders, it was prolonged by a pillar. The Egyptians turned this limitation to good account by covering the pillar with hieroglyphs. The left leg was always attached to the pillar by a tenon and the arms were fitted to the body by the same method. Only on very few statues did the arms hang free.

A statue found recently in the temple of Snofru shows the king in a much less rigid attitude. Had the Egyptian sculptors followed this example and continued along these lines they would have deprived Polycletes and Phidias of the glory of creating a truly naturalistic art. But the statue of Snofru remained an isolated experiment. The Egyptian sculptor preferred to be bound by the rigid law of frontality. This is not to say that Egyptian statues can be lined up like soldiers for review. The head and the body had to be represented in front view, but the legs, arms and hands could be allowed a wide variety of positions. Some statues have one arm hanging, while the other is stretched out towards some object, or folded across the body. Statues of scribes may have one knee on the ground, and the other at chin level.

Strictly speaking, there was no such thing as group sculpture. Two persons or more were sometimes placed against a single slab of stone, or shared the same seat, but each figure was treated as if it were a separate entity. Sometimes the woman holds her arm – somewhat elongated – behind her husband's waist. When the king is accompanied by one or more divinities no problem arises; the various personages hold each other by the hand, or the god or goddess may lay a protecting hand on the king's shoulder. During the New Kingdom, we find a great profusion of statues in which the god stands behind the king as if to protect him. Conversely, kings or private individuals may grasp a sacred object or the statue of a god or goddess in their hands, or hold it out in front of them. Occasionally, however, the figures are arranged in more intimate attitude: Isis holds the king on her knees, like a mother holding her child; Thoth, in the form of a baboon, is perched on his pedestal and is dictating a text to a scribe squatting at his feet like a well-behaved schoolboy. The sacred falcon or the sacred baboon is sometimes shown perching on the shoulders of a worshipper, or the tutor of a royal princess may be holding his charge tenderly in his lap. The Berlin Museum possesses a delightful variant of the tutor with child group: the body, arms and legs of the tutor form a sort of cube, from which only the tiny head of the child emerges. Sculptors obviously felt hampered by the traditional forms and although they did not break away from them completely, succeeded in making them rather less rigid.

It must also be admitted that Egyptian sculptors only very exceptionally displayed a knowledge of the human form comparable to that evident in Greek sculpture. The muscles of the torso, the shoulders, and the legs are only too often represented approximately, or even inaccurately. The ankles are thick, the feet clumsy; yet on occasions Egyptian sculptors were capable of depicting feet with a reasonable degree of accuracy, and they often executed hands – whether wide-open, completely closed or half closed – with meticulous care. One eventually becomes accustomed to the weaknesses of Egyptian statuary and one is pleasurably surprised by the various works in which they have been minimized. Egyptian sculpture has two main qualities: the attitudes in which the figures are represented are natural and well-balanced. But above all the master sculptors of the Memphite school succeeded in creating a series of unforgettable portraits, and, in some cases even, in extending to the whole of the body the accuracy of observation that most sculptors reserved for the face alone. Among works which have long been accepted as masterpieces should be noted first and foremost the diorite statue of Chephren, the Sheikh el-Beled, the squatting Scribe and the Salt head in the Louvre, followed by the hardly less magnificent seated statues found at Meidum of Rahotep and his wife Nofret, and the Squatting Scribe and the Kneeling Scribe in the Cairo Museum.[32] The statue of Chephren conjures up the presence of the king who ruled over the Two Lands with august majesty, as Ra ruled over the sky. The Sheikh el-Beled, so named by Mariette's workmen because of his likeness to the contemporary headman of the village, is a perfect example of the landed proprietor who, in spite of a certain corpulence, was able to make brisk tours of his vast domains. The Sitting Scribe in the Louvre is writing with his calamus on sheets of papyrus, but he keeps his acutely penetrating gaze fixed on his master, whose very thoughts he seems to be anticipating. The Salt head in the Louvre is the work of a master craftsman who had an extraordinarily acute gift of observation. By the sheer sincerity of his inspiration, he has completely transformed his not particularly attractive model. Rahotep and Nofret who sit together in the Cairo Museum in a glass cage, as if they were in their serdab, are visited every day by admiring crowds. There is a hint of anxiety in Rahotep's expression; he knew that even the great were sometimes in danger of being beaten. His wife, who has donned the wig and diadem worn on special feast-days, chastely draws her cloak over the slender contours of her breasts: she has beautiful eyes full of tenderness and her face would be quite perfect, were it not for the slightly receding chin. It must be admitted that at this period Egyptian women had no great natural beauty. Sculptors, on the whole, tended to present women with thick ankles, coarse features, and rather sulky, or vacant, expressions. It was during the Middle Kingdom, and to a greater extent during the New Kingdom, that sculptors discovered and gave artistic expression to feminine beauty.

The works just referred to have long been famous. It is almost as if the Memphite artists had been anxious for their best works to be known first. Among the indisputable masterpieces discovered more recently I should mention the group of Mycerinus and his wife, the bust of Ankhaf in the Boston Museum, the granite head of Userkaf, the Neith of Abusir and the statue of Hemiunu in the Hildesheim Museum.[33] All these works are notable for their unquestionable sincerity. The wife of Mycerinus, who is tenderly embracing her husband, has a suggestion of a smile on her face, the smile of the happily married woman. The tortured face of Ankhaf has been observed with minute care and rendered with astonishing mastery. The head of Userkaf belong to a statue which was three or four times larger than life, and which must have been tremendously impressive when it stood alone on the median axis of the temple. Hemiunu has a bull-like neck and a facial expression typical of the magisterial class whose lack of sympathy for the under-dog is mentioned a few centuries later by a king responsible for a piece of didactic literature. The body, which is heavily obese, is in perfect keeping with the head.

The sculptors found interesting models among the many dwarfs who formed part of the entourage of the king and of high-ranking personages, or who were employed as goldsmiths at Memphis. The statue of Khnumhotep has long been famous.[34] Perhaps the sculptor imagined that the double (or *Ka*) of the dwarf might feel bewildered in the presence of a normal body.[35] At any rate he portrayed his misshapen head, torso, legs and feet with great accuracy. The dwarf Seneb is represented as having even greater deformities, yet he married a woman who loved him, and who bore him normal children; they can be seen sitting naked, with their backs against the family bench and their fingers to their lips.[36] The fact that they were naked and sucking a finger was a sufficient indication that they were children. The sculptor, however, was careful to show the difference between the child's body and the adult's; this was no mean achievement, for Greek sculptors did not begin to make the distinction until the Hellenistic era.

Middle Kingdom sculptors inherited types which had been created by their ancestors, and we have examples of their work. The ten limestone statues of Sesostris found in a cache at Lisht, are no more than averagely good specimens;[37] however, the granite Sesostris found at Tanis is a splendid piece of work, in spite of the damage it sustained when an obelisk fell on top of it.[38] The statues of other kings and queens are not without a certain merit; nevertheless, the works of the first half of the Twelfth Dynasty offer little that is new, although there is a moving quality in the portraits of Sesostris III and Amenemhat III. The king is no longer a being set far above the rest of humanity and whom the subjects of Chephren gazed at in awe. Worry, set-backs, perhaps, have deepened the lines of his face, which has acquired a certain bitterness. It is most instructive to compare the fairly numerous portraits which we possess of the man who built the Labyrinth. No. 385 in the Cairo Museum shows the Pharaoh as a very young man, at once proud and wayward, and still retaining a certain youthful charm. The other statues show how age gradually deepened the lines of his face and gave it a tragic expression. [39] Before this period, Egyptian sculpture had offered no examples of subjects with faces almost obliterated by their wigs and beards, like No. 395 in the Cairo Museum which comes from the Fayum, and more especially No. 392, which was found in Tanis, in a temple which the Bubastites and the Saïtes had turned into a sculpture gallery. The latter sculpture shows two personages, kings perhaps, or priests, who are moving forward in step and bearing two tables laden with fish and lotus plants, portrayed with vigorous realism. The stern expressions of the two men match their solemn and measured tread.

When sculptors were called upon to portray divinities in human form they made no attempt to copy the features of kings or queens but looked round for the most beautiful male or female face they could find. A good example is the head of a woman with the Red Crown, probably a representation of the goddess Neith, which was found in a Fifth Dynasty temple. Later, either through flattery or because the king insisted on it, artists portrayed the gods in the likeness of the kings. A sphinx from the time of Tuthmosis III is easily recognizable by the powerful nose: Khonsu is portrayed with the effeminate features of Tutankhamen.

When gods were represented in animal form, the sculptor would add the head of a dog, a crocodile, or an ibis to the male body; to a female body he would add the head of a cow or a cobra. Statues of this type certainly existed in very early times, but those found in our museums date for the most part from later periods. The divinity could also be represented in a purely animal form: Banebded, and even Amun, appear as rams, Hathor as a cow, Wadjet as a cobra, Sobek as a crocodile, Thoueris as a female hippopotamus and Horus as a falcon. The bas-reliefs prove how skilled the Egyptians were in animal portraiture. The sculptors are responsible for several masterpieces in this genre. Among the highest achievements rank the golden hawk head from Hieraconopolis; [40] the baboon from Tanis, a representation of Khonsu seated in state on a high pedestal, shameless and cheeky;[41] the cow from Deir-el-Bahari; the Apis bull of the Serapeum and many elegant female cats. The lion was both a solar symbol and a symbol of kingship. The comparison between the king of beasts and the human king had occurred quite spontaneously to the Egyptians at the time when they were in the habit of trapping wild beasts along the fringe of the desert. The lion and the lioness, as guardians of the sun, played a part in solar mythology and symbolism. This explains how the Egyptians came to use the head and shoulders of the lion as a form for gargoyles. They had a practical as well as a symbolic function. As the lion was also the guardian of sleep, the wooden supports of beds were carved in the shape of a lion with a very elongated body, a shape which is also used as the determinative of the verb to sleep. Good examples are the bed of Osiris found at Abydos, and one of the beds found in the tomb of Tutankhamen. Sometimes a pair of lions with their front paws docilely crossed were placed at temple entrances – for example, at Soleb and Tanis; they look as if they would be ready to leap up at the slightest sound, like the archaic lions in the Cairo Museum. At an early period, sets of ivory figures in the shape of a recumbent lion were used in a certain game. The pieces were moved over a round board in the form of a coiled serpent, the markings of which were reminiscent of the wooden grids placed over the surfaces of lion traps. Lion-headed goddesses were extensively worshipped, especially near the entrances to the desert valleys at Memphis, Bubastis and in Upper Egypt. The local divinity who was called either Bastet, or Sekhmet, Mut or Pakhet, was represented in either a standing or a sitting position, with the head of a lioness. Sometimes her son was portrayed as a man or a boy with a lion's head, but instances of this are rare before the Late Period.

The sphinx can truly be called one of the most magnificent achievements of Egyptian art; it was a recumbent lion with a human head wearing a *nemes* (head-dress) like that of the Pharaohs. We do not know at what period exactly the sphinx made its appearance in Egyptian art. When the kings of the Fourth Dynasty started building their pyramids on the Giza plateau, it was noticed that a rounded limestone hillock on the fringe of the desert was shaped rather like a recumbent lion. Sculptors, perhaps even as early as Cheops' time, and later during the reign of Chephren, shaped the mass into the great sphinx about two hundred and forty feet long, which has become famous throughout the world. Looking towards the rising sun, it kept watch in front of the pyramids and saw that the enemies of Ra and the king did not disturb the movement of the sun boat when it alighted on the earth in order to take another passenger on board. During the Eighteenth Dynasty, the paws of the lion were buried under the sand, and the story goes that Prince Tuthmosis, the future Tuthmosis IV, fell asleep in the shade of the Sphinx during a hunting expedition. While he was asleep, the god appeared to him in a dream and promised to make him king if he cleared away the sand under which he, the Sphinx, was being submerged.

Several attempts to prevent encroachment by the desert sand have been made in modern times; for instance, by Mariette, before the visit of the Empress Eugénie and the guests of the Khedive, and more recently by the *Service des Antiquités* which has been able to prevent further silting up. The huge brick paws, which were built during the Roman period, do not add to the beauty of the Sphinx, which was still further marred when an Arab prince of the Middle Ages used the head as a target.

From the time of Chephren onwards, great numbers of sphinxes were set up in front of the temples. Chephren himself had a pair of sphinxes outside his valley temple.[42] They have disappeared, but the rectangular pedestals can still be seen on the paved floor of the courtyard. It was Chephren who placed two sphinxes at the entrance of the oldest temple in Avaris. Much later, they were usurped by a Hyksos king, by Merneptah and by Sheshanq I. They were discovered at the beginning of the nineteenth century, and the finer of the two, which was acquired by the collector Salt, is now in the Louvre, where it is daily admired by numerous visitors, one might almost say worshippers,[43] as it stands in a vaulted room bathed in a mysterious light. The other sphinx was brought back in fragments to Cairo in 1905 where it was somewhat inadequately restored and set up in front of the Museum. The Louvre specimen is both the oldest and the most magnificent of all the known sphinxes. The human face and the body of the lion have an incomparable grandeur. In order to convey the dual nature of the sphinx, the sculptor has delicately carved the strands of the mane on the back and neck of the lion and, on the breast, merged them into parallel lines. The animal has spread his claws on the four cartouches (*shen* in Egyptian). The cartouche consisted of a thickly outlined circle set on a flat base, and symbolized the area lit by the sun and the earth rising up at the time of the creation. The Egyptians, who were not bothered by contradictions, believed at one and the same time that the *shen* was unique and held up the sky by means of four pillars, and that there were four *shen*, the four so firmly in the sphinx's grasp.

The men who sculpted the statue certainly engraved on it the name of their sovereign – not once but most likely three or four times.

On the pedestal itself, on each side of the body, there was just room to inscribe the royal titulary; and this the artists did not fail to do. The inscriptions have been defaced by the kings who appropriated the monument. However, enough still remains on the right-hand side to establish the name of Chephren. Thus, the magnificent monument can claim to be six hundred years older than the majority of commentators have said, because they attributed it, on insufficient evidence, to Amenemhat II.

Following Chephren's example, the kings of the Fifth Dynasty, then the Middle Kingdom kings, erected sphinxes in front of their funerary monuments. As a result of a major expedition to the *bekhen* mountain, Sesostris I acquired sixty sphinxes, all of which, unfortunately, are lost. During the New Kingdom, there was a tendency to replace the human head by the head of a ram, because the ram was associated with Amun. The Egyptian sculptors continued to carve sphinxes, both large and small, right up to the Late Period. The late sphinxes, however, no longer had the majestic bearing of their illustrious predecessors.

Many Egyptologists consider a certain type of sphinx, which was found as early as the Old Kingdom and which enjoyed a certain popularity until the Eighteenth Dynasty at least, as being a straight-forward variant of the classic sphinx. The finest examples, of which there are four and which were discovered by Mariette at Sân, are now in the Cairo Museum.[44] They greatly surprised the people who were present at their discovery. They were recumbent lions and their only human element was the face framed in a broad halo of fur. The body is more squat than that of the classic sphinx. A thick mane covers the back and chest. There is even something lion-like about the face. Mariette claimed that the natives who lived in his lifetime along the shores of Lake Menzaleh had the same cast of countenance. The majority of Egyptologists since Golénischeff consider them to be portraits of Amenemhat III whose tortured countenance is well known to us from other statues. The likeness seems to me to be all the more doubtful since the four human-headed lions were actually two pairs, one of which was appropriated by Ramses II, the other by Merneptah. The faces are so different that they could hardly be attributed to the same artist. The first pair have a haughty expression on their faces; the second pair are rather more coarse-grained. Neither pair fits very easily into any of the usual categories.

About twenty years ago a human-headed lion, which is a replica on a smaller scale of the four Tanis lions, was discovered at Tell Basta in the neighbourhood of a Sixth Dynasty temple. The question of its date remains unsolved. It should be remembered that the Fourth

Dynasty kings erected a granite temple to the gods of Avaris, to which embellishments were added during the Fifth and Sixth Dynasties. The sculptors employed on this building, who were less bound by tradition than their colleagues in Memphis or the Fayum, succeeded in creating an original type of human-faced lion, a few mediocre copies of which have been found at Beirut, Thebes and El Kab. They were also responsible for the Fish-Offerers, to whom reference has already been made, and whose opulent wigs and flowing beards are also rather lion-like.[45] The local sculptors had as their ideal a human type which did not conform to the general model, and the same indications of artistic independence can be seen on examples of late sculpture discovered at Tanis. It has already been mentioned that the king was often depicted in the company of the gods, who were usually shown in a protective attitude. Occasionally, the group was posed in such a way as to indicate the Pharaoh's conception of his relationship with the god. Ramses II, who was inordinately proud, is shown seated next to Sekhmet or Anta in the same way as Rahotep is sitting next to his wife. Tutankhamen, whose trespasses had been numerous, is shown as a very tiny figure compared to Amun, who holds him between his arms and legs as if he were trying to prevent him escaping.[46]

The various divinities were also shown in groups – for instance, Osiris standing between his two sisters, Isis and Nephthys. There are innumerable representations of Isis suckling a child. Amelineau discovered a most curious work in the necropolis at Abydos, in the tomb of King Djer of the First Dynasty. It was a bed the supports of which consisted of the elongated bodies of two lions, and on which lay the body of Osiris.[47] He is copulating with Isis who has taken the form of a bird, *zerit*, in all probability a kite; four other birds, falcons, two at the head of the bed, two others at the foot, are present at the scene, which is also depicted on a bas-relief at Abydos. This is a relatively late piece of work, because we can decipher the name of a certain King Khenzer of the Twelfth Dynasty in the carved inscription. However, the episode was known at earlier periods; it was referred to in the Hymn to Osiris which dates from the Middle Kingdom.

No doubt there existed in the temples a great many sculptured representations of the various activities of the gods.

It is not my purpose to mention all the works worthy of note, which are very numerous indeed, but rather to describe the salient features of the most original creations. During the Eighteenth Dynasty both painters and sculptors began to appreciate feminine grace and charm. These were conveyed in a profusion of small-scale works made of bronze or wood, which occurred from the fourteenth to the eighth century BC. Among the many masterpieces of this kind, I must mention a statuette, now in Moscow, which has a delightful expression although the pose is rather stiff,[48] and the Lady Tui in the Louvre. A rather elaborate wig frames, but does not over-shadow, her grave yet smiling face, which has a hint of irony in its expression. Under the long robe which reaches down to her feet, we can distinguish the lines of the body which have been lovingly carved.[49] The Lady Tui was chief of the harem in the Temple of Min and were she able to speak, she would no doubt say, like the heroine of a story written in demotic: 'I am a temple slave, I am not a person of low estate.' (This implied that she could ask a high price for her favours.) The statuette of Queen Karomama, bought by Champollion in 1829, is made of bronze inlaid with gold. It is not only a superb piece of workmanship; the artist has succeeded in bringing out the proud and intelligent expression of the face. The wooden spoons, magnificent examples of which are to be seen in the Louvre, as well as in London and Berlin, are equally deserving of praise. The bowl of the spoon is sometimes given the shape of an ornamental pond, or a cartouche or a vase, and the handle is in the form of a young woman who is either completely naked or very lightly clad, swimming or sailing in a boat among the marshes, or returning laden with aquatic plants; sometimes the handle of the spoon is in the form of a male slave. In objects of this sort, as well as in the ornamentation of caskets, chests, chairs and various pieces of furniture, Egyptian art displays great sureness of technique and an imaginativeness which is in the best possible taste. Although it must be admitted that the majority of these objects were discovered in tombs, there seems little doubt that Egyptians, not only of the wealthy classes but even of modest means, had similar objects in their homes, and derived great pleasure from them.

The extraordinary developments which began during the reign of Amenophis III, and reached a peak under his successor Akhenaton, only to culminate in failure at the time of Tutankhamen, had a considerable effect on the artistic activity of Egypt. There was a break with tradition. The colossal statues which the reformer had built for his temple at Karnak at the beginning of his reign, before he moved his capital to Akhetaton, have nothing in common with the usual royal effigies. Never had a king been portrayed with such a narrow chest, such a distended belly and such swollen thighs terminating in excessively thin calves.[50] How far removed was the thin elongated face from the diorite statue of Chephren or from Sesostris, or even from his own parents, the splendid Amenophis III in the British Museum and the sullen Tiyi in the Berlin Museum![51] Yet although the figures of Akhenaton border on caricature, they arouse a certain admiration. It must also be admitted that the tendency to over-exaggeration was abandoned as soon as the court was transferred to Akhetaton, as if the change of scene had cured both the king and the sculptors whom he inspired of their complexes. Akhenaton was certainly not physically robust. Artists continued to represent him with slender limbs, sloping shoulders, and an elongated face. At least, the face is a perfect oval and the eyes elegantly drawn; a kind of smile plays around his mouth and the long, thin face indicates an introspective nature such as no Pharaoh before him had ever possessed.[52]

The worries which lined, and even ravaged, the faces of Sesostris III and Amenemhat III were of a political character, and related to the maintenance of the unity and integrity of the Kingdom and the problem of settling the rightful heir on the throne. Akhenaton was interested in metaphysical ideas, especially in the radiant star whose many arms spread a shower of gifts over all the inhabitants of the earth.

Among the statues of Nefertiti, his wife, two must be singled out; the first is the polychrome head in the Berlin Museum, the most attractive piece of sculpture ever produced by Egyptian artists, and an unfinished portrait, perhaps even more admirable still, which is in the Cairo Museum (No. 59286).[53] There are several female heads of abnormal length. Perhaps the sculptors exaggerated some structural flaw, either natural or induced, as they had done in the statues of the king at the beginning of Akhenaton's reign. Or perhaps the elongated look was simply the result of a way of dressing the hair which enjoyed a brief period of popularity. Whatever the explanation, the following three works have been the object of universal admiration: the wooden head in the Louvre (E.1455) which must originally have been an ornamental figure on a harp, the splendid female nude in University College, London (1002) which made those who saw it for the first time exclaim, 'Surely this is not Egyptian art', and the head of a child in the Louvre (E.14715) which has a thoughtful expression in spite of the youth of the subject.

The workshop of the sculptor Tuthmosis has yielded a remarkable series of plaster casts, taken either from living models, for the most part elderly people, or from the dead. Several of the plaster casts have a very moving expression, especially one in Berlin (21348), which must be a cast of the king himself. This collection is valuable from two points of view; it contains undeniably authentic portraits of those who took part in the Amarnian movement, and also it shows how conscientiously the master sculptor Tuthmosis and his disciples went about their business.

When the court was re-established at Thebes, artists reverted quite spontaneously to the traditional style. The group in the Louvre which shows Amun protecting Tutankhamen, and the Khonsu found at Karnak would have been no different, if Akhenaton and his followers had never instigated any revolutionary movement.[54] Yet it must be admitted that several of the statues and statuettes found in the famous tomb, for instance, the one of the king's head emerging from a water-lily, have an unmistakable Amarnian look.[55]

Ramses II, who was an enthusiastic builder, filled the temples with statues which depicted him, either alone or with divinities or queens and princesses, in standing, sitting or kneeling positions. In his stela of year 8, he encourages his sculptors to work zealously, for he can promise them excellent rewards for their labours. Many of the statues at Karnak, Luxor, Per-Ramses and elsewhere were executed with great speed in the workshops by skilled craftsmen. Two masterpieces should be noted: a seated figure of Ramses presenting an offering, found in the favissa at Karnak.[56] Few Egyptian monuments can rival these in gracefulness and suppleness of movement. As a young man, Ramses II must have won all hearts.

During the long reign of Ramses II, a great number of colossal statues made their appearance. This was not a new development. Leaving aside the Giza sphinx the exceptional proportions of which were dictated by nature, the sphinxes which adorned the Valley Temple of Chephren were most impressive: so too was the granite statue of Userkaf of which only the head remains. During the Middle Kingdom, monuments frequently reached a height of ten cubits. Under Amenophis III the temples were enlarged, pylons and obelisks were made higher, and the statues must have followed the same trend. Of the two stone giants which were erected in front of the tenth pylon at Karnak, only the pedestal remains: originally they were over sixty feet high. The two colossi which the king had transported from the northern to the southern Heliopolis, and which he erected in front of his funerary monument, intrigued travellers in Greek and Roman times, who engraved lines of poetry and prose on their legs. The temple has been destroyed, but the colossi, although they are now badly damaged, and have lost their crowns, are still very impressive.

Colossal statues of Ramses II, which were more than fifteen feet high are too numerous to mention; the king was anxious to equal Amenophis III at least by having colossi sixty feet high carved out of granite or hewn from the living rock. Remarkable fragments of the

giant statues have been found at Tanis, formerly Per-Ramses, and
we have documentary evidence to the effect that they were four in
number and that each one had a name – Sun of the Princes, Charm
of Egypt, Montu in the Two Lands, Ramses Beloved of Amun. They
were worshipped like gods, especially by soldiers.[57] It is not known
whether the four colossi which kept watch at Abu Simbel and whose
gaze was eternally turned towards the track leading to the gold-mines
were referred to by the same names. The recumbent colossus at
Memphis, and the one recently erected in a square in Cairo, are
splendid pieces of sculpture.

The statues which we possess from the Saïte period and the period
of the Persian domination show great technical mastery; for instance,
the cow Hathor, a statue of Osiris, the seated Isis in the Cairo
Museum, and a curious representation of Thoueris, as a female
hippopotamus standing up on its hind legs. No doubt, works such
as these are without the power to move that is possessed by so many
of the more ancient statues. We cannot fail, however, to be impressed
by the green head in the Berlin Museum, which is in no way inferior
to the best portraits of the Old Kingdom. At the end of a period of
two thousand years as at the beginning, Egypt possessed portraitists
whose work was characterized by outstanding penetration and
vigour.

We now come to the final phase of Egyptian sculpture – the
statues usually referred to as Græco-Egyptian. Although the teaching
in the various schools remained faithful to the traditional canons of
art, as is proved by pieces of sculpture found at Memphis, Tanis and
throughout the country, native sculptors, under the influence of
Greek works which appeared in great profusion at Alexandria and
in all the chief towns from the time of Ptolemy Soter onwards, began
to portray on Egyptian bodies heads resembling those of the
occupying nation – clean-shaven faces, high bold foreheads, thin
lips and a solemn expression.[58] There is no doubt that this was a
deliberate attempt at imitation. Yet Græco-Egyptian art was not so
very far removed from the portraits of the Saïte period.

It must not be forgotten that Egyptian sculptors, from the moment
they learnt to handle a chisel, proved themselves to be outstanding
portraitists. At Memphis and in many other towns, Greek sculptors
could observe the perfectly executed works of the Egyptian craftsmen
and, anxious not to be outdone by barbarians in the representation
of the truth, they began to be realistic. By imitating them, the native
Egyptians were merely reclaiming what had originally been theirs.
Sincerity was the predominating quality of Egyptian sculpture from
the time of Zoser, through the reigns of the various Amenemhats,

during the time of Akhenaton's rule and the Saïte dynasties, right up to the last of the Ptolemies.

The graphic arts

Any surface, whether large or small, curved or flat, represented for the Egyptian artist an invitation to fill it with a pattern. In the very earliest times the urge for artistic expression found an outlet on schist palettes, on wooden or ivory plaquettes then on slabs of stone. When temples were built, it was not long before they were covered from top to bottom with painted reliefs, both inside and out. Even the ribs and channels of the pillars and colonnades were eventually smoothed out in order to create more surfaces for inscriptions and hieroglyphs. The ceilings were decorated with stars and astronomical themes. The absence of decoration on the outer surfaces of the pyramid is no doubt to be explained by the peculiar awe in which the pyramids were universally held; however, artists had the two temples and the ascending causeway on which they could display their talent. The tombs of private individuals and the mastabas represent one vast open picture-book, and the same is true of the tombs in the Valley of the Kings and the Valley of the Queens, and of the tombs of the Theban nobility. Such decoration was not a privilege reserved only for the gods and the dead. The living too wanted to be surrounded with it. Too few palaces and houses belonging to private individuals remain for us to quote many instances. One, however, will suffice. In the palace of Akhenaton a scene intended to delight inhabitants and visitors alike decorated the stone flooring of a colonnaded hall. It represents a pond full of fish, carpeted with water-lilies and fringed with clumps of papyrus plants near which calves bound joyfully, while birds fly overhead.[59] Vines and convolvulus climb round the shafts of the columns and reach up to the ceiling. The whole scene gives the impression of a pergola. At Tanis, in what had probably been quite a modest house, I found plaster plaques which had fallen from the walls and were decorated with line-drawings. Egyptians lived surrounded by drawings and paintings in their homes, their temples, and finally in their tombs.

An art which had such a strong political, religious and social significance was inevitably bound by certain technical conventions. At the beginning Egyptian artists hesitated between two types of composition: a scattered presentation of animals and characters, and their arrangement according to horizontal registers. The Hieraconopolis palette, in which we see a hunter whose flute-playing has attracted a whole train of wildly gambolling animals, is an example of the first; but on the palette showing the booty from Libya, and on the majority of ivory palettes dating from this period as well as on the palette of Narmer, the space was planned out into a series of registers.

The scattered presentation which was more in keeping with the Oriental than the Egyptian mentality, was never extensively practised in the Nile Valley. Little evidence of it is found during the Old and Middle Kingdoms, although it became popular again during the Eighteenth Dynasty when there was a craze for everything Oriental. It was used mostly for depicting large-scale hunting or battle scenes. Compositions of this kind can be seen on the walls of the great temples at Luxor and Medinet-Habu. Similar representations in miniature can also be found on the chests in Tutankhamen's tomb. Such scenes make no attempt to give a truly panoramic view. The artist did not place himself at some vantage point from which he could observe the scene in its entirety or, if he did, he was not influenced by the evidence of his eyes which told him that the further away people, beasts or objects were the smaller they appeared. All the people he depicted were drawn to the same scale, as if they were all exactly the same distance away.

There is no doubt that Egyptian artists preferred to plan out the available space into a series of registers. Every form of activity depicted was broken down into scenes, in which only a very small number of figures were grouped together, and each scene followed on quite naturally from the preceding one because they were all taking place in the same setting – a field, a workshop, or a swamp – and with very short intervals between them. Generally speaking, scenes describing one particular activity filled one panel, and the division between the various panels was indicated by vertical lines. However, this convention was not always observed.

In Egypt, all the arts were influenced by the natural world. The long, low, horizontal lines of the cliffs which bordered the valley prompted architects to design temples and palaces, the general lay-out of which was in harmony with this background. Anyone going towards the desert would see pyramids, recumbent lions, or sculpted human faces. Since the Egyptian landscape was completely flat and criss-crossed by canals so narrow that two boats could not pass, and by roads which were only wide enough for one man or one beast at a time, artists tended to arrange their figures in processions. In the small towns, too, the streets were so narrow that it was impossible to get a general impression of them. Anyone walking past a row of shops could never see more than one or two at a time.

The Egyptian artist took little interest in the background of his composition. The files of offering-bearers, the symbolic personages, and groups of divinities, the processions of animals, the scenes depicting the arts and crafts, all took place in a sort of void. But in certain instances, the artist felt obliged to establish the setting, either because it was unusual, or because it was essential to the activity depicted. Hunting scenes are a case in point; they took place in the desert which was represented by a long, wavy line with, here and there, little tufts of thick-leaved plants.

The clumps of papyrus plants which figure largely in hunting and fishing scenes reach right up to the top of the wall. Down below is the water, the abode of fishes and aquatic animals such as the crocodile, the hippopotamus and the mongoose. Boats with fishermen and hunters glide across the water. Up above, in the spreading umbels of the papyrus plants, birds are trying to fight off animals such as the genet, the ichneumon and the wild cat which are climbing up the stems to attack the nests. The surface of the water, a blue rectangle crossed from top to bottom by bent black lines, is raised up as if it were a solid object, and the fish and other aquatic animals seem to be set on it. Egyptian artists had no hesitation in combining the horizontal and the vertical in one and the same painting.[60] The legs of a chair or a bed are shown in front view but the seat or the mattress are depicted as if seen from above. When the artist wishes to draw a farmyard surrounded by a fence, the latter is merely indicated by a series of uprights. Above it, the rectangular yard itself is shown from above with its central pond and its gutters. The farm labourers and live-stock are drawn upright against the rectangle.

Perspective distorts objects. It makes those which are further away appear smaller, and may even change their shape. A circle becomes an oval or a square disappears to be diamond-shaped. The Egyptian artist could not bring himself to accept this distortion. For him, living beings and objects had an ideal form from which he hardly ever departed. People were all represented as being the same size, whatever their distance from the spectator. Those who are shown as being different, and larger, in size owe this privilege to their status; they are, for instance, gods, the king, or nobles. Animals are usually drawn in profile, so as to be more easily recognizable. This does not mean that they were depicted in a set attitude. Birds fly, fold their wings when they are about to alight, hop along the ground and fight off their assailants. Oxen walk, turn their heads, scratch the ground with their feet, try to escape from boys who are en-deavouring to catch them or tip them over, and fight amongst themselves. A man in a standing position has his head drawn in profile yet the eye in front view. His head is set on two shoulders which are also presented frontally, and which merge by a skilful transition into legs and feet represented in profile. If the arms of the person are engaged in some violent or rapid action, the two shoulders are sometimes represented as one and given a curious forward movement; or again, it may happen that both shoulders are drawn in a way which would be considered almost correct by a modern artist. Incidentally, the Egyptians were not incapable of representing a silhouette almost without distortion; this occurs in drawings of statues, or in the case of figures seen full face, particularly in the middle of a group of prisoners. These exceptions, however, are neither very frequent nor particularly successful.

When figures, for instance, soldiers, animals or ships are shown in a single row or two deep, the artist depicts the nearest one as if he, or it, were standing alone. The next figure, and all the others in turn, are represented only by their front parts, but all of them are of the same size. Asses' ears, bulls' horns, the rigging of ships and soldiers' heads are all put on the same level. However, this should not be considered as a technical mistake; it is deliberate, and results from a deliberate decision to ignore perspective, and to show each being or object, as far as possible, in its classical form.

Some monuments are decorated with paintings without first being sculpted. These are the ones made of unbaked brick or carved from poor quality stone. The area to be painted was first of all carefully covered with a facing of plaster, on which the artist was then free to draw and paint. In the case of stone monuments, and particularly those made of fine white Tura limestone on the right bank opposite Memphis, the process was much more complex. It has been possible to work out its various stages by studying those monuments in which the decoration has been left in different degrees of completion, such as Akhethotep's chapel at Saqqara and the Per-neb mastaba which was removed to New York and reassembled in the Metropolitan Museum.[61] First of all, the surface was very carefully levelled and prepared. Then the outlines of the registers and panels were drawn in black, together with a number of perpendicular lines to serve as guide lines for the proportions of the figures. In some cases, squares were drawn. The artist was no doubt working from a preliminary sketch which gave both a whole picture and the details to be transferred to the wall. The lines sketching in the figures are often impeccably accurate and definite. Then a second artist made corrections which were sometimes indicated by dots. The first sculptor would then bring the figures into relief by removing the background, after which he was replaced by a more experienced colleague whose task it was to deal with the details of the figures and to correct any roughness of contour. The painters were the last to take over. The background was covered with a smooth grey-blue wash against which objects, figures, animals and hieroglyphs were boldly picked out in clean, bright colours applied without shading: red for male flesh, yellow for female flesh, blue, green, white and black for animals and objects. Each of these colours was available in several shades. The paint has worn off the bas-reliefs of the funerary temples which have been exposed to the weather. The bas-reliefs on the mastabas have fared much better. When the tomb of Ti was first discovered by Mariette, the colours were marvellously fresh and bright, but as a result of too many impressions having been made, a good deal of the paint has worn off. Still, in one or two places, enough remains to give us some idea of the extraordinary charm these old paintings had. Similarly, archaeological activities are responsible for the fact that the colours on Seti I's tomb in the Valley of Kings have faded; but visitors are still dazzled by other tombs, for instance, by that of Queen Neferkara in the Valley of Queens.[62]

A relatively limited range of scenes was depicted during the Third Dynasty.During the Fourth Dynasty, however, and especially during the Fifth, the range was greatly extended. The funerary temple of Sahure, although it is in a very dilapidated state, is the best preserved of all the temples of this period and contains religious, military, and maritime scenes, scenes depicting foreign tribute-payers and offering-bearers, hunting scenes and pictures of everyday life.

In the mastabas, the scenes of everyday life are represented in the most extraordinary detail. To begin with, artists were content to show the dead man seated in front of his table, on which were placed a few offerings (fig. 48). It was not long before men laden with offerings were shown leaving the place where the animals were slaughtered and making their way towards the master of the tomb. It then seemed quite natural, since the master had to get dressed, anoint himself with perfume, eat and drink, to portray all the various operations whereby he was supplied with both necessities and luxuries. The dead in their everlasting domain, like the living in their earthly abode, had not merely material needs nor were the people who provided both the dead and the living with the necessities of life always hard at work. They had their moments of relaxation; the ploughman would leave his plough for a while to go after a cow which had wandered off on its own; we see him hurriedly milking the cow while the cowherd is looking the other way. Boatmen exchange bantering remarks and tip each other into the water. Children take part in games, some of them merely amusing, others rather rough. Stewards of estates are being flogged (fig. 21). Just as modern caricaturists invent both the drawing and its caption, their Ancient Egyptian predecessors made the dialogue between their characters as lively as their attitudes.[63]

The best works of this kind date from the Fifth Dynasty. The Sixth Dynasty made no important additions to the stock themes on which the artists of the Middle Kingdom continued to draw, but they were no longer entirely satisfied with them, or perhaps no longer understood them in the same way as their ancestors had done, and they added scenes which might be termed historical; the most famous of these depicts the arrival of a tribe of Asiatic nomads in the Oryx Nome and their reception by the governor Khnumhotep. During the New Kingdom, viziers and high officials who had taken part in affairs of state did not hesitate to have depicted on their tombs episodes that redounded to their credit. They are shown receiving foreign embassies, for instance, long-haired Keftiu, who are presenting rhytons, goblets and vases, as well as Asiatics, southerners and even delegations from Punt who wished to curry favour with the king. We see them collecting taxes, administering justice, supervising the workshops of Amun, being rewarded by the Pharaoh and carrying out their religious duties. The old idea of the *per-zet*, or everlasting domain, seems to have completely faded out, and in the midst of all these commemorative episodes, the old stock themes no longer appear to have the same meaning. Banquets, the ritual of dressing, music and dancing occupy more space than agriculture and cattle-breeding. Painters, as well as sculptors, were appreciative of feminine beauty. We see that art has helped the lady of the house to retain the charms of her early years. As for her attendants, the female musicians and dancing girls, they are all quite irresistible! How pleasant life must have been at Thebes in the time of the Tuthmosides and the Ramessides.

Historical and religious subjects are present in almost equal proportions, in temple decoration, both in the shrines of the gods and in the hypogea on the left bank. The king is shown slaughtering his enemies; there are great battles in which the enemy, whoever he may be, is always defeated; lists of booty naturally occupy a considerable amount of space, but more specific undertakings are not neglected. There is a painting of an experimental garden at Karnak, where an attempt was made to acclimatize exotic plants. At Deir el Bahari, Hatsheput's fleet is seen going as far as the land of Punt. Gifts are exchanged with the natives, and the Egyptians fill their *kebenit* with trees and perfumes. The divine birth of the king and queen, the great festival of Opet, and the festivals of the god Min are there to remind us that the Egyptians were the most religious of men. In the tombs of the Valley of Kings, historical subjects are comparatively unimportant. One chamber of the tomb of Ramses III contains a picture of the royal treasure; in the tomb of Tuthmosis III there are portraits of the royal family; but these are exceptions, almost all the illustrations being of the other world. The artists expended all the resources of their talent on the decoration of these hypogea, on which no light was ever to shine and where no one would ever disturb the sleep of the dead Pharaoh. The result is a magnificent anthology of gods, kings, queens, and sacred animals.

Towards the end of the Bubastite period, it became the fashion for artists to model themselves on the work of the Old Kingdom, and this tendency was greatly increased during the Saïte period. The Tanis mission found many bas-reliefs, which had been used a second time in connexion with the sacred lake of Nectanebo, and which, both as regards the form of the hieroglyphs and the human figures are astonishingly close to those on the monuments of the great period.[64] It is as if the artists had slavishly copied bas-reliefs of the Fifth Dynasty. In fact, however, a new style was developing. We can see this from blocks of stone which, like those previously mentioned, were discovered in the sacred lake of Tanis, and which are fragments of one of the temples of Psammetichus, as well as on lintels which came from Delta tombs. The modest dimensions of these tombs obliged the artists to make do with a selection from the old Memphite stock of themes. These works are obvious imitations, but not mere repetitions of previous art. Although rather softer in feeling, they are distinguished by technical mastery and elegance of finish and are eagerly sought after by museums. The outstanding example of this kind of work is the Tigrane Pasha relief.[65] The Iseum of Bahbit el-Higara, which was greatly admired in the eighteenth century, when both Memphis and Upper Egypt were still unknown, is characteristic of the decline in the graphic arts which was to become more marked at the end of the Ptolemaic era and under the emperors.

The lines are still firmly and cleanly carved. Male and female profiles are still pleasing and well-finished, but it takes time and effort to appreciate the female figures in spite of their flaunted charms, because they no longer have that proud haughtiness which had previously been so well combined with ethereal gracefulness.

Independent art

After paying full tribute to the immense and varied work of all those

273

draughtsmen, sculptors and painters who, from the 'time of the god' onwards extolled the power of the gods, and the divine rôle of the Pharaoh and who created works of art to deliver great and humble alike from the fear of the other world, we may well ask if Egypt had any independent art whose sole function was to provide pleasure and emotional satisfaction. The answer is that by a judicious choice from the tombs, or even the temples, of all periods one could make an anthology in which there would be neither gods nor deceased notabilities nor bearers of offerings but only the most vivid and charming scenes of everyday life. In spite of its mutilated state, the stone flooring of the royal palace of Akhetaton, shows that art of this sort was cultivated. It is true that the Theban tombs contain pictures of lakes fringed by trees and fanned by the sweet north wind, but nowhere is there such a spontaneous expression of the love of nature as in the palace at Akhetaton, which was also graced by the wall fresco, a fragment of which is now in the Ashmolean Museum.[66] Two naked girls lying on cushions at their parents' feet are caressing each other with innocent abandon, and remind one of the princesses in Clouet's masterpiece in the Louvre. Most critics are of the opinion that this artistic spontaneity was a result of the new ideas which became current at the court during this period, and that it came to an end when those ideas were abandoned. My own view is less categorical. It seems probable that at all periods, palaces and houses were decorated with frescoes by artists whose only aim was to provide the inhabitants of these buildings with visual delight. It may even be that this decorative art, of which we have no direct knowledge, was the source of those motifs which were used to make the tombs less funereal. An indication of this is given in a tomb at Beni-Hasan[67] where an artist is shown painting an easel picture, obviously intended for a private dwelling. As a matter of fact, we do possess numerous traces of this independent art on papyrus fragments illustrated with such superb technical confidence. They present caricatures of the great civil and military compositions which filled the walls of the temples.[68] They take us into the brothels, and show us ladies of easy virtue plying their trade, as if the intention were to mock at the disgruntled scribes with their moralizings.[69] Animals are shown performing at a concert. Some of these sketches could be given titles similar to those of fables. Long before La Fontaine, scribes invented conversations between wolves and lambs, but in the case of these Egyptian works, it is rather as if we were looking at Gustave Doré's drawings, without knowing the fables they illustrate.

To the collection of humorous papyri can be added the far greater quantity of ostraca found in those places where the draughtsmen learnt and exercised their craft, chiefly at Deir el-Medineh. Before pupils were allowed to illustrate, and perhaps spoil, precious rolls of papyrus, they were given fragments of limestone on which they practised drawing all sorts of subjects, from memory, from life, or from models. Since the quality varies a great deal, we must suppose that accomplished artists were in the habit of drawing on this very

Fig. 56. Ostracon from Deir el-Medineh. Scenes of life in the women's quarters, which are not part of the religious and funerary stock themes, are often found on ostraca.

ordinary material either to supply a model or to find relaxation by taking a holiday, as it were, from the severe rules of the decorator's profession.[70] The population of Deir el-Medineh lived mainly on commissions connected with the painting of the tombs in the Valley of Kings, the Valley of Queens and the private necropolises which stretched from Kurnet-Murai to the Assassif. This is why many ostraca can be considered as sketches of subjects that are found in the tombs referred to: gods, kings, architectural motifs, hand-to-hand

275

fights, female musicians and all kinds of animals. But in most cases, these scenes are handled with a lightness of touch which is not to be found to the same extent in the most attractive of the tomb paintings. It has already been suggested that these charming sketches must have been carried out as a form of recreation by people who lived by the more austere practice of tomb and temple decoration. This explanation is no doubt valid to a certain extent, but it may also be that the artists of Deir el-Medineh were also employed as interior decorators

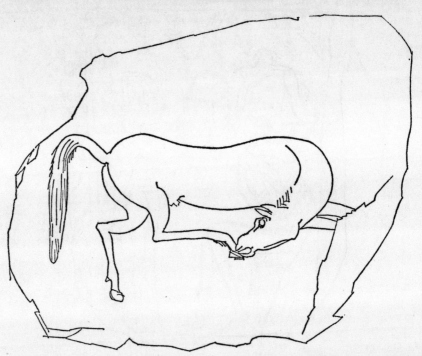

Fig. 57. A horse lying down. An ostracon from Deir el-Medineh. The horse appears in battle and recreational scenes. This sketch has all the veracity of a snap-shot.

for private houses, or as painters of easel pictures (fig. 56). It seems to me that the charming harem scenes, which are not part of the stock decoration of tombs, must have been very appropriate for the adornment of bedrooms. No doubt humorous pictures, comparable to the papyrus drawings already mentioned (foxes and monkeys, musicians, a tom-cat imitating a shepherd, a monkey holding a bag of fruit, etc.) were to be found either in antechambers or in banqueting halls, where the decoration may also have included pictures of acrobats, female musicians and horsemen. No doubt examples of this kind of picture can be found in the Theban tombs and elsewhere, but I have never seen anything comparable to the horse which is nibbling its hoof (fig. 57) or the female mandora player with bare breasts (fig. 58), or again the young girl in the rowing-boat. These are undoubtedly preliminary studies carried out by excellent artists, commissioned to execute wall paintings, not merely in tombs but in private houses and for the greater delight of their occupants. We can put them together with the stone-flooring and the frescoes of Tell el-Amarna, and the many other charming objects, such as caskets, spoons and pottery bowls, to arrive at the conclusion that Egyptian

Fig. 58. A woman playing the mandora, an ostracon from Deir el Medineh. Scantily clad dancing girls and musicians are frequently depicted on the Theban tombs. None is drawn with bolder strokes than this one.

art, going beyond the conventional restrictions which governed the decoration of temples and tombs, flourished in the houses of the living at all periods.

Jewellery and ornament

The Egyptians, who loved personal adornment, succeeded in raising it to the level of an art. Lapidaries and jewellers used, in addition to gold, stones that today are hardly considered as being semi-precious: turquoise, lapis-lazuli, quartz, cornelian, and niello. Gold was first of all purified, then distributed in ingots, ribbons or wires of all thicknesses. By methods which are still unexplained, the lapidaries managed to engrave very small hieroglyphs on very hard stones, such as amethyst, and to sculpt tiny images of the gods in agate. The methods used by the goldsmiths of the Middle Ages and the

Renaissance, such as hammering, embossing, cloisonné, inlay and niello work, were known in Egypt from very early times. [71]

The full royal attire included a variety of head-dresses, necklaces, bracelets, rings, pendants and girdles. Great ladies would often wear diadems on their jet black hair. Lords and ladies wore necklaces, throat-pieces, pendants, bracelets and rings. The diadem of Princess Khnumet is so beautiful that one is inclined to think it was not executed by human hand but by the Cabeiri, the divine sons of Ptah. The pectoral is the most characteristic item of Egyptian jewellery. Within a framework formed by the starry sky, by two plants and earth or water, or perhaps by some more simple device, is set an historical or mythological scene, or perhaps an ornamental motif. There are admirable pectorals dating from the Twelfth Dynasty and the Bubastite era. [72] At the time of the New Empire, there was a fashion for necklaces made of several rows of pearls or small metal discs, and with clasps which rested on the back of the neck and from which hung what was virtually a golden fleece. [73] According to the present state of our knowledge, the Twelfth Dynasty seems to represent the peak of achievement in Egyptian jewellery and metal-work, but it should be pointed out that we have hardly any jewellery dating from the Old Kingdom, although we know that the young women of that time were very fond of adornment. In the mastaba in the Louvre, there is a charming bas-relief showing young women who have just opened a jewel casket and are taking from it pendants and necklaces, which they are putting on with expressions of delight.

The inventiveness of Egyptian art, its diversity and its vitality are quite staggering. Architects, sculptors, painters, stone-carvers, and jewellers, without relying on any foreign models, succeeded in creating unique forms. They were as much at ease in dealing with statues of colossal dimensions as they were in working on a minute scale, and they brought to bear on all they did to extol their gods and their kings, or simply to produce aesthetic delight, an unfailing conscientiousness and a superhuman patience, which overcame all material difficulties.

CHAPTER 10

EGYPT AS SEEN BY THE ANCIENTS AND IN THE LIGHT OF MODERN RESEARCH

BEFORE concluding with some general remarks about Ancient Egypt, I feel it is necessary to give an account of the evidence supplied by those peoples who had dealings with the Egyptians: the Hebrews, the Greeks and the Romans, and then to show how, after a long period of oblivion this extraordinary ancient civilisation was re-born like the legendary Phoenix at the beginning of the nineteenth century, and became an object of special esteem on the part of scholars and archaeologists.

The Hebrews

The Pharaoh never speaks of his enemies except in the most contemptuous terms. They are 'fallen men' and even despicable fallen men, and are said to be doomed to destruction, although experience showed that they were constantly alive and active. The enemies of Egypt spoke about the country in identical terms. For instance, the king of Ashur warned Ezechias that Egypt was a broken reed and that anyone who tried to support himself by means of this broken reed would find that it pierced his hand. The sons of Israel who remained in Egypt for four centuries do not seem to have realized the splendour of the Egyptian temples; it is as if they had been struck only by what Deuteronomy XXIX, 16–17, calls 'their abominations and their idols'. They did not realize how sincerely pious the ordinary people were, and how unpretentiously simple their family life was. After the Jews had left Egypt, Moses warned them: 'After the doings of the land of Egypt, wherein ye dwelt, shall ye not do.'[1] The princes of Zoan, says the prophet Isaiah, are fools. The counsel of the wise counsellors of Pharaoh is become brutish. . . . Woe to the rebellious children that cover with a covering, but not of my spirit, that walk to go down into Egypt and have not asked at my mouth; to strengthen themselves in the strength of Pharaoh and to trust in the shadow of Egypt.[2]

The sons of Israel knew that there was some good in Egypt. When they were on their way to the Promised Land and were suffering

279

from hunger and thirst, they regretted the fish that had been theirs for the asking, the cucumbers, melons, leeks, onions and garlic. They had spread beyond the boundaries of the land of Goshen, which had been their appointed abode, and had lived in harmony with the Egyptians for a very long time. These comforts were not forgotten at the time of the terrible Nebuchadnezzar. 'And all the people both small and great, and the captains of the armies, together arose and came to Egypt, because they were afraid of the Chaldees.'[3]

The maxims of Amenemope, referred to in Chapter 8, make it possible to see how much Israel owed to her long contact with Egypt. The earliest commentators were struck by the numerous analogies between the maxims and Solomon's Proverbs, particularly in the third part. The Hebrew sage leaves out the specifically Egyptian elements which abounded in his Egyptian model, but as regards essentials he follows Egyptian teaching. Both authors declare that we are in the hand of God and both believe in the dignity of the poor, and of the blind, the halt and the lame. Ill-gotten gains do not long remain in the same hands. Parents should be respected, children chastised, and hot-tempered people avoided; one should be sparing of words and always strictly honest in the matter of boundaries, weights and measures.

The resemblances between the two works are so obvious that they have been very helpful to scholars interpreting Amenemope, as well as to recent students of the Proverbs. The Hebrew sage made no attempt to conceal his debt to his Egyptian predecessor, or indeed to the Egyptian didactic writers in general. The author of the Acts of the Apostles, VII, 22, states that Moses was learned in all the wisdom of the Egyptians. This confirms what was said by Wenamun to the king of Byblos: 'Wisdom comes from Egypt.'[4]

The Greeks and Romans

At all periods there were Greeks in Egypt, but they became more numerous under the Twenty-sixth Dynasty, and still more so under the Ptolemies. However, the Greek papyri are much more concerned with the Greeks in Egypt than with the eternal Egypt of the Egyptians. More valuable evidence is supplied by the writing of those Greeks and Romans who visited Egypt, or who simply noted down what they had heard about the country. Book II of Herodotus, Book I of Diodorus, Book XVII of Strabo, and Plutarch's treatise on Isis and Osiris are almost monographs on the subject of Egypt. Further references to Egypt occur in Homer, Juvenal, the elder Pliny, Tacitus, and many other authors.

These ancient writers, who were for the most part well disposed towards Egypt, deal with many aspects of the country. Geography, history, especially anecdotal history, the description of monuments, religion, manners and customs can all be found quaintly jumbled together in their writings. It did not escape the notice of the early travellers that Egypt was unlike any other country. The Nile rises and overflows its banks in the middle of summer, just when the rivers of Europe and Asia are at their lowest level. Egypt is a gift of the river. What they have to say about animals and plants is for the most part accurate and has been extremely useful to Egyptologists interested in natural history, and all students of Egypt without exception have taken account of what they say about the branches of the Nile, the cataracts, the nomes and the towns. They were curious about the sources of the Nile and the causes of the inundation, but the explanations given by the predecessors of Herodotus and Herodotus himself have no validity whatsoever.[5]

As regards the monuments, they were particularly impressed by the Great Pyramids, the Labyrinth, and the Colossi of Memnon. They knew that the pyramids had been built by Cheops, Chephren, and Mycerinus, but they do not seem to have suspected that dozens of similar monuments, some of which were higher than the pyramid of Mycerinus, occurred between Abu-Roash and the Fayum. Herodotus merely refers to a brick pyramid, the work of a certain Asychis, who is also said to have built the largest and finest propylea in the Temple of Ptah.[6] There are, as it happens, several brick pyramids dating from the Twelfth Dynasty, but no name resembling Asychis is to be found on them.

The Labyrinth is said to have been even more remarkable than the pyramids. Strabo saw it when it was still almost completely intact but it has now disappeared entirely. In the absence of any definite evidence, archaeologists have identified it with the funerary temple next to the pyramid of Hawara. This is no more than a guess and until further evidence is brought to light we have to make do with descriptions which are more enthusiastic than precise.

The two Colossi of the temple of Amenophis III enjoyed a surprising reputation in the ancient world. Other colossi just as big or almost as big were to be found in many towns, for instance, at Tanis, Memphis, Thebes and in Nubia. Admittedly, one of these two particular colossi produced a singing noise every morning at sunrise. It became a legend and travellers covered the legs of the colossus with verses expressive of their admiration. Many buildings, now in ruins, were still in a perfect state of preservation at the time of the emperors and the rites of the ancient gods were still celebrated there.

No doubt it was difficult for foreigners to penetrate beyond the entrances and visit the interiors. However, they commented on the obelisks, the nilometers and the attractive appearance of the temple of Bubastis. The neglect into which the temples of Heliopolis had fallen allowed Strabo to compile a general description which is on the whole quite accurate.[7] He admits their impressive size but he refuses to credit them with either charm or beauty. Germanicus, who travelled to Egypt in AD 19, visited the Labyrinth, several famous places and finally Thebes, where he had the good fortune to have as his guide an old priest who understood the language of his ancestors and was capable of translating inscriptions into Latin or Greek.[8] Similarly, in modern times, kings or visiting notabilities have had the good fortune to have the monuments explained to them not by some ignorant or garrulous dragoman, but by the Director of the *Service des Antiquités* or of the excavations at Karnak. Germanicus was thus able to obtain information about the campaigns of Ramses II, but through a curious misreading he took the list of the allies of the Hittite king to be a list of countries that Ramses had conquered, so that the Pharaoh seemed to have possessed an empire comparable to that of Alexander.

The list of kings that can be extracted from Herodotus, Book II, is very strange indeed. It begins like the Egyptian lists with Menes, the first of a series of three hundred and thirty kings, which also included a queen called Nitocris, whom modern scholars have supposed to be Neitaqert and whose reign seems to have occurred towards the end of the Sixth Dynasty.[9]

Moeris, who comes after Menes, may be identical with the builder of the Labyrinth, Amenemhat III, whose first name *Ni-maat-re* is given variously by different authors as Ameres, Lameres, or Imandes.[10]

Between Moeris and Sesostris there was apparently nothing worthy of mention. Sesostris was correctly transcribed by Manetho from the Egyptian name Sanusert, which belonged to four sovereigns of the Twelfth Dynasty; they became fused into one, whose conquests are very similar to those attributed to Ramses II by the old man of Thebes. The form Sesoosis, adopted by Diodorus,[11] is probably not a corruption of Sesostris but comes rather from Sesesu, a familiar yet respectful form of address sometimes used by Ramses II's own contemporaries. The most wildly improbable stories have grown up around this fact.

There is no point in attempting to identify the successors of Sesostris, Pheros, Proteus and Rhampsinitus[12] with actual Pharaohs. The word Pheros may have affinities with the word Pharaoh, and

Proteus with the word Paruti, a term which occurred from the New Kingdom onwards and referred to the two doors of a temple or a palace. In Rhampsinitus we can recognize Ramses-sa-Neith, Ramses son of Neith. It was usual for kings to proclaim themselves sons of one or other of the divinities in their *serekh*, or in one of their cartouches. The Bubastite kings were almost always sons of Bastet; one of the Osorkons was son of Isis. Ramses II was, according to the locality, son of Seth, Horus or Ptah. The Saïte kings, Ahmosis in particular, frequently called themselves sons of Neith, but there is no evidence that any of the Ramses ever gave themselves this appellation. But it is always possible that some document may come to light to prove that one of the Ramses was called son of Neith.

It is difficult to understand how Herodotus came to place the Cheops-Chephren-Mycerinus group after kings who, on any reckoning, belonged to a relatively more recent period. In his usual way, the Greek historian makes them the subject of amusing anecdotes which are certainly not based on fact. Maspero was probably right in believing that the stories related by Herodotus were no more than gossip current in the streets of Memphis, either among the Greek community, or among the Egyptians themselves. The tradition, according to which the kings who built the two great pyramids were tyrants, may well have been a very old one. In Herodotus' account the three illustrious names are followed by the somewhat puzzling names of Asychis, Anysis and Sethos.[13] We have to conclude that Herodotus had only a very vague idea of Pharaonic history before the time of Psammetichus, and later classical historians, even though they had the possibility of referring to Manetho's work, were hardly better informed on the subject; there is a world of difference between Usimara and the Osymandias of Diodorus. Yet I would rather have the accounts given by the classical historians than some dull and accurate list of which we have no need.

On the whole, the classical writers were better informed about the great religious festivals and the oracles than about the kings. What impressed them most was the very great antiquity of the Egyptian religion. They realized that long before the Trojan War, the Egyptians had temples and priests, and that for this reason Egypt should be called the mother of the gods. The Egyptians were the first people to celebrate great national festivals and the Greeks took over the custom from them.[14] Although the Greeks called Osiris, Isis and Nephthys by their Egyptian names (and occasionally Min, Horus, Seth, Amun and Ptah as well), being impressed with the very great antiquity they ascribed to Egyptian religion, they preferred to give Egyptian gods Greek names, not of course haphazardly but through a logical analogy with certain of their own divinities. It is not always clear on what grounds the analogy was made. Amun, king of the gods, was more or less the equivalent of Zeus, and Hathor, one of the goddesses of pleasure, of Aphrodite. But the Greeks cannot have been unaware of the fact that Hathor was represented sometimes as a cow, or sometimes as a woman with a cow's head, or with a woman's head crowned by a pair of horns. Horus, the avenger of his father, had very little in common with Apollo. Other associations are even more puzzling. Was Heracles the counterpart of Khonsu, or of Herishef? For some, Min, the ithyphallic god, was the Greek Pan, for others, Perseus; Pan, on the other hand, was compared to the god of Mendes, who was reputed to be very fond of women.

Plutarch is the best informed of all the classical authors on the subject of the gods. He wrote an account of the Osiris legend which is completely coherent and which has been invaluable to Egyptologists and indeed still is today. His account differs in certain respects from the one which can be pieced together from the Pyramid and Coffin Texts, or from various hymns. This can be explained by the fact that the Egyptian documents are based on a version of the legend which was current in Abydos, whereas Plutarch obtained his material from Busiris in the Central Delta, where the Osiris cult became established even before being adopted by the rest of Egypt.

Long before the time of Juvenal, who was frankly shocked by the Egyptian sacred animals, these beasts were a source of astonishment to the Greeks and Romans.[15] The author of the Satires, who was not well-disposed towards Egypt since he had probably lived there as an exile, considered the Egyptian worship of animals to be foolish, but his predecessors had spoken of the animal gods with a certain understanding. We should not forget that it was the evidence supplied by Strabo about the necropolis of the Apis bulls which led Mariette to the discovery of the Serapeum. The recent excavation of a huge cavern piled high with innumerable mummified bodies of ibises confirms the statement made by Herodotus to the effect that ibises were buried in the town of Hermes. The classical authors were naturally curious about the circumstances which had led to the worship of animals. Some put forward the theory that the animals had been deified because of the fear they inspired; this explanation, however, was obviously only valid in certain cases. Others explained the Egyptian beliefs by the fact that one particular divinity had become associated with a certain animal species. To say this was merely to push the problem one stage back. The explanation found in Diodorus and Plutarch is much closer to the truth.[16] According to Diodorus, the military chiefs carried images of the sacred animals fixed to their javelins, so that everyone would know to which company they belonged. Plutarch believed that it was Osiris who had had the idea of giving each section of his vast army a distinctive sign, which took the form of some animal. The animal eventually became a cult object and was worshipped as a divine creature. Since the discovery of innumerable vases and palettes dating from before the time of Menes, we have known that each clan was identified by an ensign fixed on a high pole, and that in historic times these ensigns designated a certain territory or a god, and in many cases both.

The Greeks dealt with Egyptian geographical names in the same way as they had dealt with the names of the gods. Memphis, Sais, Tanis, Thmuis and Syene were correctly transcribed from the original Egyptian: Mennefer, Sau, Zani, Tahut-Bau, and Sunu to which a Greek flexional ending was added. Others were slightly adapted to approximate to Greek names or to universally recognized barbaric names: for instance, Tahut-Ipet became Thebes; the same type of explanation is probably valid for Babylon, near Heliopolis. The majority of Egyptian towns were designated by an expression consisting of πολις and the name of the divinity, or the name of the animals venerated in the locality: Heliopolis, Diospolis, Aphroditopolis, Latopolis are examples of the first case; Hieraconopolis, Crocodolilopolis, of the second. Modern scholars have had to solve a two-fold problem; they have had to place the Greek names on the map and find their equivalents in the original Egyptian. In a few cases, for instance Anysis and Papremis, all attempts at an explanation have proved unsuccessful. Nor have we discovered the Egyptian equivalent of Terenuthis, although the Arab village of Teraneh proves that the name is very old and that it has persisted until the present day.

The information which the classical writers possessed on the subject of the after-life was more or less incoherent. They knew that all the dead were mummified, more or less elaborately, according to their social status. Herodotus has a fund of extremely useful information to offer on this subject, as well as on others, such as the cultivation of crops, the various arts and crafts, and strange customs.

Taken as a whole, the evidence supplied by the classical writers was extremely valuable to the first Egyptologists and is still very useful today. Since we now have direct sources of information at our disposal the problem is no longer the same as it used to be. We no longer accept the evidence of these authors without checking it very carefully. There are points on which we have to accept it provisionally, such as it is, and we can do this all the more confidently since it has proved reliable in some other connexions.

The information on Egypt collected by the classical writers was obtained by word of mouth only; none of them could read either the hieroglyphs or the cursive writing. Their material was supplied by Greek-speaking Egyptians, or by Greeks who had settled in Egypt and who had a smattering of the language. A few Egyptian words, correctly understood, crept into their works – for example, *Piromis*, which meant a good, upright man.[17] But the translation of a whole sentence was wide of the mark. Five signs – a child, an old man, a hawk, a fish and a hippopotamus[18] – are interpreted as meaning: 'O you who are born and who die, God hates excessive violence, for the child represents birth and the old man decay.' Not everything in this version is totally wrong. *Mesu*, derivative of the root *msy*, to be born, did indeed mean child; the fish, *bwt*, conveyed the idea of something loathsome or forbidden. The hawk, or rather the falcon, the image of Horus, could be a determinative in all divine names. Apart from this, it must be admitted that Plutarch's commentary, and generally speaking, the information he offers on the subject of Egyptian writing were not likely to put interested inquirers on the right track. Even a specialized work, such as Horapollon's study of hieroglyphs, contained too many biased, or totally inaccurate, interpretations to be of any great help.

Deciphering the hieroglyphics. Champollion

Even as early as the Renaissance, scholars were interested in Egypt and the history of the Pharaohs and anxious to discover the meaning of the hieroglyphic writing. The Jesuit, Kircher, was the best known of these pioneers. Travellers' tales and descriptions of monuments appeared in several languages, while sovereigns and princes started to collect Egyptian objects as curios. By the end of the eighteenth century, it was known that Coptic, which had been studied since the sixteenth century, was the modern form of Egyptian, and that both languages were related to the Semitic group. It had also been established that signs surrounded by a cartouche represented names of kings and that cursive forms of writing were derived from the writing on the monuments.[19] This accurate knowledge was, however, rendered null and void by the persistent belief that the hieroglyphs were symbols representing ideas.

The Egyptian expedition was soon to supply the vital key for the solution of the problem. The scholars whom Bonaparte took with him studied and measured every site and every visible monument, and finally published their findings in their great work, *La Description de l'Egypte*, which appeared between 1809 and 1816.[20] They did not confine their activities to surface exploration. In the Valley of the Kings, where eleven tombs were already accessible, they discovered the entrance to a twelfth, that of Amenophis III. Their main discovery, however, and one which was to determine the whole future course of Egyptology, occurred at Rosetta where, in 1799, Captain Bouchard unearthed a block of granite which recorded a decree issued at Memphis by Ptolemy V, in hieroglyphics, in popular writing (demotic) and in Greek. The demotic and Greek texts were almost complete. At the beginning of the hieroglyphic part of the inscription, some lines, the exact number of which is not known, are missing, and each line of the remaining portion has lost its beginning and end. The monument was transported to London in 1802, where it was studied with passionate interest. Sylvestre de Sacy and Akerblad identified the groups of demotic characters corresponding to the name Ptolemy. The hieroglyphic portion contained six examples of the name enclosed in cartouches and sometimes accompanied by epithets. With the help of this name and that of Berenice which was associated with it on one of the plates in the *Description de l'Egypte*, Thomas Young worked out the correct phonetic value of five of the fifteen signs. He indicated the groups of hieroglyphs on the Rosetta stone which corresponded to Greek words, and in fifty per cent of the cases he guessed correctly. Although these results were important, they were still inadequate and Young was not able to take them any further.

Jean-François Champollion, who succeeded in overcoming the difficulties, remains the greatest of all the names associated with the study of Egypt. He possessed to a remarkably high degree three qualities characteristic of the inventive mind: an eager and alert curiosity, a creative imagination and a sense of reality which kept his imaginativeness within bounds. From early childhood he had had a passion for Oriental studies and a premonition of the part he was to play in the revival of Ancient Egyptian culture. When in 1814, at the age of twenty-four, he published his two volumes on Egypt under the Pharaohs, he knew everything that it was possible to know about the country at that period. By 1821 he had drawn up an alphabet. He waited another year before addressing his memorable letter to M. Dacier, the Permanent Secretary of the *Académie des Inscriptions*; this letter analyses the cartouches of Ptolemy, Berenice, Cleopatra, Alexander, and several Roman emperors, as well as titles and epithets.[21] Practically no fault at all can be found with the alphabet he put forward. He established the fact that the Egyptians made very frequent use of homophones, that vowels could be indicated in a variety of ways, or even omitted altogether, and that the phonetic writing had not been created in order to designate the Greek and Roman sovereigns, but had been in use at a very early period. He added that it might even be possible to discover in Egyptian writing, if not the origins of the alphabets of the peoples of Western Asia, especially Egypt's neighbours, at least the model on which they may have been based. The decipherment of the hieroglyphs would allow the Egyptian monuments to be placed in an accurate chronological order, and make it possible to describe the institutions of Pharaonic times.

Champollion made fantastically rapid progress along these lines. He had not included his analysis of the names of Tuthmosis and Ramses in his letter to M. Dacier. The discoveries he made with regard to these names and many others were recorded in the *Précis du système hiéroglyphique des Anciens Egyptiens* which appeared in 1824. In this work Champollion not only studied the names inside cartouches but also the names of divinities and private individuals, titles and epithets. He defined the signification of more than one hundred signs and outlined a system by which others could be discovered. The close relationship between the three forms of writing, sacred, hieratic and demotic was finally proved. Kings whose existence had been disputed took their place in history. So too did Nubia which had been part of Egyptian civilisation.

Champollion now felt that he was ready to tackle the original monuments, of which there were very few in Paris. He went first to Turin to study the Drovetti collection: then, with a team of draughtsmen and French and Tuscan scholars he set off on his famous journey into Egypt and Nubia which supplied the material for his *Monuments de l'Egypte*, the *Monumenti*, and the *Notices Descriptives*, which only appeared after his death. 'Thirty years ago,' J. J. Ampère later wrote, 'these ruins were mute; now they can speak and they tell us about more than twenty centuries of Egyptian history.' When he had completed his journey, Champollion proposed that an administrative department should be created for the purpose of protecting the monuments which, as he had seen with his own eyes, were being destroyed with alarming rapidity. He also made out a most judicious list of the excavation sites in the order of urgency of exploration. When he returned to France his health was already impaired. None of his immediate pupils was able to carry on his work. He managed before he died to write his *Grammaire égyptienne* and the *Dictionnaire hiéroglyphique*,[22] thus providing his true successors, Lepsius and de Rougé, with a solid basis for further research.

Collectors and explorers. The discovery of the Serapeum

We must now go back a little to before Champollion's time. From the moment Mehemet Ali allowed Europeans access to Egypt, consuls, merchants and travellers all became collectors of antiquities. It was easy to obtain a permit from the Sultan to start excavations.[23] These amateur archaeologists bore little resemblance to the learned young men who are carefully trained by the universities in the scientific study of excavation sites and monuments. They were quite unscrupulous and were all in fierce competition with each other. The most important thing as far as they were concerned was to find objects likely to fetch a high price which they then sold to the highest bidder, without feeling in any way obliged to give preference to their own country. We should not, however, complain; the Drovetti, Salt, and Anastasy collections, not to mention many others, were the nucleus of the museums which were later established in the European capitals. At this period many extremely important discoveries enriched our knowledge of the civilisation of Ancient Egypt. Belzoni, who was called the Titan of Padua, discovered seven new tombs in the Valley of Kings, one of them being the tomb of Seti I. He had coloured reproductions made of it, which were shown in London and Paris and won for him a fame nearly as great as that Lord Carnarvon was to enjoy a hundred years later. At Giza he discovered the entrance to the second pyramid. A Genoese sailor, G. B. Caviglia, cleared the Sphinx, penetrated into the interior of the third pyramid and found, at the bottom of a muddy trench, a colossal statue of Ramses II which Herodotus may well have seen standing in the Temple of Ptah.

Far superior, from the scientific point of view, to these activities were the operations carried out by Colonel Howard Vyse and the engineer, Perring, in most of the pyramids at Giza and Meidum. Between 1842 and 1845, the large-scale Prussian expedition directed by Lepsius was to collect so many inscriptions and papyri that, on publication, they filled twelve albums. About the middle of the century, there occurred the most remarkable discovery to be recorded before that of Tutankhamen's tomb. Auguste Mariette, who had become interested in Egyptology while classifying drawings made by a relative of his, Nestor l'Hôte, one of Champollion's companions in Egypt, had been sent out to Egypt to purchase Coptic papyri. While out walking one day at Saqqara, he saw, protruding from the sand, a sphinx's head which resembled the series of sphinxes he had noticed at Alexandria and Cairo. He was immediately reminded of a passage in Strabo referring to the temple of Serapis which was situated in such a sandy area that the bodies of the sphinxes were half concealed. He had very little money, and it did not occur to him that a permit to dig might be necessary; he simply engaged about thirty workmen and set to work to clear the sand from the avenue of sphinxes, thus bringing to light not only the sphinxes themselves but also such remarkable pieces of work as the Sitting Scribe. At the hundred and thirty-fourth sphinx he came across an assembly of sages and Greek poets arranged in a semicircle. Beyond, lay more sphinxes, a statue of Bes, lions, and an Apis bull. Finally, on the 12th November 1851, in spite of various difficulties, Mariette entered the tomb of the Apis bulls, a series of underground galleries the total length of which was more than two hundred and fifty yards, and which contained twenty-four sarcophagi, as well as stelae, votive offerings and marvellous jewels.

After putting more than seven thousand pieces in the Louvre, the famous excavator set about publishing his discoveries. After a few unsuccessful attempts, the first instalment of the Serapeum of Memphis appeared. The publishers, however, very soon came up against the sort of difficulty which has always hampered publications on Egyptology – costs were underestimated, unexpected expenses occurred, and the subscribers were too few in number. The second instalment never materialized. Another edition, begun in 1864, was left unfinished. Victory is, however, in sight, since the *Centre National de la Recherche scientifique* has announced its intention of publishing Mariette's discoveries in their entirety.

Foundation of the Service des Antiquités

The year 1858 marked the beginning of a new period. The ancient remains were no longer to be left uncared for; henceforth they were to be protected, and by the very scholar who had just won fame as the discoverer of the Serapeum. Mariette was appointed *mamour* (director) of the *Service des Antiquités*, a post he was to retain until his death in 1881. He was given a salary, and was allowed to recruit assistants. He had a steam-boat at his disposal, he could conscript man-power, and from time to time was granted funds for particular purposes. He was to clear and restore the monuments, and remove the furniture and fittings to Bulaq. Although he had an extremely ambitious programme of work, his activities were in practice restricted to four excavation sites: Tanis, Memphis, Abydos and Thebes. In each case, outstanding results were obtained. We need only mention the diorite statue of Chephren, the human-faced lions, the offering-bearers, the tombs of Ti and Ptah-hotep, Rahotep and

Nofret, the treasure of Queen Ahhotep, inscriptions and king lists.

The admiration which the discovery of so many treasures aroused was accompanied in scholarly circles by a certain irritation, for the published records of Mariette's achievements did not keep pace with the actual work of excavation. Egyptologists who were eagerly awaiting the latest information had to make do with a few articles in the *Revue archéologique*, and copies of texts made without Mariette's knowing. In the end, Egyptological libraries were enriched with several fine volumes: Abydos, Dendera, Karnak and Deir-el-Bahari, the journey into Upper Egypt, and the Album of the Bulaq Museum. Mariette's *Monuments divers* appeared in 1889 with a commentary by Maspero who published a book on the mastabas of the Old Kingdom from Mariette's manuscripts. Other excavation projects were left partly unpublished, or never got beyond the planning stage: for instance, Tanis, Ti's tomb, the Serapeum and the Theban necropolis; in these various cases the work has been completed by others or will be eventually.

About 1880, an Egyptologist's library included the *Description de l'Egypte*, the *Monuments* by Champollion and Rosellini, the *Denkmäler* by Lepsius, the last part of which was devoted to the Berlin Papyrus, and *L'Histoire de l'art égyptien d'après les monuments* by Prisse d'Avennes. Lithographic reproductions had been made of the London Papyrus, the Leyden Papyrus, the Turin Papyrus, the Bulaq Museum Papyrus, and the Prisse Papyrus. Collections of inscriptions compiled by Brugsch, Duemichen and de Rougé, and the works of Mariette completed the mass of material on which decipherers, linguists and historians could work: de Rougé, Chabas and Deveria in France, Birch, Wilkinson and Goodwin in England, Leemans, Lepsius, Ebers and Brugsch in Germany. Ebers, the author of several charming novels, published an extremely attractive descriptive work on Egypt which Maspero translated into French. Ebers was also responsible for the publication of the splendid medical papyrus normally referred to by his name; Brugsch excelled in almost every field. After Champollion's death, the study of the demotic texts had been neglected. In 1855, Brugsch published a *Grammar of Demotic* which contained the general principles of the 'popular' language and writing of the Ancient Egyptians, followed by two basic works: the *Hieroglyphisch-demotisch Wörterbuch*, Leipzig 1867, and the *Geographical Dictionary of Ancient Egypt*, Leipzig, 1879–1880, which contained comparative alphabetical lists of geographical proper names found on the monuments and in the papyri. Later, in *Die Aegyptologie*, he gave a summary of the results he had achieved during his long career. The *Zeitschrift für*

Aegyptische Sprache und Altertumskunde which was the first review to be devoted to Egyptology, was founded at Leipzig in 1862, and is still in existence today. On the other hand, the *Mélanges* and the *L'Egyptologie* published by Chabas enjoyed only a short-lived success.

The *Transactions* and the *Proceedings of the Society of Biblical Archaeology*, the *Journal asiatique*, and the *Revue archéologique* have rendered great services to Egyptology.

No one now underestimates the results obtained by Champollion and his successors, who included the most renowned scholars of a period which was rich in men of outstanding intelligence. Every year more and more travellers came to Egypt. The opening of the Suez Canal attracted enormous crowds. Exhibitions in London in 1867 achieved an unmistakable success. Such, then, was the state of Egyptology at the death of Mariette in 1881.

Excavations and publications, 1881–1914

Maspero's appointment to the post which had been held by Mariette, and his departure for Egypt on the eve of the First World War, marked a new period in the history of Egyptology. Maspero had been sent to Cairo in order to help Mariette, who was already suffering from the disease from which he was to die, and in order to set up the permanent Mission that the French government had recently decided to create. His aim was to complete the training of Egyptologists and Arabic scholars who had already followed a university course, and to publish the Egyptian monuments in their entirety, instead of making a choice of those texts which were held to be the most interesting, as had been the usual practice until then. This was an admirable programme, the first fruits of which were the works devoted to the Theban tombs, the tomb of Seti I, and the Temple of Edfu; in spite of certain imperfections these have been, and still are, extremely valuable. The tomb of Ramses IX, which appeared later, would meet with the approval of the sternest critics. The publication of the Temple of Edfu, which had been interrupted after the second volume, was resumed and very nearly completed during the period between the two wars. The work is, on the whole, worthy of the monument.

Two chance discoveries, which proved to be of prime importance, kept the *Service des Antiquités* busy for several years. Even during Mariette's lifetime it had been established that the walls of the pyramids were not all blank, as had been generally believed, and that the inner chambers of some contained texts which could provide a good deal of information on the language, as well as on the earliest religious and funerary beliefs, of the Egyptians. Five pyramids in succession – those of Unas, Teti, Pepi I, Merenra and Pepi II, were entered in 1881 and 1882. Maspero, with the help of Emile Brugsch, the American Egyptologist, Wilbour, and Bouriant from the French Mission, immediately set to work to take impressings and copies of the monuments. The texts, together with a translation, appeared from 1882 onwards in the form of instalments[24] in a new review called the *Recueil de Travaux*. In the opinion of K. Sethe, the German philologist, this was Maspero's greatest service to Egyptology in all the long years of hard work he devoted to the subject.

The other discovery took place on the left bank at Thebes. Since 1875 objects which could only have come from a royal tomb had been making their appearance on the market. It soon became known that this new and profitable line of business was being carried on by men from Gurnah. They quarrelled among themselves, and one of them took the investigating officials to the vault they had discovered and were in the process of rifling. It was in the side of the hill which separates the Valley of the Kings from the agricultural land of the plain. A long corridor led from the bottom of a well thirty-five feet deep into an oblong-shaped hall. Both the corridor and the hall were crammed with coffins, boxes, vases and chests. The names of the greatest Pharaohs and queens of the New Kingdom could be read on the coffins. In a very short time the fantastic store was transported to Luxor, and from there it was taken by steamer to Bulaq. Several years elapsed before the inventory was finally completed. The mummies were unwrapped in June 1886 in the presence of the Khedive; they were measured, a description of each one was recorded and every possible precaution was taken to ensure their preservation. They were the mummies of kings and princes, originally buried amidst fabulous riches, in huge hypogea which had been hewn out of the rock and decorated. However, the wave of anarchy and pillaging which swept through Egypt during the last years of the Twentieth Dynasty forced Herihor, the High Priest of Amun, to place the mummies in very plain wooden coffins previously intended for far less important people. These were transferred from one hiding-place to another and finally ended up in the vault where they had remained undisturbed until 1875. Maspero devoted one of his most penetrating studies to the royal mummies of Deir-el-Bahari, in the first volume of the *Mémoires de la Mission française du Caire*.

From 1881 onwards, the *Service des Antiquités* no longer claimed the monopoly of archaeological exploration in Egypt. It granted excavation permits to foreign scholars, provided they had the proper qualifications. These diggers were allowed to take away half of what they found. To begin with, their activities were not subject to any specific conditions. It was only in 1912 that a regulation was introduced to the effect that foreign Egyptologists could not take away their share unless they left the sites in a satisfactory condition.

From 1882 onwards the Egypt Exploration Fund gave a powerful stimulus to Egyptological research amongst the English. Flinders Petrie was its official representative on the sites until 1894, when he founded a rival society, the Egyptian Research Account; in 1906 he started the British School of Archaeology in Egypt.

English scholars were attracted first of all to the Delta, and more especially to Pithom and the route taken by the Jews when they left Egypt, and Tanis where Mariette had stopped working in 1875. From 1883 to 1885 Flinders Petrie and F. Ll. Griffith carried out a project which Mariette had only been able to suggest as a possibility; they produced a plan and the complete texts of all the inscriptions. They brought back from Tanis two papyri, which proved to be extremely valuable in spite of their poor condition: one was a treatise on religious geography, and the other a list of hieroglyphics with their definitions.

After the excavations at the Tell of Sân, other neighbouring Tells were explored, such as Defeneh, Nebesheh and Gemaiyemi. Between 1887 and 1889, Naville, Griffith and the Rev. W. MacGregor began work on Tell Basta, which was almost as large as the Tell of Sân and contained a temple. Then explorations were undertaken at Saft, El Henneh, Tell el Maskhuta, Tell el Yahudiya, Heliopolis, the Isaeum not far from Mansura, Tell el Muqdam and Naucratis. All this work was certainly very praiseworthy but it was neither comprehensive nor consistent enough to save these famous towns from unauthorized excavators. It was clear from the beginning that the Delta remains were in a much poorer state of preservation than the surviving monuments of Upper Egypt, and so Egyptologists were irresistibly drawn towards the provinces of the south. By 1888, Flinders Petrie was exploring the pyramids of Illahun and Hawara. Going further south still, in 1891 he reached Tell el Amarna, where a peasant woman had discovered clay tablets covered with cuneiform signs while collecting *sebakh* (decomposed ancient walls of crude brick, with valuable fertilizing qualities). These tablets were in fact the diplomatic correspondence between Akhenaton and certain Asiatic monarchs, but such a discovery was so unexpected in Egypt that at first it was not taken seriously. A good third of the tablets were destroyed during transport and the major part of the rest were acquired by the British Museum.[25] In 1891–92, Flinders Petrie cleared several buildings with painted floorings which completely transformed current ideas about Egyptian art.[26]

These English scholars were no less active in the matter of publications. There appeared a series of four volumes on the tombs of Beni-Hasan, and two on those of El Bercheh. N. de Garis Davies, after making a very faithful copy of the tombs at Saqqara and Sheikh Saïd spent three years, from 1902 to 1905, making a complete copy of the tombs and stelae of El Amarna.

For a very long time, the remote past of Egypt had lain beyond any possibility of study. Civilisation seemed to have appeared, already fully developed, in the time of Zoser, just as Minerva sprang fully armed from the brow of Zeus. It is true that in 1868 the geologist Arcellin had discovered a bed of flints, which he recognized as being similar to the bed at Saint-Acheul. But for many years Egyptologists continued to argue that the Egyptian flints dated from Pharaonic times. The work carried out by de Morgan, director of the *Service des Antiquités* from 1893 onwards, showed that the Egyptian flints dated for the most part from prehistoric times. In Egypt as in Europe, the chipping of stone had preceded polishing, and polished stone implements had preceded the use of metal.

Chalcolithic Egypt was discovered about the same time as the remains of the first two dynasties. Flinders Petrie, who had been busy at Coptos, crossed the Nile and discovered, between Tukh and Ballas, tombs of a quite new type, in which the bodies were laid on their sides and surrounded by personal effects consisting of vases with decorative designs drawn in purple ink. The designs were the cause of what amounted almost to a quarrel among Egyptologists. Some thought the designs represented a village; others believed them to be boats. The latter opinion finally prevailed. After somewhat lively discussions, it was generally accepted that the new civilisation belonged to the prehistoric period.

The turn of the first two dynasties came when Amélineau, between 1895 and 1898, and Flinders Petrie, between 1899 and 1901, discovered and excavated the royal tombs of this period in a region west of Abydos. In 1897 at Negadah, de Morgan discovered a tomb which for a long time was thought to be the tomb of Menes. Quibell, who had taken part in several of Petrie's expeditions, was responsible for the discovery, in the ruins of Hieraconopolis, of the golden falcon's head, one of the marvels of Egyptian art; he also discovered the Slate Palette of Narmer and other archaic monuments. These precious finds were very soon put at the disposal of scholars in a series of works: Fl. Petrie, *Ballas and Naqada, The Royal Tombs of Abydos*;

J. de Morgan, *Recherches sur les origines de l'Egypte*, and Quibell, *Hieraconpolis*. All these works still provide the groundwork for research on primitive Egypt.

The other great archaeological events of this period took place in the regions of Memphis and Thebes. The work of excavation in the area of the Great Pyramids was shared out among Germans, Italians and Americans. Reisner found some magnificent statues in the store-houses adjoining the pyramid of Mycerinus. The Germans explored the funerary temple of Abu Gurab and the necropolis at Abusir, where the three pyramids seem to be smaller replicas of the Giza group. The excavations, which were directed with impeccable thoroughness by Borchardt, revealed the whole complex pattern of the royal funerary arrangements during the Old Kingdom. The publication, under the auspices of the Deutsche Orient Gesellschaft, of these monuments, and the bas-reliefs found in the funerary temple of Sahure, was an epoch-making event.

At Saqqara, new and important Old Kingdom tombs were discovered near Teti's Pyramid by two directors of the *Service des Antiquités*, J. de Morgan, then V. Loret. Later the *Service* decided to appoint a permanent archaeologist to this very important site. Quibell was the first man to occupy the post which he held until the outbreak of the First World War. The excavations at Dahshur, which yielded an unrivalled collection of Middle Kingdom jewels, excited universal interest.

Basing himself on Strabo's account which gives the number of royal tombs worthy of inspection as forty, V. Loret introduced a method whereby the Valley of Kings was systematically excavated by cutting right down to the virgin rock. In this way he discovered several tombs of kings and of private individuals, including the tomb of Tuthmosis III and Maherpra, and that of Amenophis II, which had been made into a hiding-place similar to the one at Deir-el-Bahari. Excavations were resumed four years later, not on this occasion under the sponsorship of the *Service des Antiquités* but thanks to the generosity of Theodore Davis, an American Egyptologist who, working in conjunction with the *Service*, waived any claim to a share of the objects found and agreed to take only such pieces as might be found in duplicate. By 1912 the number of tombs opened in the famous Valley of the Kings had risen to fifty-seven, and it seemed as if the valley had yielded up all its treasures.

It was during this same period that the systematic exploration of Karnak, under the direction of G. Legrain, was decided upon. The great event was the discovery of a favissa or cachette, not far from the sacred lake, in which the Egyptians had buried more than seven hundred statues which had been removed intact from their original settings.

The amount of material collected grew to such an extent that larger premises were needed to house it all. The museum was transferred first of all to Giza, then to Cairo, to the building which is still in use but which will probably not house it for very much longer. In 1902, Maspero and Borchardt instituted the General Catalogue of the Cairo Museum to which the majority of Egyptologists contributed. The work was rounded off with *The Excavations at Saqqara* and the *Monuments immergés de la Nubie*. The latter title is explained by the fact that, during this period, the Egyptian government decided to build a huge dam at Aswan, and as a result, the island of Philae, one of the beauty-spots of Egypt, as well as other archaeological sites situated further to the south, were submerged for part of the year. For a long time it was feared that all these monuments would be irreparably damaged. As it happened, the damage was less serious than had at first been feared, and the temples stood up quite well to being alternately submerged and exposed to the burning sun.

During this span of thirty-four years, archaeological methods were constantly improved. The real aim of the excavations was no longer to secure good museum pieces, but to study the sites. This involved drawing maps, plans and cross-sections, making a serious inventory of everything on the site, taking the necessary steps to ensure its preservation, and finally publishing all the information obtained. This meant that anyone in charge of an excavation project had to have a staff comprising an architect and several draughtsmen as well as archaeologists. Thanks to the publication of the *Annales du Service des Antiquités*, the *Recueil de Travaux*, and later of the *Journal of Egyptian Archaeology* and other reviews, the public was more speedily and more fully informed about the various discoveries than had been the case before.

Today there are Egyptologists in every country in Europe and in the United States. Historical and philological studies are in progress at the same time as excavation work continues. We should at this point mention Maspero's *Histoire des anciens peuples de l'Orient* and the research carried out, again by Maspero, on the literary texts and on religion;[28] also the edition of the *Book of the Dead* according to the New Kingdom versions by G. Naville; the researches of W. Golenischeff who acquired valuable papyri[29] for the Hermitage Museum and published them in de luxe editions; the work carried out by F. Ll. Griffith, who was responsible not only for the explanatory notes which accompanied the publications of the Egypt Exploration Fund and the Archaeological Survey of Egypt, but also for the very fine edition of Petrie's *Hieratic Papyri from Kahun and Gurob*, the deciphering of numerous demotic texts, and studies on an extremely wide variety of subjects, and in particular the Books of Wisdom. About this time W. Spiegelberg devoted much time and care to the deciphering of demotic texts.

The impressive group of Berlin scholars made a considerable contribution to the advancement of Egyptology. Stern's *Koptische Grammatik* and Ad. Erman's *Neuägyptische Grammatik* were published in 1880. In 1889, Erman also published *Die Sprache des Papyrus Westcar*, and in 1894 the *Aegyptische Grammatik*, the fourth edition of which appeared in 1928. K. Sethe, his most brilliant pupil, published *Das Aegyptische Verbum* between 1899 and 1902. All these works provide exact information about morphology – particularly the conjugation of verbs – phonetics, the relationship between Egyptian and Coptic and Egyptian and the Semitic languages, and this information has not been superseded. Although Champollion, in his letter to M. Dacier as well as in his *Précis du système hiéroglyphique*, dwelt very emphatically on the resemblances between the Egyptian alphabet and the Hebrew and Arabic alphabets, many quite famous Egyptologists, even as late as 1914, still clung to an obsolete method of transcription whereby the first four signs of the alphabet – the persnopter, the reed tuft, the arm and the chick – were taken to be vowels, whereas in actual fact they correspond to the yod, the ain and the vav. The fact that this second way of transcribing the hieroglyphs eventually won the day is undoubtedly due to Adolf Erman who published an anthology and a glossary in the same series as his grammar and who, as early as 1897, started work on a more complete, more methodical, and more reliable dictionary than that of Brugsch. At that time, many texts, both in Egypt and in museums, were still unpublished or had appeared only in fragmentary form. The first stage of the plan involved an enormous effort of revision and publication. It resulted in the appearance of the *Litterarische Texte des Mittleren Reiches*, the Peasant, Sinuhe, the Story of the Shepherd, the *Urkunden* and a carefully revised synoptic edition of the Pyramid Texts. The making of slips in connexion with all these texts was a collective effort in which many of the great specialist's pupils, both German and non-German, took part.

Like Maspero, Adolf Erman set himself the task of being proficient in all fields of Egyptology. Two of his books, *Die aegyptische Religion* and *Aegyptisches Leben in Altertum* have been translated into several languages and often reissued, and they are still classics. Another classic is J. H. Breasted's *Ancient Records of Egypt*, which contains translations and commentaries on historical studies that have come out in various countries, and special mention must be made of the work of Ed. Meyer who clarified Egyptian chronology and finally discredited those theories based on Manetho which overestimated the length of the various epochs. Wrong ideas may take a long time to die and they can only be eliminated by dint of great perseverance.

The First World War and the Egyptian Revolution

After the First World War, a new period began, during which the *Service des Antiquités* was again directed by French scholars, first P. Lacau, then Canon Drioton, who were assisted by Egyptian, French, American and English scholars. This period was brought to a close, like many other things in Egypt, between 1951–1953. It had been less easy-going than the preceding ones; new regulations were introduced in connection with excavations, and Egyptians themselves began to take part in scientific work. The law dealing with ancient remains had been made stricter in 1912. It was then decreed that permission to dig would no longer be granted to private individuals but only to learned bodies which would have to seek approval both for the personnel of their missions and for their proposed work. The excavators could no longer expect to receive half of what they found, or even any definite share. The principle adopted was as follows: any objects of which there was as yet no specimen in the national collections had to be reserved for the Cairo Museum. On the other hand, the excavators were to be allowed to present to museums in their own countries all those objects, however fine they might be, of which there were already examples in Cairo. This was a fair decision, and the excavators could count themselves satisfied since Egypt is precisely a country where numerous specimens of the same kind of object are to be found. In practice, however, the regulation did not prove altogether satisfactory.

During Mariette's lifetime, Brugsch had founded a school of archaeology, and one of his pupils, Ahmed Kamal, was for a long time one of the keepers of the Cairo Museum. The great efforts made by the Egyptian government to develop higher education eventually bore fruit, and a time came when Egyptian Egyptologists, trained in Europe or in Egypt by European scholars, swelled the ranks of Champollion's successors and organized efficient excavation work at Giza and at Tuna el Gebel. Most of these Egyptians were not content simply to collaborate with Europeans but were resolved on taking over the *Service des Antiquités* entirely, which in fact they did in stages. By 1939 the inspectors-general were all Egyptian. Very soon the same was true of the keepers, the Director-General and the architects.

W

The period opened with an awe-inspiring find. From 1917 onwards, a passionate and enlightened admirer of Egyptian art, Lord
Carnarvon, and a professional archaeologist, H. Carter, who had an
intimate knowledge of the left bank at Thebes, had been working
again in the Valley of the Kings. After the excavations of V. Loret
and Th. Davis had been completed, there was still one Pharaoh
missing and this was Tutankhamen. Since this particular king had
not been considered a model of saintly virtue, there was no special
reason to believe that his tomb would be near those of his predecessors, just as there was no evidence to the contrary. Lord
Carnarvon obtained permission to dig on conditions similar to, but
more severe than, those which had been accepted by Theodore
Davis. If any royal tomb were discovered, even though it might have
been already violated, or if any private tomb were found intact,
in both cases the objects found had to go to the Cairo Museum.

At first the search undertaken produced no result. After five years,
the excavators came back, but not optimistically, to the area near the
tomb of Ramses VI, and it was here that they discovered the entrance
to a staircase choked with rubble and blocked by a wall marked
with the seals of the Pharaoh they were looking for. Beyond the first
wall was a corridor leading to another wall, also marked with the
seals. Behind this one was the antechamber, crammed with the
most wonderful objects. This antechamber led into two adjoining
chambers and into the royal vault. Tutankhamen's richly adorned
mummy was lying in a solid gold coffin inside another double coffin,
which in turn was protected by four catafalques fitting one into the
other. This was the finest discovery of all time. For a while, the whole
world fixed its gaze on the Valley of the Kings and a team of
specialists were kept busy measuring, drawing, photographing and
removing the treasure, which was in a perfect state of preservation
and is now to be seen in the Cairo Museum.[30] P. Lacau had suggested
that since Countess Almina's father had not had the pleasure of
being present at the opening of the coffin, his daughter, as heiress
to his rights, should be given those objects which could be removed
from the collection without detracting from its scientific value. But
the Egyptian government preferred to keep everything, and to pay
the costs of the excavations.

About the same time, foreign scholars started work again on
certain excavations which had already been started and then interrupted. At Giza, to the east of the Great Pyramid, Reisner discovered
a carefully hidden shaft leading to an underground chamber which
contained Queen Hetepheres' magnificent furniture, but no mummy.[31] The Metropolitan Museum of New York sent an expedition

to Lisht and to Deir-el-Bahari. The Egypt Exploration Fund replaced the German mission at Tell el Amarna. At Arment, Sir Robert Mond, who had carried out extensive excavations at Sheikh Abd el Gurna, discovered a collective tomb of sacred bulls. Gradually English and American excavators disappeared altogether from Egypt and moved to the Sudan, where conditions were less restricting. While they still had permission to do so, French and Egyptian Egyptologists continued to carry out the operations they had undertaken at El Kab, Medamud, Tôd and Deir el-Medineh. In 1929, the present writer was granted permission to carry out excavations at Tanis. We cleared the Temple of Anat, the great eastern temple and, in 1929, discovered the necropolis of the Tanite kings inside the great enclosure wall and adjoining the temple. Robbers had broken into the tombs of Osorkon II and Shashank III but the tomb of Psusennes was virtually intact. Psusennes, one of his successors Amenemopet, and two of his companions at arms, lay in four vaults. A silver coffin with a falcon's head and containing a certain previously unknown Shashank adorned in all his finery, and two other personages, had, at some later date,[32] been placed for safety in the antechamber. The exploration of the Tanis necropolis, which had been interrupted by the Second World War, was resumed in 1945. The mission went on working until all the French excavation sites were closed down by order of the Egyptian government.

The *Service des Antiquités* devoted its activities to the two large sites which it had managed to retain. At Saqqara, C. Firth with the help of J. Ph. Lauer, who took charge of the site from 1936 onwards, had been commissioned to clear Zoser's funerary monument and to carry out a systematic excavation of it. The recent successes achieved by archaeologists at Abusir, in the Valley of the Kings and on other sites, prove beyond all doubt that Egyptologists should no longer rely on luck or their instinct, and that the work of excavation should be entrusted to well-equipped teams on whom no time limit is imposed, and who are determined to complete the operation on which they have embarked. Remarkable results were achieved at Saqqara by using this method. The monument was systematically cleared, and the underground chambers were excavated with great thoroughness. A special museum, which is by no means the least attractive feature of the vast necropolis, had to be built in order to display the vases taken from the corridors in the monument.[33]

At Karnak, where everything is on a superhuman scale, H. Chevrier adopted modern industrialized methods. He built a railway on the site and this allowed him to tip the excavated material, normally the excavator's nightmare, into the Nile. The usual practice in excavating is to cover up one sector while uncovering another, and this inevitably prolongs operations and makes them more costly. The great temple of Amun was finally cleared of the mounds of earth under which it was partly buried. The Sacred Lake, which had formerly been choked with mud and overgrown with reeds, became a gleaming expanse of water set in its surrounding wall of hewn stone and it reflected the two obelisks, the hypostyle hall and the first pylon.

In one of the temples of Amenophis IV were found powerful statues which seem to be caricatures of the king.

Another important new development was that excavations were carried out not only in the ground but within the foundations and inside the walls of the pylons. The presence of already used blocks of stone in the pylons was no new discovery, but it had not been realized that the Egyptians had adopted the practice so extensively.

Thousands of sculptured and inscribed blocks of stone – many of them in perfect condition – were removed first of all from the third pylon, then from the second. They belonged to more than ten different buildings, and it was not long before a plan was on foot for the rebuilding of several of these edifices in an open-air museum which is the only one of its kind in the world. The first building to be reassembled was the White Chapel of Sesostris I, information from which has been extensively used in the previous chapters. Others followed and more are still to come; indeed, this advantageous method should be extended to all the other Karnak pylons, and to many other buildings. I myself have found at Tanis, in the walls surrounding the Sacred Lake and in the walls of tomb III many blocks which had been used before.

Although the results of these operations were followed with great interest, some critics maintained that the method was leading to the destruction of information that the Ancient Egyptians, with great subtlety, had planted in the foundations of their buildings. This theory was first put forward at Luxor, and for a time it had a great appeal for scholars, the educated public and even professional Egyptologists. It was based on the belief that every time a Pharaoh founded a building, he was acting in conformity with a certain state of the universe and could foresee that a day would come when he would have to modify his building, or even completely transform it. The marked stones in the foundations were said to be evidence of the various alterations of plan and, moreover, contained messages that only initiates were capable of interpreting.

Since the very beginnings of Egyptology, there has been no lack of people who prefer their wild imaginings to the facts. In spite of their denials, the symbolists of Luxor were in the same category as those people before them who made great play with the dimensions of the pyramids, and they will surely have successors in the future.

All during this period, which was so rich in archaeological discoveries, publication proceeded apace. The first instalment of the *Wörterbuch* came out in 1925. The five volumes of this long awaited work contain a rich variety of hieroglyphs, with careful and well-arranged definitions of their meanings. At first, it seemed somewhat disappointing that it should contain neither examples nor references; they were, however, provided in supplementary volumes, which were rather slow in coming out. Alan H. Gardiner's *Egyptian Grammar* (Oxford 1927) is almost a treatise in Egyptology. Gardiner pays more attention to syntax than his predecessors had done, his list of signs is the most complete that has ever appeared, and he provides exercises and vocabularies to help the beginner. The opening chapters and many incidental comments are devoted to extra-grammatical questions indispensable for the understanding of the language. A new hieroglyphic fount was invented for the purposes of the book. Until then, Egyptologists had had to choose between the hollow signs of the Theinhardt fount or the black signs of the French *Imprimerie Nationale* andthe Institut Français in Cairo. Both these extremely rich collections are still in use, particularly in the case of Ptolemaic texts, in which variants are extremely numerous. They are less satisfactory for Old and Middle Egyptian, and this is why many publishers and editors have preferred to use a hand-written script, which is less attractive but more accurate. The fount used by Gardiner is based on models copied in Thebes by N. de Garis Davies, and which are at once elegant, clear and precise.

New additions have been made to the list of the Egyptologists' indispensable working tools: H. Gauthier's *Le Livre des Rois*, Ranke's *Die Aegyptische Personennamen*, Lucas's *Ancient Materials*, G. Lefebvre's *Grammaire égyptienne*, and Porter and Moss's *Topographical Bibliography*. There have also been new, reliable and handy editions of texts, as well as manuals, monographs and works of discussion. We are indebted to A. Adriaan de Buck for his *Egyptian Coffin Texts*, which forms the third great series of religious texts. Emile Chassinat has almost completed publishing his account of the temple of Edfu, which is an inexhaustible mine of religious and geographical information and he has started on the temple of Denderah. Egyptology is now in no way inferior to the older disciplines, and its magnificent publications are the pride of libraries everywhere. There is no room here to quote them all, but I should just like to mention the Robb de Tytus memorial series published by the Metropolitan

Museum in New York and the great albums devoted by the Chicago Oriental Institute to the temples of Ramses III at Medinet-Habu and Karnak. The accuracy of the copying in black and in colour is such as to satisfy the most demanding.

The present day

The picture of the last ten years presents a curious contrast. On the one hand, chairs of Egyptology have multiplied throughout the world, and there has been no slackening off in the rhythm of publication. The Institut Français is bringing out, simultaneously its account of the Temple of Denderah and that of Esna and Kom Ombo. Junker is busy with Philae. Tiy's tomb at Saqqara and the temple of Luxor, on which work has often been begun and then abandoned, will no doubt eventually see the light of day. A time will come when all, or almost all, the great monuments will have been reconnoitred for the purposes of scholarship. The same will be true of the treasures in the museums, and it can be predicted that in a few years' time there will be no unpublished material apart from the new items unearthed by the diggers. Publishers are bringing out ever greater numbers of magnificent albums, as well as popular works on the subject of Egyptology, and at the same time professional Egyptologists are classifying their material, conducting research and throwing new light on various problems. On the other hand, since the *Service des Antiquités* passed entirely under the control of the Egyptians and in spite of the excellent relations which exist between the scholars of the Nile Valley and their foreign colleagues, the latter's share in archaeological activities is smaller than before and was adversely affected by political events, just when we were hoping that it would be revived. The only notable discoveries in the last few years have been made by the Polish Mission at Athribis and by the Swiss Mission at Abusir, which found a remarkable Fifth Dynasty female head. Egyptian archaeologists must be given credit for several fine discoveries, such as Cheops' barque near the Great Pyramid, the unfinished and severely damaged pyramid of a king of the Third Dynasty at Saqqara, Sekhem-Ket and the stela of Kames in the foundations of a colossus in front of the second pylon at Karnak.

The great dam, on which work has begun a little to the south of Aswan, has caused even greater alarm that did the first Aswan dam in Egyptological circles and among all those interested in antiquity. The water-level, which already comes up to the cornice of the great pylon at Philae, is to be raised another hundred feet. Certain remains which have so far been out of reach of the water, such as the two rock-temples of Abu-Simbel and all the Nubian temples which were uncovered each year during summer, will be submerged once and for all at the bottom of an immense lake stretching beyond the frontier of the Sudan. Missions have been set up to expedite the recording of the details of the threatened monuments. Plans have been worked out to save some of them; it has been suggested that Philae might be isolated, or that some monuments could be taken to pieces and set up again in a safe place. The latter plan is, however, not applicable to the many rock temples made by Ramses II to the north of Wadi-Halfa. In the case of Abu-Simbel, two different plans have been considered: the building of a circular wall around the two rock temples or the raising of the whole cliff above water-level by means of powerful jacks two hundred feet tall. At the time of the first Aswan dam, G. Maspero wrote that the mere thought of laying a finger on a temple struck terror to the heart. It can well be imagined what he would have had to say today about the huge project which threatens the most glorious monuments of the Egypt of the Pharaohs. In itself, the phenomenon is not new. In the days of Mehemet Ali, the factories which sprang up everywhere were built with stones taken from the ancient monuments, and someone prophesied that the new would destroy the old. The devotees of progress were following the example of the Egyptians of antiquity, because even in Pharaonic times, stones had been taken from unused buildings to help in the construction of the new. A developing country cannot avoid sacrificing part at least of its inheritance. The function of Egyptologists is, precisely, to preserve what is essential in that inheritance. This is the task they have been working at now for nearly two centuries.

An evaluation of the ancient Egyptians

We have arrived at a point at which it is possible to pass judgment on the Ancient Egyptians. Their defects do not outweigh their virtues, although both are equally undeniable. Their vanity was prodigious. The slightest favour filled them with delight and their naivety in this respect made them a comparatively easy people to govern. They were hospitable, fond of good living and much given to banquets at which jokes, even crude jokes, were the order of the day. On the other hand, they were never guilty of the cruelties perpetrated by the Chaldeans and the Assyrians. They were very much attached to their towns or villages, their professions, their local gods and their feast-days; they were afraid of the Pharaoh, the priests and the scribes and, from time to time, rose against their masters, but their revolt was always short-lived.

Being extremely conscientious workers, they left an indelible mark in practically all fields of civilized activity. Admittedly, their tales, hymns and love-songs cannot be compared to the literary creations of the Greeks. In scientific thinking, their curiosity did not carry them very far. Their ancient wisdom remained very earth-bound, but it should be remembered that they had no predecessors to make things easier for them. We cannot but admire their piety; the gods were their constant companions and they never thought they had done enough to show their gratitude or to deserve new gifts. Experience had repeatedly taught them that godlessness was the source of all evil. Nothing was too good or too permanent for the dead. Each new generation eagerly accepted the burden of constructing pyramids and tombs for its lords and masters, even though the upkeep of so many previous funerary monuments was already a heavy task. Even the accomplishment of this duty did not always set their consciences at rest. From time to time a king or a prince or a private individual would be shocked at the sight of grass growing on a temple roof or a tomb being neglected, and would take the necessary steps to remedy this state of affairs, even at some cost to themselves and their heirs.

No nation has ever invented a more perfectly proportioned or more decorative form of writing than Egyptian hieroglyphics.

In the field of art, the Egyptians rival the Greeks and outshine the other peoples of antiquity. They excelled in extremes – pyramids and colossi or pectorals and pendants. Their unequalled stylistic originality is shown in their plant-columns, obelisks, pylons and avenues of sphinxes. Certain of their chapels and colonnades are reminiscent, in their perfection, of Greek temples. Some of their statues have a place among the greatest masterpieces of all time. The pictures they have left us of their daily round suggest that life must have been very enjoyable during the reigns of Cheops and Sesostris.

Such was Ancient Egypt. An Egyptologist, writing on his favourite subject, may be suspected of partiality. The present author hopes that in describing the days of Egypt's greatness and her unforgettable achievements, he has never allowed his sympathies to distort the truth.

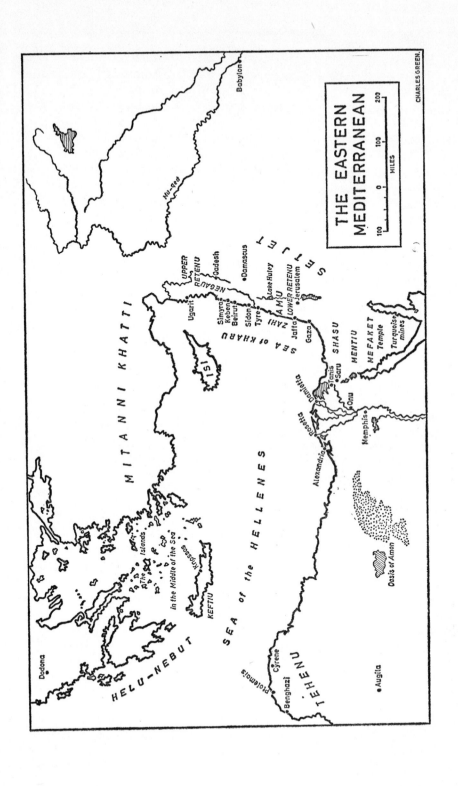

THE EASTERN
MEDITERRANEAN

CHARLES GREEN.

MILES

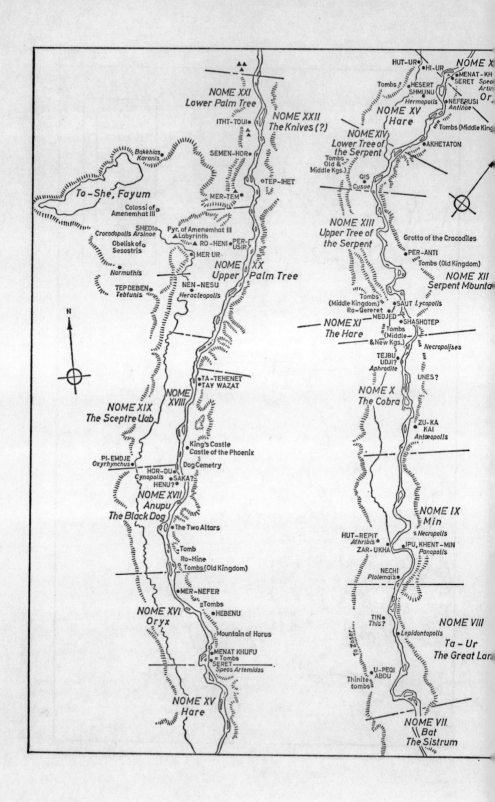

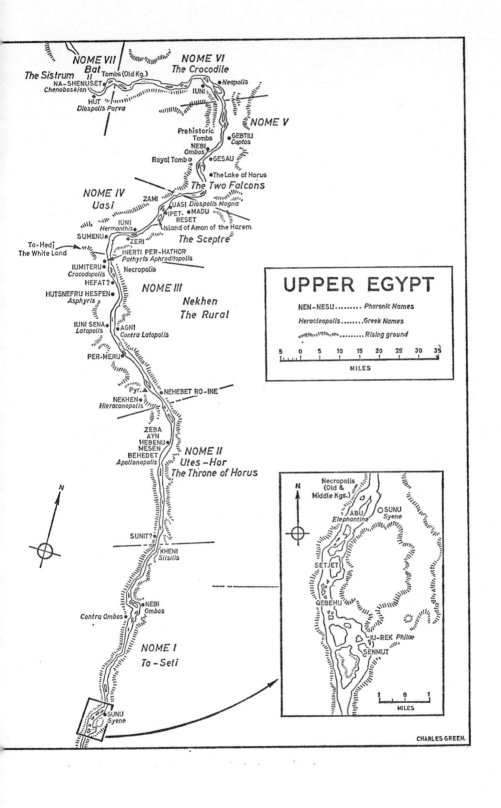

NOME VII
Bat
The Sistrum   Tombs (Old Kg.)
NA-SHENUSET
Chenoboskion
HUT
Diospolis Parva

NOME VI
The Crocodile

Neapolis
IUNI

NOME V

Prehistoric
Tombs
NEBI
Ombos
Royal Tomb
GEBTIU
Coptos
GESAU
The Lake of Horus
The Two Falcons

NOME IV
Uasi
ZAMI
UASI Diospolis Magna
IPET. MADU
RESET
Island of Amon of the Harem
IUNI
Hermonthis
SUMENU
ZERI
The Sceptre

To-Hedj
The White Land
INERTI PER-HATHOR
Pathyris Aphroditopolis
IUMITERU
Crocodopolis
HEFAT?
Necropolis

NOME III

HUTSNEFRU HESFEN
Asphyris

Nekhen
The Rural

IUNI SENA
Latopolis
AGNI
Contra Latopolis

PER-MERU

Pyr.
NEHEBET RO-INE
NEKHEN
Hieraconopolis

ZEBA
AYN
HEBENU
MESEN
BEHEDET
Apollonopolis

NOME II
Utes-Hor
The Throne of Horus

N

SUNIT?

KHENI
Silsilis

NEBI
Ombos
Contra Ombos

NOME I
To-Seti

SUNU
Syene

UPPER EGYPT

NEN-NESU .... Pharonic Names
Heracleopolis .... Greek Names
.... Rising ground

5   0   5   10   15   20   25   30   35
MILES

N

Necropolis
(Old &
Middle Kgs.)
ABU
Elephantine
SUNU
Syene

SETJET

QEBEHU

IU-REK Philae
SENMUT

1   0   1
MILES

CHARLES GREEN.

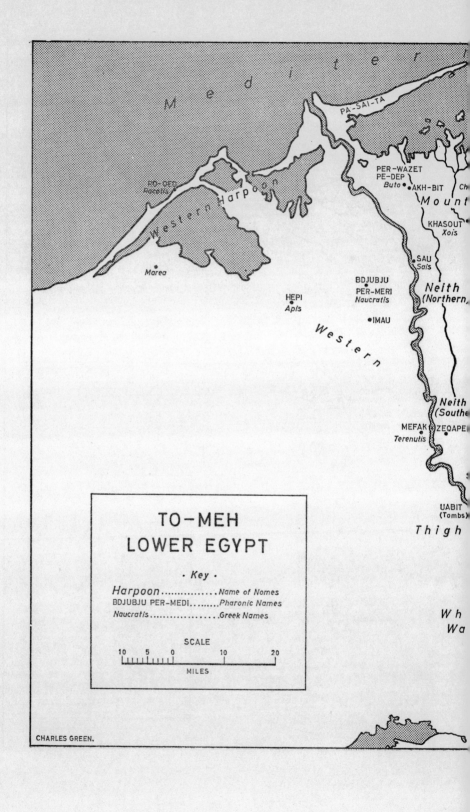

Mediterranean

PA-SAI-TA

RO-DED
Racotis

Western Harpoon

Marea

HEPI
Apis

BDJUBJU
PER-MERI
Naucratis

IMAU

PER-WAZET
PE-DEP
Buto • AKH-BIT   Ch

Mount

KHASOUT
Xois

SAU
Sais

Neith
(Northern,

Western

Neith
(Southe

MEFAK • ZEQAPE
Terenutis

UABIT
(Tombs)

Thigh

W h
Wa

TO—MEH
LOWER EGYPT

· Key ·

Harpoon..............*Name of Nomes*
BDJUBJU PER-MEDI.........*Pharonic Names*
Naucratis.................*Greek Names*

SCALE
10   5   0   10   20
MILES

CHARLES GREEN.

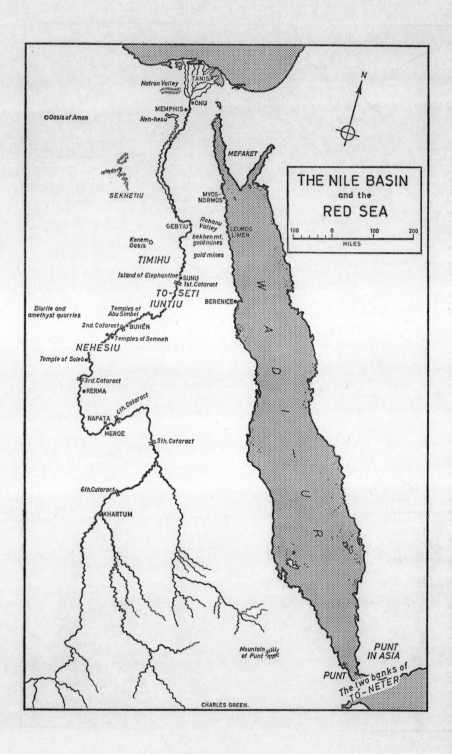

THE NILE BASIN
and the
RED SEA

100 0 100 200
MILES

Natron Valley
TANIS
MEMPHIS · ·ONU
·Oasis of Amon   *Nen-hesu*

MEFAKET

SEKHETIU

MYOS-
NORMOS
*Rohanu
Valley*
GEBTIU·   LEUKOS
LIMEN
*Kenem
Oasis*   *bekhen mt.
gold mines*
TIMIHU   *gold mines*
Island of Elephantine· SUNU
1st. Cataract
*TO-*SETI
IUNTIU
*Diorite and
amethyst quarries*   *Temples of
Abu Simbel*
BERENICE·
2nd. Cataract·· BUHEN
Temples of Semneh
NEHESIU
Temple of Soleb·

3rd. Cataract
·KERMA
4th. Cataract
NAPATA·
·MEROE
5th. Cataract

6th. Cataract
·KHARTUM

W
A
D
I
G
U
R

*Mountain
of Punt*   *PUNT
IN ASIA*
PUNT
*The two banks of
TO-NETER*

CHARLES GREEN.

NOTES

REFERENCES USED IN THE NOTES

Ann. du Serv.	Annales du Service des Antiquités de l'Egypte
Bull. Inst. fr.	Bulletin de l'Institut français d'archéologie orientale
C.R. Ac. Insc. et B.L.	Comptes-rendus de l'Académie des Inscriptions et Belles Lettres
J.E.A.	Journal of Egyptian Archæology
Kêmi	Revue de philologie et d'archéologie égyptiennes et coptes, 1928–54
Mém. Miss. fr.	Mémoires publiés par les membres de la mission archéologique française au Caire, from 1884
Urk.	Urkunden des aegyptischen Altertums, in Verbindung mit K. Sethe und H. Schäfer herausgegeben von G. Steindorff, Leipzig, 1906
	1. Urkunden der alten Reiches (4 vols.)
	2. Hieroglyphische Urkunden der griechisch-römischen Zeit (3 vols.)
	3. Urkunden der älteren Aethiopen-Könige (2 vols.)
	4. Urkunden der 18 Dynastie (4 vols.), continued by W. Helck, from 1955
Z.A.S.	Zeitschrift für Aegyptische Sprache und Altertumskunde

---

PREFACE

1. H. Gauthier, *Le Livre des Rois d'Egypte*, III, 49.
2. Abydos list in Mariette, *Abydos I*, pl. 43; Saqqara list in Mariette, *Monument divers*, pl. 58.
3. G. Farina, *Il papiro dei re ristaurato*, Roma, 1938.
4. Sethe, *Urkunden I*, 235–249.
5. *Manetho*, with an English translation by W. G. Waddell, London, 1948.

CHAPTER I: THE BLACK LAND. THE LAND OF KEM-T

1. P. Montet, *La Géographie de l'Egypte ancienne*, Paris, 1957–1961: I *Tomehu, la Basse Egypte*; II *To-chemâ, la Haute Egypte*.
2. P. Lacau and H. Chevrier, *Une chapelle de Sesostris à Karnak*, Cairo, 1956, 238.

3. Harris Papyrus I, 54 a 2.
4. V. Loret, *La Flore pharaonique*, 2nd edition, Paris, 1892; L. Keimer, *Die Gartenpflanzen im alten Aegypten*, Hamburg 1925; By the same authors, several articles in the *Annales du Service des Antiquités égyp*; the *Bulletin de l'Institut égyptien*; *Kêmi*; and the *Revue d'Egyptologie*.
5. Tomb 81 at Thebes, Wreszenski, *Atlas zur altägyptische Kulturgeschichte* I, 60 a; For the names, see Sethe, *Urkunden* IV, 73. Other beautiful gardens: British Museum No. 37983; tomb 100 at Thebes.
6. *Sallier Papyrus* I, pl. VIII, 3; A. H. Gardiner, *Late Egyptian Miscellanies*, p. 86. V. Loret in *C-R Académie des Inscriptions*, 1946, 9–15.
7. *Syria*, XVII, 285.
8. Cl. Gaillard, 'Les tâtonnements des Egyptiens de l'Ancien Empire à la recherche des animaux à domestiquer', *Rev. d'ethnogr. et de sociol.* 19, 1912.
9. Cl. Gaillard, *Recherches sur les poissons*, Cairo, 1923.
10. Hymn to Sesostris III from the Lahun papyrus, Sethe, *Lesestücke*, p. 67.
11. Exodus, VII–XI.

CHAPTER 2: THE EGYPTIANS IN THE NILE VALLEY

1. K. S. Sandford and W. J. Arkell, *Paleolithic man and the Nile-Fayum divide. Paleolithic man and the Nile Valley in Nubia and Upper Egypt, in Upper and Middle Egypt, in Lower Egypt*, Chicago Oriental Publications, X, XVII, XVIII, XLVI.
2. Bovier-Lapierre, *L'Egypte préhistorique* in *Précis d'histoire d'Egypte*, Cairo, 1932.
3. Vignard, in the *Mélanges Maspero*, Cairo, 1936, 165–75.
4. Caton-Thompson, and Gardner, *The Fayum Desert*, 2 vols., London, 1934.
5. Brunton and Caton-Thompson, *The Badarian Civilization and Predynastic Remains near Badari*, London, 1928.
6. J. Vandier, *Manuel d'archéologie égyptienne*, I, 'La préhistoire,' 230 et seq.
7. V. Loret, 'Quelques idées sur la forme primitive de certaines religions égyptiennes, *Revue égyptologique*, Paris, 1904, XI, 76–80.
8. J. Vandier, *Manuel*, I, 'La préhistoire', 573 et seq.
9. Bénédite, *Monuments Piot*, XXII, 1916, 1–34.
10. Quibell, *Hierakonpolis*, I, pl. XXVI, A–B. Ibid., I, pl. XXIX.
11. A. H. Gardiner, *Ancient Egyptian Onomastica*, 2 vols. and Atlas, Oxford University Press, 1947.
12. J. J. Clère, 'Fragment d'une nouvelle représentation du monde', *Festschrift zum 80 Geburtstag von H. Junker*, II, 1958, 32.
13. H. Junker, *Giza*, V, Vienna, 1941, 7 and seq.
14. Herodotus, II, 177. Diodorus, I, 31, and Theocritus, XVII, 82–4, give different figures.
15. Josephus, *Treatise against Apion*, I, 229.

CHAPTER 3: THE PHARAOH

1. A. H. Gardiner, *Ancient Egyptian Onomastica*, I, 13.
2. Naville, *The Temple of Deir el-Bahari*, II.
3. *Urk*, IV, 241.

4. *Sahure*, II, pl. 18.
5. Preserved in the Westcar papyrus, from 6, 20; Lefebvre, *Romans et contes égyptiens*, 80–90.
6. The Ermitage Papyrus 1116 A.
7. The Ermitage Papyrus 1116 B; cf. Posener, *Littérature et politique dans l'Egypte de la XIIème dynastie*, Paris, 1950, Ch. II.
8. Berlin Stela. Lepsius, *Denkmäler* II, 136 H.
9. *Bulletin Inst. fr.*, XLI, 31.
10. Ibid.
11. Dedicatory inscription at Abydos, 41–8.
12. Sinuhe R, 6–12.
13. Dedicatory inscription at Abydos, from line 98 to the end.
14. *Journal of Egyptian Arch.*, vol. 36, 1950, pl. 1.
15. A. H. Gardiner, 'The Coronation of King Horemheb', *Journal of Eg. Arch.*, vol. 39, 13–31.
16. Sethe, *Urk.* I, 239.
17. *Bulletin Inst. fr.*, XLI.
18. Sethe, *Urk.* I, 232.
19. Sethe, *Urk.* IV, 80.
20. *Kêmi* IV, pl. XI.
21. P. Montet, *Le drame d'Avaris*, 112.
22. *Sahure*, II, pl. 17.
23. Kuentz, *Deux stèles d'Amenophis II*, Cairo, 1925, 19–20.
24. Kuentz, 'La stèle de mariage de Ramsès II', *Ann. du Serv.*, XXV, 18
25. Mission Montet, 'La Nécropole royale de Tanis,' t. II, *Psousennès*, 139–143.
26. 'The tomb of Setau', *Journal of Egyp. Arch.*, V, 193.
27. Naville, *The Festival Hall of Osorkon II*, London, 1892.
28. Ibid.
29. A. Fakhry, 'A note on the tomb of Kheruef at Thebes', *Annales du Serv.*, XLII, 447–532.
30. Sethe, *Urk.*, I, 18–19.
31. Herodotus, II, 161–2, and IV, 159.
32. Sinuhe B, 44–76.
33. G. Posener, op. cit., 117–140.
34. Josephus, *Treatise against Apion*, I, 232.
35. Sethe, *Urk.*, I, 40–5.
36. Genesis, cc. 12.

CHAPTER 4: THE DEVELOPMENT OF EGYPT

1. *Annales du Service des antiquités de l'Egypte*, LII, 577–83.
2. Borchardt, *Sahure*, II, pl. 31.
3. Sethe, *Urk.*, I, 1–7.
4. P. Montet, *La Géographie de l'Egypte ancienne*, II, 160, 47–8, 49.
5. The chief decrees relate to the temple of Coptos, Sethe, *Urk.*, I, 280–307.
6. Sethe, *Urk.*, I, 213.
7. The Great Harris Papyrus, II, 4–11.
8. Sethe, *Urk.*, 157–8.
9. Ibid., I, 98–109.
10. G. Jéquier, *Le monument funéraire de Pépi II*, II, pl. 48, 57, 59.

11. P. Treason, *La stèle de Kouban*, 4–8.
12. P. Lacau, *Une stèle juridique de Karnak*, Cairo, 1949.
13. S. Sauneron, 'La Justice à la porte des temples', *Bull Inst. fr.*, LIV, 117–127.
14. P. Montet, *La Géographie de l'Egypte ancienne : I, To-mehou la Basse Egypte ; II, La Haute Egypte*.
15. Sethe, *Urk.*, I, 253–5.
16. Newberry, *Beni-Hasan I*, pl. 25, I.13 et seq.
17. J. Vandier, *Moalla*, insc. no. 2.
18. Newberry, *Beni-Hasan*, I, pl. 8.
19. Ibid., I, pl. 28–31.
20. J. Vandier, *La famine dans l'Egypte ancienne*, Cairo, 1936.
21. P. Barguet, *La Stèle de la Famine à Sehel*, Cairo, 1953.
22. Sethe, *Urk.*, I, 16.
23. P. Montet, *Les Scènes de la Vie privée dans les tombeaux de l'Ancien Empire*, Paris 1925; Junker, *Giza*, 12 vols., and several articles by Keimer. P. Montet, *La vie quotidienne en Egypte au temps des Ramsès*, Paris, 1942; Posener, Sauneron, Yoyotte, *Dictionnaire de la civilisation égyptienne*, Paris, 1959.
24. Garis Davies, *The Tomb of Nakht*, pl. xx. Similar subject matter on the tomb of Khamhat No. 571 and Djeserkaresenb No. 38. For modern times, see Lebeuf, *L'habitation des Fâli*, Paris, 1961.
25. Couyat et Montet, *Les inscriptions du Ouadi Hammamat*, Cairo, 1912, No. 1.
26. The Great Harris Papyrus, I, 28, 3–5; 46, 1–2; 48, 2; cf. V. Loret, *La résine de térébinthe*, Cairo, 1949, 32–4.
27. K. Sethe, *Die Bau-und Denkmalsteine der alten Aegypter und ihre Namen*, Berlin, 1933.
28. Couyat et Montet, *Hammamat*; G. Goyon, *Nouvelles inscriptions rupestres du Ouadi Hammamat*, Paris, 1957.
29. *The Instruction of Ptah-hotep*, verse 58–9.
30. A. H. Gardiner, 'The map of the gold mines in a Ramesside papyrus at Turin', *The Cairo Scientific Journal*, 19, 41–6.
31. S. Clarke and R. Engelbach, *Ancient Egyptian Masonry*, London, 1930.
32. The section concerning Snofru on the Palermo Stone, *Urk.*, I, 236.
33. Brief description in *Orientalia*, 25 (1956), fasc. 3.
34. Daressy, *Fouilles de la Vallée des Rois*, pl. x, No. 2401.
35. G. Maspero, *Guide des visiteurs du Musée du Cairo*, 2ème édition, 384.
36. Herodotus, III, 37.
37. G. E. Smith, *Royal Mummies*, Cairo, 1912.

CHAPTER 5:

THE EXPANSION OF EGYPT AND THE REACTIONS OF
NEIGHBOURING PEOPLES

1. *Pyramidentexte*, 511.
2. Tomb of Kheruf at Thebes, *Ann. Serv.*, XLII, pl. 39; tombs 57, 48, and 42 at Thebes.
3. *Pyramidentexte*, 1588–95.
4. *Sahura*, II, pl. 5.
5. Tacitus, *Ann. II*, 60.

6. Herodotus, II, 164.
7. Plutarch, *De Iside et Osiride*, 15–17.
8. P. Montet, *Byblos et l'Egypte*, Paris, 1927; Dunand, *Fouilles de Byblos* – 2 volumes have appeared since 1927.
9. A. H. Gardiner, *The Admonitions of an Egyptian Sage*, 3, 6–9; cf. *Kêmi*.
10. G. Lefebvre, *Romans et Contes égyptiens*, 208–20.
11. On the stela of Yehavmelek, Collection de Clercq, Perrot-Chipiez, *Histoire de l'Art dans l'antiquité*, III, 68.
12. Loud, *Meggido*, II, pl. 265–7; A. M. Blackmann, *Journal of Egyptian Archaeology*, II, J3.
13. A. Rowe, *The Four Canaanite Temples of Beth-Shan*.
14. Du Mesnil du Buisson, 'L'ancienne Qatna', *Syria*, IX, 10 et seq.
15. Cl. Schaeffer, *Ugaritica*, I-III.
16. P. Montet, *Les reliques de l'art syrien*, Paris, 1937.
17. A. H. Gardiner, Peet and Cerny, *The Inscriptions of Sinai*, Second Edition.
18. V. Loret in *Kêmi*, I, 99–114.
19. A. H. Gardiner, in *Journ. of Eg. Arch.*, IV, 28–39.
20. Lucas, *Ancient Egyptian Materials and Industries*, Second Edition, 353. Misson Montet, *Psousennès*, 139–143.
21. P. Montet, *Le Drame d'Avaris*, ch. II and III.
22. Ch. Kuentz, *La Bataille de Qadech*, Cairo, 1928.
23. *Ann. du Serv.*, XXXVIII, 369–396.
24. Sethe, *Urkunden*, I, 124–131.
25. Sethe, *Lesestücke*, 83–5.
26. N. de G. Davies and A. H. Gardiner, *The Tomb of Huy*, The Theban Tombs Series, IV.
27. Sethe, *Urkunden*, I, 246.
28. M. Alliot in *Revue d'Egyptologie*, VIII, 1–7.
29. W. M. Flinders Petrie, *Tanis*, II, pl. 42.
30. P. Montet, *Le Drame d'Avaris*, 26.
31. Couyat et Montet, *Les inscriptions du ouadi Hammamat*, No. 114.
32. Ed. Naville, *The Temple of Deir el Bahari*, III, 69–86.
33. The Great Harris Papyrus, I, 77, 8–13.
34. Herodotus, II, 159; IV, 43.
35. Borchardt, *Sahuřě*, II, pl. I.
36. The Harpason Stela in the Louvre gives the line of descent from Buyuwawa through several generations.
37. Herodotus, II, 152–4.
38. The Stela of the year III of Amasis, *Rec. de trav.*, XXII, 2.
39. *Urk.*, II, 153–4, 197.
40. *Pyr.*, 629.
41. W. S. Smith, *Sculpture and Paintings in the Old Kingdom*, pl. 39 and p. 157.
42. Vercoutter, *Les Haou-nebout, Bull. Inst. fr.*, XLVI, 125–148, and XLVIII, 107–209. A. H. Gardiner, *Anc. Eg. Onomastica*, I, 206.
43. *Rev. Arch.*, 28, 1947, 143; 34, 1949, 143.
44. See Ch. 8.
45. Triumphal Stela of Amasis, *Urk.*, IV, 17.
46. Wreszinski, *Atlas*, II, 62.
47. *The Odyssey*, XIV, 244 et seq.

48. Herodotus, II, 91.
49. Ibid., II, 56–8.
50. Aeschylus, *The Suppliants*, 1018.
51. Vercoutter, *L'Egypte et le monde égéen préhellénique*, Cairo, 1956.
52. Poem of Qadesh, 6; cf. Yoyotte in *Kêmi*, X, 679.
53. *Medinet-Habu*, I, pl. 39–44.

CHAPTER 6: ON THE NATURE OF GODS AND PIETY

1. Herodotus, II, 37.
2. Juvenal, *Sat.*, XV, 1–4.
3. Cairo, No. 27820 (Egyptian Museum, I, pl. 111).
4. Herodotus, II, 42.
5. *De Iside et Osiride*, 16.
6. Stela of the year 400, *Kêmi*, IV, pl. XIV.
7. Horus-Seth, Chester Beatty Papyrus, I, 9, 10–10, 1, Sallier Papyrus, IV, recto, 2: *De Iside et Osiride*, 19.
8. Mendes Stela, *Urk.*, II, 48–51.
9. Kuentz, 'Quelques monuments du culte de Sobek', *Bull. Inst. fr.*, XXVIII, 133 et seq.
10. *Urk.*, I, 20, 237 (Palermo Stone).
11. P. Montet, *Géographie de l'Eg. anc.*, II, 185.
12. Ibid., I, 69.
13. *Edf.*, I, 329.
14. Horus-Seth, 5, 6–6, 1.
15. *Kêmi*, X, 48.
16. Lacau-Chevrier, *Une chapelle de Sesostris Ier à Karnak.*
17. The gate of Ptolemy Evergetes at Karnak is an example of this.
18. S. Sauneron, *Les prêtres de l'ancienne Egypte.*
19. P. Montet in *Journal of Near Eastern Studies*, IX, 1950, 18 et seq.
20. P. Montet, *Géographie*, I, 178.
21. P. Bucher, in *Kêmi*, I, 41 et seq.
22. Herodotus, II, 59–60.
23. Ibid., II, 63.
24. Stela of Ikher-nopet, Schaefer in *Untersuchungen*, IV, 2.
25. Bas-relief at Luxor, Wreszinski, Atlas II, 69–70.
26. P. Montet, 'Le fruit défendu', in *Kêmi*, XI, 85.
27. J. Vandier, *Le papyrus Jumilhac*, 123–4.
28. *De Iside et Osiride*, 72.
29. P. Montet, *Scènes de la vie privée dans les tombeaux de l'ancien Empire*, 6–7.
30. Borchardt, *Sahurê*, II, pl. 30.
31. Labib Habachi, in *Ann. du Serv.*, L, 501.
32. *Le conte des deux frères et l'histoire d'Horus-Seth*, French translation in Lefebvre, *Romans et contes égyptiens.*
33. J. Vandier, *La religion égyptienne*, Coll. Marna, 45–6.
34. S. Sauneron and J. Yoyotte, *La naissance du monde selon l'Egypte ancienne*, in *Sources orientales*, 1, 17 et seq.
35. Naos d'Ismailia, *Kêmi*, VI, 1–42.
36. *Comptes-rendus Acad. des Inscrip.*, 1960, 172–80.
37. Carnarvon tablet I in *J.E.A.*, III, 95 et seq.

38. Hymn on the tomb of Ai in N. de Garis Davies, *El Amarna*, VI, pl. XXVII and XLI, cf. Ad. Erman, *Religion égyptienne*, 640–2.
39. P. Montet, *Le Drame d'Avaris*, Ch. IV.
40. The Harris Papyrus I is, generally speaking, an inventory of the gifts which Ramses III offered to the gods.
41. P. Montet, op. cit., Ch. V.
42. Harris Papyrus I, 75.
43. J. Vandier, *Le papyrus Jumilhac*, 129–130.
44. Ch. Kuentz, *La bataille de Qadech*, 243.
45. Tomb 172 at Thebes, Wreszinski, Atlas I, 356.
46. Tombs of Nakht, Khaemhat (No. 575 of Zeserkaresenb, No. 38); cf. Lebeuf, *L'habitation des Fali*, 544.
47. Sallier Papyrus, I, VIII; cf. Loret, *Comptes-rendus, Acad. des Inscrip.*, 1946, 9–15.
48. Ad. Erman, *La religion égyptienne*, Ch. X.
49. P. Lacau, *Les statues guérisseuses*, in *Monuments Piot*, XXV.
50. Et. Drioton, *La religion égyptienne*, in Brillant and Aigrin, *Hist. des Rel.*, 3, 25 et seq.
51. K. Sethe, *Lesestücke*, 73.

CHAPTER 7: HUMAN DESTINY AND CARING FOR THE DEAD

1. Tomb of Pinehas at Thebes, No. 16. Wreszinski, *Atlas*, I, 114, and Tomb of Anerifer, Posener, *Dictionnaire de la civilisation égyptienne*, p. 10. Papyrus of Nebked, ibid., 289, Maspero, *Hist.*, I, 198.
2. Borchardt, *Sahurê*, II, pl. 17.
3. Cairo 259; J. de Morgan, *Fouilles de Dahchour*, I, pl. XXXIII–XXXV.
4. P. Montet, *Scènes de la vie privée*, 66.
5. *Urk.*, IV, 937–8.
6. Sarcophagus of Merneptah appropriated by Psusennes, *Nécropole royale de Tanis*, II, 117–9.
7. *Pyr.*, 835.
8. Ad. Erman, *La religion ég.*, 248–9.
9. Quibell, *The Tomb of Hesy*, Cairo, 1913.
10. Firth, Quibell, *Step Pyramid*, 2 vols., Cairo, 1936; Lauer, *La pyramide à degrés*, 3 vols., Cairo, 1936–9.
11. Lauer, *Observations sur les pyramides*, Cairo, 1960, 73–83.
12. *Urk.*, I, 209.
13. A. Fakhry, 'The Bent Pyramid of Dahshur', *Ann. du Serv.*, LI.
14. Al. Varille, *A propos des pyramides de Snofru*, Cairo, 1947.
15. G. Jéquier, *Mastabat Faraoun*, Cairo, 1928.
16. J. Vandier, *Manuel*, II, vol. I, 151.
17. J. Leclant in *Orientalia*, 1956, vol. 25, pl. XLV–XLVIII.
18. J. Vandier, *Manuel* II, vol. 2, 582.
19. *Editio princeps*, Maspero, *Les inscriptions des pyramides de Saqqarah*, Paris, 1894; K. Sethe, *Die altaeg. Pyramidentexte*, Leipzig, 1908–22; *Ubersetzung und Kommentar um den altaeg. Pyr. texten*, 4 vols. (unfinished). Also to be consulted: Jéquier, *Le monument funéraire de Pépi II*, vol. I. Fragments of the Pyramid of Teti are in process of publication.
20. Carl Wilke, in *Zeitschrift für Aegyptische Sprache*, LXX, 56 et seq.

21. *Urk.*, I, 117. Other instances in *Kêmi*, XIV, 92.
22. W. S. Smith, *The Tomb of Hetepheres, the mother of Cheops*, Cambridge (Massachusetts), 1955.
23. Et. Drioton, *Pages d'égyptologie*, Cairo, 1957, 72 et seq.
24. G. Jéquier, op. cit., pl. 12.
25. The arrangements which the owner of a tomb made for his funeral ceremony are listed in several Old Kingdom inscriptions, *Urk.*, I, 11, 27, 37.
26. Inscription of the contract on tomb I at Siut.
27. *Urk.*, I, 75.
28. *Urk.*, I, 119; cf. *Kêmi*, X, 82.
29. Text and translation in A. H. Gardiner, *Eg. Gram.*, 168–9.
30. *Kêmi*, IV, 46–8.
31. Hermitage Papyrus III 6 A, 51–7; J. Yoyotte in *Sources orientales*, IV, *Le jugement des morts*, 34.
32. Maspero, *Les contes populaires de l'Egypte ancienne* (4th edit.), 158 et seq.
33. Ch. Maystre, *Les déclarations d'innocence*, Cairo, 1937.
34. Ibid.
35. Stela of Uriage, now in the Grenoble Museum; *Urk.*, IV, 1021.
36. Cairo stela 48831; *Bull. Inst. fr.*, XLV, 155 et seq.
37. *De Iside et Osiride*, 27.
38. Berlin 1204; Schäfer, *Die Osirismysterien in Abydos*, 1904.
39. Erman, *Religion égyptienne*, 101.
40. *Z.A.S.*, XLVII, 165.
41. De Buck, *The Egyptian Coffin Texts*, I, 13.
42. Ibid., I, 146.
43. Ibid., I, 151.
44. *Bibliotheca aegyptica*, VII, 38.
45. Zed-her's inscription on his statue, in Cairo 46341, I, 146–7.
46. Al. Plankoff, *Le livre du jour et de la nuit*, Cairo, 1942.
47. Lefébure, *Le tombeau de Séti I*, Part IV, pl. XXXVI.
48. H. Carter, *The Tomb of Tutankhamen*, 3 vols., London, 1933.
49. Mission Montet: *La Nécropole royale de Tanis*, vol. I, Osorkon II; vol. 2, Psusennes; vol. 3, Shashank III. Paris, 1948–1950–1960.
50. Cairo 34003, Lacau, *Steles du Nouvel Empire*, pl. II–III.
51. J. Capart and A. H. Gardiner, *Le papyrus Léopold II et le papyrus Amherst*, Brussels, 1939.
52. G. Daressy, *Cercueils des cachettes royales* (Cairo 61001–61004), Cairo, 1909.
53. Ad. Erman, *Gespräch eines Lebensmüden mit Seiner Seele*, Berlin, 1896.
54. Harris Papyrus 500, No. 6.
55. Tomb 50 of Gurneh: Bénédite in *Mém. Miss. fr.*, V, pl. II and IV.
56. Herodotus, II, 78.
57. G. Lefebvre, *Romans et Contes ég.*, 173–7; A. H. Gardiner, *Late Egyptian Stories*, 39–94.

CHAPTER 8: INTELLECTUAL ACHIEVEMENTS

1. A. H. Gardiner, *Egyptian Grammar*, Sign-list.
2. Ibid., p. 27.
3. G. Möller, *Hieratische Paleographie*, 3 vols., Leipzig, 1912.
4. Chester Beatty Papyrus, ed. A. H. Gardiner, IV, No. 3.

5. Harris Papyrus 500, No. 6.
6. G. Posener, 'Les richesses inconnues de la littérature égyptienne';
   Rev. d'egypt, VI, 27.
7. Ch. Kuentz, *La bataille de Qadech*, Cairo, 1928.
8. E. Dévaud, *Maximes de Ptahhotep*, Freiburg.
9. P. Montet, *Les scènes de la vie privée dans les tombeaux égyptiens de l'Ancien
   Empire*, Paris, Strasburg, 1925.
10. De Buck, *The Egyptian Coffin Texts*, II, 389–495; cf. Drioton, *Rev. du
    Caire*, 1942.
11. *Musée égyptien*, II, 29–53; *Urk.*, I, 235–250.
12. *Urk.*, I, 103.
13. *Urk.*, I, 128.
14. Ad. Erman, *Die Märchen des Papyrus Westcar*, translation in Lefebvre,
    Romans et Contes égyptiens, 75 et seq.
15. Posener in *Rev. d'égypt*, vol. II.
16. A. H. Gardiner, *The Admonitions of an Egyptian Sage*, Leipzig, 1909.
17. Ad. Erman, *Gespräch eines Lebensmüden mit seiner Seele*, Berlin, 1896.
18. Posener, *Littérature et politique dans l'Egypte de la XIIème dynastie*, Paris,
    1956.
19. Translation in Lefebvre, op. cit.
20. For example, the Hymn to Osiris in the *Bibliothèque Nationale*, and the
    many hymns to Min during the Middle Kingdom.
21. At the beginning of the Eighteenth Dynasty, King Ahmosis, with a
    fine lyrical gesture, pointed to the ostriches dancing in the rising
    sun, cf. Kuentz, in *Bull. Inst. fr.*, XXIII, 85; Dautheville, ibid.,
    XX, 226.
22. S. Schott, French translation by P. Krieger in *L'Orient ancien illustré*, 9.
23. Cairo 34010 in *Urk.*, IV, 614.
24. Kuentz, *La bataille de Qadech*.
25. Harris Papyrus I, 75–9.
26. A. H. Gardiner, *Late Egyptian Stories*, 61–76; G. Lefebvre, *Romans et
    Contes égyptiens*, 204–20.
27. *Urk.*, III, 1–56.
28. Herodotus, II, 121.
29. Pap. IV de Bulaq, IV.
30. Pap. 10474 from British Museum. Trad. H.O. Lange; *Das Weisheits-
    buch des Amenemope*, Copenhagen, 1925; Griffith in *J.E.A.*, XII,
    191–237.
31. Brooklyn Papyrus No. 47, 218, 135; G. Posener Paper read before the
    International Conference of Orientalists, Moscow, 1962.
32. Et. Drioton, *Le théâtre égyptien*, *Pages d'égyptologie*, Cairo, 1952.
33. A. Rey, *La science orientale avant les Grecs*, Paris, 1942, Book III, *La
    Science égyptienne*.
34. Tomb 15, cf. *Bull. Inst. fr.*, IX, 14.
35. Lauer, *Observations sur les pyramides*, Cairo, 1960.
36. Chester Beatty Papyrus No. 1, on the back of C.1.
37. Decree of Canopus, *Urk.*, II.
38. *Z.A.S.* 37,99.
39. Ebers Papyrus. I. *verso*.
40. *Urk.*, IV, 827.
41. P. Montet, *Le Drame d'Avaris*, p. 111.

42. Ebers Papyrus 18, 2; 61, 4–5; 61, 15. Berlin Medical Papyrus, 11, 12; Hearst Papyrus, 2, 17; 10, 11.
43. Fl. Petrie, *Tanis*, II, pl. XLII.
44. Herodotus, II, 19 et seq.
45. Herodotus, IV, 42.
46. L. Keimer, *Les Limites de l'observation naturaliste dans quelques représentations animales de l'Egypte antique*, Cairo, 1953.
47. Homer, *Odyssey*, IV, 229–232; Herodotus, II, 84; III, 1.
48. J. H. Breasted, *The Edwin Smith Surgical Papyrus*, 2 vols. Chicago, 1930; G. Lefebvre, *Essai sur la médecine égyptienne de l'époque pharaonique*, Paris, 1956.
49. This interpretation has been suggested by V. Loret, *Mélanges Maspero*, I, 85.

CHAPTER 9: ART

1. P. E. Newberry, *Beni-Hasan*, I, pl. 26.
2. Ed. Naville, *Bubastis*, pl. LI.
3. Engelbach, *The Aswan Obelisk*, Cairo, 1912; *The Problem of Obelisks*.
4. Inscription of the year VIII of Ramses II, *Ann. du Serv.*, XXXVIII, 219–230.
5. Al Varille, in *Ann. du Serv.*, XXXIII, 85–94.
6. P. Montet, 'Les statues de Ramses II à Tanis,' *Mélanges Maspero*, I, 497–508.
7. *Urk.*, I, 153.
8. N. de Garis Davies, *Puyemre*, I, pl. XXXVII.
9. N. de Garis Davies, *Two Ramesside Tombs at Thebes*, pl. XXXVII.
10. N. de Garis Davies, *The Tomb of Ken-Amon at Thebes*, pl. XIII–XX.
11. Junker, *Die Gesellschaftliche Stellung den äg Künstler im alten Reich*, Ak. Wien, 1959.
12. *Urk.*, I, 23.
13. Daressy, in *Mém. Inst. ég.*, III, 525; the editors of the tomb of Merruka, and Junker, op. cit.
14. This was the opinion of Ad. Erman and Davies; cf. *Z.A.S.*, XXXVIII, 1–2.
15. Ostracon 21447 in Berlin.
16. *Urk.*, IV, 395–418. The portrait of Senmut in H. E. Winlock, *Excavations at Deir-el-Bahari*, New York, 1942, pl. 63.
17. *Urk.*, IV, 420–430.
18. Cl. Robichon and Al. Varille, *Le temple d'Amenhotep, fils de Hapou*, Cairo, 1931.
19. Br. Mus. No. 475.
20. Couyat et Montet, *Hammamat*, pl. 22.
21. Firth and Quibell, *The Step Pyramid*, 2 vols., Cairo, 1936; Ph. Lauer, *La pyramide à degrés*, 3 vols., Cairo, 1936–9.
22. *Ann. du Serv.*, VII, 260–86; VIII, 201–10; XII, 57–63.
23. G. Jéquier, *L'architecture et la décoration*, I, pl. 2 and 3.
24. Ibid., I, pl. 6 and 7.
25. Ibid., I, pl. 10.
26. Ibid., I, pl. 65–8.
27. Ibid., I, pl. 12, 30–1.

28. P. Lacau and H. Chevrier, *Une chapelle de Sesostris Ier à Karnak*; H. Chevrier in *Ann. du Serv.*, XXXVIII, pl. CII–CIII.

29. Ch. Kuentz, *Obélisques*, Cairo, 1932.

30. P. Barguet, in *Ann. du Serv.*, L, 269.

31. The Artemidos Speos to the south of Beni-Hasan, G. Jéquier, op. cit., I, pl. 27.

32. Cairo 14 and 34; Louvre N. 2289; Cairo 33–4, 36, 119, in Vandier, *La statuaire égyptienne*, Paris, 1958.

33. Boston 11738 and 27442; Cairo 52501; *Orientalia*, vol. 27, pl. VII; Hildesheim, 1962.

34. Cairo 144.

35. Maspero, *Essais sur l'art égyptien*, Paris, 1912, 83–9.

36. H. Junker, *Giza*, V, pl. 9.

37. G. Jéquier, op. cit., I, pl. 16.

38. *Ann. du Serv.*, XXXVII, pl. I and II.

39. Heads from the Nubar and Gulbenkian collections in Vandier, *La statuaire égyptienne*, pl. LXVI.

40. Cairo 52701, Vernier, *Bijoux et orfèvrerie*, pl. LVIII–LXI.

41. *Kêmi*, XII, pl. III–IV.

42. J. Vandier, *Manuel*, II, p. 51, fig. 32.

43. G. Jéquier, op. cit., I, pl. 18; *Editions Tel, Antiquités égyptiennes du musée du Louvre*, pl. 56–7.

44. Cairo, 393 and 394; 530 and 1243.

45. Cairo 392.

46. Louvre, E 11609.

47. Cairo 32090; Maspero, *Guide* (1914), 174, fig. 51.

48. Moscow, 2099 f.

49. *Editions Tel*, pl. 85.

50. *Ann. du Serv.*, XXVIII, pl. IV, and XXXI, pl. 10.

51. Brit. Mus. 416; Berlin 21834.

52. Louvre, E 11076; Louvre, N 831.

53. Berlin 21223; Cairo 44869, 44870.

54. Louvre 11609; Cairo 38488.

55. Cairo T.16, T.14.

56. Cairo 42142.

57. J. J. Clère, in *Kêmi*, XI, 24–46.

58. P. Montet in *Monuments Piot*, L, 1–10.

59. Fl. Petrie, *Tell el Amarna*, pl. II-IV.

60. Especially in very early times; see Quibell, *The Tomb of Hesi*, pl. XI, gaming table, pl. XVIII, chairs, pl. XIX, bed.

61. Caroline Ranson Williams, *The Decoration of the Tomb of Per-neb*, New York, 1932.

62. It is now possible to find excellent publications of Egyptian paintings in which the colouring is accurately reproduced. N. de Garis Davies, *Ancient Egyptian Paintings*, Chicago, 1916; N. de Garis Davies, *Robb de Peyster Tytus Memorial Series*, New York, 1917–1927; Mekhitarian, *La peinture égyptienne*, in Skira, *Les grands siècles de la peinture*, 1954.

63. P. Montet, *Les scènes de la vie privée dans les tombeaux égyptiens de l'ancien Empire*, Strasburg, 1925.

64. Most of these are as yet unpublished c.f. *Kêmi*, XII, 68–70.

65. Bissing-Bruckmann, *Denkmäler*, pl. 101.
66. Mekhitarian, *La peinture égyptienne*, 116. English edition.
67. *Bull. Inst. fr.*, IX, pl. VII.
68. Lepsius, *Answahl der Wichtigsten Urkunden*, pl. XXIII.
69. Pleyte and Rossi, *Papyrus de Turin*, pl. CXLV.
70. J. Vandier d'Abbadie, *Catalogue des ostraca figurés de Deir el-Medina*, Cairo, 1936–59.
71. Em. Vernier, *La bijouterie et la joaillerie égyptiennes*, Cairo, 1907.
72. *Nécropole royale de Tanis*, II, No. 219 (coloured plate).
73. Ibid., Nos. 482–487.

CHAPTER 10:

EGYPT AS SEEN BY THE ANCIENTS AND IN THE LIGHT OF MODERN RESEARCH

1. Lev., XVIII, 3.
2. Isaiah, XIX, 11, 13; XXX, 1–2.
3. II Kings, XXV, 26.
4. Wenamon, 2, 22–3.
5. Herodotus, II, 20–28. The author admits that he had been unable to obtain any information from the Egyptians themselves. The only person to give him an answer was a scribe from the temple of Saïs who replied somewhat jocularly to his questions.
6. Herodotus, II, 136.
7. Strabo, XVII, 28.
8. Tacitus, *Annals*, II, 59–60.
9. Herodotus, II, 100.
10. Gauthier, *Livre des Rois*, I, 319; Vergote in *Z.A.S.*, 87, 66–76.
11. Diodorus, I, 53; cf. P. Montet, *Germanicus et le vieillard de Thèbes*, Strasburg, 1947, p. 51.
12. Herodotus, II, 124 et seq.
13. Ibid., II, 136–137.
14. Ibid., II, 58, 50.
15. Ibid., II, 67.
16. Diodorus, I, 86; Plutarch, *De Iside et Osiride*, 72; cf. V. Loret in *Rev. égyp.*, t.X, p. 101.
17. Herodotus, II, 143.
18. Plutarch, *De Iside et Osiride*, 32.
19. David, C. F., *Ac. Insc. et B.L.*, 1961.
20. *La Description de l'Egypte*, ed. Imprimerie Nationale, 9 vols. text, and 14 vols. plates, Paris, 1809–1828; ed. Panckoucke, 24 vols. in octavo, and 12 vols. plates, Paris, 1821–1829.
21. Champollion le Jeune, *Lettre à M. Dacier relative à l'alphabet des hiéroglyphes*, Paris, 1822; *éd. du centenaire* with an introductory study on the deciphering of hieroglyphs by H. Sottas, Paris, 1922.
22. Champollion le Jeune, *Grammaire égyptienne en écriture hiéroglyphique*, Paris, 1843.
23. P. Montet, *Isis ou la recherche de l'Egypte ensevelie*, Paris, 1956.
24. They were published in one volume, *Les Inscriptions des pyramides de Saqqara*, Paris, 1894.
25. The tablets have been published by Knudtzon, *Die el Amarna Tafeln*,

Leipzig, 1907, and Mercer, *The Tell el Amarna Tablets*, Toronto, 1939.

26. Fl. Petrie, *Tell el Amarna*, London, 1894.
27. Legrain, *Statues et statuettes de Rois et de particuliers*, Cairo, 1906 et seq.
28. *Etudes égyptiennes*, 2 vols.; *Etudes de mythologie et d'archéologie égyptiennes*, 9 vols.; *Les contes populaires de l'Egypte ancienne*, 4th ed., 1911.
29. Hieratic Papyri, 1115, 1116 A and 1116 B in the Hermitage Museum in Leningrad, 1913.
30. Carter, *The Tomb of Tutankhamen*, 3 vols., London, 1923–1933.
31. Reisner, *The Tomb of Hetepheres, the mother of Cheops*.
32. *La Nécropole royale de Tanis:* I, Osorkon II; II, Psusennes; III, Shashank III; Paris, 1947–1960.
33. C. Firth, *The Step Pyramid*, 2 vols., and Lauer, *La Pyramide à degrés*, 3 vols., Cairo, 1936–1939.
34. See Chevrier's annual reports in the *Annales du Service des Antiquités*, XXXVIII et seq.

BIBLIOGRAPHY

The bibliography of Ancient Egypt is extremely extensive. Many of the works used by the author have been referred to in the notes. In Chapter 10, which contains an outline of the history of Egyptology, attention was drawn to a large number of publications, original texts and monuments, as well as to those studies which marked important stages in the development of the subject. While omitting works dealing with particular features of Ancient Egypt, I should like here to indicate most of those that any reader anxious to improve his knowledge of Ancient Egypt might consult with advantage. For convenience of reference, they have been grouped in sections: language and writing, literature, history, religion, the sciences, the arts, archaeology and customs.

Language and Writing

There is no need to make further reference to the grammars by Erman, Sir Alan H. Gardiner and G. Lefebvre or to the writings of Sethe; they are, together with the *Wörterbuch* by Erman and Grapow, the basic works. To them may be added: B. Gunn, *Studies in Egyptian Syntax*, Paris, 1924; W. Spiegelberg, *Die demotische Grammatik*, 1925; G. Möller, *Hieratische Paläographie*, 3 vols., Leipzig, 1912.

Literature

The literary documents of Ancient Egypt have been made available to the modern reader in a number of English, German and French works: G. Maspero, *Les contes populaires de l'Egypte ancienne*, 4th ed., Paris, 1912; Budge, *Egyptian Tales and Romances*, London, 1931; Ad. Erman, *Die Literatur der Aegypter*, Leipzig, 1923; K. Sethe, *Dramatische Texte zur altäg. Mysterienspielen*, Leipzig, 1928; A. H. Gardiner, *Egyptian Letters to the Dead*, London, 1928; Et. Drioton, *Le Théâtre égyptien*, Cairo, 1942; G. Lefebvre, *Romans et contes égyptiens de l'époque pharaonique*, Paris, 1949; Schott, *Altäg. Liebeslieder*, Zurich, 1950.

327

History

Many writers have undertaken the task of compiling histories of Egypt. Some have dealt more particularly with chronology and the activities of the Pharaohs; others have concentrated on institutions and customs. In the first category we should add to the works of G. Maspero and Ed. Meyer already quoted: W. Fl. Petrie, *A History of Egypt*, 3 vols., London, 10th ed., 1923; E. Parker, *The Calendars of Ancient Egypt*, Chicago, 1950; Drioton-Vaudier, *Egypte*, Coll. Clio, 4th ed., 1962 (very useful and well documented). The third edition of the Cambridge Ancient History is now in the press. J. H. Breasted's *Ancient Records of Egypt*, Chicago, 1905–7, which contains the historical documents discovered up to that date, in translation and with a commentary, has proved extremely useful. It should be completed with more recent discoveries, as should Gauthier's *Le Livre des Rois*. We may quote, in the second category: Al. Moret, *Le Nil et la civilisation égyptienne*, Vol. VII in the series *Evolution de l'humanité*, Paris, 1926 (somewhat out of date) and J. Pirenne, *Histoire de la civilisation de l'Egypte ancienne*, Neufchatel, 1961–63, 3 vols., magnificently illustrated but only to be used with caution. For the Middle Kingdom, Posener should be consulted: *Littérature et politique dans l'Egypte de la XIIe dynastie*, Paris, 1956.

Religion

Of all the aspects of Egyptian civilisation, religion is that which has been studied most assiduously. In the general works already quoted readers will find chapters devoted to the subject. Ad. Erman's *Die Religion der Ägypter*, Berlin, 1934, although out of date on some points, can still be consulted with advantage, since the translations are very carefully done. The same can be said of J. H. Breasted's *Development of Religion and Thought in Ancient Egypt*, New York, 1912. For the early period, K. Sethe's *Urgeschichte und älteste Religion der Ägypter*, Leipzig, 1930, remains a basic work. The reader should consult, in addition, Th. Hoppfner, *Fontes historiae religionis aegyptiacae*, Bonn, 1922–25; G. Roeder, *Urkunden zur Religion der alten Ägypten*, Jena, 1923; Spiegel, *Die Idee vom Totengericht in den aeg. Religion*, Leipzig, 1935; H. Frankfort, *Ancient Egyptian Religion*, New York, 1948; J. Vandier, *La religion égyptienne*, collection Mana, Paris, 1949; H. Bonnet, *Reallexicon der äg. religionsgeschicht*, Berlin, 1952; J. Sainte Fare Garnot, *La vie religieuse dans l'ancienne Egypte*, Paris, 1948; H. Kees, *Götterglaube in alten aeg.*, 2nd edition, Berlin, 1956, and, by the same author, *Totenglaube und Jenseitsvorstellung der alten Ag.*, Berlin,

1956; S. Mercer, *The Pyramid Texts in Translation, and Commentary*, 4 vols.

The following are more specialized works: W. Wolf, *Das Schöne Fest von Opet*, Leipzig, 1931; H. Gauthier, *Les fêtes du dieu Min*, Cairo, 1934; S. Sauneron, *Les fêtes religieuses d'Esna aux derniers siècles du paganisme*, Cairo, 1962; M. Alliot, *Le culte d'Horus à Edfu*, Cairo, 1954.

A recently formed team of young research workers has begun publishing studies of particular points connected with the ancient civilisations, under the title *Sources orientales*, Editions du Seuil, Paris. In the volumes that have already appeared—*La Naissance du Monde, Les Songes, Les Pèlerinages, Le Jugement des Morts*—Egypt is compared with other countries.

The Sciences

A comprehensive survey can be found in A. Rey, *La science orientale avant les Grecs*, in the series *Evolution de l'humanité*. Paris, 1942. Additional works are: Er. Peet, *The Rhind Mathematical Papyrus*, London, 1923; J. H. Breasted, *The Smith Surgical Papyrus*, Chicago, 1930; G. Lefebvre, *La médecine égyptienne*, Paris. Quite recently, H. Grapow and his associates completed the publication of a *Grundriss der Medecin der alten Aegypt*, 8 vols., Berlin, 1958–1962, which marks a decisive stage in the clarification of the medical knowledge of the Ancient Egyptians.

The Arts

The *Topographical Bibliography* by B. Porter and R. Moss is a catalogue of all the monuments and other contents and gives an extremely comprehensive bibliography. The monuments are carefully studied in the *Manuel d'archéologie égyptienne* by J. Vaudier, five volumes of which have appeared so far, 1952–58. For the pyramids, the reader should refer to Edwards, *The Pyramids of Egypt*, London, 1947, and Ph. Lauer, *Histoire monumentale des pyramides d'Egypte*, vol. I, 1962 (further volumes to be published). Many works have been devoted to sculpture: Von Bissing, *Denkmäler äg. Sculptur*, Munich, 1911–14; H. G. Evers, *Staat aus dem Stein*, Munich, 1929; Smith, *A History of Egyptian Sculpture and Painting in the Old Kingdom*, Boston, London, 1946; J. Capart, *Leçons sur l'art égyptien*, Liège, 1920, *Propos sur l'art égyptien*, Bruxelles, 1930.

Many magnificent albums illustrating Egyptian art are now to be found in the principal libraries and museums.

Archaeology

W. M. Fl. Petrie, *The Arts and Crafts of Ancient Egypt*, London, 1923; A. Lucas, *Ancient Egyptian Materials and Industries*, 2nd ed., London, 1934; P. Montet, *Les Scènes de la vie privée dans les tombeaux égyptiens de l'ancien empire*, Paris and Strasbourg, 1925; P. Montet, *La vie quotidienne en Egypte au temps des Ramsès*, Paris, 1946 (translated into English, German, Italian, Spanish, Portuguese, Dutch and Hebrew); G. Posener, in collaboration with S. Sauneron and J. Yoyotte, *Dictionnaire d'archéologie égyptienne*, Paris, 1959.

INDEX